EXCITING NEW TITLES FO ACHIEVING SUCCESS IN LEAVING CERT ENGLISH

- Written by experienced teachers and examiners
- Exam focus with sample answers to develop effective writing skills
- Fresh and engaging design

Textbook

FREE eBook*

Digital resources on www.gillexplore.ie

*Included with the textbook

GILL EDUCATION

'Poetry can break open locked chapters of possibility ...'
Adrienne Rich

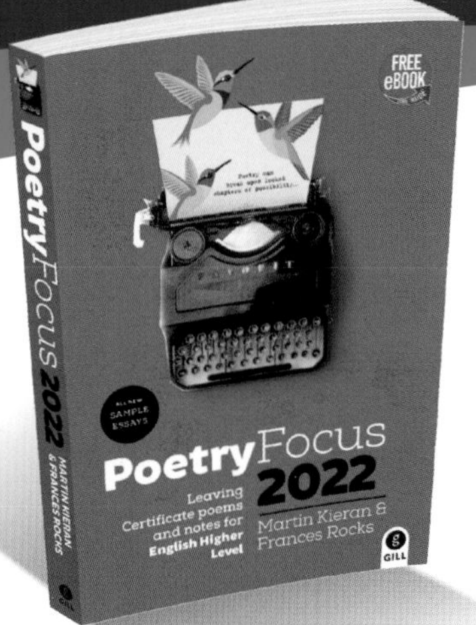

This established poetry anthology for Leaving Certificate Higher Level English is the definitive guide to achieving top marks in the 2022 exam.

For each poet, *Poetry Focus 2022* provides these unique exam-focused features:

- **Critical Literacy** notes on each poem provide a focused discussion on theme and style.
- **Writing About the Poem** sections provide **sample paragraphs** with **Examiner's Comments**, which help students articulate their responses to the highest standard.
- Examination-style **class/homework exercises** develop effective writing skills.
- **Revision Overviews** provide summaries and visual memory aids for exam preparation.
- Guidelines and sample questions and answers for the **Unseen Poetry** question.
- UPDATED: **Sample Leaving Cert questions, full essays, plans, marking scheme guidelines and Examiner's Comments**.
- A suite of digital resources is available on **www.gillexplore.ie.**

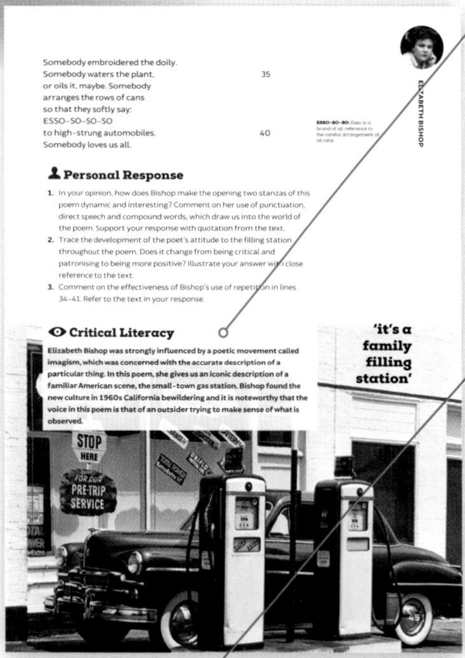
Somebody embroidered the doily.
Somebody waters the plant,
or oils it, maybe. Somebody
arranges the rows of cans
so that they softly say:
ESSO–SO–SO–SO
to high-strung automobiles.
Somebody loves us all.

ESSO–SO–SO–SO: Esso is a brand of oil; reference to the careful arrangement of oil cans.

ELIZABETH BISHOP

Personal Response

1. In your opinion, how does Bishop make the opening two stanzas of this poem dynamic and interesting? Comment on her use of punctuation, direct speech and compound words, which draw us into the world of the poem. Support your response with quotation from the text.
2. Trace the development of the poet's attitude to the filling station throughout the poem. Does it change from being critical and patronising to being more positive? Illustrate your answer with close reference to the text.
3. Comment on the effectiveness of Bishop's use of repetition in lines 34–41. Refer to the text in your response.

Critical Literacy

Elizabeth Bishop was strongly influenced by a poetic movement called imagism, which was concerned with the accurate description of a particular thing. In this poem, she gives us an iconic description of a familiar American scene, the small-town gas station. Bishop found the new culture in 1960s California bewildering and it is noteworthy that the voice in this poem is that of an outsider trying to make sense of what is observed.

'it's a family filling station'

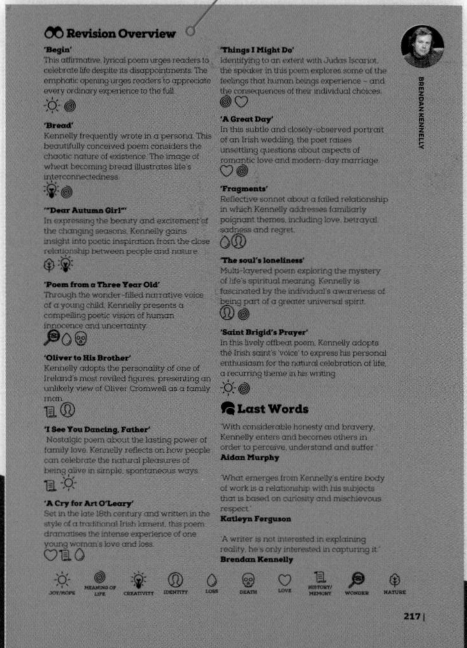
Revision Overview

'Begin'
This affirmative, lyrical poem urges readers to celebrate life despite its disappointments. The emphatic opening urges readers to appreciate every ordinary experience to the full.

'Bread'
Kennelly frequently wrote in a persona. This beautifully conceived poem considers the chaotic nature of existence. The image of wheat becoming bread illustrates life's interconnectedness.

'"Dear Autumn Girl"'
In expressing the beauty and excitement of the changing seasons, Kennelly gains insight into poetic inspiration from the close relationship between people and nature.

'Poem from a Three Year Old'
Through the wonder-filled narrative voice of a young child, Kennelly presents a compelling poetic vision of human innocence and uncertainty.

'Oliver to His Brother'
Kennelly adopts the personality of one of Ireland's most reviled figures, presenting an unlikely view of Oliver Cromwell as a family man.

'I See You Dancing, Father'
Nostalgic poem about the lasting power of family love. Kennelly reflects on how people can celebrate the natural pleasures of being alive in simple, spontaneous ways.

'A Cry for Art O'Leary'
Set in the late 18th century and written in the style of a traditional Irish lament, this poem dramatises the intense experience of one young woman's love and loss.

'Things I Might Do'
Identifying to an extent with Judas Iscariot, the speaker in this poem explores some of the feelings that human beings experience – and the consequences of their individual choices.

'A Great Day'
In this subtle and closely-observed portrait of an Irish wedding, the poet raises unsettling questions about aspects of romantic love and modern-day marriage.

'Fragments'
Reflective sonnet about a failed relationship in which Kennelly addresses familiarly poignant themes, including love, betrayal, sadness and regret.

'The soul's loneliness'
Multi-layered poem exploring the mystery of life's spiritual meaning. Kennelly is fascinated by the individual's awareness of being part of a greater universal spirit.

'Saint Brigid's Prayer'
In this lively offbeat poem, Kennelly adopts the Irish saint's 'voice' to express his personal enthusiasm for the natural celebration of life, a recurring theme in his writing.

Last Words

'With considerable honesty and bravery, Kennelly enters and becomes others in order to perceive, understand and suffer.'
Aidan Murphy

'What emerges from Kennelly's entire body of work is a relationship with his subjects that is based on curiosity and mischievous respect.'
Katleyn Ferguson

'A writer is not interested in explaining reality, he's only interested in capturing it.'
Brendan Kennelly

JOY/HOPE · MEANING OF LIFE · CREATIVITY · IDENTITY · LOSS · DEATH · LOVE · HISTORY/MEMORY · WONDER · NATURE

BRENDAN KENNELLY

217 |

POETRY FOCUS

The Unseen Poem

'Students should be able ... to read poetry conscious of its specific mode of using language as an artistic medium.'
(DES English Syllabus, 4.5.1)

Note that responding to the unseen poem is an exercise in aesthetic reading. It is especially important, in assessing the responses of the candidates, to guard against the temptation to assume a 'correct' reading of the poem.

Reward the candidates' awareness of the patterned nature of the language of poetry, its imagery, its sensuous qualities, and its suggestiveness.

SEC Marking Scheme

In the Unseen Poem 20-mark question, you will have 20 minutes to read and respond to a short poem that you are unlikely to have already studied. Targeted reading is essential. **Read over the questions** first to focus your thoughts and feelings.

In your **first reading** of the poem:
- Aim to get an initial sense of what the poet is saying and think about why the poet is writing about that particular subject.
- What is happening? Who is involved? Is there a sense of place and atmosphere?
- Underline interesting words or phrases that catch your attention. Avoid wasting time worrying about any words that you don't understand. Instead, **focus on what makes sense** to you.

Read through the poem **a second time**:
- Who is speaking in the poem? Is it the poet or another character?
- Is the poet describing a scene?
- Or remembering an experience?
- What point is the poet making?
- What do you notice about the poet's language use?
- How does the poem make you feel?
- Did it make you wonder? Trust your own reaction.

| 422

THE AUTHORS

MARTIN KIERAN and **FRANCES ROCKS** are experienced teachers and examiners who have wri
Language Lessons (HL) and the *Gill Shakespeare Focus* series. Martin has worked for many years
Certificate (HL) English. Frances delivers in-service **workshops** for second-level teachers of Englis

'O, beware, my lord, of jealousy; it is the green-eyed monster, which doth mock the meat it feeds on.'

The latest play in the trusted Gill Shakespeare Focus series, this new and beautifully illustrated edition of *Othello* expertly assists students in understanding Shakespeare's great drama and thoroughly prepares them for achieving top marks in the Leaving Certificate exam.

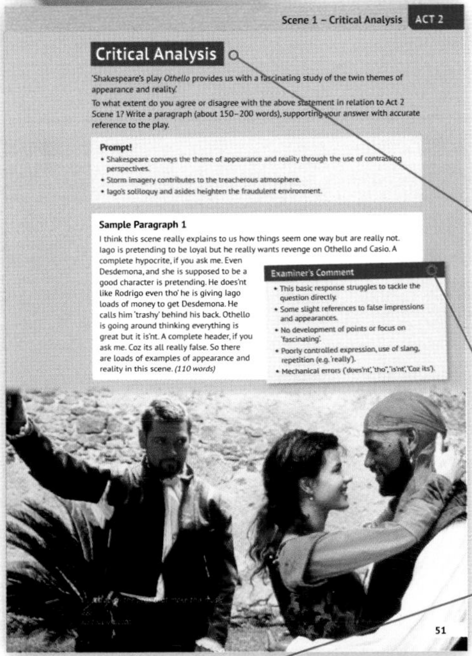
Scene 1 – Critical Analysis ACT 2

Critical Analysis

'Shakespeare's play *Othello* provides us with a fascinating study of the twin themes of appearance and reality.'

To what extent do you agree or disagree with the above statement in relation to Act 2 Scene 1? Write a paragraph (about 150–200 words), supporting your answer with accurate reference to the play.

Prompt!
- Shakespeare conveys the theme of appearance and reality through the use of contrasting perspectives.
- Storm imagery contributes to the treacherous atmosphere.
- Iago's soliloquy and asides heighten the fraudulent environment.

Sample Paragraph 1

I think this scene really explains to us how things seem one way but are really not. Iago is pretending to be loyal but he really wants revenge on Othello and Casio. A complete hypocrite, if you ask me. Even Desdemona, and she is supposed to be a good character is pretending. He does'nt like Rodrigo even tho' he is giving Iago loads of money to get Desdemona. He calls him 'trashy' behind his back. Othello is going around thinking everything is great but it is'nt. A complete header, if you ask me. Coz its all really false. So there are loads of examples of appearance and reality in this scene. *(110 words)*

Examiner's Comment
- This basic response struggles to tackle the question directly.
- Some slight references to false impressions and appearances.
- No development of points or focus on 'fascinating'.
- Poorly controlled expression, use of slang, repetition (e.g. 'really').
- Mechanical errors ('does'nt', 'tho'', 'is'nt', 'Coz its').

51

Detailed scene-by-scene analysis:
- Introductory **overview**.
- **Summary** and in-depth **Critical Analysis**.
- Study of **Shakespeare's Language**.
- **Key Quotes** plus commentary.
- Exam-style questions and **Sample Paragraphs** with Examiner's Comments.

Essential study notes:
- **Characters** – analytical study.
- Central **Themes and Issues**.
- **Dramatic Techniques** (Irony, Soliloquies).
- ***Othello* as a Comparative Text** – modes defined, exemplar paragraphs with Examiner's Comments.
- **Exam Technique** – giving guidance on how to **achieve top marks**, with notes on purposeful use of key scenes, paragraphing succinctly and quoting effectively.
- **Full Sample Essays** – marked and graded with invaluable Examiner's Comments.
- Sample **answer plans** and **paragraphs** enable students to scaffold successful answers.
- Sample Leaving Certificate **exam questions**.
- A suite of digital resources is available on **www.gillexplore.ie**.

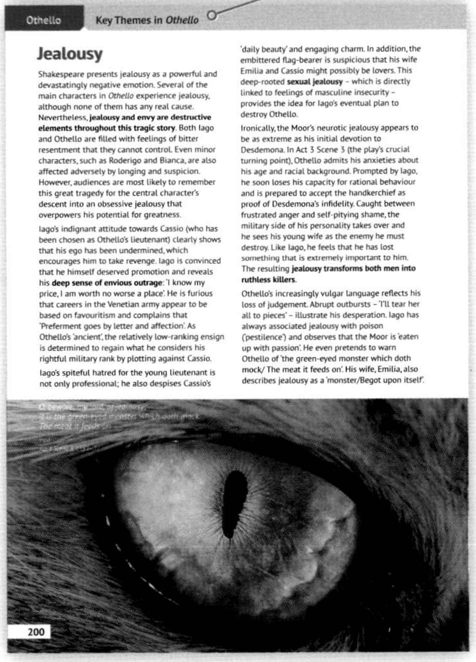
Othello Key Themes in *Othello*

Jealousy

Shakespeare presents jealousy as a powerful and devastatingly negative emotion. Several of the main characters in *Othello* experience jealousy, although none of them has any real cause. Nevertheless, **jealousy and envy are destructive elements throughout this tragic story**. Both Iago and Othello are filled with feelings of bitter resentment that they cannot control. Even minor characters, such as Roderigo and Bianca, are also affected adversely by longing and suspicion. However, audiences are most likely to remember this great tragedy for the central character's descent into an obsessive jealousy that overpowers his potential for greatness.

Iago's indignant attitude towards Cassio (who has been chosen as Othello's lieutenant) clearly shows that his ego has been undermined, which encourages him to take revenge. Iago is convinced that he himself deserved promotion and reveals his **deep sense of envious outrage**: 'I know my price, I am worth no worse a place'. He is furious that careers in the Venetian army appear to be based on favouritism and complains that 'Preferment goes by letter and affection'. As Othello's 'ancient', the relatively low-ranking ensign is determined to regain what he considers his rightful military rank by plotting against Cassio.

Iago's spiteful hatred for the young lieutenant is not only professional; he also despises Cassio's 'daily beauty' and engaging charm. In addition, the embittered flag-bearer is suspicious that his wife Emilia and Cassio might possibly be lovers. This deep-rooted **sexual jealousy** – which is directly linked to feelings of masculine insecurity – provides the idea for Iago's eventual plan to destroy Othello.

Ironically, the Moor's neurotic jealousy appears to be as extreme as his initial devotion to Desdemona. In Act 3 Scene 3 (the play's crucial turning point), Othello admits his anxieties about his age and racial background. Prompted by Iago, he soon loses his capacity for rational behaviour and is prepared to accept the handkerchief as proof of Desdemona's infidelity. Caught between frustrated anger and self-pitying shame, the military side of his personality takes over and he sees his young wife as the enemy he must destroy. Like Iago, he feels that he has lost something that is extremely important to him. The resulting **jealousy transforms both men into ruthless killers**.

Othello's increasingly vulgar language reflects his loss of judgement. Abrupt outbursts – 'I'll tear her all to pieces' – illustrate his desperation. Iago has always associated jealousy with poison ('pestilence') and observes that the Moor is 'eaten up with passion'. He even pretends to warn Othello of 'the green-eyed monster which doth mock/ The meat it feeds on'. His wife, Emilia, also describes jealousy as a 'monster/Begot upon itself'.

200

...veral Leaving Certificate English textbooks, including ... Senior Advising and **Chief Advising** for Leaving ...ghout the country.

GILL EDUCATION

The one-stop guide to Ordinary Level English Paper 1.

***Language Lessons* Ordinary Level is a focused and practical guide to achieving top marks in Ordinary Level English Paper 1.**

- Written by an **experienced Ordinary Level teacher** with the **specific needs** of the Ordinary Level student in mind.
- **Scaffolding, prompts for beginning an answer** and **accessible tips** for picking up marks provide solutions for the recurring difficulties that may be experienced by Ordinary Level students.
- **Wide range of extracts** on modern and topical issues relevant to Leaving Cert students in the **Comprehending Section**.
- Essential **grammar and spelling** revision.
- Focus on **visual literacy**.
- Consistent focus on **PCLM** marking scheme.
- **Practical, student-focused approach bridges the gap** between **Junior Cycle** and **Leaving Cert English**, developing OL students' ability to compose **longer and more structured** answers.
- **Past exam questions** with realistic **sample** and **modelled answers**.
- Clear guides on the appropriate **structure** and **register** required for **each genre in Composing Section.**
- **Write-in element** encourages self-editing and guides students towards confidence in answering exam questions.
- A suite of digital resources is available on **www.gillexplore.ie.**

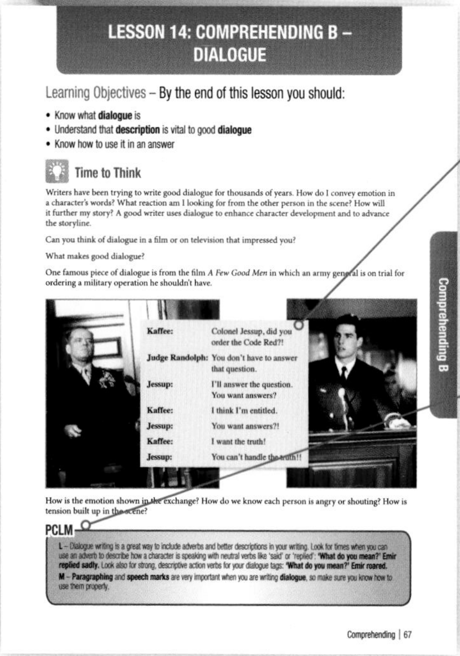
LESSON 14: COMPREHENDING B – DIALOGUE

Learning Objectives – By the end of this lesson you should:

- Know what **dialogue** is
- Understand that **description** is vital to good **dialogue**
- Know how to use it in an answer

Time to Think

Writers have been trying to write good dialogue for thousands of years. How do I convey emotion in a character's words? What reaction am I looking for from the other person in the scene? How will it further my story? A good writer uses dialogue to enhance character development and to advance the storyline.

Can you think of dialogue in a film or on television that impressed you?

What makes good dialogue?

One famous piece of dialogue is from the film *A Few Good Men* in which an army general is on trial for ordering a military operation he shouldn't have.

Kaffee:	Colonel Jessup, did you order the Code Red?!
Judge Randolph:	You don't have to answer that question.
Jessup:	I'll answer the question. You want answers?
Kaffee:	I think I'm entitled.
Jessup:	You want answers?!
Kaffee:	I want the truth!
Jessup:	You can't handle the truth!!

How is the emotion shown in the exchange? How do we know each person is angry or shouting? How is tension built up in the scene?

PCLM

L – Dialogue writing is a great way to include adverbs and better descriptions in your writing. Look for times when you can use an adverb to describe how a character is speaking with neutral verbs like 'said' or 'replied': **'What do you mean?' Emir replied sadly.** Look also for strong, descriptive action verbs for your dialogue tags: **'What do you mean?' Emir roared.**

M – **Paragraphing** and **speech marks** are very important when you are writing **dialogue**, so make sure you know how to use them properly.

Comprehending B

Comprehending | 67

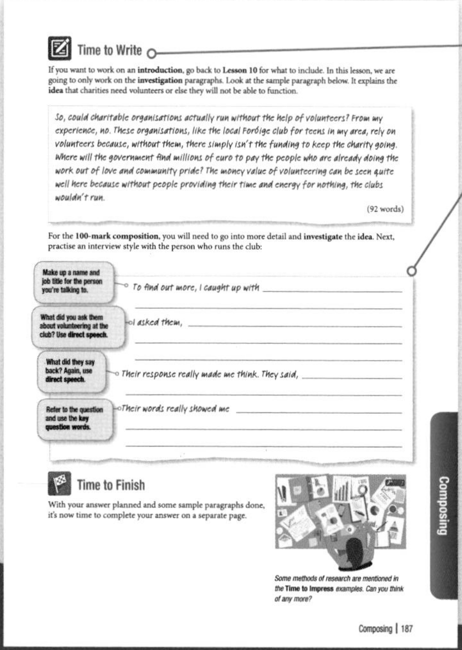
Time to Write

If you want to work on an **introduction**, go back to **Lesson 10** for what to include. In this lesson, we are going to only work on the **investigation** paragraphs. Look at the sample paragraph below. It explains the **idea** that charities need volunteers or else they will not be able to function.

So, could charitable organisations actually run without the help of volunteers? From my experience, no. These organisations, like the local Foróige club for teens in my area, rely on volunteers because, without them, there simply isn't the funding to keep the charity going. Where will the government find millions of euro to pay the people who are already doing the work out of love and community pride? The money value of volunteering can be seen quite well here because without people providing their time and energy for nothing, the clubs wouldn't run.

(92 words)

For the **100-mark composition**, you will need to go into more detail and **investigate** the **idea**. Next, practise an interview style with the person who runs the club:

Make up a name and job title for the person you're talking to. — *To find out more, I caught up with* ______

What did you ask them about volunteering at the club? Use **direct speech.** — *I asked them,* ______

What did they say back? Again, use **direct speech.** — *Their response really made me think. They said,* ______

Refer to the question and use the **key question words.** — *Their words really showed me* ______

Time to Finish

With your answer planned and some sample paragraphs done, it's now time to complete your answer on a separate page.

Some methods of research are mentioned in the **Time to Impress** *examples. Can you think of any more?*

Composing

Composing | 187

HIGHER LEVEL ALSO AVAILABLE

THE AUTHOR

DAN STYNES is a teacher with 12 years' experience working in St Paul's CBS, in Dublin 1. He has also taught for 10 years in the Institute of Education, Leeson Street, where he delivers classes focused on intense revision, with a strong emphasis on practical tips and advice for tackling the exam.

WE'RE HERE TO HELP!

GILL EDUCATION

For more information on this title, contact your local sales representative.
You will find their contact details on **gilleducation.ie/sales-reps-secondary**.
Follow **@GillEducation** on Twitter, Facebook and Instagram

GILL SHAKESPEARE FOCUS

OTHELLO

Leaving Certificate English

Text, analysis, commentary notes and sample essays

MARTIN KIERAN AND FRANCES ROCKS

GILL EDUCATION

Gill Education
Hume Avenue
Park West
Dublin 12
www.gilleducation.ie

Gill Education is an imprint of M.H. Gill & Co.

ISBN: 9780 7171 88277

Cover design: O'Brien Creative

For permission to reproduce photographs, the authors and publisher gratefully acknowledge the following:

© Alamy: ii, viii, ixT, x, xiiC, xiiB, xiiiT, xiv, 17, 32, 49B, 51, 68, 80, 96, 97B, 128, 137B, 139, 153, 177, 179, 182, 187, 188, 193, 205, 208, 209, 215, 230, 239, 244, 257, 267, 271; © ArenaPAL: xiiiC, xiiiB, 1, 13, 20, 49T, 50, 57, 70, 72, 82, 97T, 114, 123, 124, 144, 168, 169T, 170, 190, 194, 195, 198, 207, 215, 225, 231, 234, 235, 251, 258, 261, 269; © Getty Images: i, 33, 34, 36, 55, 69, 98, 102, 103, 110, 111, 136, 140, 147, 169B, 197, 224, 228, 242, 263; © iStock/Getty Premium: iii, iv, v, ixB, 38, 39, 54, 79, 113, 146, 155, 175, 202, 204, 206, 212, 233, 238, 241, 246, 253, 259, 265; © Nashville Shakespeare Festival, photographer Jeff Frazier and designer Chris Keegan: 218; © Royal National Theatre: 221; © RSC/Keith Pattison: 125, 137T, 152, 192, 196, 201, 249; © RSC/Manuel Harlan: 75; © RSC/Reg Wilson: xiiT, 7; © RSC/Simon Annand: 156; © Sean Gray/Long Beach Playhouse: 227; © Shutterstock: 11, 12, 19, 37, 73, 74, 78, 81, 126, 127, 172, 173, 199, 200, 203, 210, 211, 213, 254; © Théâtre de la Tempête, graphic design Isabelle Durand: 229.

The authors and publisher have made every effort to trace all copyright holders, but if any have been inadvertently overlooked we would be pleased to make the necessary arrangement at the first opportunity.

The paper used in this book is made from the wood pulp of managed forests. For every tree felled, at least one tree is planted, thereby renewing natural resources.

Contents

*** N.B. Key scenes requiring close, detailed study**

ACT 5

* N.B. Key scenes requiring close, detailed study

CHARACTER STUDIES

KEY THEMES IN *OTHELLO*

DRAMATIC TECHNIQUES IN *OTHELLO*

SHAKESPEARE'S LANGUAGE

EXAM TECHNIQUE

SAMPLE ESSAYS AND PLANS

USING *OTHELLO* AS A COMPARATIVE TEXT

Introduction

- *Othello* is one of Shakespeare's greatest plays. Set in Venice and Cyprus, its passionate characters and controversial issues continue to excite audiences around the world. Written in 1603, the story focuses on a Moorish general in the Venetian army and Iago, his disloyal ensign (flag-bearer).
- The play has been seen primarily as a domestic or private tragedy concerned with intense relationships. It speaks clearly to contemporary audiences, partly because it deals with such crucial modern issues as prejudice, gender, multi-culturalism, and how misunderstanding and miscommunication can affect relations between couples.
- Most Leaving Certificate exam questions on the Shakespearean text relate to characters, themes and dramatic techniques, all of which are closely interrelated. A close knowledge of the play's key or most revealing scenes will provide a solid basis for answering questions successfully.
- In studying *Othello*, it is worth remembering that the text was written specifically for theatrical performance. Despite any inconsistencies regarding the plot or timescale, audiences are more likely to fully appreciate this intriguing stage drama by fully accepting the 'new reality' that Shakespeare has created.

Othello: Plot Overview

Stage by Stage

1. Iago is angry that Othello, the Venetian army general, has insulted him by promoting an inexperienced soldier, Michael Cassio, to be his lieutenant.
2. Othello secretly marries Desdemona, the daughter of a senator in Venice.
3. Iago tells Desdemona's father about the marriage to cause trouble for Othello.
4. Desdemona's father is unhappy that his daughter has married Othello. He complains to the Duke of Venice, but his objection is unsuccessful.
5. The Duke sends Othello to Cyprus to lead the Venetian forces against an impending Turkish invasion. Desdemona, Iago and Cassio join him there.
6. Iago tricks Cassio into getting drunk while on guard duty. Cassio ends up in a street brawl and is demoted by Othello from his position as lieutenant.
7. Iago begins to make Othello suspicious about his wife's relationship with Cassio. He gets a handkerchief belonging to Desdemona and leaves it in Cassio's room, arguing that it is proof of Desdemona's unfaithfulness.
8. Unaware of Iago's scheming, Desdemona pleads with her husband to reappoint Cassio. However, Othello believes that her behaviour is further proof that she is Cassio's lover.
9. Iago continues to manipulate Othello, who becomes so enraged with jealousy that he murders Desdemona as punishment for her apparent infidelity.
10. The truth emerges that Iago has lied. Othello finally realises his tragic mistake and kills himself.

Time and Place in *Othello*

In *Othello*, events happen in a shorter time sequence than is usual in Shakespeare's plays. To some extent, the first act (which takes place over one night) can be seen as **a prologue to the main story** set in Cyprus. The effect is to make the tragedy seem much more intense. The drama is also heightened due to the lack of a significant subplot and the almost total absence of comic relief.

From Act 2 onwards, there is a rush of activity: Othello's wedding celebrations, Cassio's dismissal, Desdemona's pleading on his behalf, Iago's increasing influence, Othello's growing suspicion and its inevitable tragic outcome. Although Othello's whole world seems to disintegrate very quickly, **characters make comments that suggest a much longer timescale**. For example, Bianca complains to Cassio that he has avoided her for 'seven days and nights'.

The **contrasting settings** are also important. The city of Venice has a sophisticated social class system, which welcomes Othello as a military commander but rejects him as a son-in-law. The Moor has little understanding of the finer points of social behaviour and Iago has no trouble convincing him that women in Venice are all immoral.

By contrast, **Cyprus is symbolically located halfway between the civilised and heathen worlds**. Within this claustrophobic setting, where Othello is in absolute command, he becomes the focus of attention. It is in this unfamiliar location that passions are let loose and order disappears.

Critics have commented on the **'double time' of *Othello***. The play's main action occurs over just two days, but Shakespeare makes us think the time is actually longer. Fortunately, theatre audiences are largely unaware of any inconsistencies, primarily because they are caught up in the psychological intensity of the play. Of course, to fully appreciate *Othello*, a willing suspension of disbelief is a vital part of the contract between audience and playwright.

Locations in *Othello*

The island of Cyprus, directly south of Turkey, is part of the Venetian Republic in Othello *and subject to invasion by the Turks. Later it became part of the Turks' Ottoman Empire.*

Shakespeare's Life

Since William Shakespeare lived more than 400 years ago, the little we know about his life comes mainly from public records. For example, we are sure that he was baptised in Stratford-upon-Avon, 100 miles north-west of London, on 26 April 1564.

We also know that Shakespeare's life revolved around two locations: Stratford and London. He grew up, had a family and bought property in Stratford, but he worked in London, the centre of English theatre. As an actor, playwright and a partner in a leading acting company, he soon became prosperous and well-known.

1564	Born in Stratford-upon-Avon
1582	Marries Anne Hathaway
1583	His daughter Susannah is born
1584	Birth of twins, Judith and Hamnet
1585	Moves to London
1590s	Writes first plays, *Richard III* and *Henry VII*
1593–96	Continues to write, including *Richard II* and *Romeo and Juliet*
1596	Death of his son Hamnet
1599	Invests in the Globe Theatre
1603	Writes *Othello*
1604	First known performance of *Othello*
1605–6	Writes *King Lear* and *Macbeth*
1609	Becomes part-owner of the new Blackfriars Theatre
1612	Retires and returns to Stratford-upon-Avon
1616	Dies on 23 April, aged 52, and buried in Holy Trinity Church, Stratford-upon-Avon

(Dates for plays are approximate.)

Shakespeare's Theatre

Throughout Shakespeare's lifetime, professional theatre was a highly successful business that provided popular entertainment for people of all backgrounds. Shakespeare wrote for a specific acting company, known first as the Lord Chamberlain's Men and later as the King's Men.

Plays were performed in the royal courts, as well as in town squares, churches and guildhalls around the country. In London, the largest theatres were open-air arenas with room for several thousand people. These buildings were made mainly of wood. Indoor playhouses accommodated up to 500 people, all of whom were given seats. Lighting was provided by candles, making indoor theatres suitable for winter and evening productions.

William Shakespeare (1564–1616)

The Swan

Built in 1595–6, the Swan Theatre was located in the Southwark district of London, close to the River Thames. It had a capacity for 3,000 spectators and was described by Johannes de Witt, a Dutchman visiting the English capital, as 'the finest and biggest of the London theatres'. De Witt also drew a sketch of the building and a copy of this famous drawing is probably the single most reliable source of information about the interior layout of Elizabethan London theatres.

The Globe

From 1599, London's most important outdoor theatre was the Globe, also in Southwark, where Shakespeare's best-known dramas were first produced. The building was about 36 feet high and had a diameter of 84 feet. The inside of the structure contained three tiers of galleries that surrounded an uncovered yard roughly 56 feet in diameter.

The grounds surrounding the theatre would have been bustling with playgoers and local people. Stallholders sold merchandise and refreshments, creating a lively market-day atmosphere. The Globe would have particularly attracted young people and there were many complaints of apprentices avoiding work in order to go to the theatre.

Staging

The bare stages of Shakespeare's day had very little scenery and few props except for objects required by the plot. Setting and mood were suggested by the power of the play's language.

There was a roof over the stage, but no curtain. Rhyming couplets signalled the end of a scene. Colourful costumes were common, often denoting a character's social status or nationality. Exits and entrances were in plain view of the audience, but actors could also descend from the 'heavens' above the stage or enter and exit from the 'hell' below through a trapdoor.

The Actors

Women never performed in stage dramas (acting was seen as a disreputable profession), and young boys usually played female characters. During Elizabethan times, there was a fast turnover of plays – and little or no time for rehearsal – so actors needed to have excellent recall. Indeed, they sometimes received scripts just hours before the play started and relied on prompters who sat behind the curtains and whispered the lines.

Actors performed on a stage space that thrust into the yard area and had three sides where audience members could watch the action. Acoustics were poor and actors were often forced to shout their lines and use exaggerated theatrical gestures. Speech patterns were heightened for dramatic effect.

A 1596 sketch of a performance on the thrust stage (extending into the auditorium) of the Swan Theatre

Audiences

Shakespeare's theatre was full of life. Poorer people ('groundlings') would pay a few pennies to stand in front of the stage while the better-off paid more for places in the sheltered side galleries. A trumpeter, perched on the roof, would hurry latecomers into the theatre when a performance was due to begin.

Plays were staged in the afternoon and the audience would talk, wander around and eat and drink during performances, so authors had to come up with ways of holding their attention. Since there were no backdrops or artificial lighting, audiences used their imagination to believe the dramas being presented on the stage.

The New Globe

The continuing popularity of Shakespeare's plays means that the Globe Theatre lives on, with a modern reconstruction close to the original site in Southwark. Completed in 1997, the theatre serves not only as a museum, but also as a working playhouse.

The new Globe Theatre

Othello Fact File

- Shakespeare's *Othello* was inspired by a story entitled *Hecatommithi*, written by an Italian author, Giraldi Cinthio. It was published in Venice in 1565.
- The two earliest printed versions of Shakespeare's *Othello* differ greatly. *Othello* first appeared in Shakespeare's quarto (or pocket-sized book) in 1622, along with several of his other plays. In 1623 it appeared again in Shakespeare's folio, with about 160 additional lines that were not in the first version. Conversely, the folio lacked a dozen lines that only appeared in the quarto.
- In *Othello*, the title character is called 'the Moor' because he is from North Africa. However, in Shakespeare's time, this term was commonly used to describe anyone who came from Africa or Arabia.
- These days we usually say 'I'm going to see a play'. However, back in Elizabethan times, people talked about 'going to hear a play'.
- One performance of *Othello* in 1660 starred an actress (reportedly named Margaret Hughes) in the role of Desdemona. This production marked the first time that a woman was accepted on the English stage. Before this, all characters, male and female, were played exclusively by men.
- Some critics have pointed out the satanic references in the names of Othello and Desdemona – 'hell' and 'demon'.
- The word 'honesty' (or variations of it) is used 52 times over the course of the play. Ironically, it is said most often by, or about, Iago.
- The play consists of roughly 3,320 lines. Iago speaks almost 1,100 of these, about 250 more than Othello himself.
- In the United States, the first ever onstage kiss between a black man and a white woman occurred in a 1943 Broadway production of *Othello*, starring Paul Robeson and Uta Hagen.
- *Othello* introduced several new phrases into the English language. These include 'foregone conclusion', 'jealousy ... the green-eyed monster' and 'wear my heart upon my sleeve'.

Uta Hagen and Paul Robeson in the 1943/4 Broadway production of Othello

Shakespeare's Text and Line Numbers

Over the years, Shakespeare's plays have been printed in various formats. Most popular versions of *Othello* have some modernised spelling and punctuation. Line numbers may also differ slightly, depending on the particular edition.

How the Single Text Shakespeare Question Is Marked

The Single Test English (Higher Level) question is allocated 60 minutes in the exam and worth **60 marks** in total. These are awarded by reference to the **PCLM** criteria for assessment (i.e. 3 x 18 marks for each of P, C and L plus 6 marks for M):

P = Clarity of **Purpose**:	18 (30%)
C = **Coherence** of Delivery:	18 (30%)
L = Efficiency of **Language** Use:	18 (30%)
M = Accuracy of **Mechanics**:	6 (10%)

P

In assessing 'Clarity of Purpose', examiners will judge how successfully the candidate has addressed the question and engaged with the set task. This refers to the quality of engagement, relevance, focus, originality and understanding of the appropriate genre.

The marks awarded for 'Coherence of Delivery' and 'Efficiency of Language Use' will not normally be higher than 'Clarity of Purpose'. (In exceptional cases, e.g. where the candidate has written in the wrong genre, the marks for 'C' and/or 'L' may be higher than 'P'.)

C

In awarding the marks for 'Coherence of Delivery', examiners will assess how well the candidate has sustained the response and developed the entire answer. This refers to the quality and management of ideas, supporting points, sequencing, and engagement with texts.

L

Marks for 'Efficiency of Language Use' are awarded for the management and control of language. This refers to the quality of language used to achieve clear communication in terms of vocabulary, paragraph structure, syntax, punctuation, fluency, style and expression appropriate to the task.

Marks for 'L' are awarded in so far as the candidate's answering is considered 'appropriate to the delivery of the task'.

The standard of both 'Coherence of Delivery' and 'Efficiency of Language Use' informs the marks awarded for 'Clarity of Purpose'.

M

Marks awarded for 'Accuracy of Mechanics' refer to spelling and grammar appropriate to the register. Marks for 'M' are essentially independent of 'P', 'C' and 'L' marks.

Essential Scenes in *Othello*

In preparing for the Single Text *Othello* question, it is important to **become familiar with the entire play** through a close reading of the text. Your written work should show creative thought, supporting the points you make with good reference to key scenes. Some moments in the drama (including the six scenes listed below) are particularly revealing and worth studying in detail.

◆ Act 1 Scene 1

The opening scene takes place on a street in Venice late at night. Iago talks to Roderigo about his hatred for Cassio and Othello. He informs Brabantio that his daughter Desdemona has secretly married the Moor Othello, a general in the Venetian army.

◆ Act 1 Scene 3

The Duke of Venice and his senators prepare for war against the Turks. Othello answers Brabantio's accusations of bewitching his daughter and is sent to Cyprus on military duty. Iago initiates his scheme of revenge against the Moor.

◆ Act 2 Scene 1

Othello, Desdemona and Iago arrive in Cyprus. A storm at sea has destroyed the Turkish fleet. Iago involves Roderigo in his plan to discredit Cassio and replace him as Othello's lieutenant. He also swears to ruin the happiness of the newlyweds.

◆ Act 2 Scene 3

Cassio gets involved in a drunken brawl and loses his position as lieutenant. Iago convinces him that his only hope of reinstatement is to ask Desdemona to plead on his behalf. The ensign delights in his plan to trick Othello into jealously misunderstanding Desdemona's interest in Cassio.

◆ Act 3 Scene 3

Desdemona pleads with her husband to reinstate Cassio, who has been dismissed from his post for drinking on duty. Iago persuades Othello that Desdemona and Cassio are secret lovers. Consumed by jealousy, the Moor is increasingly controlled by Iago.

◆ Act 5 Scene 2

Othello murders Desdemona in her bed. Emilia reveals the truth about Iago's evil plot. Realising his terrible foolishness, the Moor then kills himself, leaving an unrepentant Iago to be punished by Cassio, who remains in Cyprus as the new governor.

Writing about the Play

Remember that all commentaries and **study guides are there to be challenged**. There is no single 'correct way' to interpret *Othello*.

In responding to exam questions, **have confidence in developing your own ideas** and always express yourself clearly. Identify the main elements of the question, so that your answer is coherent and well structured.

Make sure to **avoid unfocused narrative**. Wherever possible, find your own examples from the text to support your views and use accurate quotations when appropriate.

Characters

DUKE of Venice

BRABANTIO – a senator, Desdemona's father

GRATIANO – Brabantio's brother

LODOVICO – Brabantio's cousin

OTHELLO – the Moor (a general in the military service of Venice)

CASSIO – lieutenant to Othello

IAGO – an ensign (standard bearer) to Othello

RODERIGO – a Venetian gentleman

MONTANO – governor of Cyprus (before Othello)

CLOWN – servant to Othello

DESDEMONA – Othello's wife

EMILIA – Iago's wife

BIANCA – Cassio's mistress

SENATORS, SAILORS, OFFICERS, GENTLEMEN, MESSENGERS, MUSICIANS, HERALDS, ATTENDANTS

Act 1
Scene 1*

INTRODUCTION

- On a street in Venice, Roderigo and Iago quarrel over money.
- Iago complains bitterly about Othello's behaviour towards him.
- Brabantio is informed that his daughter has eloped with the Moor.
- The outraged father organises a search party.

* **Key scene requiring close, detailed study**

Venice: A street at night

Enter Roderigo and Iago

Roderigo
Tush! Never tell me; I take it much unkindly
That thou, Iago, who hast had my purse
As if the strings were thine, shouldst know of this.

Iago
'Sblood, but you will not hear me:
If ever I did dream of such a matter,
Abhor me.

Roderigo
Thou told'st me thou didst hold him in thy hate.

Iago
Despise me, if I do not. Three great ones of the city,
In personal suit to make me his lieutenant,
Off-capped to him: and, by the faith of man,
I know my price, I am worth no worse a place:
But he; as loving his own pride and purposes,
Evades them, with a bombast circumstance
Horribly stuffed with epithets of war;
And, in conclusion,
Nonsuits my mediators; for, 'Certes,' says he,
'I have already chosen my officer.'
And what was he?
Forsooth, a great arithmetician,
One Michael Cassio, a Florentine,
A fellow almost damned in a fair wife;
That never set a squadron in the field,
Nor the division of a battle knows
More than a spinster: unless the bookish theoric,
Wherein the toged consuls can propose
As masterly as he: mere prattle, without practice,
Is all his soldiership. But he, sir, had the election:
And I, of whom his eyes had seen the proof
At Rhodes, at Cyprus and on other grounds
Christian and heathen, must be be-lee'd and calmed
By debitor and creditor: this counter-caster,
He, in good time, must his lieutenant be,
And I – God bless the mark!– his Moorship's ancient.

Roderigo
By heaven, I rather would have been his hangman.

Iago
Why, there's no remedy; 'tis the curse of service.
Preferment goes by letter and affection,
And not by old gradation, where each second
Stood heir to the first. Now, sir, be judge yourself,
Whether I in any just term am affined
To love the Moor.

---

1 Tush: *Come on!*
1 much unkindly: *rather badly*
3 this: *Othello and Desdemona's elopement and secret marriage*
4 'Sblood: *by God's blood (a swear word)*
7 him: *Othello*
9 suit: *appeal, petition – three important citizens have asked Othello to promote Iago*
10 Off-capped: *respectfully removed their caps*
11 price: *value, worth*
12 he: *Othello, unnamed, is verbally abused by Iago*
13 bombast circumstance: *elaborate excuse*
14 epithets of war: *military language*
16 Nonsuits my mediators: *blocks the request of my supporters*
16 Certes: *certainly*
19 arithmetician: *theorist, academic (with little military experience)*
20 Florentine: *person from the city of Florence*
21 almost … wife: *a ladies' man*
22 set a squadron: *led a company of soldiers*
24 spinster: *inexperienced person*
25 toged consuls: *senators wearing robes of peace*
26 prattle: *idle talk*
27 had the election: *was chosen*
29 Rhodes: *island in the Mediterranean Sea*
29 Cyprus: *island in the Mediterranean Sea*
30 be-lee'd: *pacified, unable to move*
31 counter-caster: *accountant*
33 Moorship's: *contemptuous reference to Othello's background*
33 ancient: *old advise ensign, flag-bearer*
36 Preferment: *promotion*
36 letter and affection: *qualifications and favouritism*
37 old gradation: *promotion based on army experience*
39 affined: *bound*

Roderigo I would not follow him then.

Iago O, sir, content you;
I follow him to serve my turn upon him:
We cannot all be masters, nor all masters
Cannot be truly followed. You shall mark
Many a duteous and knee-crooking knave,
That, doting on his own obsequious bondage,
Wears out his time, much like his master's ass,
For nought but provender, and when he's old, cashiered.
Whip me such honest knaves. Others there are
Who, trimmed, in forms and visages of duty,
Keep their hearts attending on themselves,
And throwing but shows of service on their lords,
Do well thrive by them and when they have lined their coats
Do themselves homage: these fellows have some soul
And such a one do I profess myself. For, sir,
It is as sure as you are Roderigo,
Were I the Moor, I would not be Iago:
In following him, I follow but myself;
Heaven is my judge, not I for love and duty,
But seeming so, for my peculiar end:
For when my outward action doth demonstrate
The native act and figure of my heart
In compliment extern, 'tis not long after
But I will wear my heart upon my sleeve
For daws to peck at: I am not what I am.

Roderigo What a full fortune does the thick-lips owe
If he can carry't thus!

Iago Call up her father,
Rouse him: make after him, poison his delight,
Proclaim him in the streets; incense her kinsmen,
And, though he in a fertile climate dwell,
Plague him with flies: though that his joy be joy,
Yet throw such vexations on't
As it may lose some colour.

Roderigo Here is her father's house; I'll call aloud.

Iago Do, with like timorous accent, and dire yell,
As when, by night and negligence, the fire
Is spied in populous cities.

Roderigo What ho! Brabantio! Signior Brabantio, ho!

Iago Awake! What ho, Brabantio! Thieves, thieves, thieves!
Look to your house, your daughter, and your bags!
Thieves! thieves!

43 serve my turn: *aid my own purposes*
46 duteous: diligent
46 knee-crooking: *bowing, excessively attentive*
46 knave: *serving man*
47 obsequious bondage: *slavish behaviour*
49 provender: *food and drink*
49 cashiered: *dismissed from service*
51 trimmed ... visages of duty: *dressed up in false appearances of loyalty*
54 lined their coats: *enriched themselves*
55 Do themselves homage: *serve their own interests*
58 Were I the Moor, I would not be Iago: *cryptic remark by Iago, who admits that if he were Othello, he would have nothing to do with such a self-serving person as Iago*
61 peculiar end: *personal purpose*
63 native act and figure: *natural appearance*
64 compliment extern: *outward show*
66 daws: *jackdaws*
67 full fortune ... owe: *great riches Othello will own*
68 If ... thus: *if Othello can succeed*
71 Proclaim him: *denounce Othello*
73 Plague him with flies: *destroy his happiness*
77 timorous accent: *terrifying tones*
82 bags: *moneybags*

Brabantio appears above, at a window

Brabantio What is the reason of this terrible summons?
What is the matter there?

Roderigo Signior, is all your family within?

Iago Are your doors locked?

Brabantio Why, wherefore ask you this?

Iago 'Zounds, sir, you're robbed; for shame, put on your gown;
Your heart is burst, you have lost half your soul;
Even now, now, very now, an old black ram
Is tupping your white ewe. Arise, arise;
Awake the snorting citizens with the bell,
Or else the devil will make a grandsire of you:
Arise, I say.

Brabantio What, have you lost your wits?

Roderigo Most reverend signior, do you know my voice?

Brabantio Not I: what are you?

Roderigo My name is Roderigo.

Brabantio The worser welcome:
I have charged thee not to haunt about my doors:
In honest plainness thou hast heard me say
My daughter is not for thee; and now, in madness,
Being full of supper and distempering draughts,
Upon malicious bravery, dost thou come
To start my quiet.

Roderigo Sir, sir, sir–

Brabantio But thou must needs be sure
My spirit and my place have in them power
To make this bitter to thee.

Roderigo Patience, good sir.

Brabantio What tell'st thou me of robbing? This is Venice;
My house is not a grange.

Roderigo Most grave Brabantio,
In simple and in pure soul I come to you.

Iago 'Zounds, sir, you are one of those that will not serve God, if the devil bid you. Because we come to do you service and you think we are ruffians, you'll have your daughter covered with a Barbary horse; you'll have your nephews neigh to you; you'll have coursers for cousins and gennets for germans.

88 wherefore: *why*
89 'Zounds: *by God's wounds (a swear word)*
92 tupping: *enjoying sex with*
92 white ewe: *Desdemona*
93 snorting: *snoring*
94 devil: *insulting reference to Othello*
94 grandsire: *grandfather*
101 charged ... doors: *ordered you to stay away*
104 distempering draughts: *alcohol*
106 start my quiet: *disturb my rest*
109 place: *position*
113 grange: *remote country house*
119 covered ... Barbary horse: *another insult that Desdemona is mating with an Arabic horse (Othello)*
121 coursers: *large powerful horses*
121 gennets: *small Spanish horses*
121 germans: *close relatives*

Brabantio What profane wretch art thou?

Iago I am one, sir, that comes to tell you your daughter
and the Moor are now making the beast with two backs.

Brabantio Thou art a villain.

Iago Thou art a senator.

Brabantio This thou shalt answer; I know thee, Roderigo.

Roderigo Sir, I will answer any thing. But, I beseech you,
If it be your pleasure and most wise consent,
As partly I find it is, that your fair daughter,
At this odd-even and dull watch o' the night,
Transported, with no worse nor better guard
But with a knave of common hire, a gondolier,
To the gross clasps of a lascivious Moor –
If this be known to you, and your allowance,
We then have done you bold and saucy wrongs;
But if you know not this, my manners tell me
We have your wrong rebuke. Do not believe
That, from the sense of all civility,
I thus would play and trifle with your reverence:
Your daughter, if you have not given her leave,
I say again, hath made a gross revolt;
Tying her duty, beauty, wit and fortunes
In an extravagant and wheeling stranger
Of here and everywhere: straight satisfy yourself.
If she be in her chamber or your house,
Let loose on me the justice of the state
For thus deluding you.

Brabantio Strike on the tinder, ho!
Give me a taper! Call up all my people!
This accident is not unlike my dream:
Belief of it oppresses me already.
Light, I say, light!

Exit

Iago Farewell; for I must leave you:
It seems not meet, nor wholesome to my place,
To be produced as, if I stay, I shall
Against the Moor: for, I do know, the state,
However this may gall him with some cheque,
Cannot with safety cast him, for he's embarked
With such loud reason to the Cyprus wars,
Which even now stand in act, that, for their souls,
Another of his fathom they have none,
To lead their business: in which regard,
Though I do hate him as I do hell-pains.

124 making the beast with two backs: *having sex*

131 odd-even: *just after midnight*

134 gross clasps: *indecent embraces*

134 lascivious: *sex-obsessed*

136 saucy: *insolent, cheeky*

140 trifle: *play*

142 gross revolt: *blatant act of rebellion*

144 wheeling: *of no fixed place*

149 Strike on the tinder: *make a light*

150 taper: *candle*

155 wholesome to my place: *good for my position (as Othello's servant)*

158 gall: *hurt*

158 cheque: *scolding*

159 cast: *dismiss*

160 loud reason: *strong support from the Senate*

162 fathom: *capability*

165 life: *occupation*
166 flag: *outward appearance*
168 Sagittary: *a well-known tavern or inn*
171 despised: *dishonoured*
181 charms: *spells, love potion*
182 property: *correct nature*
194 deserve your pains: *reward you for your trouble*

Yet, for necessity of present life,
I must show out a flag and sign of love,
Which is indeed but sign. That you shall surely find him,
Lead to the Sagittary the raised search;
And there will I be with him. So farewell.

Exit

Enter Brabantio and Servants with torches

Brabantio It is too true an evil. Gone she is;
And what's to come of my despised time
Is nought but bitterness. Now, Roderigo,
Where didst thou see her? O unhappy girl!
With the Moor, say'st thou? Who would be a father!
How didst thou know 'twas she? O she deceives me
Past thought! What said she to you? Get more tapers:
Raise all my kindred. Are they married, think you?

Roderigo Truly, I think they are.

Brabantio O heaven! How got she out? O treason of the blood!
Fathers, from hence trust not your daughters' minds
By what you see them act. Is there not charms
By which the property of youth and maidhood
May be abused? Have you not read, Roderigo,
Of some such thing?

Roderigo Yes, sir, I have indeed.

Brabantio Call up my brother. O, would you had had her!
Some one way, some another. Do you know
Where we may apprehend her and the Moor?

Roderigo I think I can discover him, if you please,
To get good guard and go along with me.

Brabantio Pray you, lead on. At every house I'll call;
I may command at most. Get weapons, ho!
And raise some special officers of night.
On, good Roderigo; I'll deserve your pains.

Exeunt

Key Scene Extended Commentary

A heated argument (lines 1–34)

On a dimly lit street in Venice, two men are engaged in a noisy quarrel. Roderigo, a rich Venetian, is hopelessly in love with the beautiful Desdemona. He has been paying Iago to arrange a marriage between himself and Desdemona, but he feels cheated after hearing that she has eloped with Othello, a Moor and a general in the Venetian army. Roderigo is enraged that Iago – who is Othello's junior army officer – did not let him know, 'I take it much unkindly'.

Iago explains that he hates Othello because he has been passed over for promotion despite references from his 'mediators'. He sneers at Othello's choice of lieutenant, the inexperienced Michael Cassio, who 'never set a squadron in the field' and who is in a casual relationship with a courtesan. Iago claims that he has been ignored by Othello, even though 'his eyes had seen the proof' of him on the battlefield. In contrast, Cassio's so-called soldiership is 'mere prattle, without practice'.

Clever manipulation (lines 35–68)

Iago skilfully manipulates the gullible Roderigo by focusing on the hatred they both have for their common enemy, Othello. He explains how the 'curse of service' depends on connections and favouritism rather than seniority, 'Preferment goes by letter and affection'. Iago cynically praises those who pretend to be loyal servants while secretly enriching themselves, 'lined their coats'. He also reveals his own devious nature, 'I follow him to serve my turn upon him'. Iago is intent on taking revenge on the Moor. The scheming hypocrite openly admits, 'I am not what I am'. However, Roderigo is unaware of what Iago has confessed. He has stopped listening and is still fixated on Othello's success in winning Desdemona's love.

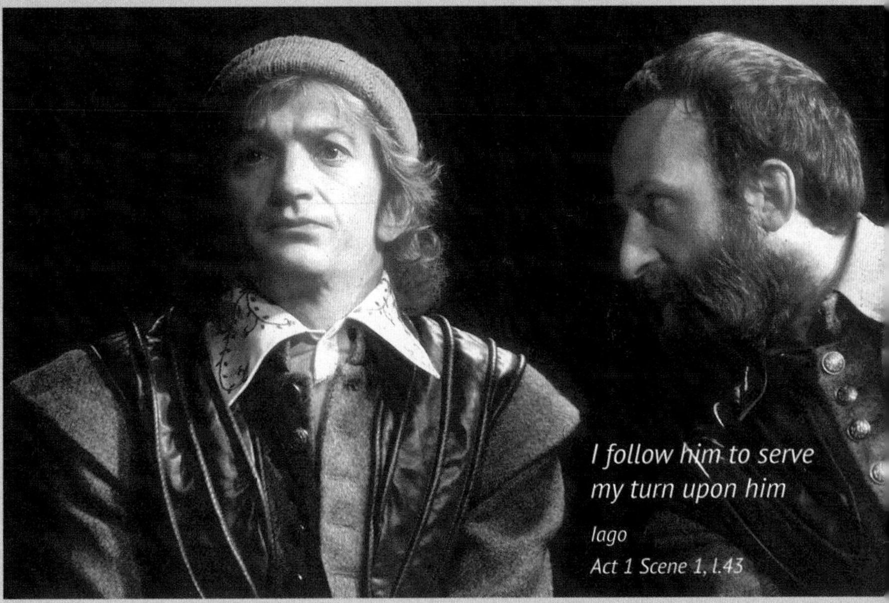

I follow him to serve my turn upon him

Iago
Act 1 Scene 1, l.43

The cunning plan (lines 69–79)

With fiendish ingenuity, Iago suggests to the foolish Roderigo that he should waken Senator Brabantio, Desdemona's father, to inform him of his daughter's secret marriage to Othello, so that he will arrange a search party to apprehend the couple. This will also prevent Othello from enjoying time with his new bride; it will 'Plague him with flies'. Iago instructs Roderigo to yell as loudly as if fire had broken out in the densely populated city.

Raising the search party (lines 80–153)

On the street outside Brabantio's residence, Roderigo and Iago begin to roar, 'Thieves, thieves!/ Look to your house, your daughter, and your bags!' Brabantio appears at an upstairs window, demanding to know 'the reason of this terrible summons'. Roderigo politely addresses the senator, 'is all your family within?' Iago is contemptuous of Roderigo's politeness. He rudely interrupts the old senator, making crudely offensive remarks about his daughter and Othello. He declares that the Moor, 'an old black ram', is going to make 'a grandsire' of Brabantio. The naive Roderigo reveals himself to the senator, but the distraught father thinks Roderigo is drunk, 'full of supper and distempering draughts', and has simply come to make mischief. Brabantio had already ordered Roderigo from his house on an earlier occasion and rejected his marriage proposal to Desdemona, 'My daughter is not for thee'.

Meanwhile, Iago slyly remains in the shadows, shouting racist insults, 'you'll have your daughter covered with a Barbary horse'. Roderigo also paints a graphic picture of Desdemona's 'gross revolt' into the arms of the 'lascivious Moor'. It seems that Roderigo is genuinely shocked at Desdemona's choice of husband, 'Tying her duty, beauty, wit and fortunes' to Othello. After some consideration, Brabantio decides to take action. He calls for light, 'Strike on the tinder' and organises a full-scale search for his daughter.

Various exits (lines 154–194)

Conniving as always, Iago insists that he cannot be seen with the search party because he has to pretend that he is loyal to Othello; it would not be 'wholesome to my place'. But he is unable to conceal how much he abhors the Moor, 'I do hate him as I do hell-pains'. Once more he instructs Roderigo, ordering him to lead the searchers to the Sagittary Inn where the newlyweds are staying. Iago then slips away quietly to 'support' Othello.

Meanwhile Brabantio is feeling sorry for himself and lamenting his fate, 'Who would be a father!' He is devastated by Desdemona's actions and regards her elopement as 'treason of the blood'. Brabantio wonders if his daughter has been stolen from him by magic 'charms'. He even wishes that she had married Roderigo rather than the Moor. The scene ends with Brabantio and Roderigo setting off with a group of armed men in search of Othello.

Shakespeare's Dramatic Style

The dramatic opening sets the scene and creates an **edgy atmosphere**. Shakespeare presents his audience with an angry exchange between Roderigo and Iago, about a nameless man whom they both hate. The poorly lit street setting adds to the sense of intrigue. Before long, there are ominous signs of trouble ahead – resulting from both Iago's resentment towards Othello and Roderigo's envy over Desdemona's elopement. Brabantio's fury at his daughter's secret life and his acceptance of hearsay rather than evidence foreshadow Othello's tragic behaviour.

Neither of the main characters, Othello or Desdemona, appears in this opening scene, although the dialogue and action centres on the couple. Several **questions engage the audience**. Who exactly is this mysterious Moor whom the state of Venice relies on so heavily? Why is he subjected to so much racial abuse? How has Othello charmed the daughter of one of the leading citizens of this sophisticated city? And why did the lovers elope?

Tone is used to great effect in this opening scene. Iago swears frequently (''Sblood', 'Forsooth') to browbeat and control the less assured Roderigo, 'Thou toldst me thou didst hold him in thy hate'. Iago's injured pride, 'I know my price', gives way to contempt as he sneers at Michael Cassio, the 'arithmetician', who has secured a prestigious position as Othello's lieutenant. Iago begins to win over the audience by complaining bitterly about the loss of traditional values such as loyalty and professional experience. He seems to have a plausible grievance.

Like a poisonous spider, however, Iago is weaving his web within this complex tangle of personal relationships. Whom will he ensnare? What methods will he use to 'serve' his 'turn'? Are Othello, Desdemona and Cassio all in danger? **Tension is established between opposites**: dark/light, black/white, words/actions, good/evil, male/female, secret love/secret hate, passionate impulse/civilised control, order/anarchy. The scene is set. What will happen next?

Critical Analysis

Discuss how Shakespeare's use of language, including imagery, plays an important part in developing our understanding of the setting and atmosphere of Act 1 Scene 1 of the play *Othello*.

Write a paragraph (about 150–200 words), supporting your answer with reference to the play.

Prompt!

- Shakespeare introduces the audience to a shadowy world of intrigue and menace where nothing is as it appears to be. Iago is the master of deception.
- Animal imagery and racist language contribute to the coarse atmosphere.
- Sharp contrasts show a divided, morally ambivalent world.

Sample Paragraph 1

Shakespeare protrays an exciting opening in Othello. He starts with the image of an argument by Iago and Roderigo because he thinks Iago has been scamming him by taking his money and not letting on what's really going on. They both hate Othello who is not even in the scene. They decide to go to Barbantio's house who is the father of Desdemona who has run off with Othello and tell him. Roderigo loves her, but she married Othello, an African army leader. They wake up Barbantio and use bad language to get him so angry so he gets his soldiers to look for the couple who have elloped. They all go to the local inn to arrest him. This is an exciting setting for the start of the play. *(130 words)*

Examiner's Comment

- This basic response fails to take on the question directly.
- Some slight references to conflict and the excited atmosphere.
- No focus on language or imagery.
- Repetitive expression, some awkward expression and spelling errors ('protrays', 'Barbantio', 'elloped').

Sample Paragraph 2

The opening scene of 'Othello' by William Shakespeare is set in Venice. Iago and Roderigo fight in a public street. Their angry language sets a violent mood. Iago is jealous that Cassio has been promoted to the senior position he wanted. Iago despises him because he has no wartime experience, 'he never set a squadron'. Cassio only knows the theory of battle, 'great arithmetician'. Iago is more vulgar than Roderigo, although he describes Desdemona's secretive elopement to really annoy her father, making crude jokes about the 'gross clasps of a lecherous Moor'. There are many contrasts in this uneasy scene, such as between daylight and darkness ('dull watch o' the night'). The tense mood is also caused by the racial insults against Othello by his white enemies. This shows how everything is breaking down and there is 'gross revolt' in the civilised city of Venice. *(145 words)*

Examiner's Comment

- This mid-grade response makes a solid attempt to address the question.
- Some reasonably focused comments linking abusive language with the uneasy mood.
- The point about tension is good but deserves further development.
- Generally controlled expression throughout.
- More supportive reference and quotation would have improved the answer.

Sample Paragraph 3

A murky world of intrigue is seen at the start of 'Othello'. Set late at night on a dimly lit Venetian street, two men engage in a heated argument, 'Never tell me'/ 'but you will not hear me'. Iago vents his anger against Othello, 'I do hate him as I do hell-pains',/ ''Sblood'. Coarse imagery adds to the crude atmosphere, as he and Roderigo taunt Brabantio about Desdemona's secret marriage to the Moor, 'your daughter covered with a Barbary horse'. Shakespeare has cleverly positioned his audience as eavesdroppers to Iago's tale of bitter disappointment at failing to gain promotion to lieutenant. This morally unstable society is further drawn by his contrasting accounts of 'service'. Loyalty and openness go unrewarded, 'shows of service ... Do well thrive'. The scene concludes with the deceitful Iago slipping away, under cover of darkness, having instigated a search for Othello and Desdemona. He tells the gullible Roderigo that he 'must show out a flag, and sign of love' to his hated master, Othello. The midnight elopement highlights the contrast between passionate impulse and civilised control. Venice represents order, but beneath its surface, all is not as it appears. Iago, the master of deception, symbolises this ambivalent atmosphere, 'I am not what I am'. *(210 words)*

Examiner's Comment

- This successful top-grade answer tackles the question directly and engages well with the text.
- Focused discussion of night-time setting, language and symbolism in creating atmosphere.
- Some well-supported development of points on moral ambivalence, using apt reference and quotation.
- Impressive expression and varied vocabulary ('morally unstable society', 'passionate impulse and civilised control').

Class/Homework Exercise

What is your initial impression of Iago? Has he a plausible grievance against Othello or is he a skilful manipulator who enjoys causing trouble for others?

Write a paragraph (about 150–200 words), giving reasons for your views and supporting your response with accurate quotation from the text.

Prompt!

Plausible grievance:

- Iago feels insulted that Othello has promoted an inexperienced officer, Cassio, in preference to him, whom Othello has seen in action on the battlefield. Three influential persons from Venice have spoken on Iago's behalf, but have been ignored. Seniority and experience have been unfairly cast aside for someone knowledgeable in only the theory of war.

Skilful manipulator:

- Iago cleverly extricates himself from Roderigo's claim of obtaining money from him with false promises. He convinces the foolish Roderigo that he is just as outraged at Othello and Desdemona's elopement. He forces Roderigo into telling Desdemona's father the news of his daughter's secret marriage. In contrast to Roderigo, Iago keeps himself hidden, shouting vulgar comments from the shadows. Having started the trouble, he is shrewd enough not to be found in the middle of it.

Revision Overview

Iago has been taking money from Roderigo, to help him win Desdemona's love. But she has eloped with Othello, a Moor and a general in the Venetian army. Although Roderigo is disappointed and angry, Iago succeeds in regaining his trust by explaining how and why he also hates Othello. He is resentful because he has been passed over for promotion by Othello and only serves him to exact revenge.

Roderigo envies Othello's success in winning Desdemona. Iago instructs Roderigo to waken Brabantio to tell him of his daughter's secret marriage. They succeed in upsetting the old senator, who at first orders Roderigo away from his home, as he has done before. But the two men continue to harass Brabantio and he enlists the help of Roderigo in organising a search for the couple. Iago has now managed to place both Roderigo and Brabantio in direct opposition to Othello while he sneaks off to maintain favour with the general who is of such importance to the Venetian state.

Exam Focus

Act 1 Scene 1 can be used successfully in response to a range of examination questions about the play's central themes, characters, relationships and the playwright's dramatic style.

This **key scene** has significant dramatic functions:

- Establishes the cosmopolitan setting of Venice, a place of hushed conversations where there is a mood of intrigue and dark practices.
- Presents initial views of Iago, Roderigo and Brabantio.
- Offers first impressions of Othello and Desdemona.
- Introduces themes of hatred, jealousy, racism, dishonour and love.
- Uses animal imagery to cause offence and incite prejudice.
- Involves the audience in the emerging conspiratorial plot.

- **Theme: Appearance and reality –** Iago's paradoxical statement 'I am not what I am' emphasises the ambiguity of his complex identity. It also highlights the disorder beneath the appearance of civilisation in the Venetian world.
- **Characters: Iago –** embittered, experienced soldier, elusive, devious manipulator, coarse, prejudiced.
  Roderigo – rich, disappointed suitor to Desdemona, gullible, privileged, believes money can buy everything, including love.
  Brabantio – Venetian senator, rich, respectable, trusting, can be persuaded without proof.

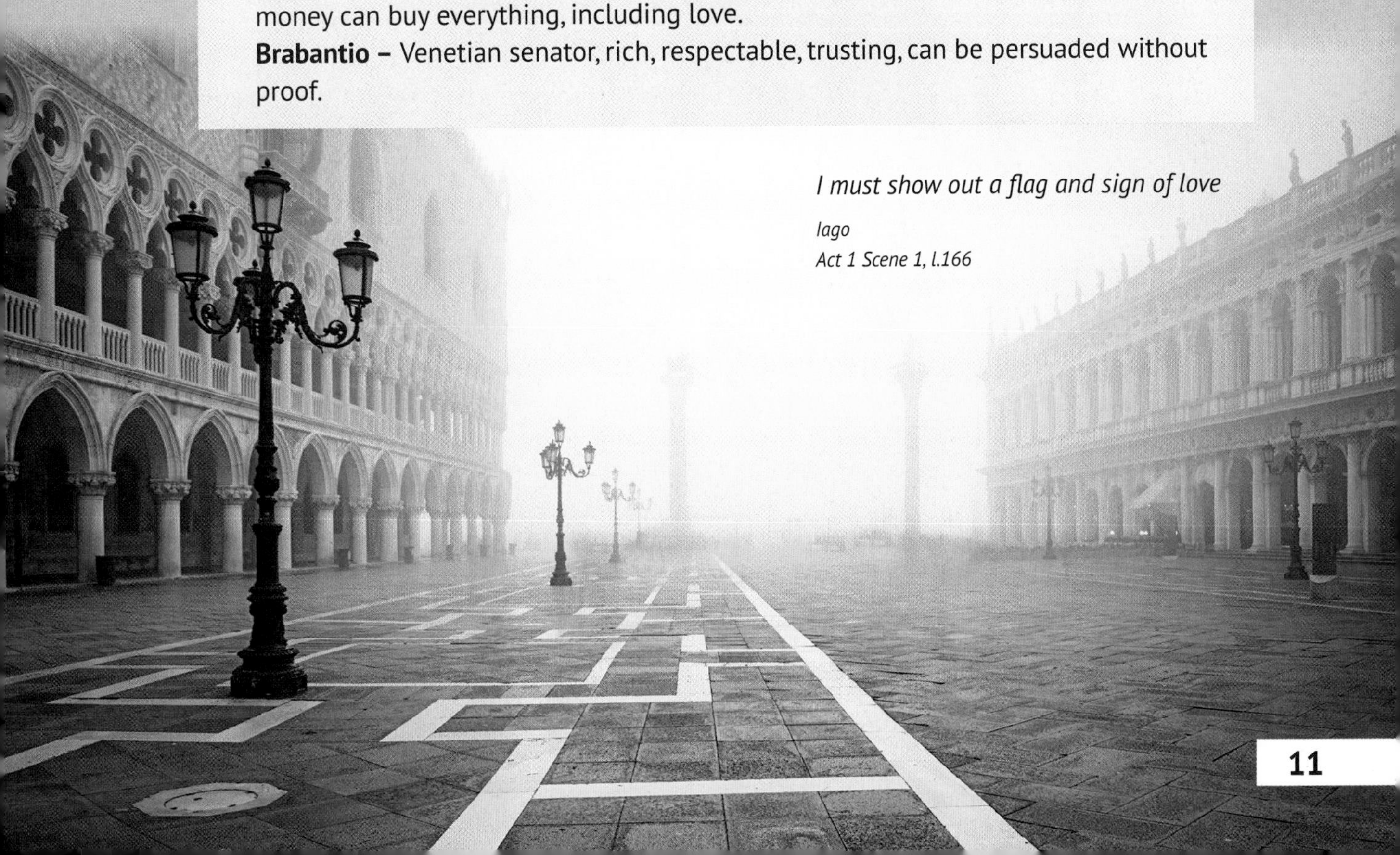

I must show out a flag and sign of love

Iago
Act 1 Scene 1, l.166

Key Quotes

I follow him to serve my turn upon him *(Iago to Roderigo) l.43*	Iago's determined tone shows how intent he is on reversing the power dynamic between himself and Othello. Bitter at being passed over for promotion, he will take his revenge by merely pretending to be loyal while really looking out for himself. He will make use of Roderigo to destroy Othello, almost as if he is playing a game.
I am not what I am *(Iago to Roderigo) l.66*	Establishes the evil nature of Iago's character. His outward appearance conceals his true self. He is really a cold, calculating genius. The line also references the duplicitous nature of Venice, which is about to be exposed.
an old black ram *Is tupping your white ewe* *(Iago to Brabantio) l.91–2*	In reducing Othello to the level of a beast in this coarse metaphor, Iago reveals his racist outlook. There is also a sense of the patriarchal culture in Venice – Desdemona does not belong to herself, but to the men around her. The metaphor uses animal imagery coupled with reference to Othello's Moorish descent to illustrate hostility towards his ethnicity.
To the gross clasps of a lascivious Moor *(Roderigo to Brabantio) l.134*	Seething sibilance and long vowel sounds convey Roderigo's self-pitying resentment. Rejected by Desdemona, he resorts to abusing Othello. Roderigo's exaggerated language also reflects his social snobbery and racism.
Who would be a father! *(Brabantio) l.174*	Brabantio's disjointed speech reveals his shattered state of mind. He is torn between love for his daughter and anguish at her deception. Shocked by her elopement, he wavers between blaming her 'treason' and excusing her as a victim of dark arts. However, Brabantio has rushed to judgement without proof, which foreshadows tragic events later in the play.

Scene 2

INTRODUCTION

- Hypocritical Iago warns Othello against both Roderigo and Brabantio.
- Othello remains calm and refuses to be provoked.
- Brabantio seeks justice, believing his daughter has been tricked by the Moor.
- The Duke of Venice and the Senate will decide Othello's fate.

2 very stuff o' the conscience: *as a matter of moral decency*
3 contrived: *planned*
3–4 I lack iniquity ... service: *sometimes I'm not evil enough for my own good*
5 yerked him: *stabbed Roderigo*
7 prated: *chattered, babbled*
8 scurvy and provoking terms: *offensive and despicable insults*
11 forbear: *tolerate*
12 fast: *legally*
13 magnifico: *nobleman (referring to Brabantio)*
14–15 a voice potential ... duke's: *as powerful an influence as the Duke of Venice*
18 cable: *rights*
20 signiory: *Venetian government*
21 out-tongue: *outweigh, offset*
23 promulgate: *make public*
23–24 fetch ... royal siege: *descended from kings*
24 demerits: *traits, qualities*
25 unbonneted: *on equal terms*
28 my unhoused free condition: *my status as a bachelor*
29 circumscription and confine: *restriction*
30 raised: *angry and alarmed*
34 parts: *abilities*
34 perfect soul: *clear conscience*
36 Janus: *two-faced Roman god*

Venice: Outside the Sagittary Inn

Enter Othello, Iago and attendants with torches

Iago
Though in the trade of war I have slain men,
Yet do I hold it very stuff o' the conscience
To do no contrived murder: I lack iniquity
Sometimes to do me service: nine or ten times
I had thought to have yerked him here under the ribs.

Othello
'Tis better as it is.

Iago
Nay, but he prated,
And spoke such scurvy and provoking terms
Against your honour
That, with the little godliness I have,
I did full hard forbear him. But, I pray you, sir,
Are you fast married? Be assured of this,
That the magnifico is much beloved,
And hath in his effect a voice potential
As double as the duke's. He will divorce you,
Or put upon you what restraint and grievance
The law, with all his might to enforce it on,
Will give him cable.

Othello
Let him do his spite:
My services which I have done the signiory
Shall out-tongue his complaints. 'Tis yet to know –
Which, when I know that boasting is an honour,
I shall promulgate – I fetch my life and being
From men of royal siege, and my demerits
May speak unbonneted to as proud a fortune
As this that I have reached. For know, Iago,
But that I love the gentle Desdemona,
I would not my unhoused free condition
Put into circumscription and confine
For the sea's worth. But look what lights come yond!

Iago
Those are the raised father and his friends:
You were best go in.

Othello
Not I; I must be found.
My parts, my title and my perfect soul
Shall manifest me rightly. Is it they?

Iago
By Janus, I think no.
Enter Cassio and certain officers with torches

Othello
The servants of the duke, and my lieutenant!
The goodness of the night upon you, friends.
What is the news?

Cassio The duke does greet you, general,
And he requires your haste-post-haste appearance,
Even on the instant.

Othello What is the matter, think you?

Cassio Something from Cyprus as I may divine.
It is a business of some heat. The galleys
Have sent a dozen sequent messengers
This very night at one another's heels;
And many of the consuls, raised and met,
Are at the duke's already. You have been
hotly called for,
When, being not at your lodging to be found,
The senate hath sent about three several quests
To search you out.

Othello 'Tis well I am found by you.
I will but spend a word here in the house,
And go with you.

Exit

Cassio Ancient, what makes he here?

Iago 'Faith, he to-night hath boarded a land carrack:
If it prove lawful prize, he's made for ever.

Cassio I do not understand.

Iago He's married.

Cassio To who?

Re-enter Othello

Iago Marry, to – Come, captain, will you go?

Othello Have with you.

Cassio Here comes another troop to seek for you.

Iago It is Brabantio. General, be advised,
He comes to bad intent.

Enter Brabantio, Roderigo and officers with torches and weapons

Othello Holla, stand there!

Roderigo Signior, it is the Moor.

Brabantio Down with him, thief!

They draw on both sides

Iago You, Roderigo! Come, sir, I am for you.

Othello Keep up your bright swords, for the dew will rust them.
Good signior, you shall more command with years
Than with your weapons.

41 haste-post-haste: *immediate*
44 divine: *guess*
45 heat: *urgency*
46 sequent: *successive*
48 consuls: *senators*
49 hotly: *urgently*
51 several quests: *separate search parties*
57 land carrack: *treasure ship (Desdemona)*
58 lawful prize: *legal capture*
70 am for you: *will fight you*
71 Keep up: *put away*

Brabantio
O thou foul thief, where hast thou stowed my daughter?
Damned as thou art, thou hast enchanted her;
For I'll refer me to all things of sense,
If she in chains of magic were not bound,
Whether a maid so tender, fair and happy,
So opposite to marriage that she shunned
The wealthy curled darlings of our nation,
Would ever have, to incur a general mock,
Run from her guardage to the sooty bosom
Of such a thing as thou – to fear, not to delight.
Judge me the world, if 'tis not gross in sense
That thou hast practised on her with foul charms,
Abused her delicate youth with drugs or minerals
That weaken motion: I'll have it disputed on;
'Tis probable and palpable to thinking.
I therefore apprehend and do attach thee
For an abuser of the world, a practiser
Of arts inhibited and out of warrant.
Lay hold upon him: if he do resist,
Subdue him at his peril.

Othello
Hold your hands,
Both you of my inclining, and the rest.
Were it my cue to fight, I should have known it
Without a prompter. Where will you that I go
To answer this your charge?

Brabantio
To prison, till fit time
Of law and course of direct session
Call thee to answer.

Othello
What if I do obey?
How may the duke be therewith satisfied,
Whose messengers are here about my side,
Upon some present business of the state
To bring me to him?

First Officer
'Tis true, most worthy signior;
The duke's in council and your noble self,
I am sure, is sent for.

Brabantio
How! the duke in council!
In this time of the night! Bring him away:
Mine's not an idle cause: the duke himself,
Or any of my brothers of the state,
Cannot but feel this wrong as 'twere their own;
For if such actions may have passage free,
Bond-slaves and pagans shall our statesmen be.

Exeunt

76 refer me ... sense: *appeal to common sense*
79 opposite to marriage: *uninterested in getting married*
80 curled darlings: *privileged Venetian men*
81 incur a general mock: *subject herself to public ridicule*
82 guardage: *guardianship (of her father)*
82 sooty bosom: *derogatory reference to Othello's colour*
84 gross in sense: *quite obvious*
88 probable and palpable to thinking: *easily proven*
91 arts inhibited: *black magic*
91 out of warrant: *against the law*
95 of my inclining: *who support me*
96 cue: *correct moment*
100 course of direct session: *normal legal process*
105 present: *critical, important*
112 idle cause: *insignificant wrong*
113 brothers of the state: *fellow senators*
115 passage free: *no consequences*
116 Bond-slaves and pagans: *slaves and heathens*

Commentary

False information (lines 1–35)

On a street outside the Saggitary Inn, Iago pretends to be outraged at Roderigo's 'scurvy and provoking terms' against Othello's 'honour'. Iago also warns Othello that Brabantio is a powerful man who could have the secret marriage annulled. The general remains controlled, however, and is clearly confident of his importance as a military commander to the Venetian state, 'My services ... Shall out-tongue his complaints'. Othello is obviously proud of his distinguished family background, stating that he is descended from 'men of royal siege'. He declares his feelings for his new bride with sincerity, 'I love the gentle Desdemona', insisting that this is the only reason he married and gave up his personal freedom, 'unhoused free condition'. A characteristically insincere Iago offers to save Othello from the approaching search party, 'You were best go in'. However, Othello rejects his advice and chooses to stand his ground, 'I must be found'.

Important state business (lines 36–67)

The first search party arrives, led by Cassio, who brings urgent news from the Senate that Turkish forces seem intent on capturing Cyprus, a strategic island under the control of Venice. Othello is 'hotly called for', confirming his importance to the security of the state. After Othello's hasty departure, Iago describes the Moor's 's love for Desdemona in crude terms, 'he to-night hath boarded a land carrack'. This compares Othello to a pirate who has stolen Desdemona's love.

Important personal business (lines 68–116)

A second search party arrives, headed by Brabantio and Roderigo, who are both keen to arrest Othello. Weapons are quickly drawn. Othello calmly takes charge of the situation, however, defusing a physical confrontation with words alone, 'Keep up your bright swords, for the dew will rust them'. Brabantio accuses Othello of practising dark arts to win his daughter, 'thou hast enchanted her'. The frantic father is at a loss to understand how Desdemona 'shunned/ The wealthy curled darlings' of Venice and instead chose Othello's 'sooty bosom'.

Were it my cue to fight,
I should have known it
Without a prompter

Othello
Act 1 Scene 2, l.96–7

Othello refuses to be provoked by these racist insults, 'Were it my cue to fight, I should have known it', and promises to 'answer' all of Brabantio's accusations. The two men agree to go to the Duke, who is 'in council' on account of the developing threat by the Turks. Brabantio is certain that his case will be supported by the members of the Senate, who will 'feel this wrong as 'twere their own'. The audience is left to decide where their sympathies lie. With Desdemona's loving husband, Othello? Or with her enraged father, who feels that his daughter has been wronged?

Dramatic Significance of Act 1 Scene 2

Scene 2 heightens the atmosphere of confusion established at the start of the play. Two search parties find Othello. Their arrival **combines the public threat to Venice by Turkey and the private dispute over Desdemona's marriage**. The audience is now positioned to judge Othello from his own words and actions.

He appears confident and considered, 'My parts, my title, and my perfect soul/ Shall manifest me rightly'. The picture of a lewd practitioner of 'foul charms' begins to disappear. **Shakespeare subtly subverts racial bigotry by showing its injustice.** The audience realises that Othello was being described by a rejected suitor, a demoted subordinate and an angry father. When characters judge one another, they often define themselves more than they define the other person.

It is interesting that Othello is staying at the Saggitary Inn. The zodiac sign of Saggitarius is associated with a warlike individual who regards life as a grand adventure. It is also appropriate that the duplicitous Iago swears by the two-headed Roman god, Janus. The comment reflects his two-faced character. On several occasions, we witness the ensign's quick wit in action, always turning events to his advantage. Act 1 Scene 2 highlights **growing dramatic tension** within the unsettled world of Venice.

Class/Homework Exercise

Shakespeare examines society's treatment of the outsider in his play *Othello*.

Compare the presentation of the character of Othello in Act 1 Scene 1 and Act 1 Scene 2 of the play. Write a paragraph (about 150–200 words), supporting your answer with reference to the two scenes.

Prompt!

- Scene 1 contains abusive references to ethnicity, 'the Moor'; racial stereotype, 'the thick-lips;' and character defects, 'loving his own pride and purposes'.
- Iago and Roderigo expect that Brabantio will view his daughter's elopement with Othello as shameful and unacceptable within Venetian society.
- In Scene 2, Brabantio accuses Othello of practising dark arts 'in chains of magic' and drugs. Demeaning racial slurs, 'a thing'.
- Scene 2 presents Othello's actual words – confident of his 'services' to Venice, secure in his love for Desdemona, he refuses to run away, ''Tis well I am found by you', will not brawl in public.

Revision Overview

Iago seeks out Othello and pretends to be outraged at Roderigo's behaviour. He warns Othello of the influential power of Desdemona's angry father. But Othello is confident that his military service to Venice and his royal birth will be valued by the Senate. Cassio arrives, leading the first search party, and informs Othello that he is urgently required to attend the Senate, which is in session because of the Turkish threat to the state. The second search party arrives, led by an angry Brabantio, who insults Othello with charges of using magic and drugs to seduce his naive daughter. Othello tries to pacify him and they agree to ask the Senate to resolve the matter. Brabantio is a respected senator and feels confident that he will be vindicated when he presents his case against Othello before the Duke of Venice.

- **Theme: Appearance and reality –** who is speaking the truth? Iago? Othello? Brabantio?
- **Characters: Iago –** hypocritical play-maker, influencing other characters and events.
  Othello – quiet, dignified, self-confident, authoritative presence.
  Brabantio – an angry father seeking justice, hysterical, racist, superstitious.

Key Quotes

My services which I have done the signiory Shall out-tongue his complaints *(Othello to Iago) l.20–21*	Othello is confident of his importance to the Senate. As a successful army general who has defended the state, he believes that his good reputation and royal connections will protect him against any false accusations by Brabantio. His calm tone reflects his important position as a respected figure who has assimilated well into Venetian society.
You have been hotly called for *(Cassio to Othello) l.49*	Cassio's urgent message confirms the Senate's dependence on Othello's military expertise to protect them from the Turkish threat to Cyprus.
he to-night hath boarded a land carrack *(Iago to Cassio) l.57*	The cynical Iago sees Othello's love for Desdemona in sea-faring terms – boarding a large treasure ship. He compares his general's marriage to an act of piracy similar to seizing a ship at sea. Iago cannot imagine a relationship based on love. Instead, he regards the marriage as something that benefits Othello's future.
So opposite to marriage that she shunned The wealthy curled darlings of our nation *(Brabantio to Othello) l.79–80*	Brabantio feels wronged and he struggles to understand his daughter's elopement with Othello. He believes that Desdemona was never interested in marriage and that she had already rejected several rich Venetian gentlemen – such as Roderigo.
Were it my cue to fight, I should have known it Without a prompter *(Othello) l.96–7*	Othello uses a theatrical expression to show his authority. He defuses an explosive situation by calmly stating that he does not need a signal from anyone to tell him when to fight. This use of imagery and his controlled tone suggest a sophisticated individual.

Act 1
Scene 3*

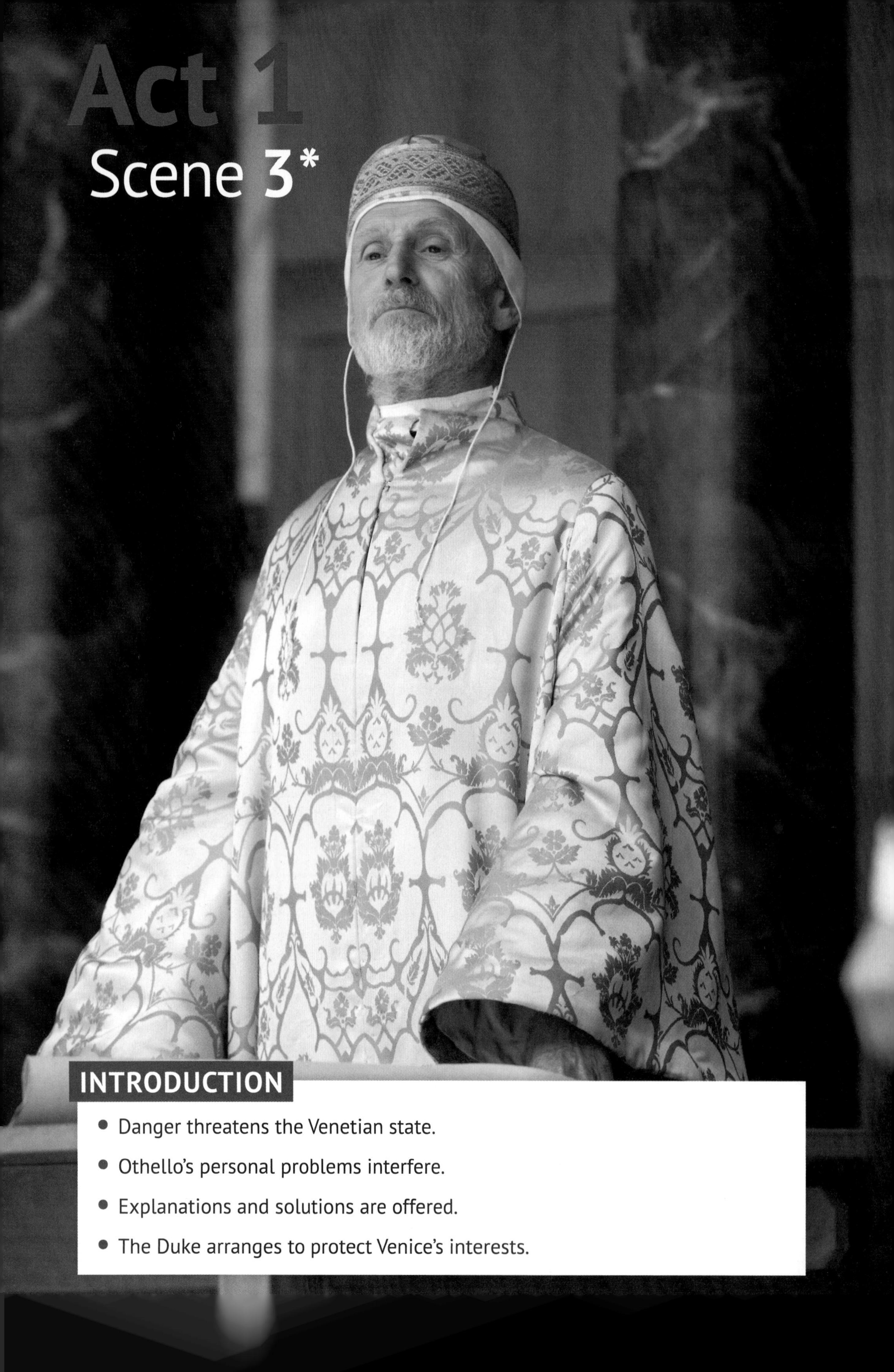

INTRODUCTION

- Danger threatens the Venetian state.
- Othello's personal problems interfere.
- Explanations and solutions are offered.
- The Duke arranges to protect Venice's interests.

Venice: A council-chamber

The Duke and Senators sitting at a table with lights. Officers attending.

Duke of Venice There is no composition in these news
That gives them credit.

First Senator Indeed, they are disproportioned.
My letters say a hundred and seven galleys.

Duke of Venice And mine, a hundred and forty.

Second Senator And mine, two hundred:
But though they jump not on a just account
As in these cases, where the aim reports,
'Tis oft with difference – yet do they all confirm
A Turkish fleet, and bearing up to Cyprus.

Duke of Venice Nay, it is possible enough to judgment:
I do not so secure me in the error,
But the main article I do approve
In fearful sense.

Sailor [*Within*] What, ho! What, ho! What, ho!

First Officer A messenger from the galleys.

Enter a Sailor

Duke of Venice Now, what's the business?

Sailor The Turkish preparation makes for Rhodes;
So was I bid report here to the state
By Signior Angelo.

Duke of Venice How say you by this change?

First Senator This cannot be,
By no assay of reason: 'tis a pageant,
To keep us in false gaze. When we consider
The importancy of Cyprus to the Turk,
And let ourselves again but understand,
That as it more concerns the Turk than Rhodes,
So may he with more facile question bear it,
For that it stands not in such warlike brace,
But altogether lacks the abilities
That Rhodes is dressed in: if we make thought of this,
We must not think the Turk is so unskilful
To leave that latest which concerns him first,
Neglecting an attempt of ease and gain,
To wake and wage a danger profitless.

Duke of Venice Nay, in all confidence, he's not for Rhodes.

First Officer Here is more news.

Enter a Messenger

1 composition: *consistency, agreement*
2 gives them credit: *makes the reports believable*
3 disproportioned: *inconsistent, changeable*
7 jump not on a just account: *do not agree precisely*
8 where the aim reports: *where they are just estimates*
10 bearing up: *sailing towards*
12 secure me: *feel confident*
13 approve: *accept, believe*
14 In fearful sense: *as a cause for alarm*
23 assay of reason: *reasonable trial or analysis*
23 pageant: *pretence, trick*
24 false gaze: *deceived, confused*
29 brace: *readiness, preparation*
31 dressed in: *equipped with*
35 wage: *risk*

38 Ottomites: *Turks (from the Ottoman Empire)*

40 injointed ... fleet: *linked up with another fleet of ships*

42 restem: *retrace, change direction*

46 free duty: *respect*

53 straight: *straight away*

62 engluts: *engulfs, overwhelms*

69 mountebanks: *tricksters, quacks*

71 Sans: *without*

73 beguiled: *charmed, tricked*

Messenger The Ottomites, reverend and gracious,
Steering with due course towards the isle of Rhodes,
Have there injointed them with an after fleet.

First Senator Ay, so I thought. How many, as you guess?

Messenger Of thirty sail: and now they do restem
Their backward course, bearing with frank appearance
Their purposes toward Cyprus. Signior Montano,
Your trusty and most valiant servitor,
With his free duty recommends you thus,
And prays you to believe him.

Duke of Venice 'Tis certain, then, for Cyprus.
Marcus Luccicos, is not he in town?

First Senator He's now in Florence.

Duke of Venice Write from us to him; post-post-haste dispatch.

First Senator Here comes Brabantio and the valiant Moor.

Enter Brabantio, Othello, Iago, Roderigo and Officers

Duke of Venice Valiant Othello, we must straight employ you
Against the general enemy Ottoman.

[***To Brabantio***]

I did not see you; welcome, gentle signior;
We lacked your counsel and your help tonight.

Brabantio So did I yours. Good your grace, pardon me;
Neither my place nor aught I heard of business
Hath raised me from my bed, nor doth the general care
Take hold on me, for my particular grief
Is of so flood-gate and o'erbearing nature
That it engluts and swallows other sorrows
And it is still itself.

Duke of Venice Why, what's the matter?

Brabantio My daughter! O, my daughter!

Senators Dead?

Brabantio Ay, to me;
She is abused, stolen from me and corrupted
By spells and medicines bought of mountebanks;
For nature so preposterously to err,
Sans witchcraft could not.

Duke of Venice Whoe'er he be that in this foul proceeding
Hath thus beguiled your daughter of herself
And you of her, the bloody book of law
You shall yourself read in the bitter letter

After your own sense, yea, though our proper son
Stood in your action.

Brabantio Humbly I thank your grace.
Here is the man, this Moor, whom now, it seems,
Your special mandate for the state-affairs
Hath hither brought.

Duke of Venice [***With Senators***] We are very sorry for it.

Duke of Venice [***To Othello***] What, in your own part, can you say to this?

Brabantio Nothing, but this is so.

Othello Most potent, grave, and reverend signiors,
My very noble and approved good masters,
That I have taken away this old man's daughter,
It is most true; true, I have married her:
The very head and front of my offending
Hath this extent, no more. Rude am I in my speech,
And little blessed with the soft phrase of peace:
For since these arms of mine had seven years' pith,
Till now some nine moons wasted, they have used
Their dearest action in the tented field,
And little of this great world can I speak,
More than pertains to feats of broil and battle,
And therefore little shall I grace my cause
In speaking for myself. Yet, by your gracious patience,
I will a round unvarnish'd tale deliver
Of my whole course of love: what drugs, what charms,
What conjuration and what mighty magic –
For such proceeding I am charged withal –
I won his daughter.

Brabantio A maiden never bold;
Of spirit so still and quiet, that her motion
Blushed at herself; and she, in spite of nature,
Of years, of country, credit, everything,
To fall in love with what she feared to look on?
It is a judgment maimed and most imperfect
That will confess perfection so could err
Against all rules of nature, and must be driven
To find out practices of cunning hell,
Why this should be. I therefore vouch again
That with some mixtures powerful o'er the blood
Or with some dram conjured to this effect
He wrought upon her.

76 After your own sense: *as you wish*
77 Stood in your action: *was the person you accused*
80 mandate: *order*
89 head and front: *extent*
90 Rude: *rough, uncultured*
92 pith: *strength, growth*
94 field: *battlefield*
97 grace: *advance*
101 conjuration: *spells, tricks*
105 motion: *movement, desires*
107 credit: *reputation*
109 maimed: *flawed, tarnished*
113 vouch: *claim*
115 dram: *magic potion*

119 thin habits: *weak accusations*

120 modern seeming: *common beliefs, rumours*

128 foul: *evil, wicked*

146 disastrous chances: *dangerous events*

147 by flood and field: *on sea and on land*

148 the imminent deadly breach: *at the very point of death*

152 antres: *caves*

152 idle: *empty*

156 Anthropophagi: *cannibals, man-eaters*

Duke of Venice To vouch this is no proof,
Without more wider and more overt test
Than these thin habits and poor likelihoods
Of modern seeming do prefer against him.

First Senator But, Othello, speak:
Did you by indirect and forced courses
Subdue and poison this young maid's affections?
Or came it by request and such fair question
As soul to soul affordeth?

Othello I do beseech you,
Send for the lady to the Sagittary,
If you do find me foul in her report,
The trust, the office I do hold of you,
Not only take away, but let your sentence
Even fall upon my life.

Duke of Venice Fetch Desdemona hither.

Othello Ancient, conduct them: you best know the place.

Exeunt Iago and Attendants

And, till she come, as truly as to heaven
I do confess the vices of my blood,
So justly to your grave ears I'll present
How I did thrive in this fair lady's love,
And she in mine.

Duke of Venice Say it, Othello.

Othello Her father loved me; oft invited me;
Still questioned me the story of my life,
From year to year, the battles, sieges, fortunes,
That I have passed.
I ran it through, even from my boyish days,
To the very moment that he bade me tell it;
Wherein I spake of most disastrous chances,
Of moving accidents by flood and field
Of hair-breadth scapes i' the imminent deadly breach,
Of being taken by the insolent foe
And sold to slavery, of my redemption thence
And portance in my travels' history:
Wherein of antres vast and deserts idle,
Rough quarries, rocks and hills whose heads touch heaven
It was my hint to speak – such was the process
And of the Cannibals that each other eat,
The Anthropophagi and men whose heads
Do grow beneath their shoulders. This to hear
Would Desdemona seriously incline;

But still the house-affairs would draw her thence:
Which ever as she could with haste dispatch,
She'd come again, and with a greedy ear
Devour up my discourse; which I observing,
Took once a pliant hour, and found good means
To draw from her a prayer of earnest heart
That I would all my pilgrimage dilate,
Whereof by parcels she had something heard,
But not intentively: I did consent,
And often did beguile her of her tears
When I did speak of some distressful stroke
That my youth suffered. My story being done,
She gave me for my pains a world of sighs:
She swore, in faith, 'twas strange,
'twas passing strange,
'Twas pitiful, 'twas wondrous pitiful:
She wished she had not heard it, yet she wished
That heaven had made her such a man. She
thanked me,
And bade me, if I had a friend that loved her,
I should but teach him how to tell my story,
And that would woo her. Upon this hint I spake:
She loved me for the dangers I had passed,
And I loved her that she did pity them.
This only is the witchcraft I have used:
Here comes the lady; let her witness it.

Enter Desdemona, Iago, and Attendants

Duke of Venice I think this tale would win my daughter too.
Good Brabantio, take up this mangled matter at the best:
Men do their broken weapons rather use
Than their bare hands.

Brabantio I pray you, hear her speak:
If she confess that she was half the wooer,
Destruction on my head, if my bad blame
Light on the man! Come hither, gentle mistress:
Do you perceive in all this noble company
Where most you owe obedience?

Desdemona My noble father,
I do perceive here a divided duty:
To you I am bound for life and education;
My life and education both do learn me
How to respect you; you are the lord of duty;
I am hitherto your daughter. But here's my husband,
And so much duty as my mother showed
To you, preferring you before her father,

162 Devour ... discourse: *eagerly listen to me*
163 pliant: *convenient, favourable*
165 dilate: *tell at length*
166 by parcels: *in parts, not the whole story*
167 intentively: *completely*
168 beguile: *entice, coax*
172 passing: *surpassingly, exceedingly*
176 bade: *implored*
178 spake: *spoke up, declared myself*
182 witness: *verify, confirm*
184 mangled: *confused, unclear*
190 Light on: *condemns*
196 learn: *teach*

201 challenge: *claim*

203 God be wi' you: *God be with you (goodbye)*

205 get: *create a child of my own*

212 clogs: *wooden blocks tied to horses' legs to restrain them*

214 grise: *support, staircase*

221 Patience ... makes: *endurance helps us cope with loss*

223 bootless: *useless*

230 sugar: *sweeten*
230 gall: *poison*
231 equivocal: *debatable, ambiguous*

236 fortitude: *strength*

237 substitute: *replacement*

241 slubber: *spoil, smear*

242 stubborn and boisterous: *tough and violent*

So much I challenge that I may profess
Due to the Moor my lord.

Brabantio God be wi' you! I have done.
Please it your grace, on to the state-affairs.
I had rather to adopt a child than get it.
Come hither, Moor:
I here do give thee that with all my heart
Which, but thou hast already, with all my heart
I would keep from thee. For your sake, jewel,
I am glad at soul I have no other child,
For thy escape would teach me tyranny
To hang clogs on them. I have done, my lord.

Duke of Venice Let me speak like yourself, and lay a sentence
Which as a grise or step may help these lovers
Into your favour.
When remedies are past, the griefs are ended
By seeing the worst which late on hopes depended.
To mourn a mischief that is past and gone
Is the next way to draw new mischief on.
What cannot be preserved when fortune takes,
Patience her injury a mockery makes.
The robbed that smiles steals something from the thief;
He robs himself that spends a bootless grief.

Brabantio So let the Turk of Cyprus us beguile;
We lose it not, so long as we can smile.
He bears the sentence well that nothing bears
But the free comfort which from thence he hears,
But he bears both the sentence and the sorrow
That, to pay grief, must of poor patience borrow.
These sentences, to sugar, or to gall,
Being strong on both sides, are equivocal:
But words are words; I never yet did hear
That the bruised heart was pierced through the ear.
I humbly beseech you, proceed to the affairs of state.

Duke of Venice The Turk with a most mighty preparation makes for Cyprus. Othello, the fortitude of the place is best known to you; and though we have there a substitute of most allowed sufficiency, yet opinion, a sovereign mistress of effects, throws a more safer voice on you: you must therefore be content to slubber the gloss of your new fortunes with this more stubborn and boisterous expedition.

Othello
The tyrant custom, most grave senators,
Hath made the flinty and steel couch of war
My thrice-driven bed of down: I do agnise
A natural and prompt alacrity
I find in hardness, and do undertake
These present wars against the Ottomites.
Most humbly therefore bending to your state,
I crave fit disposition for my wife.
Due reference of place and exhibition,
With such accommodation and besort
As levels with her breeding.

Duke of Venice
If you please,
Be it at her father's.

Brabantio
I'll not have it so.

Othello
Nor I.

Desdemona
Nor I; I would not there reside,
To put my father in impatient thoughts
By being in his eye. Most gracious duke,
To my unfolding lend your prosperous ear;
And let me find a charter in your voice,
To assist my simpleness.

Duke of Venice
What would you, Desdemona?

Desdemona
That I did love the Moor to live with him,
My downright violence and storm of fortunes
May trumpet to the world: my heart's subdued
Even to the very quality of my lord:
I saw Othello's visage in his mind,
And to his honour and his valiant parts
Did I my soul and fortunes consecrate.
So that, dear lords, if I be left behind,
A moth of peace, and he go to the war,
The rites for which I love him are bereft me,
And I a heavy interim shall support
By his dear absence. Let me go with him.

Othello
Let her have your voices.
Vouch with me, heaven, I therefore beg it not,
To please the palate of my appetite,
Nor to comply with heat the young affects
In me defunct and proper satisfaction,
But to be free and bounteous to her mind:
And heaven defend your good souls, that you think
I will your serious and great business scant
For she is with me: no, when light-wing'd toys

245 thrice-driven bed of down: *soft feather bed*
245 agnise: *acknowledge*
246 alacrity: *eagerness*
248 Ottomites: *Turks*
250 disposition: *arrangements*
251 exhibition: *respect, support*
252 besort: *servants*
262 let me find a charter in your voice: *give me your support*
266 downright violence: *open rebellion*
269 visage: *face*
284 scant: *neglect*

286 seal: *fill*

287 speculative ... instruments: *physical and mental powers*

288 disports: *sexual pleasures*

289 skillet: *saucepan*

289 helm: *helmet*

290 indign: *unworthy, sinful*

301 import: *concern*

303 honest: *first use of ironic term to describe Iago*

310 delighted: *outstanding*

312 use: *treat*

319 in the best advantage: *at the first opportunity*

Of feathered Cupid seal with wanton dullness
My speculative and officed instruments,
That my disports corrupt and taint my business,
Let housewives make a skillet of my helm,
And all indign and base adversities
Make head against my estimation!

Duke of Venice Be it as you shall privately determine,
Either for her stay or going: the affair cries haste,
And speed must answer it.

First Senator You must away to-night.

Othello With all my heart.

Duke of Venice At nine in the morning here we'll meet again.
Othello, leave some officer behind,
And he shall our commission bring to you;
With such things else of quality and respect
As doth import you.

Othello So please your grace, my ancient;
A man he is of honest and trust:
To his conveyance I assign my wife,
With what else needful your good grace shall think
To be sent after me.

Duke of Venice Let it be so.
Good night to everyone.
[*To Brabantio*]
And, noble signior,
If virtue no delighted beauty lack,
Your son-in-law is far more fair than black.

First Senator Adieu, brave Moor, use Desdemona well.

Brabantio Look to her, Moor, if thou hast eyes to see:
She has deceived her father, and may thee.

Othello My life upon her faith!

Exeunt Duke, Brabantio, Cassio, Senators and Attendants

Othello Honest Iago,
My Desdemona must I leave to thee:
I prithee, let thy wife attend on her:
And bring them after in the best advantage.
Come, Desdemona: I have but an hour
Of love, of worldly matters and direction,
To spend with thee: we must obey the time.

Exeunt Othello and Desdemona

Roderigo Iago.

Iago What say'st thou, noble heart?

Roderigo What will I do, thinkest thou?

Iago Why, go to bed, and sleep.

Roderigo I will incontinently drown myself.

Iago If thou dost, I shall never love thee after. Why, thou silly gentleman?

Roderigo It is silliness to live when to live is torment: and then have we a prescription to die when death is our physician.

Iago O villainous! I have looked upon the world for four times seven years; and since I could distinguish betwixt a benefit and an injury, I never found man that knew how to love himself. Ere I would say, I would drown myself for the love of a guinea-hen, I would change my humanity with a baboon.

Roderigo What should I do? I confess it is my shame to be so fond, but it is not in my virtue to amend it.

Iago Virtue! A fig! 'Tis in ourselves that we are thus or thus. Our bodies are our gardens, to the which our wills are gardeners. So that if we will plant nettles, or sow lettuce, set hyssop and weed up thyme, supply it with one gender of herbs or distract it with many, either to have it sterile with idleness, or manured with industry, why, the power and corrigible authority of this lies in our wills. If the balance of our lives had not one scale of reason to poise another of sensuality, the blood and baseness of our natures would conduct us to most preposterous conclusions. But we have reason to cool our raging motions, our carnal stings, our unbitted lusts, whereof I take this that you call love to be a sect or scion.

Roderigo It cannot be.

Iago It is merely a lust of the blood and a permission of the will. Come, be a man. Drown thyself? Drown cats and blind puppies. I have professed me thy friend, and I confess me knit to thy deserving with cables of perdurable toughness; I could never better stead thee than now. Put money in thy purse. Follow thou these wars; defeat thy favour with an usurped beard. I say, put money in thy purse. It cannot be that Desdemona should long continue her love to the Moor – put money in thy purse – nor he

327 incontinently: *instantly*

336 guinea-hen: *prostitute*

337 baboon: *ape*

343–4 hyssop, thyme: *aromatic herbs*

344 gender: *type, kind*

347 corrigible authority: *ability to control*

349 poise: *counterbalance*

352 carnal strings: *sexual urges*

353 unbitted: *uncontrollable*

354 sect: *offshoot*

354 scion: *cutting*

360 perdurable: *long-lasting*

361 stead thee: *help you*

367 sequestration: *separation, divorce*

370 locusts: *fruit of the carob tree*

371 coloquintida: *bitter apple*

372 sated with: *tired of*

378 super-subtle: *refined*

380 pox: *plague*

388 conjunctive: *allied, combined*

389 cuckold: *suspect his wife of adultery*

392 Traverse: *march, get going*

his to her. It was a violent commencement, and thou shalt see an answerable sequestration – put but money in thy purse. These Moors are changeable in their wills – fill thy purse with money. The food that to him now is as luscious as locusts, shall be to him shortly as bitter as coloquintida. She must change for youth; when she is sated with his body, she will find the error of her choice. Therefore put money in thy purse. If thou wilt needs damn thyself, do it a more delicate way than drowning. Make all the money thou canst. If sanctimony and a frail vow betwixt an erring barbarian and a super-subtle Venetian not too hard for my wits and all the tribe of hell, thou shalt enjoy her – therefore make money. A pox of drowning thyself! It is clean out of the way. Seek thou rather to be hanged in compassing thy joy than to be drowned and go without her.

Roderigo Wilt thou be fast to my hopes, if I depend on the issue?

Iago Thou art sure of me. Go, make money. I have told thee often, and I retell thee again and again, I hate the Moor. My cause is hearted: thine hath no less reason. Let us be conjunctive in our revenge against him. If thou canst cuckold him, thou dost thyself a pleasure, me a sport. There are many events in the womb of time which will be delivered. Traverse! Go, provide thy money. We will have more of this to-morrow. Adieu.

Roderigo Where shall we meet in the morning?

Iago At my lodging.

Roderigo I'll be with thee betimes.

Iago Go to; farewell. Do you hear, Roderigo?

Roderigo What say you?

Iago No more of drowning, do you hear?

Roderigo I am changed.

Iago Go to; farewell. Put money enough in your purse.

Roderigo I'll sell all my land.

Exit

Iago Thus do I ever make my fool my purse:
For I mine own gained knowledge should profane,
If I would time expend with such a snipe.
But for my sport and profit. I hate the Moor:
And it is thought abroad, that 'twixt my sheets
He has done my office. I know not if it be true
Yet I, for mere suspicion in that kind,
Will do as if for surety. He holds me well:
The better shall my purpose work on him.
Cassio's a proper man: let me see now:
To get his place and to plume up my will
In double knavery. How, how? Let's see.
After some time, to abuse Othello's ear
That he is too familiar with his wife;
He hath a person and a smooth dispose
To be suspected, framed to make women false.
The Moor is of a free and open nature,
That thinks men honest that but seem to be so,
And will as tenderly be led by the nose
As asses are.
I have't. It is engender'd. Hell and night
Must bring this monstrous birth to the world's light.
Exit

405 snipe: *idiot*
407 thought abroad: *generally rumoured*
408 done my office: *slept with my wife*
412 proper: *handsome, popular*
413 plume up my will: *have some fun, glorify myself*
416 familiar: *intimate*
423 engender'd: *formed, created*

Key Scene Extended Commentary

Public matters (lines 1–52)

The Duke and senators discuss the Turkish threat to the state. Venice was a thriving port and its wealthy merchants required safe sea routes around the Mediterranean for transporting goods. The state employed naval boats and mercenary troops to protect their commercial interests. However, conflicting reports 'with difference' arrive regarding the Turkish fleet, which seems to be en route to Cyprus. The tension is increased by the deceptive manoeuvres of the Turks. The Duke considers the evidence and decides that their likely intention is to invade Cyprus.

Domestic turmoil (lines 53–103)

'Valiant Othello' is greeted warmly by the Duke, who expresses the state's urgent need of their great general, 'we must straight employ you'. Not surprisingly, the focus is on Venice's own interests. Brabantio interrupts the state's business with a torrent of extravagant accusations that his daughter has been 'corrupted' with 'spells and medicines'. At first the Duke promises swift justice, 'the bloody book of law'. The mood changes, however, when Brabantio points to the offender, 'Here is the man, this Moor'. The Duke requests Othello to tell his 'part'. In contrast to his hysterical father-in-law, Othello adopts a solemn sincerity and immediately accepts responsibility, confessing, 'I have married her'. He also claims that he is 'Rude' in speech, because he has been a soldier for much of his life. Ironically, he then makes a sophisticated speech. Othello appeals to the 'potent, grave, and reverend signiors'. He crafts his points eloquently, claiming that he 'won' Brabantio's daughter by fair means, not foul.

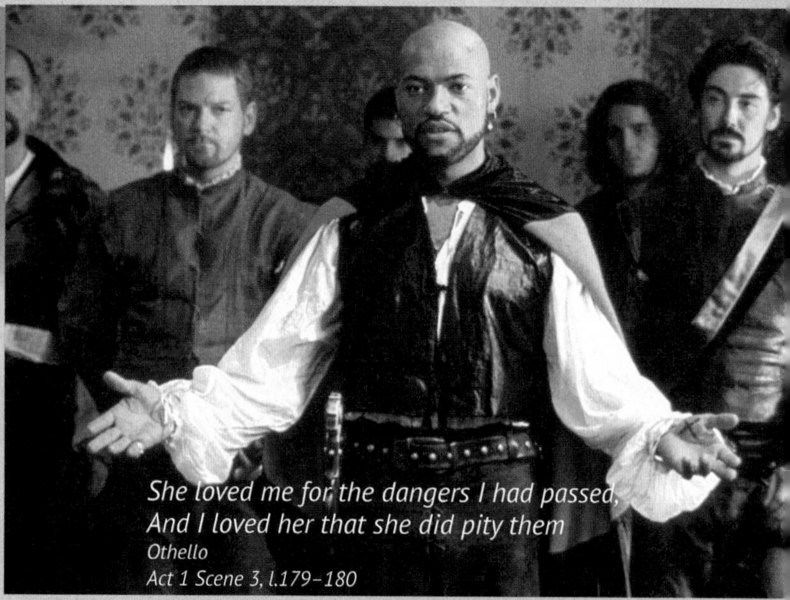

She loved me for the dangers I had passed,
And I loved her that she did pity them
Othello
Act 1 Scene 3, l.179–180

Divided positions (lines 104–234)

Brabantio refuses to accept that his daughter, 'A maiden never bold', should fall in love 'with what she feared to look at'. He insists that this inter-racial marriage is so unnatural that Othello must have used 'some mixtures powerful o'er the blood' to win Desdemona. Othello is so confident of his position, however, that he instructs the senators to 'Send for the lady'. He wishes Desdemona to testify before her father and to support his evidence.

Othello then informs the Senate about how he and his wife first met, recalling that Brabantio frequently 'invited' him to his home to tell 'the story of my life'. It was his tales of war and 'the dangers' he had experienced that attracted her. Desdemona initiated the relationship by declaring that if Othello would teach a friend of his to tell such a story, then 'that would woo her'. In response, the Duke gives his considered verdict, 'I think this tale would win my daughter too'. He offers practical advice to Brabantio about making the best of this 'mangled matter'. The incredulous father refuses to believe that Desdemona was 'half the wooer'. We are left wondering if Brabantio ever really knew his daughter.

Desdemona herself is quietly assertive, tactfully acknowledging 'a divided duty'. She acknowledges the debt she owes her 'noble father', but just as her mother left home to marry Brabantio, she has done likewise in choosing Othello. The distraught father is forced to admit defeat, but he adds a cruel jibe, 'I had rather to adopt a child than get it'.

I had rather to adopt a child than get it
Brabantio
Act 1 Scene 3, l.205

New arrangements (lines 235–322)

The Duke urges Othello to lead Venice's 'stubborn and boisterous expedition' against the Turks. Desdemona pleads to be allowed to accompany Othello on his campaign. She is prepared to publicly 'trumpet' her love for the Moor. This is a very different woman from the one described by her father as 'still and quiet'. Othello promises that he will not neglect his official duties if his wife goes with him. The Duke agrees to let the couple 'privately determine' and emphasises the immediate threat to the state that 'cries haste'. Othello declares that 'honest' Iago and his wife Emilia will accompany Desdemona to Cyprus. As Brabantio departs, his final comment foreshadows the play's tragic outcome. He casts doubt on his daughter's character, 'She has deceived her father, and may thee'. Othello's response is ironic, 'My life upon her faith!'

I saw Othello's visage in his mind

Desdemona
Act 1 Scene 3, l.269

Cynical opportunist (lines 323–402)

A heartbroken Roderigo threatens suicide because he cannot now marry Desdemona. Iago immediately counsels him to accompany Othello and the Venetian forces against the Turks, 'Follow these wars'. He reassures him, pointing out that the Moors are 'changeable', that Desdemona will seek a younger man, 'change for youth', and that the marriage cannot last, 'she will find the error of her choice'. Iago is dependent on Roderigo's wealth and repeatedly urges him, 'Put money in thy purse'. He expresses his cynical view on life – everything has a price, so Desdemona can be bought. Iago also provides a more convincing motive for Roderigo to believe him, 'I hate the Moor'. He suggests joining forces 'in our revenge'. The master of improvisation uses everything to his advantage. As always, Roderigo is easily convinced, 'I am changed', and immediately resolves to 'sell all my land'.

A monstrous birth (lines 403–424)

Iago's soliloquy allows an insight into the workings of his warped mind as he devises his 'monstrous' plan of revenge. It is only in his soliloquies that we can be sure that he is speaking the truth. Iago operates on self-interest alone. He has a talent for spotting the weaknesses of other people and coolly lists each character's flaws. Roderigo is despised as a 'fool', a 'purse' and a 'snipe'. Iago acknowledges the Moor's 'frank and open nature', which he intends to use for his own degenerate 'purpose'. He understands that Othello 'holds me well', so he can turn that to his advantage also. He knows Cassio is a 'proper man' whose refinement and sophistication, 'smooth dispose', would be appealing to women.

There are other reasons for Iago's obsessive hatred. He believes that his wife Emilia and Othello have been lovers, although he has no proof, only 'mere suspicion'. He also wishes to oust Cassio from his influential position as lieutenant and destroy the Moor, 'abuse Othello's ear', with insinuations that Cassio is also 'too familiar with his wife'. Iago is aware that Othello judges on appearance, 'thinks men honest that but seem to be so', therefore the Moor can be easily manipulated, 'led by the nose/ As asses are'. Iago's vengeful plan is finally in place, 'It is engender'd'. Will this villain be successful in exploiting and corrupting the weaknesses and insecurities of others?

Hell and night
Must bring this monstrous birth
to the world's light
Iago
Act 1 Scene 3, l.423–4

Shakespeare's Dramatic Style

Repetition heightens the distinction between appearance and reality throughout Act 1 Scene 3. 'The verb 'beguile' is used on several occasions. The Duke is concerned that Brabantio's daughter has been blinded, 'beguiled ... of herself'. Othello admits that his tales of dangerous adventures induced Desdemona to cry, 'beguile her of her tears'. Brabantio wryly suggests that the Turks could trick the Venetians out of Cyprus because, following the Duke's logic, 'We lose it not, so long as we can smile'. However, Desdemona sees beyond physical appearance and judges Othello not on outward show but on his character, 'I saw Othello's visage in his mind'. Will she be proven right?

Is Shakespeare playing with the **audience's emotions** by almost convincing them of Iago's world view that we have 'reason to cool our raging motions'? His solution to every problem is 'put money in thy purse'. He reduces everything to physical and material terms. It is his open admission of enjoyment of evil for its own sake, however, that really chills the audience. Iago advises Roderigo to have an affair with Desdemona and 'cuckold' Othello not only for his own 'pleasure' but to give Iago 'sport'. He is prepared to destroy three people to 'plume up my will/ In double knavery'.

As the scene concludes, Shakespeare succeeds in stirring up a tremendous **sense of foreboding**. The audience is now in possession of all the significant facts of character and incident. Iago's soliloquy allows us to witness the origins of Othello's downfall. We can begin to trace the turbulent emotional journey of a great but vulnerable man who is setting out on a collision course with an undeclared enemy, 'honest' Iago. Act 1 Scene 3 is both fascinating and appalling for its range of sinister aspects: the Turkish threat looms, Iago plots, Brabantio issues a dire warning and romantic love is in danger of being blinded by excessive feeling.

Critical Analysis

Identify and discuss an insight or a variety of insights you gained into the subject of identity through your engagement with Act 1 Scene 3 of Shakespeare's play *Othello*.

Write a paragraph (about 150–200 words), supporting your answer with reference to the text.

Prompt!

- Identity refers to individuality, uniqueness and character – who and what a person is.
- Qualities, values, gender, class, race, status, etc. can shape identity.
- Characters can sometimes exhibit both true and false identities.

Sample Paragraph 1

Othello is hated by Iago and Barbanto. Just because he is different. Barbanto cant belive his daughter chose this man for her husband. She will lose her good name. Iago pretends to be honest. But is plotting against Othello in secret behind his back with Rodrigo to get back revenge at Desdemona because he hates 'the moor' because he gave away his job to Cassio that Iago wanted so badly. So Barbanto hates Othello because the daughter is marrying a man whose from a different race and Iago hates Othello because he didnt get the job. This is Othello's foriegn identity as a royle African prince who comes to Venice to fight for Venice against the Turkish army in Cyprus. This is the true insight into Othello as his identity is away from his home. *(135 words)*

Examiner's Comment

- Mainly narrative summary with slight references to identity towards the end.
- Little or no developed discussion.
- Repetitive expression, punctuation errors, some awkward expression and spelling flaws ('Barbanto', 'belive', 'foriegn', 'royle').
- Basic response that fails to tackle the question directly.

Sample Paragraph 2

I learned that a person who is from a different background can be treated unfairly because of unfair-minded racial stereotyping. Othello is a Moor from North Africa and is now in Venice. He is not well educated, 'Rude am I in my speech'. He has spent his life on the battlefield so is not used to the advanced sophisticated Venetian ways. Brabantio accuses him of drugging Desdemona and using 'evil witchcraft' to seduce her into marriage. He typecasts Othello because he is so shocked she should marry 'a Moor' that he would prefer to 'adopt' a child than have one of his own. Iago also labels Othello and is prejudiced against outsiders. He judges Othello as lecherous, which is a common insult, because he suspects Othello of having a love affair with his wife. Neither Iago nor Brabantio have any proof for their unfair accusations against Othello, only their prejudice. *(150 words)*

Examiner's Comment

- Solid mid-grade response that attempts to take on the question.
- Some focused points about Othello's status as an 'outsider'.
- The point about tension is good, but deserves further development.
- Developed discussion and accurate quotation would have improved the answer.
- Expression is generally controlled throughout.

Sample Paragraph 3

In Act 1 Scene 3, Othello is unaware of racial discrimination, believing that his reputation and good name will protect him against any accusations. He is at ease in his own identity, believes in himself. Yet Othello is defined by race by his bitter ensign, Iago. However, the Duke employs Othello as an army commander to protect Venice's interests. A black general is accepted and needed. Desdemona also refuses to judge by outer appearances, 'I saw Othello's visage in his mind'. Like the Duke, she concentrates on Othello's unique abilities, 'his honour and his valiant parts'. But her father is bigoted and judges by racial stereotype, and he will not accept the Moor's marriage to Desdemona which, in his opinion, is 'against all rules of nature'. He concentrates on racial identity. The equally hypocritical Iago refers to Othello as an 'erring barbarian' and makes a sweeping racial judgement, 'The Moors are changeable in their wills'. In this revealing scene, morally dubious characters identify by racial prejudice while open-minded characters, such as the Duke and Desdemona, judge others by their personal characteristics. They respect other people, using a person's name, highlighting that person's individuality. *(190 words)*

Examiner's Comment

- Competent top-grade response addressing the question directly and engaging well with the play.
- Good focused discussion of Othello's dual role as an outsider who has military status in Venice.
- Clear expression and varied vocabulary ('concentrates on Othello's unique abilities', 'sweeping racial judgement').
- Some cogent development of points on moral ambivalence, backed by suitable reference and accurate quotation.

Class/Homework Exercise

Shakespeare's play *Othello* introduces us to a world where evil and disorder are juxtaposed with the forces of goodness and order.

Write a paragraph (about 150–200 words), giving reasons for your views and supporting your response with accurate quotation from Act 1 Scene 3 of the play.

Prompt!

Evil and disorder:

- Turkish threat to the state of Venice
- Blurred distinction between appearance and reality
- Racial bigotry
- Jealousy
- Lust
- Hatred
- Iago, Roderigo, Brabantio

Goodness and order:

- Duke and senators
- Legal solutions to challenging problems
- Tolerance
- Trust
- Honour
- Duty
- Love
- Othello, Desdemona

to his honour and his valiant parts
Did I my soul and fortunes consecrate

Desdemona
Act 1 Scene 3, l.270–271

Revision Overview

The Duke and senators discuss the Turkish threat to the state and hope that Othello will deal with it successfully. When Brabantio accuses Othello of using magic to win Desdemona, the couple explain to the Duke how their love developed. The Duke is sympathetic but is more concerned with the possible crisis in Cyprus and the security of the Venetian state. Othello agrees to leave immediately for Cyprus, requesting that Desdemona accompany him. Iago concocts a plan to make Othello jealous by suggesting that Desdemona and Cassio are secret lovers.

- **Theme: Appearance and reality –** there are rumours that Turkish ships are creating diversions at sea to trick the Venetians into 'false gaze'. Brabantio makes untrue accusations against Othello. Iago's public appearance and private plotting keep everyone confused.
- **Characters: Othello –** eloquent, respected, dutiful, proud, lacking self-knowledge.
  Desdemona – romantic, idealistic, assertive.
  Iago – cunning, manipulative, delights in evil.
  Brabantio – emotional, judgemental, bitter.
  The Duke – calm, authoritative, considered, shrewd.
  Roderigo – depressed, rash, gullible.

Exam Focus

Act 1 Scene 3 can be used successfully in response to a range of examination questions about the play's central themes, characters, relationships and the playwright's dramatic style.

This **key scene** has significant dramatic functions:

- Establishes sense of urgency and unease through the night-time setting. The senators are in emergency session to discuss the military crisis with Turkey.
- Presents Desdemona as a more complex character who seems aware of Othello's vulnerability.
- Develops themes of jealousy, racism, love, duty, appearance and reality.
- Informs the audience of Iago's determined plan for vengeance.
- Increases dramatic tension through irony and foreshadowing.

Let us be conjunctive in our revenge against him

Iago
Act 1 Scene 3, l.388–389

Key Quotes

Valiant Othello, we must straight employ you, *Against the general enemy Ottoman* (Duke to Othello) l.53–54	Although Brabantio enters first, the Duke greets Othello much more warmly. This highlights the crucial importance of the general to Venice. The city's trade routes depend on defeating the Turks. There is no time to be lost.
I saw Othello's visage in his mind, *And to his honour and his valiant parts* *Did I my soul and fortunes consecrate* (Desdemona) l.269–271	Desdemona uses sacred language to describe the spiritual aspect of the couple's relationship. She is the only character who judges Othello beyond appearance. Desdemona looks past his outer form to his inner qualities. She is romantic and trusting.
Look to her, Moor, if thou hast eyes to see: *She has deceived her father, and may thee* (Brabantio to Othello) l.313–4	Having dismissed the Duke's practical advice, Brabantio is angry and bitter. He undermines Desdemona's character and foreshadows the ironic tragedy that lies ahead.
My life upon her faith! (Othello to Brabantio) l.315	At this stage, Othello is the loyal husband who swears an oath on his wife's good reputation. This passionate and trusting pledge will be dismissed later by Iago as a 'frail vow'.
It is engender'd (Iago) l.423	Shakespeare has allowed the audience to watch the inner workings of Iago's villainous mind. We see his talent for identifying the qualities and flaws of others. He will take advantage of Othello's trusting nature to convince him that Cassio is having an affair with Desdemona. Iago has now created his 'monstrous' plan for revenge against both Othello and Cassio.

Act 2
Scene 1*

INTRODUCTION

- A new setting; the remote island of Cyprus.
- Will all the travellers survive the storm and arrive safely?
- Is the Turkish fleet still a threat to Venice?
- Characters reveal more about themselves to the audience.

* **Key scene requiring close, detailed study**

A quayside in Cyprus

Enter Montano and two Gentlemen

Montano What from the cape can you discern at sea?

First Gentleman Nothing at all; it is a high-wrought flood.
I cannot, 'twixt the heaven and the main,
Descry a sail.

Montano Methinks the wind does speak aloud at land,
A fuller blast ne'er shook our battlements.
If it hath ruffianed so upon the sea,
What ribs of oak, when mountains melt on them,
Can hold the mortise? What shall we hear of this?

Second Gentleman A segregation of the Turkish fleet:
For do but stand upon the banning shore,
The chidden billow seems to pelt the clouds;
The wind-shaked surge, with high and monstrous mane,
seems to cast water on the burning Bear,
And quench the guards of the ever-fixed Pole:
I never did like molestation view
On the enchafed flood.

Montano If that the Turkish fleet
Be not ensheltered and embayed, they are drowned:
It is impossible they bear it out.

Enter a third Gentleman

Third Gentleman News, lads! Our wars are done:
The desperate tempest hath so banged the Turks,
That their designment halts. A noble ship of Venice
Hath seen a grievous wreck and sufferance
On most part of their fleet.

Montano How! Is this true?

Third Gentleman The ship is here put in,
A Veronesa; Michael Cassio,
Lieutenant to the warlike Moor Othello,
Is come on shore; the Moor himself at sea,
And is in full commission here for Cyprus.

Montano I am glad on't; 'tis a worthy governor.

Third Gentleman But this same Cassio, though he speak of comfort
Touching the Turkish loss, yet he looks sadly,
And prays the Moor be safe; for they were parted
With foul and violent tempest.

1 cape: *headland*
1 discern: *see*
2 high-wrought: *very rough*
4 Descry: *make out*
7 ruffianed: *raged*
8 ribs of oak: *wooden boats*
9 hold the mortise: *survive*
10 segregation: *scattering*
11 banning: *foaming*
12 chidden billow: *noisy waves*
14–15 Bear, Pole: *constellations of stars*
16–17 like molestation ... enchafed flood: *never seen such disturbed seas*
19 ensheltered and embayed: *safe in harbour*
20 bear it out: *survive*
22 banged: *damaged*
23 designment halts: *plans are ruined*
24 sufferance: *destruction*
28 Veronesa: *Italian ship*
34 Touching: *concerning*

Montano Pray heavens he be;
For I have served him, and the man commands
Like a full soldier. Let's to the seaside, ho!
As well to see the vessel that's come in
As to throw out our eyes for brave Othello,
Even till we make the main and the aerial blue
An indistinct regard.

Third Gentleman Come, let's do so:
For every minute is expectancy
Of more arrivance.

Enter Cassio

Cassio Thanks, you the valiant of this warlike isle,
That so approve the Moor! O, let the heavens
Give him defence against the elements,
For I have lost us him on a dangerous sea.

Montano Is he well shipped?

Cassio His bark is stoutly timbered, his pilot
Of very expert and approved allowance;
Therefore my hopes, not surfeited to death,
Stand in bold cure.

A cry within: 'A sail, a sail, a sail!'

Enter a fourth Gentleman

Cassio What noise?

Fourth Gentleman The town is empty; on the brow o' the sea
Stand ranks of people, and they cry 'A sail!'

Cassio My hopes do shape him for the governor.

Guns heard

Second Gentleman They do discharge their shot of courtesy:
Our friends at least.

Cassio I pray you, sir, go forth,
And give us truth who 'tis that is arrived.

Second Gentleman I shall.

Exit

Montano But, good lieutenant, is your general wived?

Cassio Most fortunately: he hath achieved a maid
That paragons description and wild fame;
One that excels the quirks of blazoning pens,
And in the essential vesture of creation
Does tire the ingener.

42 main: *sea*
42 aerial blue: *sky*
43 An indistinct regard: *indistinguishable*
49 elements: *weather*
53 allowance: *reputation*
54–55 not surfeited ... cure: *are not very high*
59 shape him for: *imagine him to be*
65 wived: *married*
67 paragons: *surpasses*
68 quirks ... pens: *written praise*
69–70 essential ... ingener: *no one can do her beauty justice*

75 guttered: *jagged*
75 congregated: *heaped*
76 ensteeped: *submerged*
76 guiltless keel: *unknowing ship*
78 mortal: *deadly*
83 footing: *arrival*
84 se'nnight's speed: *a week ahead*
88 extincted spirits: *fears*
92 let her have your knees: *kneel before her*
95 Enwheel: *encircle*
101 contention: *storm*
103 citadel: *fortress (Cyprus)*

Re-enter second Gentleman

How now! who has put in?

Second Gentleman 'Tis one Iago, ancient to the general.

Cassio Has had most favourable and happy speed:
Tempests themselves, high seas, and howling winds,
The guttered rocks and congregated sands,
Traitors ensteeped to clog the guiltless keel,
As having sense of beauty, do omit
Their mortal natures, letting go safely by
The divine Desdemona.

Montano What is she?

Cassio She that I spake of, our great captain's captain,
Left in the conduct of the bold Iago,
Whose footing here anticipates our thoughts
A se'nnight's speed. Great Jove, Othello guard,
And swell his sail with thine own powerful breath,
That he may bless this bay with his tall ship,
Make love's quick pants in Desdemona's arms,
Give renewed fire to our extincted spirits
And bring all Cyprus comfort!

Enter Desdemona, Emilia, Iago, Roderigo, and Attendants

O, behold,
The riches of the ship is come on shore!
Ye men of Cyprus, let her have your knees.
Hail to thee, lady! And the grace of heaven,
Before, behind thee, and on every hand,
Enwheel thee round!

Desdemona I thank you, valiant Cassio.
What tidings can you tell me of my lord?

Cassio He is not yet arrived: nor know I aught
But that he's well and will be shortly here.

Desdemona O, but I fear – how lost you company?

Cassio The great contention of the sea and skies
Parted our fellowship. But, hark, a sail!

Second Gentleman They give their greeting to the citadel;
This likewise is a friend.

Cassio See for the news.

Exit Gentleman

Good ancient, you are welcome.

To Emilia

Welcome, mistress.
Let it not gall your patience, good Iago,
That I extend my manners; 'tis my breeding
That gives me this bold show of courtesy.

Kissing her

Iago Sir, would she give you so much of her lips
As of her tongue she oft bestows on me,
You'll have enough.

Desdemona Alas, she has no speech.

Iago In faith, too much;
I find it still, when I have list to sleep:
Marry, before your ladyship, I grant,
She puts her tongue a little in her heart,
And chides with thinking.

Emilia You have little cause to say so.

Iago Come on, come on; you are pictures out of doors,
Bells in your parlours, wild-cats in your kitchens,
Saints in your injuries, devils being offended,
Players in your housewifery, and housewives in your beds.

Desdemona O, fie upon thee, slanderer!

Iago Nay, it is true, or else I am a Turk:
You rise to play and go to bed to work.

Emilia You shall not write my praise.

Iago No, let me not.

Desdemona What wouldst thou write of me, if thou shouldst
praise me?

Iago O gentle lady, do not put me to't;
For I am nothing, if not critical.

Desdemona Come on, assay. There's one gone to the harbour?

Iago Aye, madam.

Desdemona I am not merry; but I do beguile
The thing I am, by seeming otherwise.
Come, how wouldst thou praise me?

Iago I am about it; but indeed my invention
Comes from my pate as birdlime does from frieze;
It plucks out brains and all: but my muse labours,
And thus she is delivered.
If she be fair and wise, fairness and wit,
The one's for use, the other useth it.

108 gall: *annoy*
112 bestows on: *gives out to*
114 has ... speech: *is soft-spoken*
116 have list: *want*
119 chides with thinking: *scolds silently*
121 pictures: *silent beauties*
122 Bells: *noisy*
124 Players: *lazy home-makers*
124 housewives: *shameless*
134 assay: *try*
136 beguile: *pretend I am*
139 I am about it: *I am thinking about it*
140 pate: *mind*
140 birdlime ... frieze: *with great difficulty (like trying to catch birds)*
141 muse: *inspiration*
142 delivered: *slowly produced*
143 wit: *intelligence*

Desdemona Well praised! How if she be black and witty?

Iago If she be black, and thereto have a wit,
She'll find a white that shall her blackness fit.

Desdemona Worse and worse.

Emilia How if fair and foolish?

Iago She never yet was foolish that was fair;
For even her folly helped her to an heir.

Desdemona These are old fond paradoxes to make fools laugh i' the alehouse. What miserable praise hast thou for her that's foul and foolish?

Iago There's none so foul and foolish thereunto,
But does foul pranks which fair and wise ones do.

Desdemona O heavy ignorance! thou praisest the worst best. But what praise couldst thou bestow on a deserving woman indeed, one that, in the authority of her merit, did justly put on the vouch of very malice itself?

Iago She that was ever fair and never proud,
Had tongue at will and yet was never loud,
Never lacked gold and yet went never gay,
Fled from her wish and yet said 'Now I may',
She that being angered, her revenge being nigh,
Bade her wrong stay and her displeasure fly,
She that in wisdom never was so frail
To change the cod's head for the salmon's tail;
She that could think and ne'er disclose her mind,
See suitors following and not look behind,
She was a wight, if ever such wight were—

Desdemona To do what?

Iago To suckle fools and chronicle small beer.

Desdemona O most lame and impotent conclusion! Do not learn of him, Emilia, though he be thy husband. How say you, Cassio? is he not a most profane and liberal counsellor?

Cassio He speaks home, madam: You may relish him more in the soldier than in the scholar.

Iago [*Aside*] He takes her by the palm: ay, well said, whisper: with as little a web as this will I ensnare as great a fly as Cassio. Ay, smile upon her, do; I will catch you in your own courtesies. You say true; 'tis so, indeed: if such tricks as these strip you out of your lieutenantry, it had been better you had not kissed your three fingers so

152 fond paradoxes: *foolish jokes*

159–160 one that ... itself: *a woman who didn't worry about what others say*

171 wight: *lover*

173 chronicle ... beer: *be concerned with trivial matters*

176 profane and liberal: *vulgar and immoral*

178 home: *bluntly*

182 ensnare: *trap*

oft, which now again you are most apt to play the
sir in. Very good; well kissed! An excellent
courtesy! 'Tis so, indeed. Yet again your fingers
to your lips? Would they were clyster-pipes for your sake!

Trumpet within

The Moor! I know his trumpet.

Cassio 'Tis truly so.

Desdemona Let's meet him and receive him.

Cassio Lo, where he comes!

Enter Othello and Attendants

Othello O my fair warrior!

Desdemona My dear Othello!

Othello It gives me wonder great as my content
To see you here before me. O my soul's joy!
If after every tempest come such calms,
May the winds blow till they have wakened death!
And let the labouring bark climb hills of seas
Olympus-high and duck again as low
As hell's from heaven! If it were now to die,
'Twere now to be most happy; for, I fear,
My soul hath her content so absolute
That not another comfort like to this
Succeeds in unknown fate.

Desdemona The heavens forbid
But that our loves and comforts should increase,
Even as our days do grow!

Othello Amen to that, sweet powers!
I cannot speak enough of this content;
It stops me here; it is too much of joy:
And this, and this, the greatest discords be
[***Kissing her***]
That e'er our hearts shall make!

Iago [***Aside***] O, you are well tuned now!
But I'll set down the pegs that make this music,
As honest as I am.

Othello Come, let us to the castle.
News, friends; our wars are done, the Turks are
  drowned.
How does my old acquaintance of this isle?
Honey, you shall be well desired in Cyprus;
I have found great love amongst them. O my sweet,
I prattle out of fashion, and I dote
In mine own comforts. I prithee, good Iago,

190 clyster-pipes: *tubes used in medical operations*

201 bark: *ship*

201–2 hills ... Olympus-high: *as tall as a legendary mountain*

203 If it were now to die: *if I died now*

217 set down the pegs: *loosen the strings – to cause disharmony*

224 I dote: *I'm not making sense*

226 coffers: *luggage*
227 master: *man in command*
234 list: *listen to*
239 Lay thy finger thus: *put your finger to your lips and be quiet*
243 Her eye must be fed: *she needs a good-looking lover*
244-5 the devil: *Othello*
246 sport: *love-making*
249 defective: *lacking*
251 heave the gorge: *become sick of it*
254-5 pregnant ... position: *obviously true*
256 voluble: *eloquent*
257-9 putting on ... affection: *puts on a show of good manners to hide his real desires*
260 subtle slippery: *smoothly treacherous*
261-2 can ... advantages: *that is opportunistic*
264 requisites: *requirements*
265 green minds: *foolish girls*
265 pestilent: *dangerous*
266 the woman: *Desdemona*

Go to the bay and disembark my coffers:
Bring thou the master to the citadel;
He is a good one, and his worthiness
Does challenge much respect. Come, Desdemona,
Once more, well met at Cyprus.

Exeunt Othello, Desdemona, and Attendants

Iago Do thou meet me presently at the harbour. Come hither. If thou be'st valiant – as, they say, base men being in love have then a nobility in their natures more than is native to them – list me. The lieutenant tonight watches on the court of guard: – first, I must tell thee this – Desdemona is directly in love with him.

Roderigo With him! why, 'tis not possible.

Iago Lay thy finger thus, and let thy soul be instructed. Mark me with what violence she first loved the Moor, but for bragging and telling her fantastical lies: and will she love him still for prating? let not thy discreet heart think it. Her eye must be fed; and what delight shall she have to look on the devil? When the blood is made dull with the act of sport, there should be, again to inflame it and to give satiety a fresh appetite, loveliness in favour, sympathy in years, manners and beauties; all which the Moor is defective in: now, for want of these required conveniences, her delicate tenderness will find itself abused, begin to heave the gorge, disrelish and abhor the Moor; very nature will instruct her in it and compel her to some second choice. Now, sir, this granted – as it is a most pregnant and unforced position – who stands so eminently in the degree of this fortune as Cassio does? a knave very voluble; no further conscionable than in putting on the mere form of civil and humane seeming, for the better compassing of his salt and most hidden loose affection? why, none; why, none: a subtle slippery knave, a finder of occasions, that has an eye can stamp and counterfeit advantages, though true advantage never present itself; a devilish knave. Besides, the knave is handsome, young and hath all those requisites in him that folly and green minds look after: a pestilent complete knave; and the woman hath found him already.

Roderigo I cannot believe that in her; she's full of most blessed condition.

Iago Blessed fig's-end! The wine she drinks is made of grapes: if she had been blessed, she would never have loved the Moor. Blessed pudding! Didst thou not see Her paddle with the palm of his hand? Didst not mark that?

Roderigo Yes, that I did; but that was but courtesy.

Iago Lechery, by this hand; an index and obscure prologue to the history of lust and foul thoughts. They met so near with their lips that their breaths embraced together. Villainous thoughts, Roderigo! When these mutualities so marshal the way, hard at hand comes the master and main exercise, the incorporate conclusion, Pish! But, sir, be you ruled by me: I have brought you from Venice. Watch you to-night; for the command, I'll lay it upon you. Cassio knows you not. I'll not be far from you: do you find some occasion to anger Cassio, either by speaking too loud, or tainting his discipline; or from what other course you please, which the time shall more favourably minister.

Roderigo Well.

Iago Sir, he is rash and very sudden in choler, and haply may strike at you: provoke him, that he may; for even out of that will I cause these of Cyprus to mutiny; whose qualification shall come into no true taste again but by the displanting of Cassio. So shall you have a shorter journey to your desires by the means I shall then have to prefer them; and the impediment most profitably removed, without the which there were no expectation of our prosperity.

Roderigo I will do this, if I can bring it to any opportunity.

Iago I warrant thee. Meet me by and by at the citadel:
I must fetch his necessaries ashore. Farewell.

Roderigo Adieu.

Exit

Iago That Cassio loves her, I do well believe it;
That she loves him, 'tis apt and of great credit:
The Moor, howbeit that I endure him not,
Is of a constant, loving, noble nature,
And I dare think he'll prove to Desdemona
A most dear husband. Now, I do love her too;
Not out of absolute lust, though peradventure
I stand accountant for as great a sin,
But partly led to diet my revenge,
For that I do suspect the lusty Moor

269 fig's-end: *rubbish*
272 paddle with: *caress*
274 prologue: *introduction, lead-in*
278 mutualities: *intimate exchanges*
279–280 incorporate conclusion: *physical consummation, sex*
285 tainting: *mocking*
289 in choler: *when angry*
292–3 whose … Cassio: *which will not end until Cassio loses his position as lieutenant*
295 prefer: *advance*
300 necessaries: *belongings*
303 apt … credit: *likely and believable*
304 howbeit: *even though*
308 peradventure: *perhaps*
309 accountant … sin: *also guilty of lusting after her*

312 leaped into my seat: *made love to my wife*
313 inwards: *guts*
319 trace: *follow after, befriend*
320 stand the putting on: *does what I tell him*
321 on the hip: *at my mercy*
322 rank garb: *foul manner*
325 egregiously an ass: *a complete fool*
326 practising upon: *plotting against*
328 Knavery's: *villainy's*

Hath leaped into my seat; the thought whereof
Doth, like a poisonous mineral, gnaw my inwards;
And nothing can or shall content my soul
Till I am evened with him, wife for wife,
Or failing so, yet that I put the Moor
At least into a jealousy so strong
That judgment cannot cure. Which thing to do,
If this poor trash of Venice, whom I trace
For his quick hunting, stand the putting on,
I'll have our Michael Cassio on the hip,
Abuse him to the Moor in the rank garb –
For I fear Cassio with my night-cap too –
Make the Moor thank me, love me and reward me.
For making him egregiously an ass
And practising upon his peace and quiet
Even to madness. 'Tis here, but yet confused:
Knavery's plain face is never seen, till used.

Exit

Key Scene Extended Commentary

Tense anticipation (lines 1–46)

A violent storm rages while the outgoing governor of Cyprus and others wait anxiously on the windswept quayside for the arrival of the new governor, Othello. The sea is a 'high-wrought flood' making it impossible to 'Descry a sail'. The only comfort is that the turbulent weather has destroyed the Turkish fleet. Othello's great soldierly qualities ('warlike Moor', 'brave Othello') are repeatedly praised.

First arrival (lines 47–89)

Michael Cassio, Othello's lieutenant, arrives first. He increases the dramatic tension when he reports that the convoy of ships were 'parted'. His heartfelt prayer for Othello's safe arrival, 'O, let the heavens/ Give him defence against the elements', denotes the close friendship between the general and his officer. Cassio reports on Othello's recent marriage and describes his new bride, Desdemona, in glowing terms, 'a maid/ That paragons description'. He refers to her as 'our captain's captain' and hopes that she will soon be reunited with Othello 'And bring all Cyprus comfort!'

Revealing conversation (lines 90–194)

Cassio's polished manner is evident in the extravagant language he uses to greet Desdemona's arrival, 'The riches of the ship is come on shore', and his demand that due respect should be paid to the new governor's wife, 'let her have your knees'. In contrast, Iago's contempt for women is clear from his description of them as beautiful and silent when in company, 'pictures out of doors', but noisy 'wild-cats' and cold 'housewives' at home. Desdemona challenges his jaundiced view of women by calling him a 'slanderer'.

I am not merry; but I do beguile
The thing I am, by seeming otherwise

Desdemona
Act 2 Scene 1, l.136–7

Surprisingly, she and Iago engage in clever wordplay and mild flirtation while they await the arrival of Othello. Several times she asks him how he would 'praise' her. Does this fit in with the audience's previous impression of Desdemona? Is she the quiet 'maiden' described by her father? Or is she the strong-willed character who defied her father and society to follow her heart and who eloquently pleaded her case in the Senate to accompany her husband to Cyprus?

with as little a web as this will I
ensnare as great a fly as Cassio

Iago
Act 2 Scene 1, l.181–2

Listening to Iago's coarse comments, the audience can see why Othello chose the courteous Cassio as his lieutenant. In an ominous aside, the scorned ensign vows to 'catch' Cassio 'in your own courtesies'. Iago is skilled at turning situations to his advantage and intends to use Cassio's elegant manners to dislodge him from his position as lieutenant.

Happy reunion (lines 195–230)

Othello arrives and the newlyweds are happily reunited, 'O my soul's joy!' Although their mutual love seems obvious, the audience is caught between several responses: relief at the safe arrival of Othello, delight at the lovers' reunion and mounting anxiety at Iago's malicious schemes. In another aside, Iago vows to avenge himself against Othello, 'to set down the pegs'. He will use Othello's great love for Desdemona to ruin him. Unaware of the threat, Othello declares that all is 'well met at Cyprus'.

The plot thickens (lines 231–328)

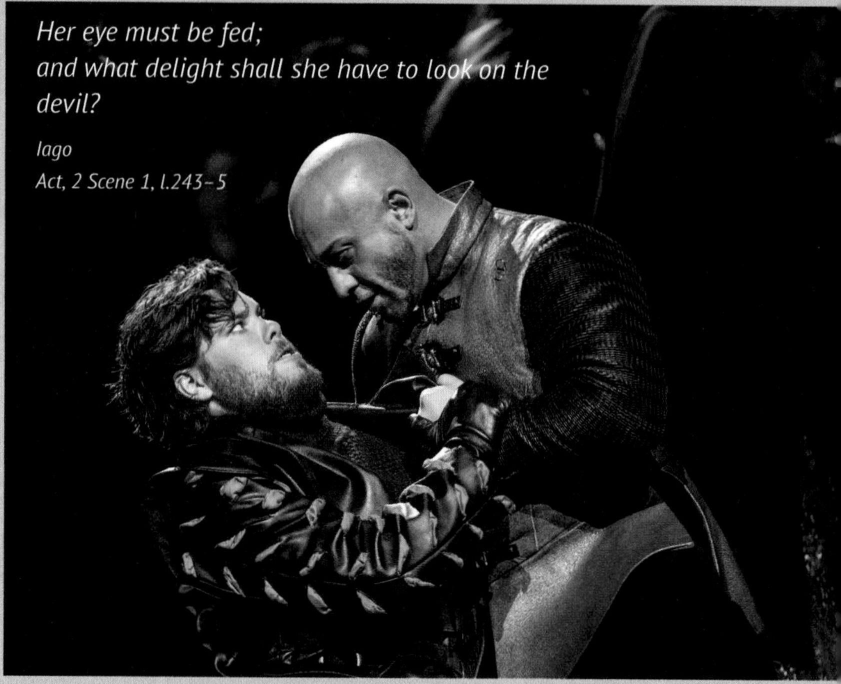

Her eye must be fed;
and what delight shall she have to look on the devil?
Iago
Act, 2 Scene 1, l.243–5

Iago and Roderigo are left alone together while the others proceed to the castle. Iago immediately casts doubt on Desdemona's reputation by claiming that she is having a secret affair with Cassio, 'Desdemona is directly in love with him'. He belittles Othello's character by accusing him of boasting and 'telling fantastical lies'. Roderigo finds it hard to believe Iago's insinuations because he worships Desdemona, whom he regards as 'full of most blessed condition'. Yet Iago succeeds in his insinuations that 'the subtle slippery knave' Cassio had an ulterior motive in his shows of gallantry.

Iago deliberately twists Cassio's actions, 'Didst thou not see/ Her paddle with the palm of his hand?' He convinces the credulous Roderigo to provoke Cassio, who is easily angered, 'very sudden in choler', while he will then 'cause these of Cyprus to mutiny'. If the plan to discredit Cassio works, he will be relieved of his position as lieutenant.

This key scene concludes with another revealing soliloquy from Iago. He is well aware of Othello's positive qualities, 'constant, loving, noble'. Iago's stated motives for revenge are that he suspects both Othello and Cassio of being his wife's lovers. Yet there is no real evidence that Emilia has been unfaithful. But Iago believes the worst about people and labels them as he sees fit, contemptuously dismissing Roderigo as 'poor trash of Venice'. He intends to make an 'ass' out of Othello by putting him in 'a jealousy so strong/ That judgment cannot cure'. His twisted plan is almost ready, 'Knavery's plain face is never seen, till used'.

Shakespeare's Dramatic Style

The action moves to Cyprus where it will remain for the rest of the play. It is a dangerous, uncertain **setting**, far removed from cultured, cosmopolitan Venice. The stormy weather heightens the mood of wild impulse and unrestrained passion. The 'guttered rocks and congregated sands' are 'Traitors'. Vivid description, 'wind-shaked surge', and violent verbs ('shook', 'ruffianed') convey the intensity.

Shakespeare also uses the setting to **foreshadow** the confusion that is about to wreak havoc in the lives of the central characters. Othello's passionate declaration of love to Desdemona is ironic, 'If it were now to die/ 'Twere now to be most happy'. Little does he know what the future holds for him and his wife.

Vivid **imagery** emhasises Iago's cruel plans. He is like the spider weaving a web of deceit by turning a character's best qualities against him. He observes Desdemona and Cassio, who 'takes her by the palm' and snidely remarks, 'with as little a web as this will I ensnare as great a fly as Cassio'. He sneers at the harmony evident between Othello and his wife, 'you are well tuned now' and coldly resolves to destroy their love by loosening the 'pegs that make this music' to throw all into chaos.

Critical Analysis

'Shakespeare's play *Othello* provides us with a fascinating study of the twin themes of appearance and reality.'

To what extent do you agree or disagree with the above statement in relation to Act 2 Scene 1? Write a paragraph (about 150–200 words), supporting your answer with reference to the play.

Prompt!

- Shakespeare conveys the theme of appearance and reality through the use of contrasting perspectives.
- Storm imagery contributes to the treacherous atmosphere.
- Iago's soliloquy and asides heighten the fraudulent environment.

Sample Paragraph 1

I think this scene really explains to us how things seem one way but are really not. Iago is pretending to be loyal but he really wants revenge on Othello and Casio. A complete hypocrite, if you ask me. Even Desdemona, and she is supposed to be a good character is pretending. He does'nt like Rodrigo even tho' he is giving Iago loads of money to get Desdemona. He calls him 'trashy' behind his back. Othello is going around thinking everything is great but it is'nt. A complete header, if you ask me. Coz its all really false. So there are loads of examples of appearance and reality in this scene. *(110 words)*

Examiner's Comment

- This basic response struggles to tackle the question directly.
- Some slight references to false impressions and appearances.
- No development of points or focus on 'fascinating'.
- Poorly controlled expression, use of slang, repetition (e.g. 'really').
- Mechanical errors ('does'nt', 'tho'', 'is'nt', 'Coz its').

I'll set down the pegs that make this music

Iago

Act 2 Scene 1, l.217

Sample Paragraph 2

Act 2 Scene 1 shows the difference between what is seen and what is really happening. We see the safe arrival of Cassio, Desdemona, Iago and Othello, 'well met at the island', after the terrible storm. But the real storm is just beginning, but the only ones who know are Iago and Roderigo. Iago is determined to get revenge on Othello and Cassio because he suspects them of being lovers of his wife, they, according to him, 'leapt into his bed'. But he has no evidence, he just decides that this is the way because he has such a low opinion of everyone. He paints everything with his cynical viewpoint. Everything should be great, the wars are finished, everyone arrived on the island safely despite the storm, but Iago is plotting to make sure that this will not be the case. *(140 words)*

Examiner's Comment

- Mid-grade response that addresses some aspects of the question.
- Reasonably focused commentary about Iago's secret obsession with revenge.
- The final point about irony is good, but it lacks development.
- Little emphasis on the fascination of the scene.
- Accurate quotation would also have improved the answer.

Sample Paragraph 3

In Act 2 Scene 1, Shakespeare presents an intriguing view of the difference between outward show and actuality. Cassio describes the deceptive seas around Cyprus, 'The guttered rocks and congregated sands' that threaten Desdemona's ship. This foreshadows the coming treachery that lies ahead. Even Desdemona herself confesses to pretending, 'I do beguile/ The thing I am'. She takes part in Iago's coarse teasing while waiting anxiously for the safe arrival of her husband. However, it is Iago, the master of deception, in his sneering asides and an alarming soliloquy, who truly represents the difference between appearance and reality. He confides that he intends to 'ensnare' Cassio by using his 'courtesies' against him. He plans to turn Othello's love for Desdemona against him by causing Othello to feel 'a jealousy so strong' that all reason disappears. Through such dramatic conflict, foreshadowing, hidden feelings, asides and irony, the audience is given an absorbing study of appearance and reality. *(155 words)*

Examiner's Comment

- A successful top-grade answer that takes on the full question directly and engages well with the scene.
- Focused discussion of the dangerous maritime setting in foreshadowing the play's tragic outcome.
- Well-supported development of points on Desdemona's hidden fears and Iago's secret plans for revenge, supported by apt reference and quotation.
- The final sentence provides an impressive concluding overview and there is clear expression throughout the paragraph.

Class/Homework Exercise

Shakespeare uses dramatic irony to great effect in Act 2 Scene 1. (This is where the full significance of a character's words or actions is clear to the audience, but not to the character.)

Write a paragraph (about 150–200 words) in response to this statement.

Prompt!
- Cassio's happy celebration of Desdemona's safe arrival.
- Othello's exuberant speeches to Desdemona on their reunion.
- The end of the storm and the Turkish wars.
- Desdemona's trust in Iago.
- Othello's positive opinion of Iago and Cassio.

Revision Overview

The setting has moved from the city of Venice to the island of Cyprus. A fierce storm has scattered the Turkish fleet. All the main characters begin to arrive on the island in quick succession. Cassio announces Othello's marriage and praises his new bride, Desdemona. He welcomes her courteously while they anxiously await Othello's arrival. Othello lands and announces that the Turkish threat is over and the wars are 'done'. He is happily reunited with Desdemona. Iago secretly plots with Roderigo to destroy Othello and Cassio by exploiting their weaknesses. He will ruin Othello through jealousy and Cassio through rashness.

- **Theme: Appearance and reality –** Desdemona makes an intriguing statement as she waits on the quayside for the arrival of her husband, 'I do beguile/ The thing I am, by seeming otherwise'. Is she simply saying that she is more than a pretty face? Or admitting that she is secretly worried about Othello's safety?
- **Characters: Cassio –** courteous, gallant, cheerful.
  Desdemona – admired, strong, witty, romantic, happy.
  Othello – respected, emotional, confident, decisive, joyful.
  Iago – bitter, cynical, misogynistic, manipulative, cruel.
  Roderigo – obsessive, credulous, easily manipulated.

Exam Focus

Act 2 Scene 1 can be used successfully in response to a range of examination questions about the play's central themes, characters, relationships and the playwright's dramatic style.

This **key scene** has significant dramatic functions:
- Establishes a new setting – the island of Cyprus, a remote outpost of the Venetian empire, far removed from the city's civilising forces.
- Develops our understanding of the play's main characters.
- The storm's practical function removes the public theme of the Turkish threat to Venice, allowing the playwright to concentrate on the personal domestic tragedy.
- Storm imagery foreshadows Othello's raging jealousy.
- Repulsive imagery, bird-snaring, asses, spider, wild-cats are used to reflect Iago's cynical view of the world.
- Advances themes of order/disorder, love/hatred, appearance and reality.
- Iago's asides and soliloquy inform the audience of his evil plans.

Key Quotes

I am not merry; but I do beguile The thing I am, by seeming otherwise *(Desdemona) l.136–7*	In her casual conversation with Iago, Desdemona reveals new aspects of her personality. She can be witty and flirtatious. She also admits that there is much more to her character than others realise.
with as little a web as this will I ensnare as great a fly as Cassio *(Iago) l.181–2*	Driven by vengeance, Iago delights in controlling the lives of others. Using venomous imagery, he reveals how he will ruin the lieutenant by casting suspicion on him.
O my fair warrior! *My dear Othello!* *(Othello and Desdemona greet each other) l.195–6*	The reunited lovers show their deep mutual affection. Othello addresses Desdemona as a 'warrior'. Is he comfortable only using the language of the battlefield? Or does he think she has been brave in defying father and society to be with him? Desdemona greets her new husband tenderly. Is she aware that he is not as confident as he likes to pretend?
O, you are well tuned now! *But I'll set down the pegs that make this music* *(Iago) l.216–7*	Iago means to destroy Othello's happiness by creating disharmony between him and Desdemona. He revels in being the vengeful Machiavellian manipulator producing conflict between the happy couple.
Her eye must be fed; and what delight shall she have to look on the devil? *(Iago) l.243–5*	Iago's cynical world view tarnishes Desdemona's reputation through his suggestion that she will soon desire someone more attractive than the Moor. His racial comments are aimed at convincing Roderigo that he might still have a chance of winning Desdemona's love.
he is rash and very sudden in choler *(Iago to Roderigo) l.289*	Iago is a clever judge of character. He knows that Cassio is prone to anger and acts without thinking. Iago will instruct Roderigo to trick the lieutenant into losing control, so that Othello will then have to dismiss him from his post.

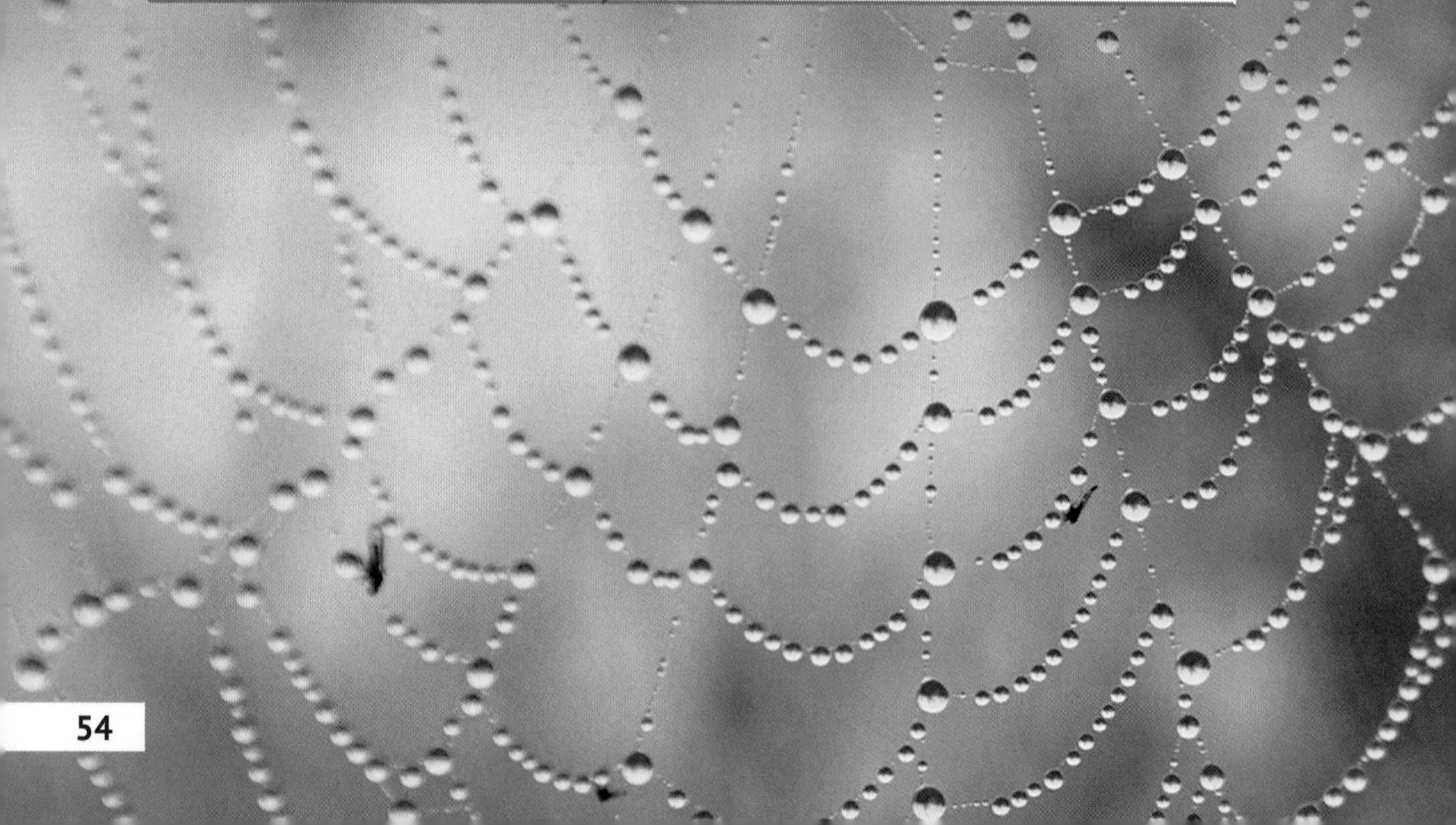

Act 2
Scene 2

INTRODUCTION

- A joyful announcement.
- Othello orders a night of merrymaking to celebrate victory over the Turks and his recent marriage to Desdemona.

A street

Enter a Herald with a proclamation. People following.

Herald It is Othello's pleasure, our noble and valiant general, that, upon certain tidings now arrived, importing the mere perdition of the Turkish fleet, every man put himself into triumph; some to dance, some to make bonfires, each man to what sport and revels his addiction leads him: for, besides these beneficial news, it is the celebration of his nuptial. So much was his pleasure should be proclaimed. All offices are open, and there is full liberty of feasting from this present hour of five till the bell have told eleven. Heaven bless the isle of Cyprus and our noble general Othello!

Exeunt

3 importing: *making known*
3 mere perdition: *total destruction*
4 put himself into triumph: *get ready to celebrate*
9 offices: *kitchens, food stores*
9–10 full liberty of: *freedom for*
11 told: *struck*

Commentary

Double celebrations (lines 1–12)

On a street in Cyprus, a herald announces 'beneficial news', the destruction of the Turkish fleet and the recent marriage of Othello and Desdemona. The night is declared a holiday with 'full liberty' of feasting and celebrations from five o'clock until eleven.

Dramatic Significance

Scene 2 is **a joyful interlude**. Peace has descended on the island with the removal of the threat of war, 'perdition of the Turkish fleet'. Othello and Desdemona are now free to enjoy their married life together, 'the celebration of his nuptial'.

The scene is also highly ironic. Othello has given his soldiers freedom to enjoy 'a night of revels' – something that will become the opportunity for Iago's hidden mischief and villainy. He is about to disturb the peace again and throw all into chaos, just as he had done in Venice when he awoke Brabantio.

Dramatically, this mood of celebration is in strong **contrast to the tragedy that awaits** the unsuspecting Moor. The audience is all too aware that this scene marks a very short break before the destructive power of evil is unleashed.

Key Quote

Heaven bless the isle of Cyprus and our noble general Othello!

(Herald) l.11–12

The herald ends his announcement with a prayer for all. However, while the destruction of the Turkish fleet and the marriage of Othello and Desdemona are cause for celebration, there is dramatic irony here. The audience knows all about Iago's evil schemes, while those onstage are oblivious to the coming danger.

Act 2
Scene 3*

INTRODUCTION

- Cyprus celebrates Othello's marriage and the end of the Turkish threat.
- Impulsive actions lead to dire consequences.
- Iago's cunning plans are put in motion.
- Will evil triumph over good?

* **Key scene requiring close, detailed study**

2 honourable stop: *proper self-control*
3 outsport discretion: *celebrate too much*
11 the fruits are to ensue: *we can now enjoy a night of love*
12 profit: *pleasure*
16 cast: *dismissed*
18 made ... her: *made love to her*
19 Jove: *king of the gods, a lover of many women*
20 exquisite: *attractive*
21 game: *tricks*
23-24 parley of provocation: *invitation to lust*
26 alarm: *signal*
29 stoup: *jug, tankard*
29-30 a brace of Cyprus gallants: *a couple of local men*
30 fain have a measure: *like to drink a toast*
32-33 poor ... drinking: *problems with alcohol*

A hall in the castle

Enter Othello, Desdemona, Cassio, and Attendants

Othello Good Michael, look you to the guard to-night:
Let's teach ourselves that honourable stop,
Not to outsport discretion.

Cassio Iago hath direction what to do;
But, notwithstanding, with my personal eye
Will I look to it.

Othello Iago is most honest.
Michael, good night: to-morrow with your earliest
Let me have speech with you.

To Desdemona

Come, my dear love,
The purchase made, the fruits are to ensue;
That profit's yet to come 'tween me and you.
Good night.

Exeunt Othello, Desdemona, and Attendants

Enter Iago

Cassio Welcome, Iago; we must to the watch.

Iago Not this hour, lieutenant; 'tis not yet ten o' the clock. Our general cast us thus early for the love of his Desdemona; who let us not therefore blame: he hath not yet made wanton the night with her; and she is sport for Jove.

Cassio She's a most exquisite lady.

Iago And, I'll warrant her, full of game.

Cassio Indeed, she's a most fresh and delicate creature.

Iago What an eye she has! Methinks it sounds a parley of provocation.

Cassio An inviting eye; and yet methinks right modest.

Iago And when she speaks, is it not an alarm to love?

Cassio It is indeed perfection.

Iago Well, happiness to their sheets! Come, lieutenant, I have a stoup of wine; and here without are a brace of Cyprus gallants that would fain have a measure to the health of black Othello.

Cassio Not to-night, good Iago: I have very poor and unhappy brains for drinking: I could well wish courtesy would invent some other custom of entertainment.

Iago O, they are our friends; but one cup: I'll drink for you.

Cassio I have drunk but one cup to-night, and that was
craftily qualified too, and, behold, what innovation
it makes here: I am unfortunate in the infirmity,
and dare not task my weakness with any more.

Iago What, man! 'Tis a night of revels: the gallants
desire it.

Cassio Where are they?

Iago Here at the door; I pray you, call them in.

Cassio I'll do it; but it dislikes me.

Exit

Iago If I can fasten but one cup upon him,
With that which he hath drunk to-night already,
He'll be as full of quarrel and offence
As my young mistress' dog. Now, my sick fool Roderigo,
Whom love hath turned almost the wrong side out,
To Desdemona hath to-night caroused
Potations pottle-deep; and he's to watch:
Three lads of Cyprus, noble swelling spirits,
That hold their honours in a wary distance,
The very elements of this warlike isle,
Have I to-night flustered with flowing cups,
And they watch too. Now, amongst this flock of drunkards,
Am I to put our Cassio in some action
That may offend the isle. But here they come:
If consequence do but approve my dream,
My boat sails freely, both with wind and stream.

Re-enter Cassio; with him Montano and Gentlemen; servants following with wine

Cassio 'Fore God, they have given me a rouse already.

Montano Good faith, a little one, not past a pint,
As I am a soldier.

Iago Some wine, ho!

Sings

And let me the canakin clink, clink;
And let me the canakin clink
A soldier's a man;
A life's but a span;
Why, then, let a soldier drink.
Some wine, boys!

Cassio 'Fore God, an excellent song.

38 craftily qualified: *carefully diluted*
38 innovation: *bad effect*
39 infirmity: *intolerance*
41 revels: *celebration*
45 dislikes: *displeases*
51 caroused: *drunk*
52 Potations pottle-deep: *many mugs of wine*
54 hold their honours in a wary distance: *are quick to protect their honour*
55 elements: *foundations*
56 flustered: *confused*
60 consequence: *future events*
62 rouse: *drink*
66 canakin: *drinking can, tankard*

74 potent in potting: *heavy drinkers*
75 swag-bellied Hollander: *fat Dutchman*
78 with facility: *with ease*
79 Almain: *German*
80 ere ... pottle: *before another tankard*
86 breeches: *trousers*
87 held: *considered*
88 lown: *lout*
89 wight: *man*
90 degree: *status*
92 auld: *old*
94 exquisite: *superb*

Iago I learned it in England, where, indeed, they are most potent in potting: your Dane, your German, and your swag-bellied Hollander – Drink, ho! – are nothing to your English.

Cassio Is your Englishman so expert in his drinking?

Iago Why, he drinks you, with facility, your Dane dead drunk; he sweats not to overthrow your Almain; he gives your Hollander a vomit, ere the next pottle can be filled.

Cassio To the health of our general!

Montano I am for it, lieutenant; and I'll do you justice.

Iago O sweet England!
King Stephen was a worthy peer,
His breeches cost him but a crown;
He held them sixpence all too dear,
With that he called the tailor lown.
He was a wight of high renown
And thou art but of low degree:
'Tis pride that pulls the country down;
Then take thine auld cloak about thee.
Some wine, ho!

Cassio Why, this is a more exquisite song than the other.

Iago Will you hear it again?

Cassio No; for I hold him to be unworthy of his place that does those things. Well, God's above all; and there be souls must be saved, and there be souls must not be saved.

Iago It's true, good lieutenant.

Cassio For mine own part – no offence to the general, nor any man of quality – I hope to be saved.

Iago And so do I too, lieutenant.

Cassio Ay, but, by your leave, not before me; the lieutenant is to be saved before the ancient. Let's have no more of this, let's to our affairs. Forgive us our sins! Gentlemen, let's look to our business. Do not think, gentlemen, I am drunk, this is my ancient, this is my right hand, and this is my left: I am not drunk now, I can stand well enough, and speak well enough.

All Excellent well.

Cassio Why, very well then; you must not think then that I am drunk.

Exit

Montano To the platform, masters; come, let's set the watch.

Iago You see this fellow that is gone before;
He is a soldier fit to stand by Caesar
And give direction: and do but see his vice;
'Tis to his virtue a just equinox,
The one as long as the other: 'tis pity of him.
I fear the trust Othello puts him in.
On some odd time of his infirmity,
Will shake this island.

Montano But is he often thus?

Iago 'Tis evermore the prologue to his sleep:
He'll watch the horologe a double set,
If drink rock not his cradle.

Montano It were well
The general were put in mind of it.
Perhaps he sees it not; or his good nature
Prizes the virtue that appears in Cassio,
And looks not on his evils: is not this true?

Enter Roderigo

Iago [*Aside to him*] How now, Roderigo!
I pray you, after the lieutenant; go.

Exit Roderigo

Montano And 'tis great pity that the noble Moor
Should hazard such a place as his own second
With one of an ingraft infirmity:
It were an honest action to say
So to the Moor.

Iago Not I, for this fair island:
I do love Cassio well; and would do much
To cure him of this evil. But, hark! What noise?

Cry within: 'Help! help!'

Re-enter Cassio, driving in Roderigo

Cassio You rogue! You rascal!

Montano What's the matter, lieutenant?

Cassio A knave teach me my duty!
I'll beat the knave into a twiggen bottle.

Roderigo Beat me!

Cassio Dost thou prate, rogue?

Striking Roderigo

Montano Nay, good lieutenant;

114 platform: *lookout post*
114 set the watch: *mount the guard*
116 stand by Caesar: *be the famous Roman's right-hand man*
117 give direction: *issue orders*
118 a just equinox: *an exact equivalent*
121 infirmity: *drunken behaviour*
124 prologue to his sleep: *habit before bedtime*
125–6 watch ... cradle: *not sleep unless he's drunk*
128 put in mind: *informed*
135 hazard: *risk*
136 ingraft infirmity: *deep-rooted weakness*
145 twiggen bottle: *pulp, bottle made of wicker*
147 prate: *rant*

151 mazzard: *head*

154 cry a mutiny: *call out that there is a street fight happening*

158 Diablo: *the devil*

159 rise: *wake up*

160 shamed: *disgraced*

168–9 Are we turned Turks … Ottomites?: *Are we attacking ourselves just as the Turks would have done?*

171 carve for his own rage: *stab someone in anger*

172 Holds his soul light: *doesn't value his life*

174 propriety: *peace and quiet*

178 quarter: *order*

179 Devesting them: *undressing themselves*

181 tilting: *thrusting, lunging*

183 peevish odds: *foolish quarrel*

Staying him

I pray you, sir, hold your hand.

Cassio Let me go, sir,
Or I'll knock you over the mazzard.

Montano Come, come, you're drunk.

Cassio Drunk!

They fight

Iago [***Aside to Roderigo***] Away, I say; go out, and cry a mutiny.

Exit Roderigo

Nay, good lieutenant – alas, gentlemen –
Help, ho! Lieutenant. Sir. Montano.
Help, masters! Here's a goodly watch indeed!

Bell rings

Who's that which rings the bell? Diablo, ho!
The town will rise: God's will, lieutenant, hold!
You will be shamed for ever.

Enter Othello, and gentlemen with weapons

Othello What is the matter here?

Montano 'Zounds, I bleed still; I am hurt to the death.

Othello Hold for your lives!

Iago Hold, ho! Lieutenant, sir, Montano, gentlemen,
Have you forgot all sense of place and duty?
Hold! The general speaks to you; hold, hold, for shame!

Othello Why, how now, ho! From whence ariseth this?
Are we turned Turks, and to ourselves do that
Which heaven hath forbid the Ottomites?
For Christian shame, put by this barbarous brawl:
He that stirs next to carve for his own rage
Holds his soul light; he dies upon his motion.
Silence that dreadful bell: it frights the isle
From her propriety. What is the matter, masters?
Honest Iago, that looks dead with grieving,
Speak, who began this? on thy love, I charge thee.

Iago I do not know: friends all but now, even now,
In quarter, and in terms like bride and groom
Devesting them for bed; and then, but now –
As if some planet had unwitted men –
Swords out, and tilting one at other's breast,
In opposition bloody. I cannot speak
Any beginning to this peevish odds;
And would in action glorious I had lost
Those legs that brought me to a part of it!

Othello How comes it, Michael, you are thus forgot?

Cassio I pray you, pardon me; I cannot speak.

Othello Worthy Montano, you were wont be civil;
The gravity and stillness of your youth
The world hath noted, and your name is great
In mouths of wisest censure: what's the matter,
That you unlace your reputation thus
And spend your rich opinion for the name
Of a night-brawler? Give me answer to it.

Montano Worthy Othello, I am hurt to danger:
Your officer, Iago, can inform you,
While I spare speech, which something now
  offends me,
Of all that I do know: nor know I aught
By me that's said or done amiss this night;
Unless self-charity be sometimes a vice,
And to defend ourselves it be a sin
When violence assails us.

Othello Now, by heaven,
My blood begins my safer guides to rule;
And passion, having my best judgment collied,
Assays to lead the way: if I once stir,
Or do but lift this arm, the best of you
Shall sink in my rebuke. Give me to know
How this foul rout began, who set it on;
And he that is approved in this offence,
Though he had twinned with me, both at a birth,
Shall lose me. What! In a town of war,
Yet wild, the people's hearts brimful of fear,
To manage private and domestic quarrel,
In night, and on the court and guard of safety!
'Tis monstrous. Iago, who began it?

Montano If partially affined, or leagued in office,
Thou dost deliver more or less than truth,
Thou art no soldier.

Iago Touch me not so near:
I had rather have this tongue cut from my mouth
Than it should do offence to Michael Cassio;
Yet, I persuade myself, to speak the truth
Shall nothing wrong him. Thus it is, general.
Montano and myself being in speech,
There comes a fellow crying out for help:
And Cassio following him with determined sword,
To execute upon him. Sir, this gentleman

188 wont be civil: *usually well-mannered*
189 gravity and stillness: *discipline and restraint*
191 censure: *judgement*
192 unlace your reputation: *undo your good name*
197 spare speech ... offends me: *do not speak because it hurts me*
198 aught: *anything*
199 amiss: *wrong*
200 self-charity: *self-defence*
202 assails: *strikes*
205 collied: *shattered*
206 Assays: *tries*
208 rebuke: *reprimand, judgement*
209 foul rout: *disgraceful brawl*
209 set it on: *started it*
210 approved: *guilty*
214 manage: *engage in*
217 partially ... office: *you take his side or fear the lieutenant*
220 Touch me not: *do not accuse me*

229 entreats his pause: *begs him to stop*
231 Lest ... clamour: *in case the uproar*
233 Outran my purpose: *was too fast*
233 returned: *came back here*
235 high in oath: *shouting abuse*
245 strange indignity: *unexpected insult*
248 mince this matter: *downplay what happened*
249 light: *favourable*
260 balmy slumbers: *soothing sleep*
263 Marry: *indeed!*
264 reputation: *good name*
265 immortal: *timeless, illustrious*
266 bestial: *repulsive*

Steps in to Cassio, and entreats his pause:
Myself the crying fellow did pursue,
Lest by his clamour – as it so fell out –
The town might fall in fright: he, swift of foot,
Outran my purpose; and I returned the rather
For that I heard the clink and fall of swords,
And Cassio high in oath; which till to-night
I ne'er might say before. When I came back –
For this was brief – I found them close together,
At blow and thrust; even as again they were
When you yourself did part them.
More of this matter cannot I report:
But men are men; the best sometimes forget:
Though Cassio did some little wrong to him,
As men in rage strike those that wish them best,
Yet surely Cassio, I believe, received
From him that fled some strange indignity,
Which patience could not pass.

Othello I know, Iago,
Thy honesty and love doth mince this matter,
Making it light to Cassio. Cassio, I love thee
But never more be officer of mine.

Re-enter Desdemona, attended

Look, if my gentle love be not raised up!
I'll make thee an example.

Desdemona What's the matter?

Othello All's well now, sweeting; come away to bed.
Sir, for your hurts, myself will be your surgeon:
Lead him off.

To Montano, who is led off

Iago, look with care about the town,
And silence those whom this vile brawl distracted.
Come, Desdemona: 'tis the soldier's life
To have their balmy slumbers waked with strife.

Exeunt all but Iago and Cassio

Iago What, are you hurt, lieutenant?

Cassio Ay, past all surgery.

Iago Marry, heaven forbid!

Cassio Reputation, reputation, reputation! O, I have lost my reputation! I have lost the immortal part of myself, and what remains is bestial. My reputation, Iago, my reputation!

Iago As I am an honest man, I thought you had received some bodily wound; there is more sense in that than in reputation. Reputation is an idle and most false imposition: oft got without merit, and lost without deserving: you have lost no reputation at all, unless you repute yourself such a loser. What, man! There are ways to recover the general again: you are but now cast in his mood, a punishment more in policy than in malice, even so as one would beat his offenceless dog to affright an imperious lion: sue to him again, and he's yours.

Cassio I will rather sue to be despised than to deceive so good a commander with so slight, so drunken, and so indiscreet an officer. Drunk? and speak parrot? and squabble? swagger? swear? and discourse fustian with one's own shadow? O thou invisible spirit of wine, if thou hast no name to be known by, let us call thee devil!

Iago What was he that you followed with your sword? What had he done to you?

Cassio I know not.

Iago Is't possible?

Cassio I remember a mass of things, but nothing distinctly; a quarrel, but nothing wherefore. O God, that men should put an enemy in their mouths to steal away their brains! That we should, with joy, pleasance revel and applause, transform ourselves into beasts!

Iago Why, but you are now well enough: how came you thus recovered?

Cassio It hath pleased the devil drunkenness to give place to the devil wrath; one unperfectness shows me another, to make me frankly despise myself.

Iago Come, you are too severe a moraler: as the time, the place, and the condition of this country stands, I could heartily wish this had not befallen; but, since it is as it is, mend it for your own good.

Cassio I will ask him for my place again; he shall tell me I am a drunkard! Had I as many mouths as Hydra such an answer would stop them all. To be now a sensible man, by and by a fool, and presently a beast! O strange! Every inordinate cup is unblessed and the ingredient is a devil.

270–1 an idle and most false imposition: *a useless, deceptive idea*

273 repute: *believe*

275 cast in his mood: *dismissed in anger*

277 affright: *scare*

277 imperious: *majestic*

277 sue: *appeal*

281 speak parrot: *talk nonsense*

282–3 discourse fustian: *speak pompously*

291 nothing wherefore: *not what it was about*

300 severe a moraler: *hard on yourself*

305 Hydra: *mythological snake that grew additional heads*

308 inordinate: *excessive, overflowing*

310 familiar creature: *a friend*
313 approved: *shown*
318 denotement: *observation*
318 parts: *qualities*
319 importune: *beg*
321 apt: *capable*
322 vice: *fault, sin*
324 entreat … splinter: *ask her to restore the friendship*
325 lay: *bet*
330 betimes: *early*
338 Probal: *reasonable*
340 inclining: *sympathetic*
341 framed as fruitful: *naturally generous*
342 free elements: *earth, air, fire and water*
343 baptism: *Christian redemption*
344 seals and symbols: *the cross and other religious images*
345 enfettered: *enslaved*
346 list: *pleases*
347 her appetite: *his desire for her*
348 weak function: *natural desire*
349 counsel: *advise*
349 parallel: *similar*
350 Divinity … hell: *Satan's religion*
352 suggest: *pretend, tempt*

Iago Come, come, good wine is a good familiar creature
if it be well used: exclaim no more against it.
And, good lieutenant, I think you think I love you.

Cassio I have well approved it, sir. I drunk!

Iago You or any man living may be drunk! at a time, man.
I'll tell you what you shall do. Our general's wife
is now the general: may say so in this respect, for
that he hath devoted and given up himself to the
contemplation, mark, and denotement of her parts and
graces: confess yourself freely to her; importune
her help to put you in your place again: she is of
so free, so kind, so apt, so blessed a disposition,
she holds it a vice in her goodness not to do more
than she is requested: this broken joint between
you and her husband entreat her to splinter; and, my
fortunes against any lay worth naming, this
crack of your love shall grow stronger
than it was before.

Cassio You advise me well.

Iago I protest, in the sincerity of love and honest kindness.

Cassio I think it freely; and betimes in the morning I will
beseech the virtuous Desdemona to undertake for me:
I am desperate of my fortunes if they check me here.

Iago You are in the right. Good night, lieutenant; I
must to the watch.

Cassio Good night, honest Iago.

Exit

Iago And what's he then that says I play the villain?
When this advice is free I give and honest,
Probal to thinking and indeed the course
To win the Moor again? For 'tis most easy
The inclining Desdemona to subdue
In any honest suit: she's framed as fruitful
As the free elements. And then for her
To win the Moor – were it to renounce his baptism,
All seals and symbols of redeemed sin,
His soul is so enfettered to her love,
That she may make, unmake, do what she list,
Even as her appetite shall play the god
With his weak function. How am I then a villain
To counsel Cassio to this parallel course,
Directly to his good? Divinity of hell!
When devils will the blackest sins put on,
They do suggest at first with heavenly shows,

As I do now: for whiles this honest fool
Plies Desdemona to repair his fortunes
And she for him pleads strongly to the Moor,
I'll pour this pestilence into his ear,
That she repeals him for her body's lust;
And by how much she strives to do him good,
She shall undo her credit with the Moor.
So will I turn her virtue into pitch,
And out of her own goodness make the net
That shall enmesh them all.

Re-enter Roderigo

How now, Roderigo!

Roderigo I do follow here in the chase, not like a hound that hunts, but one that fills up the cry. My money is almost spent; I have been to-night exceedingly well cudgelled; and I think the issue will be, I shall have so much experience for my pains, and so, with no money at all and a little more wit, return again to Venice.

Iago
How poor are they that have not patience!
What wound did ever heal but by degrees?
Thou know'st we work by wit, and not by witchcraft;
And wit depends on dilatory time.
Does it not go well? Cassio hath beaten thee.
And thou, by that small hurt, hast cashiered Cassio:
Though other things grow fair against the sun,
Yet fruits that blossom first will first be ripe:
Content thyself awhile. By the mass, 'tis morning;
Pleasure and action make the hours seem short.
Retire thee; go where thou art billeted:
Away, I say; thou shalt know more hereafter:
Nay, get thee gone.

Exit Roderigo

Two things are to be done:
My wife must move for Cassio to her mistress;
I'll set her on;
Myself the while to draw the Moor apart,
And bring him jump when he may Cassio find
Soliciting his wife: ay, that's the way:
Dull not device by coldness and delay.

Exit

356 pestilence: *poison*
357 repeals: *supports*
358 strives: *tries*
359 undo ... Moor: *lose her husband's trust*
360 pitch: *filth*
362 enmesh: *trap*
365 one that fills up the cry: *like a lost hunting dog*
367 cudgelled: *beaten, battered*
373 dilatory: *slowly dragging*
375 cashiered: *dismissed*
380 billeted: *stationed, sleeping*
384 move: *plead*
386 the while: *meantime*
387 bring ... jump: *arrange*
388 Soliciting: *petitioning*
389 Dull ... delay: *there's no time to waste*

Key Scene Extended Commentary

A clear warning (lines 1–13)

Othello leaves Cassio on guard duty during the celebrations, reminding him not to allow the soldiers to drink to excess. He particularly emphasises the importance of responsible self-control, 'that honourable stop'. As the new governor of Cyprus, he is concerned that if a public disturbance broke out, it would alarm the island's citizens. Othello then retires with his new bride to enjoy their delayed honeymoon.

Time to celebrate (lines 14–45)

Iago attempts to establish a soldierly friendship with his intended victim, Cassio. He engages in coarse conversation about Othello's wedding night, making comments about Desdemona as a temptress who is 'full of game'. Cassio remains chivalrous, however, insisting that the governor's wife is an 'exquisite lady' and a 'delicate creature'. Iago then makes a bold move to put his vengeful plot into play. He proposes that he and Cassio share a drink to Othello's health with 'a brace of Cyprus gallants'. At first Cassio declines, confessing that he does not have a good head for alcohol, 'I have very poor and unhappy brains for drinking'. But Iago persists, exploiting Cassio's interest in socialising. The ensign tells him that it is, 'a night of revels: the gallants desire it'. Cassio enjoys being popular and is very easily persuaded, 'I'll do it; but it dislikes me'. Will such half-hearted agreement prove to be his ruination?

'Tis a night of revels: the gallants desire it.

Iago

Act 2 Scene 3, l.41–2

The drinking scene (lines 46–113)

Clearly aware of other people's weaknesses, Iago uses every opportunity presented to advance his warped schemes. He knows Cassio becomes easily angered when drunk, so he resolves to 'fasten but one cup upon him' in addition to what the lieutenant has already had. His 'sick fool Roderigo' is already intoxicated, as are 'Three lads of Cyprus'. The riotous scene is set and Iago is about to unleash mayhem, 'here they come'. He calls for more wine and performs two rousing drinking songs during which Cassio becomes progressively incoherent while insisting, 'I am not drunk now'.

Street fight (lines 114–161)

Montano, the previous governor of Cyprus, is a sober contrast to Cassio, who is reckless and immature. Iago slyly 'confides' in Montano about the lieutenant's 'infirmity' for alcohol, yet continues to praise Cassio – 'a soldier fit to stand by Caesar'. Concerned by what he hears about the lieutenant, Montano immediately declares that Othello should be informed, 'put in mind of it'. Meanwhile, the ensign manipulates everyone around him, particularly Roderigo – who has also been drinking. The atmosphere suddenly changes when Cassio and Roderigo get involved in a fight. Other soldiers join in and a huge brawl develops. Montano attempts to intervene, 'Come, come, you're drunk', but the lieutenant turns on him as well. Iago again dispatches Roderigo, this time to 'cry a mutiny'. The ensign's plan to cause public disorder confirms Othello's worst fears. The alarm bell rings. Iago pretends to calm the commotion and tells Cassio, 'You will be shamed for ever'.

Anger and shame **(lines 162–250)**

Honest Iago, that looks dead with grieving, Speak, who began this?
Othello
Act 2 Scene 3, l.175–176

Othello is incensed at the outbreak of public disorder and demands to know, 'What is the matter here?' He turns to 'honest Iago' for an explanation of 'this barbarous brawl'. The ensign lies at first, 'I do not know', while Cassio is so ashamed he 'cannot speak'. Othello is becoming increasingly furious, 'What! In a town of war ... To manage private and domestic quarrel,/ In night'. Iago then knowingly reveals Cassio's fault while pretending to excuse it, 'I had rather have this tongue cut from my mouth/ Than it should do offence to Michael Cassio'. He succeeds in undermining the unreliable Cassio through his treacherous efforts to defend him, 'the best sometimes forget'. Othello acts decisively, dismissing the young lieutenant, 'Cassio, I love thee/ But never more be officer of mine'.

A crucial development
(lines 251–335)

As Desdemona arrives, Othello acts protectively towards her, saying that conflict is a normal part of military life. He also orders that Montano's wounds are attended to and puts Iago in charge of restoring peace in Cyprus. In the meantime, a distraught Cassio considers his shattered reputation, 'the immortal part of myself'. He bitterly regrets his excessive drinking – something that can 'transform ourselves into beasts'. Iago cleverly seizes another opportunity and advises Cassio to ask Desdemona for support to have him reinstated. He argues that apart from being naturally helpful, 'she holds it a vice in her goodness not to do more than she is requested'. Desdemona also has huge influence over Othello, 'Our general's wife is now the general'. Not for the first time, Cassio is instantly persuaded that 'honest' Iago has his best interests at heart, 'in the morning I will beseech the virtuous Desdemona to undertake for me'.

Ominous revelation (lines 336–389)

Addressing the audience directly, Iago can barely conceal his intense satisfaction in plotting against the Moor. After all, who can accuse him of villainy when he offers such helpful advice to his friends? He has succeeded in persuading both Othello and Cassio that he is to be trusted. This allows him to take full advantage of their good qualities in order to trap them: Othello's devotion to his new wife; Cassio's desire to restore his reputation. Unlike the other characters, Iago is acutely aware that appearances can be deceptive. The ensign will gradually convince the Moor that Desdemona pleads for Cassio because she is in love with him. A dejected Roderigo interrupts Iago's thoughts, complaining that his 'money is almost spent' – and for no obvious benefit. Iago responds by asking him to be patient ands reminds him that Cassio has already been successfully 'cashiered', so there is still a chance of winning Desdemona. The scene ends with Iago reverting to his malevolent plot, contriving to force his own wife, Emilia, to appeal to Desdemona on Cassio's behalf. He also hopes to place Othello in a position where he can actually observe Cassio 'Soliciting his wife'. The web of deceit grows.

O, I have lost my reputati
I have lost the immortal
of myself, and what rema
is bestial
Cassio
Act 2 Scene 3, l.264–6

Shakespeare's Dramatic Style

An atmosphere of deception pervades Act 2 Scene 3. The audience watches in growing frustration while Iago misleads Roderigo, Montano, Cassio and Othello. The fight scene is central to the duplicity, almost a **small-scale play within the play**. Iago becomes scriptwriter, producer and main actor. The chameleon-like villain quickly adapts to changing circumstances, so that he always ingratiates himself with others. He is Cassio's faithful supporter in times of need. No wonder we feel dismayed as the grateful lieutenant tells Iago, 'You advise me well'.

The real Iago only emerges in the concluding **soliloquy**. He brazenly flings an audacious challenge to the audience, 'And what's he then that says I play the villain?' His confident, vigorous tone emphasises his deep enjoyment of evil-doing, 'So will I turn her virtue into pitch'. In targeting Desdemona's compassionate nature, it is clear that Iago will readily abuse the virtues of others rather than their weaknesses to create chaos.

Act 2 Scene 3 marks **a turning point** in the play. Othello's loss of temper clearly signifies that he is no longer fully in control of himself. 'My blood begins my safer guides to rule'. He is now driven by passion rather than judgement. Cassio is given little opportunity to defend himself and the general even sounds vindictive when he says, 'I'll make thee an example'. Othello's language is also changing and his exasperation is evident in his unrestrained expressions ('Are we turned Turks', ''Tis monstrous'), suggesting further loss of self-assurance.

Critical Analysis

'Throughout the play *Othello* Shakespeare makes use of a variety of dramatic techniques to evoke an atmosphere of deception and corruption.'

Discuss this statement with reference to Act 2 Scene 3. Write a paragraph (about 150–200 words), supporting your answer with reference to the text.

Prompt!

- Soliloquies – involve audience in corrupt world of Iago's duplicity.
- Foreshadowing – heightens the sense of inevitable tragedy.
- Contrasts – expose evil and good, Cassio/Iago, Montano/Cassio, Desdemona/Iago, etc.
- Play within the play – Iago is director, scriptwriter and actor – intensifies mood of treachery.
- Vivid imagery and aural effects – add to the vindictive atmosphere.

Sample Paragraph 1

Act 2, scene three is a very exciting scene to watch. It has both a drinking scene and fight scene. I liked the drink scene when Iago starts to sing about how good each country is at drinking, 'clink, clink'. He is having a laugh. Cassio should of tried to stay half sober at least. Iago has used the technique of tricking him through drink. Then in comes Rodrigo pushing Cassio in the chest with his sword. Cassio then fights with Montanno hitting him on the 'mazzard' which is the old word for his head. The bell rings. Othello is mad at his outburst and wants to know exactly whats going on. Iago's technique works because Cassio is given his marching papers. This exciting scene by Shakespeare is full of deception and corruption. It is full of trickery as well. *(140 words)*

Examiner's Comment

- Basic response that lacks focus on dramatic techniques.
- Some narrative summary with slight references to deception.
- Little or no analysis.
- Poorly controlled expression and mechanical flaws ('Rodrigo', 'Montanno', 'should of', 'whats').

Sample Paragraph 2

Shakespeare uses the dramatic technique of the small drama within the main scene and this is a symbol of the evil atmosphere. Iago is fully in control. Shakespeare has created a mini scene where he is the puppet master getting Cassio drunk and then in a fight on the street setting. He has encouraged Cassio to become so drunk so that he will lose his officer position. Iago directs Roderigo telling him to 'go out and cry a mutiny'. He even pretends to be an unwilling witness to Cassio's so-called crime. In fact, Iago controls everyone. He becomes Cassio's adviser. He encourages Cassio to use Desdemona to get to Othello so that he can lay the blame on them both in Othello's eyes. Cassio is delighted and vows to 'beseech the virtuous Desdemona'. Shakespeare shows Iago moving characters around as if they were on a chessboard so that it suits him. I think this highlights the evil world of the play. *(160 words)*

Examiner's Comment

- Reasonable attempt to link one dramatic device to the evil atmosphere.
- Further developed discussion would have improved the answer.
- Expression is note-like, repetitive and strained at times.
- This mid-grade response makes a solid effort at addressing the question.

Sample Paragraph 3

Throughout Act 2 Scene 3, Shakespeare makes effective use of one key dramatic device, the soliloquy, to create a disturbing world of pretence and villainy. Iago's first soliloquy places the audience as observer of his schemes to coax Cassio into losing self-control, 'If I can but fasten one cup upon him ... He'll be as full of quarrel ... As my young mistress' dog'. The second soliloquy deepens the sense of corruption. Here Iago tries to convince the audience by putting forward a rational argument, 'Probal to thinking'. He is correct to suggest using the 'inclining Desdemona' to plead with Othello on Cassio's behalf. Isn't she the general's 'general'? Shakespeare gives Iago powerful alliterative phrases and hissing sibilance to emphasise his evil world, 'I'll pour this pestilence into his ear, / That she repeals him for her body's lust'. Not only has Iago created a 'net' to 'enmesh' the characters in the play, he has also involved the audience by almost inviting them to be accomplices to his devious plans. We are all corrupted in Iago's world of perversion and treachery. *(175 words)*

Examiner's Comment

- Impressive top-grade response tackles the question directly and engages effectively with the text.
- Focused and supported discussion of the atmosphere created by soliloquies.
- Convincing discussion of the poetic language used to reveal Iago's malicious nature.
- Clear expression and varied vocabulary ('deepens the sense of corruption', 'hissing sibilance to emphasise his evil world').

Class/Homework Exercise

'In the play *Othello* audiences are both fascinated and repelled by Iago's inventive villainy.'

Write a paragraph (about 150–200 words), giving reasons for your views and supporting your response with quotation from Act 2 Scene 3 of the play.

Prompt!

Iago fascinates and intrigues through his clever multi-layered schemes:

- Outwits Cassio to get him dismissed by exploiting his weaknesses.
- Expertly manipulates gullible Roderigo to further his vengeful plans.
- Turns every opportunity to his advantage.

Iago repels and disgusts through his devious and convoluted conspiracies:

- Takes obvious delight in practising evil.
- Cynically exploits various character qualities – Cassio's sociability, Desdemona's decency, Othello's desire for justice.
- Lies and half-truths obscure reality for others, but not for him.

How am I then a villain
To counsel Cassio to this
parallel course

Iago
Act 2 Scene 3, l.348–349

Revision Overview

Cyprus celebrates freedom from the Turkish threat. Although Cassio is in charge of the military guard, Iago entices him to start drinking. The ensign knows that Cassio is prone to anger when drunk. He also plays on the young lieutenant's desire to please others. Cassio soon becomes involved in a public brawl with Roderigo and Montano. An angry Othello demands to know the reason for the disturbance, but Iago pretends to be reluctant to say exactly what happened. However, he further implicates Cassio while pretending to excuse him. Othello immediately dismisses Cassio from his position, leaving the lieutenant shattered. Iago consoles Cassio, suggesting that he ask Desdemona to intervene on his behalf. Iago's aim is to undermine Othello's trust in his wife's faithfulness. He also decides to use his own wife, Emilia, to persuade Desdemona to help Cassio.

- **Themes: Appearance and reality –** Iago is the only character who is aware of the boundaries between reality and appearance. 'When devils will the blackest sins put on,/ They do suggest at first with heavenly shows'. Othello, Cassio, Montano and Roderigo are all fooled by 'honest Iago'.
  Reputation – Cassio loses his reputation. Desdemona is about to have her good name tarnished. Othello acts to ensure his reputation is as a strong, decisive governor. Meanwhile, Iago has an undeserved reputation for being 'honest'.
- **Characters: Cassio –** easily led, good-natured, eager to please, irresponsible, concerned with social status.
  Desdemona – virtuous, sympathetic, vulnerable.
  Roderigo – disappointed in love, easily controlled, persists in self-delusion.
  Othello – impulsive, decisive, wants to be seen to act justly, deceived by appearances.
  Iago – man of many parts – lively drinking partner, concerned friend, wise observer, scheming manipulator, trusted by all as 'honest'.

Exam Focus

Act 2 Scene 3 can be used successfully in response to a range of examination questions about the play's central themes, characters, relationships and the playwright's dramatic style.

This **key scene** has significant dramatic functions:

- Presents a clear victory of the force of evil over good.
- Illustrates the opportunistic villain's manipulation of characters and events.
- Involves audience as unwilling co-conspirators in expanding web of deceit.
- Use of violence, irony, humour, contrast and foreshadowing heightens the theatrical experience.

So will I … make the net
That shall enmesh them all
Iago
Act 2 Scene 3, l.351–3

Key Quotes

I fear the trust Othello puts him in *(Iago to Montano) l.120*	Iago purposely damages Cassio's reputation with Montano, former governor of Cyprus. The ensign also succeeds in tarnishing Othello's judgement.
Honest Iago, that looks dead with grieving, *Speak, who began this?* *(Othello to Iago) l.175–6*	Othello, like everyone else, is completely fooled by his ensign. The Moor judges by appearances. He assumes Iago is sincere just because he looks dejected at what has happened.
O, I have lost my reputation! *I have lost the immortal part of myself, and what remains is bestial* *(Cassio to Iago) l.264–6*	Cassio's feelings are expressed in prose to underline his descent to a sub-human level because of his drunken behaviour. Does he also lapse into melodramatic self-pity here? He regards his good name as a divine quality that he has carelessly thrown away.
How am I then a villain *To counsel Cassio to this parallel course,* *Directly to his good?* *(Iago) l.348–50*	Iago poses a rhetorical question directly to the audience. He challenges us to criticise him for advising Cassio on a course of action that should benefit him. The audience is aware that Iago does not act out of good intentions; he is deliberately creating confusion.
Dull not device by coldness and delay *(Iago) l.389*	The deadening alliteration underscores Iago's utter determination to proceed with his evil plans for revenge as quickly as possible. It is a chilling conclusion to this dynamic scene.

Act 3
Scene 1

INTRODUCTION

- Cyprus, the morning after the night's disruptive street brawl.
- Can Cassio's meeting with Desdemona bring about his reinstatement?
- Will Iago's evil plans continue to gather pace?

1 content your pains: *pay you for your trouble*

4 i' the nose: *a pun on the nasal accent of Naples and the poor sound of the music*

23 quillets: *jokes*

26 entreats: *begs*

31 In happy time: *just in time*

Before the castle

Enter Cassio and some Musicians

Cassio Masters, play here; I will content your pains;
Something that's brief; and bid 'Good morrow, general.'

Music. Enter Clown

Clown Why masters, have your instruments been in Naples, that they speak i' the nose thus?

First Musician How, sir, how!

Clown Are these, I pray you, wind-instruments?

First Musician Ay, marry, are they, sir.

Clown O, thereby hangs a tail.

First Musician Whereby hangs a tale, sir?

Clown Marry, sir, by many a wind-instrument that I know. But, masters, here's money for you: and the general so likes your music, that he desires you, for love's sake, to make no more noise with it.

First Musician Well, sir, we will not.

Clown If you have any music that may not be heard, to it again: but, as they say to hear music the general does not greatly care.

First Musician We have none such, sir.

Clown Then put up your pipes in your bag, for I'll away: go; vanish into air; away!

Exeunt Musicians

Cassio Dost thou hear, my honest friend?

Clown No, I hear not your honest friend; I hear you.

Cassio Prithee, keep up thy quillets. There's a poor piece of gold for thee: if the gentlewoman that attends the general's wife be stirring, tell her there's one Cassio entreats her a little favour of speech: wilt thou do this?

Clown She is stirring, sir: if she will stir hither, I shall seem to notify unto her.

Cassio Do, good my friend.

Exit Clown

Enter Iago

In happy time, Iago.

Iago You have not been abed then?

Cassio Why, no; the day had broke
Before we parted. I have made bold, Iago,
To send in to your wife: my suit to her
Is, that she will to virtuous Desdemona
Procure me some access.

Iago I'll send her to you presently;
And I'll devise a mean to draw the Moor
Out of the way, that your converse and business
May be more free.

Cassio I humbly thank you for it.

Exit Iago

I never knew
A Florentine more kind and honest.

Enter Emilia

Emilia Good morrow, good Lieutenant: I am sorry
For your displeasure; but all will sure be well.
The general and his wife are talking of it;
And she speaks for you stoutly: the Moor replies,
That he you hurt is of great fame in Cyprus,
And great affinity, and that in wholesome wisdom
He might not but refuse you; but he protests he loves you
And needs no other suitor but his likings
To take the safest occasion by the front
To bring you in again.

Cassio Yet, I beseech you,
If you think fit, or that it may be done,
Give me advantage of some brief discourse
With Desdemona alone.

Emilia Pray you, come in;
I will bestow you where you shall have time
To speak your bosom freely.

Cassio I am much bound to you.

Exeunt

38 presently: *at once*
39 mean to draw: *plan to lure*
40 converse: *discussion*
41 more free: *private*
44 Florentine: *native of Florence*
46 displeasure: *unhappy experience*
48 stoutly: *loyally*
49 he: *Montano*
50 great affinity: *well liked*
51 refuse you: *reject your appeal*
53 occasion: *opportunity*
54 bring you in again: *reinstate you as lieutenant*
57 Give ... discourse: *allow me to speak*
60 bestow: *arrange*
61 bosom: *feelings*
62 bound: *obliged, indebted*

Commentary

Musical interlude (lines 1–20)

In an effort to improve his standing in Othello's eyes, Cassio pays a group of musicians to serenade the newlyweds, Othello and Desdemona, with 'Something that's brief' in accordance with Elizabethan custom. However, Othello sends a clown from the castle to dismiss the musicians. Is he still angry after the events of the previous night?

A request (lines 21–42)

Cassio now pays the clown to send Emilia, Desdemona's maidservant, to her mistress, because he wishes to ask her 'a little favour of speech'. Suddenly Iago arrives and agrees to fetch his wife himself. He also promises to distract Othello, 'I'll devise a mean to draw the Moor/ Out of the way', so that Cassio can speak freely with Desdemona, Cassio is impressed.

A promise (lines 43–62)

Emilia has good news for Cassio, 'all will sure be well'. Desdemona is already pleading Cassio's case on his behalf. Although the Moor considers the wounding of Montano a serious matter, he still regards Cassio highly and is likely to reinstate him at a later stage. But Cassio is not satisfied and desires to speak with 'Desdemona alone'. Emilia agrees to help, unwittingly aiding her husband's vengeful plans. Cassio is indebted to her.

Dramatic Significance

A very brief musical interlude gives a little **comic relief** after the dark, violent mood of the previous scene. However, an **ominous note** is also struck when the clown reveals that it is Othello who has ordered the music to stop. Is he still furious over the embarrassing disturbances and Cassio's drunken antics? Cassio fails to understand the significance of Othello's gesture. Instead of waiting for the situation to settle, he insists on involving Desdemona on his behalf.

Act 3 Scene 2 **contrasts the characters of Iago and Cassio**. The ensign is adept at reading situations and he turns the young officer's impatience to his own vengeful advantage. Cassio is relatively shallow and easily manipulated because he is preoccupied with restoring his good name. His lack of judgement is evident in his assessment of Iago's character, 'I never knew/ A Florentine more kind and honest'. It is also apparent when he insists on meeting with Desdemona rather than accepting reassurances that she is already speaking 'stoutly' in his defence. The scene concludes with another ironic comment from Cassio, 'I am bound to thee'.

O, thereby hangs a tail

Clown
Act 3 Scene 1, l.8

Key Quotes

I'll devise a mean to draw the Moor Out of the way *(Iago to Cassio) l.39*	Iago pretends to do everything in his power to help the former lieutenant regain his position. Yet the audience knows that he is secretly accelerating his plan to damn the gullible Cassio and the innocent Desdemona in Othello's eyes. Ironically, nobody suspects Iago.
I never knew A Florentine more kind and honest *(Cassio) l.43–4*	This statement shows Cassio's lack of judgement. Only the audience is aware of Iago's true character. The manipulative puppet master's limitless capacity for deception is slowly entrapping everyone around him. We watch in disbelief as events continue to work in Iago's favour.
I will bestow you where you shall have time To speak your bosom freely *(Emilia to Cassio) l.60–1*	Emilia is used by Iago to trap Cassio and Desdemona. She is unaware of her husband's devious plans. Her well-intentioned interference will prove tragically disastrous. Through her action, Iago will be able to present their innocent meeting to Othello in the worst possible light, damaging not only Cassio but also Desdemona's reputation for ever.

INTRODUCTION

- A new order has been established on the island of Cyprus.

A room in the castle

Enter Othello, Iago and Gentlemen

Othello These letters give, Iago, to the pilot,
And by him do my duties to the senate.
That done, I will be walking on the works,
Repair there to me.

Iago Well, my good lord, I'll do it.

Othello This fortification, gentlemen, shall we see it?

Gentleman We'll wait upon your lordship.

Exeunt

2 do my duties: *show my loyalty*

3 works: *fortifications*

4 Repair: *go*

Commentary

Changed times (lines 1–7)

In this short scene, Othello inspects the island's defences against possible attack from foreign armies or fleets. It is Iago who now accompanies the busy general, not the disgraced Cassio, whom he has just replaced.

The purpose of the scene appears to be mainly to show the passing of time as Othello takes control of his military duties. He gives Iago a number of official letters to deliver, again illustrating his increasing reliance on his new second-in-command.

Act 3 Scene 2 adds to the play's dramatic irony. The audience is aware of Iago's secret obsession with bringing about the Moor's downfall. Othello may be successful in dealing with threats to Cyprus, but he fails completely to recognise his personal enemy.

I will be walking on the works
Othello
Act 3 Scene 2, l.3

Act 3
Scene 3*

INTRODUCTION

- Cassio's impatience for reinstatement affects both Desdemona and Othello.
- Iago continues to skilfully manipulate the Moor.
- Othello's character is suddenly transformed.
- An embroidered handkerchief becomes an important element in the tragic story.

* **Key scene requiring close, detailed study**

The garden of the the castle

Enter Desdemona, Cassio, and Emilia

Desdemona
Be thou assured, good Cassio, I will do
All my abilities in thy behalf.

Emilia
Good madam, do, I warrant it grieves my husband,
As if the case were his.

Desdemona
O, that's an honest fellow. Do not doubt, Cassio,
But I will have my lord and you again
As friendly as you were.

Cassio
Bounteous madam,
Whatever shall become of Michael Cassio,
He's never anything but your true servant.

Desdemona
I know it. I thank you. You do love my lord,
You have known him long, and be you well assured,
He shall in strangeness stand no further off
Than in a polite distance.

Cassio
Ay, but, lady,
That policy may either last so long,
Or feed upon such nice and waterish diet,
Or breed itself so out of circumstance,
That I being absent, and my place supplied,
My general will forget my love and service.

Desdemona
Do not doubt that: before Emilia here
I give thee warrant of thy place: assure thee
If I do vow a friendship, I'll perform it
To the last article; my lord shall never rest,
I'll watch him tame, and talk him out of patience;
His bed shall seem a school, his board a shrift,
I'll intermingle every thing he does
With Cassio's suit; therefore be merry, Cassio,
For thy solicitor shall rather die
Than give thy cause away.

Emilia
Madam, here comes my lord.

Cassio
Madam, I'll take my leave.

Desdemona
Why, stay, and hear me speak.

Cassio
Madam, not now, I am very ill at ease,
Unfit for mine own purposes.

Desdemona
Well, do your discretion.
Exit Cassio
Enter Othello and Iago

Iago
Ha! I like not that.

2 All my abilities: *all I possibly can*

3 warrant: *believe*

13–14 He shall ... distance: *he will distance himself from you for a short time*

16 policy: *plan*

17 feed ... diet: *last longer*

18 breed ... circumstance: *continue by accident*

19 my place supplied: *my position filled*

22 warrant: *guarantee*

24 article: *detail*

25 watch him tame: *keep him awake*

26 board a shrift: *dining table will be like a confessional*

29 solicitor: *one who pleads a case*

36 your discretion: *as you think best*

Othello What dost thou say?

Iago Nothing, my lord, or if – I know not what.

Othello Was not that Cassio parted from my wife?

Iago Cassio, my lord! No, sure, I cannot think it,
That he would steal away so guilty-like,
Seeing you coming.

Othello I do believe 'twas he.

Desdemona How now, my lord!
I have been talking with a suitor here,
A man that languishes in your displeasure.
Why, your lieutenant, Cassio. Good my lord,
If I have any grace or power to move you,
His present reconciliation take;
For if he be not one that truly loves you,
That errs in ignorance and not in cunning,
I have no judgment in an honest face:
I prithee, call him back.

Othello Went he hence now?

Desdemona Yes, faith, so humbled
That he has left part of his grief with me,
To suffer with him. Good love, call him back.

Othello Not now, sweet Desdemona; some other time.

Desdemona But shall it be shortly?

Othello The sooner, sweet, for you.

Desdemona Shall it be tonight at supper?

Othello No, not to-night.

Desdemona Tomorrow dinner, then?

Othello I shall not dine at home;
I meet the captains at the citadel.

Desdemona Why, then, tomorrow night, or Tuesday morn,
On Tuesday noon, or night, or Wednesday morn:
I prithee, name the time, but let it not
Exceed three days: in faith, he's penitent;
And yet his trespass, in our common reason –
Save that, they say, the wars must make examples
Out of their best – is not almost a fault
To incur a private check. When shall he come?
Tell me, Othello: I wonder in my soul,
What you would ask me, that I should deny,
Or stand so mammering on. What! Michael Cassio,
That came a-wooing with you, and so many a time,

47 languishes: *suffers*

50 present reconciliation take: *accept his apology*

52 errs in ignorance: *was mistaken by accident*

70 penitent: *sorry*

71 trespass: *error*

72 Save: *except*

74 check: *scolding*

77 mammering: *hesitating*

When I have spoke of you dispraisingly,
Has taken your part; to have so much to do
To bring him in! Trust me, I could do much—

Othello Prithee, no more, let him come when he will,
I will deny thee nothing.

Desdemona Why, this is not a boon,
'Tis as I should entreat you wear your gloves,
Or feed on nourishing dishes, or keep you warm,
Or sue to you to do a peculiar profit
To your own person: nay, when I have a suit
Wherein I mean to touch your love indeed,
It shall be full of poise and difficult weight
And fearful to be granted.

Othello I will deny thee nothing:
Whereon, I do beseech thee, grant me this,
To leave me but a little to myself.

Desdemona Shall I deny you? No, farewell, my lord.

Othello Farewell, my Desdemona: I'll come to thee straight.

Desdemona Emilia, come. Be as your fancies teach you;
Whatever you be, I am obedient.

Exeunt Desdemona and Emilia

Othello Excellent wretch! Perdition catch my soul,
But I do love thee! And when I love thee not,
Chaos is come again.

Iago My noble lord—

Othello What dost thou say, Iago?

Iago Did Michael Cassio, when you wooed my lady,
Know of your love?

Othello He did, from first to last. Why dost thou ask?

Iago But for a satisfaction of my thought.
No further harm.

Othello Why of thy thought, Iago?

Iago I did not think he had been acquainted with her.

Othello O yes, and went between us very oft.

Iago Indeed!

Othello Indeed! Indeed: discernest thou aught in that?
Is he not honest?

Iago Honest, my lord!

81 bring him in: *reinstate him*
84 boon: *favour*
87 peculiar profit: *personal benefit*
88 suit: *request*
90 poise: *confidence*
97 fancies: *wishes*
99 wretch: *rascal (used affectionately)*
99 Perdition: *damnation*
101 Chaos: *Armageddon, catastrophe*
111 between us: *acted as an intermediary*
113 discernest thou aught: *do you see anything strange*

Othello Honest! Ay, honest.

Iago My lord, for aught I know.

Othello What dost thou think?

Iago Think, my lord!

Othello Think, my lord! By heaven, he echoes me,
As if there were some monster in his thought
Too hideous to be shown. Thou dost mean something:
I heard thee say even now, thou lik'st not that,
When Cassio left my wife: what didst not like?
And when I told thee he was of my counsel
In my whole course of wooing, thou cried'st 'Indeed!'
And didst contract and purse thy brow together,
As if thou then hadst shut up in thy brain
Some horrible conceit: if thou dost love me,
Show me thy thought.

Iago My lord, you know I love you.

Othello I think thou dost,
And, for I know thou art full of love and honesty,
And weighest thy words before thou givest them breath,
Therefore these stops of thine fright me the more:
For such things in a false disloyal knave
Are tricks of custom, but in a man that's just
They are close denotements, working from the heart
That passion cannot rule.

Iago For Michael Cassio,
I dare be sworn I think that he is honest.

Othello I think so too.

Iago Men should be what they seem,
Or those that be not, would they might seem none!

Othello Certain, men should be what they seem.

Iago Why, then, I think Cassio's an honest man.

Othello Nay, yet there's more in this:
I prithee, speak to me as to thy thinkings,
As thou dost ruminate, and give thy worst of thoughts
The worst of words.

Iago Good my lord, pardon me:
Though I am bound to every act of duty,
I am not bound to that all slaves are free to.
Utter my thoughts? Why, say they are vile and false:
As where's that palace whereinto foul things
Sometimes intrude not? Who has a breast so pure,
But some uncleanly apprehensions

125 of my counsel: *in my confidence*
126 wooing: *courting*
127 purse thy brow: *raise your eyebrows*
129 conceit: *idea*
137 tricks of custom: *common deceptions*
138 close denotements: *secret hints*
144 would they might seem none: *I wish they would not be false*
148 thy thinkings: *your thoughts*
149 ruminate: *think*
155 whereinto: *into which*
157 uncleanly apprehensions: *unpleasant thoughts*

Keep leets and law-days and in session sit
With meditations lawful?

Othello Thou dost conspire against thy friend, Iago,
If thou but thinkest him wronged and makest his ear
A stranger to thy thoughts.

Iago I do beseech you –
Though I perchance am vicious in my guess,
As, I confess, it is my nature's plague
To spy into abuses, and oft my jealousy
Shapes faults that are not – that your wisdom yet,
From one that so imperfectly conceits,
You would take no notice, nor build yourself a trouble
Out of my scattering and unsure observance.
It were not for your quiet nor your good,
Nor for my manhood, honesty, or wisdom,
To let you know my thoughts.

Othello What dost thou mean?

Iago Good name in man and woman, dear my lord,
Is the immediate jewel of their souls:
Who steals my purse steals trash; 'tis something, nothing,
'Twas mine, 'tis his, and has been slave to thousands:
But he that filches from me my good name
Robs me of that which not enriches him
And makes me poor indeed.

Othello By heaven, I'll know thy thoughts.

Iago You cannot, if my heart were in your hand;
Nor shall not, whilst 'tis in my custody.

Othello Ha!

Iago O, beware, my lord, of jealousy;
It is the green-eyed monster which doth mock
The meat it feeds on. That cuckold lives in bliss
Who, certain of his fate, loves not his wronger;
But, O, what damned minutes tells he o'er
Who dotes, yet doubts, suspects, yet strongly loves!

Othello O misery!

Iago Poor and content is rich and rich enough,
But riches, fineless, is as poor as winter
To him that ever fears he shall be poor.
Good heaven, the souls of all my tribe defend
From jealousy!

Othello Why, why is this?
Thinkest thou I would make a life of jealousy,
To follow still the changes of the moon

158 leets: *local courts*
158 law-days: *days when courts are in session*
161–2 makest ... thoughts: *do not allow him to enter your mind*
164 vicious in my guess: *possibly wrong*
165 nature's plague: *natural personality*
168 conceits: *imagines things*
170 scattering and unsure observance: *uncertain observations*
171 quiet: *peace of mind*
179 filches: *steals*
188 cuckold: *husband who has a cheating wife*
189 certain of his fate: *knows for sure*
191 dotes: *loves*
194 fineless: *endless*

204 exsufflicate and blown surmises: *exaggerated suspicions*
205 Matching thy inference: *just as you are suggesting*
217 franker: *more open*
220 Wear your eye thus: *look at her like this*
222 self-bounty: *natural kindness*
223 country disposition: *native ways*
224 pranks: *bad behaviour*
225 best conscience: *sense of right and wrong*
233 seeming: *pretence*
234 seal: *blind*
234 close as oak: *like an oak tree*
238 bound: *indebted*

With fresh suspicions? No, to be once in doubt
Is once to be resolved: exchange me for a goat,
When I shall turn the business of my soul
To such exsufflicate and blown surmises,
Matching thy inference. 'Tis not to make me jealous
To say my wife is fair, feeds well, loves company,
Is free of speech, sings, plays and dances well;
Where virtue is, these are more virtuous:
Nor from mine own weak merits will I draw
The smallest fear or doubt of her revolt,
For she had eyes, and chose me. No, Iago,
I'll see before I doubt; when I doubt, prove,
And on the proof, there is no more but this –
Away at once with love or jealousy!

Iago I am glad of it, for now I shall have reason
To show the love and duty that I bear you
With franker spirit. Therefore, as I am bound,
Receive it from me. I speak not yet of proof.
Look to your wife, observe her well with Cassio,
Wear your eye thus, not jealous nor secure.
I would not have your free and noble nature,
Out of self-bounty, be abused, look to it:
I know our country disposition well;
In Venice they do let heaven see the pranks
They dare not show their husbands: their best conscience
Is not to leave it undone, but keep unknown.

Othello Dost thou say so?

Iago She did deceive her father, marrying you;
And when she seem'd to shake and fear your looks,
She loved them most.

Othello And so she did.

Iago Why, go to then;
She that, so young, could give out such a seeming,
To seal her father's eyes up close as oak –
He thought 'twas witchcraft – but I am much to blame;
I humbly do beseech you of your pardon
For too much loving you.

Othello I am bound to thee for ever.

Iago I see this hath a little dashed your spirits.

Othello Not a jot, not a jot.

Iago I' faith, I fear it has.
I hope you will consider what is spoke
Comes from my love. But I do see you're moved,

I am to pray you not to strain my speech
To grosser issues nor to larger reach
Than to suspicion.

Othello I will not.

Iago Should you do so, my lord,
My speech should fall into such vile success
As my thoughts aim not at. Cassio's my worthy friend –
My lord, I see you are moved.

Othello No, not much moved:
I do not think but Desdemona's honest.

Iago Long live she so! And long live you to think so!

Othello And yet, how nature erring from itself—

Iago Ay, there's the point: as – to be bold with you –
Not to affect many proposed matches
Of her own clime, complexion, and degree,
Whereto we see in all things nature tends –
Fie! one may smell in such a will most rank,
Foul disproportion, thoughts unnatural.
But pardon me: I do not in position
Distinctly speak of her, though I may fear
Her will, recoiling to her better judgment,
May fall to match you with her country forms
And happily repent.

Othello Farewell, farewell:
If more thou dost perceive, let me know more;
Set on thy wife to observe: leave me, Iago.

Iago [***Going***] My lord, I take my leave.

Othello Why did I marry? This honest creature doubtless
Sees and knows more, much more, than he unfolds.

Iago [***Returning***] My lord, I would I might entreat
your honour
To scan this thing no further, leave it to time:
Though it be fit that Cassio have his place,
For sure, he fills it up with great ability,
Yet, if you please to hold him off awhile,
You shall by that perceive him and his means:
Note, if your lady strain his entertainment
With any strong or vehement importunity,
Much will be seen in that. In the meantime,
Let me be thought too busy in my fears –
As worthy cause I have to fear I am –
And hold her free, I do beseech your honour.

244 strain: *exaggerate*
245 reach: *extent*
249 vile success: *evil consequence*
257 affect: *accept*
257 proposed matches: *marriage proposals*
258 clime: *country*
261 Foul disproportion: *improper behaviour*
264 recoiling: *returning*
265 fall ... country forms: *prefer her own countrymen*
266 happily repent: *take back her love for you*
278 means: *behaviour, antics*
279 strain his entertainment: *urges his reinstatement*
280 importunity: *pleading*

285 government: *reaction*

289 haggard: *unfaithful*

290 jesses: *ties to me*

291 whistle ... wind: *free her*

292 pray at fortune: *survive as best she may*

292 Haply, for: *perhaps because*

293 soft parts of conversation: *social graces*

294 chamberers: *gentlemen*

295 vale of years: *middle age*

296 abused: *betrayed*

298 delicate: *refined*

300 vapour: *foul air*

303 Prerogatived: *privileged*

303 base: *those of humble birth*

304 unshunnable: *inevitable*

305 forked: *the sign for a deceived husband*

306 do quicken: *are born*

316 watching: *staying up late*

Othello Fear not my government.

Iago I once more take my leave.

Exit

Othello This fellow's of exceeding honesty,
And knows all qualities, with a learned spirit,
Of human dealings. If I do prove her haggard,
Though that her jesses were my dear heartstrings,
I'ld whistle her off and let her down the wind,
To pray at fortune. Haply, for I am black
And have not those soft parts of conversation
That chamberers have, or for I am declined
Into the vale of years – yet that's not much –
She's gone. I am abused, and my relief
Must be to loathe her. O curse of marriage,
That we can call these delicate creatures ours,
And not their appetites! I had rather be a toad,
And live upon the vapour of a dungeon,
Than keep a corner in the thing I love
For others' uses. Yet, 'tis the plague of great ones
Prerogatived are they less than the base,
'Tis destiny, unshunnable, like death:
Even then this forked plague is fated to us
When we do quicken. Desdemona comes:

Re-enter Desdemona and Emilia

If she be false, O, then heaven mocks itself!
I'll not believe it.

Desdemona How now, my dear Othello!
Your dinner, and the generous islanders
By you invited, do attend your presence.

Othello I am to blame.

Desdemona Why do you speak so faintly?
Are you not well?

Othello I have a pain upon my forehead here.

Desdemona 'Faith, that's with watching, 'twill away again:
Let me but bind it hard, within this hour
It will be well.

Othello Your napkin is too little:

He puts the handkerchief from him, and it drops.

Let it alone. Come, I'll go in with you.

Desdemona I am very sorry that you are not well.

Exeunt Othello and Desdemona

Emilia
I am glad I have found this napkin:
This was her first remembrance from the Moor:
My wayward husband hath a hundred times
Wooed me to steal it, but she so loves the token,
For he conjured her she should ever keep it,
That she reserves it ever more about her
To kiss and talk to. I'll have the work taken out,
And give it Iago: what he will do with it
Heaven knows, not I;
I nothing but to please his fantasy.

Re-enter Iago

Iago
How now! What do you here alone?

Emilia
Do not you chide, I have a thing for you.

Iago
A thing for me? It is a common thing—

Emilia
Ha!

Iago
To have a foolish wife.

Emilia
O, is that all? What will you give me now
For that same handkerchief?

Iago
What handkerchief?

Emilia
What handkerchief!
Why, that the Moor first gave to Desdemona,
That which so often you did bid me steal.

Iago
Hast stolen it from her?

Emilia
No, 'faith; she let it drop by negligence.
And, to the advantage, I, being here, took it up.
Look, here it is.

Iago
A good wench, give it me.

Emilia
What will you do with it, that you have been
So earnest to have me filch it?

Iago
[***Snatching it***] Why, what's that to you?

Emilia
If it be not for some purpose of import,
Give it me again: poor lady, she'll run mad
When she shall lack it.

Iago
Be not acknown on it. I have use for it.
Go, leave me.

Exit Emilia

I will in Cassio's lodging lose this napkin,
And let him find it. Trifles light as air
Are to the jealous confirmations strong
As proofs of holy writ: this may do something.

322 napkin: *handkerchief*
323 remembrance: *keepsake*
324 wayward: *stubborn*
326 conjured her: *made her swear*
328 work taken out: *the embroidery copied*
331 please his fantasy: *keep him happy*
333 chide: *scold*
344 by negligence: *carelessly*
345 to the advantage: *as luck would have it*
351 purpose of some import: *important use*
354 Be not acknown on: *do not admit*
357 Trifles: *unimportant things*
359 holy writ: *the Bible*

The Moor already changes with my poison:
Dangerous conceits are, in their natures, poisons,
Which at the first are scarce found to distaste,
But with a little act upon the blood.
Burn like the mines of sulphur. I did say so.
Look, where he comes!

Re-enter Othello

Not poppy, nor mandragora,
Nor all the drowsy syrups of the world,
Shall ever medicine thee to that sweet sleep
Which thou owedst yesterday.

Othello Ha! ha! False to me?

Iago Why, how now, general! No more of that.

Othello Avaunt! Be gone! Thou hast set me on the rack:
I swear 'tis better to be much abused
Than but to know it a little.

Iago How now, my lord!

Othello What sense had I of her stolen hours of lust?
I saw it not, thought it not, it harmed not me:
I slept the next night well, was free and merry;
I found not Cassio's kisses on her lips:
He that is robbed, not wanting what is stolen,
Let him not know it, and he's not robbed at all.

Iago I am sorry to hear this.

Othello I had been happy, if the general camp,
Pioners and all, had tasted her sweet body,
So I had nothing known. O, now, for ever
Farewell the tranquil mind! Farewell content!
Farewell the plumed troop, and the big wars,
That make ambition virtue! O, farewell!
Farewell the neighing steed, and the shrill trump,
The spirit-stirring drum, the ear-piercing fife,
The royal banner, and all quality,
Pride, pomp and circumstance of glorious war!
And, O you mortal engines, whose rude throats
The immortal Jove's dead clamours counterfeit,
Farewell! Othello's occupation's gone!

Iago Is it possible, my lord?

Othello Villain, be sure thou prove my love a whore,
Be sure of it, give me the ocular proof,
Or by the worth of man's eternal soul,
Thou hadst been better have been born a dog
Than answer my waked wrath!

361 conceits: *imaginings*
364 mines of sulphur: *hell fire*
366 poppy, nor mandragora: *sleep-inducing drugs*
369 thou owedst: *you enjoyed*
372 Avaunt: *go away*
372 rack: *instrument of torture*
383 general camp: *whole army*
384 Pioners: *ordinary soldiers*
389 trump: *trumpet*
392 circumstance: *ceremony*
393 engines: *cannons*
394 Jove's dead clamours: *loud thunderbolts*
395 occupation's gone: *career is over*
398 ocular proof: *visible evidence*

Iago Is it come to this?

Othello Make me to see it; or, at the least, so prove it,
That the probation bear no hinge nor loop
To hang a doubt on; or woe upon thy life!

Iago My noble lord –

Othello If thou dost slander her and torture me,
Never pray more, abandon all remorse.
On horror's head horrors accumulate;
Do deeds to make heaven weep, all earth amazed;
For nothing canst thou to damnation add
Greater than that.

Iago O grace! O heaven forgive me!
Are you a man? have you a soul or sense?
God be wi' you; take mine office. O wretched fool,
That livest to make thine honesty a vice!
O monstrous world! Take note, take note, O world,
To be direct and honest is not safe.
I thank you for this profit; and from hence
I'll love no friend, since love breeds such offence.

Othello Nay, stay; thou shouldst be honest.

Iago I should be wise, for honesty's a fool
And loses that it works for.

Othello By the world,
I think my wife be honest and think she is not;
I think that thou art just and think thou art not.
I'll have some proof. Her name, that was as fresh
As Dian's visage, is now begrimed and black
As mine own face. If there be cords, or knives,
Poison, or fire, or suffocating streams,
I'll not endure it. Would I were satisfied!

Iago I see, sir, you are eaten up with passion:
I do repent me that I put it to you.
You would be satisfied?

Othello Would! nay, I will.

Iago And may: but, how? How satisfied, my lord?
Would you, the supervisor, grossly gape on –
Behold her topped?

Othello Death and damnation! O!

Iago It were a tedious difficulty, I think,
To bring them to that prospect: damn them then,
If ever mortal eyes do see them bolster
More than their own! What then? how then?

404 probation: *proof*
415 office: *job*
419 profit: *lesson*
428 Dian's visage: *goddess of the moon*
430 suffocating streams: *rivers of lava*
431 satisfied: *certain*
438 topped: *with a lover*
440 tedious difficulty: *hard thing to arrange*
442 bolster: *share a pillow*

446 prime: *lecherous*
447 salt: *lusty*

What shall I say? Where's satisfaction?
It is impossible you should see this,
Were they as prime as goats, as hot as monkeys,
As salt as wolves in pride, and fools as gross
As ignorance made drunk. But yet, I say,
If imputation and strong circumstances,
Which lead directly to the door of truth,
Will give you satisfaction, you may have it.

Othello Give me a living reason she's disloyal.

453 office: *task*

Iago I do not like the office:
But, since I am entered in this cause so far,
Pricked to it by foolish honesty and love,
I will go on. I lay with Cassio lately,
And, being troubled with a raging tooth,
I could not sleep.
There are a kind of men so loose of soul,
That in their sleeps will mutter their affairs.
One of this kind is Cassio.
In sleep I heard him say 'Sweet Desdemona,
Let us be wary, let us hide our loves!'
And then, sir, would he gripe and wring my hand,
Cry 'O sweet creature!' and then kiss me hard,
As if he plucked up kisses by the roots
That grew upon my lips: then laid his leg
Over my thigh, and sighed, and kissed; and then
Cried 'Cursed fate that gave thee to the Moor!'

464 gripe: *grab, clutch*

Othello O monstrous! Monstrous!

Iago Nay, this was but his dream.

472 denoted: *showed what had taken place*
473 shrewd doubt: *penetrating guess*
474 thicken: *reinforce*

Othello But this denoted a foregone conclusion:
'Tis a shrewd doubt, though it be but a dream.

Iago And this may help to thicken other proofs
That do demonstrate thinly.

Othello I'll tear her all to pieces.

Iago Nay, but be wise, yet we see nothing done,
She may be honest yet. Tell me but this,
Have you not sometimes seen a handkerchief
Spotted with strawberries in your wife's hand?

Othello I gave her such a one, 'twas my first gift.

Iago I know not that, but such a handkerchief –
I am sure it was your wife's – did I today
See Cassio wipe his beard with.

Othello If it be that—

Iago If it be that, or any that was hers,
It speaks against her with the other proofs.

Othello O, that the slave had forty thousand lives!
One is too poor, too weak for my revenge.
Now do I see 'tis true. Look here, Iago,
All my fond love thus do I blow to heaven.
'Tis gone.
Arise, black vengeance, from thy hollow cell!
Yield up, O love, thy crown and hearted throne
To tyrannous hate! Swell, bosom, with thy fraught,
For 'tis of aspics' tongues!

Iago Yet be content.

Othello O, blood, blood, blood!

Iago Patience, I say; your mind perhaps may change.

Othello Never, Iago. Like to the Pontic sea,
Whose icy current and compulsive course
Never feels retiring ebb, but keeps due on
To the Propontic and the Hellespont,
Even so my bloody thoughts, with violent pace,
Shall ne'er look back, ne'er ebb to humble love,
Till that a capable and wide revenge
Swallow them up. Now, by yond marble heaven,

Kneels

In the due reverence of a sacred vow
I here engage my words.

Iago Do not rise yet.

Kneels

Witness, you ever-burning lights above,
You elements that clip us round about,
Witness that here Iago doth give up
The execution of his wit, hands, heart,
To wronged Othello's service! Let him command,
And to obey shall be in me remorse,
What bloody business ever.

They rise

Othello I greet thy love,
Not with vain thanks, but with acceptance bounteous,
And will upon the instant put thee to it:
Within these three days let me hear thee say
That Cassio's not alive.

Iago My friend is dead:
'Tis done at your request. But let her live.

495 fraught: *burden of hatred*
496 aspics: *poisonous snakes*
500 Pontic sea: *Black Sea*
503 Propontic: *Sea of Marmara*
503 Hellespont: *Dardanelles*
506 capable: *massive*
507 marble heaven: *hard sky*
512 clip: *surround*
514 execution: *activities*
517 What bloody business ever: *however murderous it gets*
519 acceptance bounteous: *generous reward*

Othello Damn her, lewd minx! O, damn her!
Come, go with me apart. I will withdraw,
To furnish me with some swift means of death
For the fair devil. Now art thou my lieutenant.

Iago I am your own for ever.

Exeunt

Key Scene Extended Commentary

A fateful meeting (lines 1–36)

Desdemona, Cassio and Emilia meet in the garden of the castle. Desdemona promises her support to have Cassio reinstated, using 'All my abilities in thy behalf'. Cassio is impatient, afraid that Othello 'will forget my love and service'. While Desdemona's promise might be admirable, her decision to interfere in her husband's public duty is questionable. Cassio was dismissed by his commanding officer for a serious breach of duty in a time of emergency for the island. Cassio sees Othello and Iago enter and he slips away, still too ashamed to face his general.

Insinuation and a plea (lines 37–98)

Iago seizes the opportunity to spread suspicion by innuendo, saying, 'Ha! I like not that'. The temptation of Othello has begun. Iago pretends he does not think it could be Cassio because he would not 'steal away so guilty-like'. Desdemona immediately begins her plea on Cassio's behalf, 'shall it be shortly?' At first her husband is indulgent, 'The sooner, sweet, for you'. But the more she persists, his mood changes. Othello reminds her that he has military duties to attend to, but Desdemona continues in a coy, flirtatious way, 'I wonder in my soul,/ What you would ask me, that I should deny?' Othello eventually gives in to her persuasion, 'I will deny thee nothing'. He wearies of the conversation and asks 'leave me but a little to myself'. The tone of his wife's reply is interesting, 'I am obedient'. Does it show the first strain in their relationship?

I have been talking with a suitor here,
A man that languishes in your
displeasure

Desdemona
Act 3 Scene 3, l.46–7

Seeds of doubt (lines 99–286)

Iago immediately sets to work, insidiously spreading confusion. Using the formal language of a court, he asks Othello, 'Did Michael Cassio, when you wooed my lady,/ Know of your love?' Iago's dark mysterious comments exasperate the Moor, who demands to know more, 'Show me thy thought'. But Iago 'plays' his victim, biding his time. In contrast to Desdemona's simple methods of persuasion, he skilfully manipulates Othello to conjure up for himself a 'monster in his thought', jealousy. Consumed by the 'green-eyed monster', Othello becomes increasingly suspicious.

O, beware, my lord of jealousy;
It is the green-eyed monster

Iago
Act 3 Scene 3, l.186–7

More than anything, the Moor craves certainty, 'to be once in doubt/ Is once to be resolved'. He lists Desdemona's good qualities; she is 'fair, feeds well, loves company'. He consoles himself that she chose him and dismisses his jealousy. But Iago has other trump cards and he tells Othello that Moors are outsiders while Desdemona is a Venetian lady – 'In Venice they do let heaven see the pranks/ They dare not show their husbands'. In other words, she is an unreliable wife. Disoriented and completely out of his depth, Othello responds, 'Dost thou say so?'

Iago's confidence grows. He reminds the Moor of his wife's ability to mislead, 'She did deceive her father, marrying you'. Othello instantly accepts this undeniable truth; 'And so she did'.

The Moor tries to contain his raging feelings, pretending that he is 'not much moved'. But his trust is broken. He instructs Iago to have Emilia spy on Desdemona, 'Set on thy wife to observe'. Left alone and heartbroken, he wonders 'Why did I marry?' He suspects that Iago knows much more than he 'unfolds'. Iago briefly returns, pretending to beg Othello to take no action and 'scan this thing no further' to see how Desdemona responds.

She did deceive her father,
marrying you

Iago
Act 3 Scene 3, l.228

Confusion reigns (lines 287–308)

In his soliloquy, Othello repeats his belief in Iago's 'exceeding honesty'. He tortures himself by listing all his insecurities. He is an outsider, he lacks refinement and he is much older than his wife. The Moor judges himself on colour, class and age. Two simple statements, 'She's gone. I am abused', reveal the extent of his torment. Yet when he sees Desdemona returning, his great love for her surfaces again and he refuses to believe she is 'false'.

The handkerchief plot (lines 309–507)

Othello expresses his anguish by complaining of a headache. Desdemona tries to soothe him, but drops her handkerchief. Shortly afterwards, Emilia finds it and recounts how it was Desdemona's first token of love from Othello. She also reveals that Iago has repeatedly asked her to steal it from her mistress. Iago enters and begins immediately to scold her. He snatches the handkerchief from his wife, saying he has 'use for it'. His secret intention is to place it in Cassio's lodging as evidence that Desdemona is the lieutenant's lover. Iago is aware that these 'Trifles light as air' can be used as 'proofs' to the suspicious.

A distraught Othello enters, accusing Iago of setting him 'on the rack'. Because he now knows of Desdemona's 'stolen hours of lust', his peace of mind is shattered. The Moor has lost all that was important to him – particularly his proud military successes. He demands 'ocular proof' from Iago that his wife is a 'whore', otherwise the consequences for Iago will be disastrous. In response, Iago pretends to be hurt; he is being punished for being 'direct and honest'.

Othello struggles helplessly, caught in the ensign's vengeful web. Iago then tells the Moor a bold lie, claiming that he observed Cassio moaning in his sleep for 'Sweet Desdemona'. At this point, Othello loses all self-control, swearing to 'tear her all to pieces'. Iago now produces the final piece of 'evidence', the embroidered handkerchief, which he claims he saw Cassio using to wipe his beard. Othello now craves, 'blood, blood, blood!' Iago's plan has succeeded.

Shakespeare's Dramatic Style

By the end of Act 3 Scene 3, the 'temptation scene', Iago is dominant. Convinced that he has been betrayed by Desdemona, Othello is in despair and intent on violent revenge. The play's tragic outcome is unavoidable. Shakespeare ends this **pivotal scene** with the Moor and his ensign kneeling together in what resembles a mock wedding ceremony, each promising to take vengeance on Desdemona and Cassio. Iago's concluding pledge ominously references the language of love and marriage: 'I am your own for ever'.

Over the course of this lengthy sequence, **Shakespeare develops both of the play's central characters**. While Iago gains confidence in executing his villainous plans, we see how vulnerable Othello is. He craves certainty ('Give me a living reason she's disloyal') and wants to act decisively. Like Desdemona, he mixes public life with private concerns. The Moor uses the language of the battlefield when considering emotions. He is egotistical, Desdemona 'chose me'. Yet he is also is conscious of his

I am your own for ever

Iago
Act 3 Scene 3, l.529

inexperience in matters of love, lacking the 'soft parts of conversation'. It's clear that he no longer thinks for himself, but echoes Iago's words. His vivid imagination is prodded by the devious ensign to conjure up a 'monster in his thought'. Ironically, Othello cannot imagine that Iago is deceiving him.

Othello's **language** highlights his degradation in this traumatic scene. Unable to see reality, he acts as judge and executioner without giving Cassio or Desdemona a chance to voice their side of Iago's story. Othello's use of bestial imagery ('toad', 'aspics' tongues') mirrors Iago's coarse speech ('hot as monkeys'). He has descended to his ensign's level.

Nobody suspects the truth about Iago. whose 'honest' character is repeatedly mentioned – particularly by Othello. Only the audience is aware of Iago's duplicity. **Dramatic irony** is used to anticipate future developments. Othello exclaims 'when I love thee not,/ Chaos is come again'. He has indeed become 'bound' to Iago for ever because he has been blinded by Iago's skill in awakening the 'green-eyed monster' of jealousy within him. The use of **sight imagery** highlights this. Othello demands 'ocular proof'. Iago advises him to 'Look to your wife' while Othello tries to hold on to his sanity by consoling himself that 'she had eyes, and chose me'. As we watch the tense cat-and-mouse exchanges between the Moor and his ensign, Shakespeare succeeds in simultaneously fascinating and disturbing his audience.

Critical Analysis

'In his play *Othello*, Shakespeare presents revealing insights into appearance and reality.'

Discuss this view, supporting your opinions with reference to Act 3 Scene 3. Write a paragraph (about 150–200 words), supporting your answer with reference to the play.

Prompt!

- Characters are easily misled by appearances.
- Personal fears and insecurities affect perceptions of truth.
- Language can be manipulated to obscure actuality.
- Circumstantial evidence – especially if unverifiable – often obscures reality.
- Self-deception blinds Othello and Desdemona to Iago's true nature.

Sample Paragraph 1

I think Shakespeare shows us the madness that comes when people start to believe in lies. Othello beleves all of Iago's false lies about Cassio and his bride Desdemona. I think Iago was clever because he hopped onto anything that he could use such as when Emilia found the hankerchef or napkin that Othello gave Desdemona as a pre-nup gift. Shakespeare is just showing us just how clever Iago is because he is going to put it in Cassio's room so that he will find it and this will be more evidence against him of them having an affair along with the dream he made up all of which was pure lies. He tells Othello about Cassio's dream and Othello starts to shout for blood. He has now excepted Iago's story. I think he just doesn't know the truth anymore. *(140 words)*

Examiner's Comment

- Basic response that fails to take on the question of insights.
- Some references to Iago's deception of Othello.
- Poor expression and some spelling errors ('beleves', 'hankerchef', 'excepted').

Sample Paragraph 2

In Act 3 Scene 3 Iago puts doubts into Othello's mind about his friend Cassio and his wife Desdemona. He manages to make Othello into 'a green-eyed monster' by disturbing his peace of mind. Othello tries to hold on to reality by saying 'I'll see before I ever doubt her' and he won't simply accept Iago's untrue claim that his wife is unfaithful until he has received 'ocular proof'. But Shakespeare shows us that people can be quickly deceived by appearances. 'The Moor already changes' with Iago's 'poison'. I was interested that Othello never asked either Cassio or Desdemona what they had to say about all this. Instead he accepts Iago's story of Cassio's dream and his so-called proof that he saw Cassio wiping his beard with Desdemona's handkerchief, her first precious gift from Othello. Now Othello loses his grip on reality, 'All of my fond love do I blow to heaven'. He also abandons his career and becomes a blood-thirsty avenger. He has entered Iago's hellish reality. *(170 words)*

Examiner's Comment

- This mid-grade response summarises the scene and refers mainly to one insight ('people can be deceived').
- More focus on other aspects of the theme would have improved the answer.
- Some misquotes, but good general engagement with the scene.
- Expression is clear and controlled throughout.

Sample Paragraph 3

Shakespeare explores the blurred distinction between appearance and reality through Iago's clever deception. The key to his success is the carefully cultivated assumption accepted by all, especially Othello, that he is 'honest'. Yet Iago colours Othello's perception of Cassio's hasty exit by assuring him that it could not surely be him sneaking away 'so guilty-like'. We are made aware of how a character's insecurities can divert him from the truth. Iago reminds Othello that his wife has already practised deception by 'marrying you'. He is creating an alternative reality through innuendo and lies. We are seeing planned misinformation. Shakespeare allows us to witness the terrible consequences of this descent into 'Chaos' for the once noble Othello who now mirrors Iago's coarse language, imagining himself as 'a toad' living on 'the vapour of a dungeon'. For the first time, the Moor lies by pretending he is 'not much moved' by Iago's 'revelations'. A fictitious account of a dream is unsubstantiated evidence that completes Iago's scheme to make Othello 'see' what is not – Desdemona's adultery. The playwright also shows us the torment of one who has lost his 'tranquil mind' through the machinations of a character who 'shapes' events to distort reality. *(200 words)*

Examiner's Comment

- Clearly illustrated discussion focusing on insights about appearance and reality.
- Supported development of points on insecurity, misinformation and the trauma caused by deception.
- Impressive vocabulary ('blurred distinction', 'designed misinformation', 'unsubstantiated evidence').
- A well-organised and successful top-grade standard.

Class/Homework Exercise

'In the play *Othello,* Iago both fascinates and repels us as he creates clever schemes to take revenge against the Moor.'

Discuss this statement with particular reference to Act 3 Scene 3. Write a paragraph (about 150–200 words), giving reasons for your views and supporting your response with suitable quotation from the text.

Prompt!

- 'Honest Iago' – an intriguing mix of bitterness and vengeance.
- His cynical charm fools everyone.
- An inventively treacherous sociopath.
- A skilled manipulator who delights in evil.
- Iago's actions and compelling language dominate this scene.

Revision Overview

Cassio is eager to be reinstated as lieutenant and insists on seeking Desdemona's help. However, he refuses to face Othello directly. Naively, Desdemona persists in persuading her husband, but Othello asks her to leave him alone. Iago seizes his chance to raise doubts about Cassio's hasty departure. His hesitant replies to Othello's questions are designed to suggest that the lieutenant has something to hide. Othello becomes more and more suspicious.

Iago advises Othello not to become jealous, while at the same time making vague hints about Desdemona's unfaithfulness. In response, Othello lies for the first time, pretending that the ensign's insinuations have not really affected him. Iago then suggests directly that the general's wife and Cassio are secret lovers. When Desdemona reappears, Othello's doubts seem to vanish. However, he tells a second lie, claiming that he has a headache. During Desdemona's efforts to comfort him, he accidently drops her handkerchief, his first gift to her.

When the couple leave, Emilia finds the handkerchief and shows it to Iago, who takes it from her. He intends to place it in Cassio's lodgings as incriminating evidence. Othello returns, demanding more proof of his wife's infidelity. Iago invents another story about how Cassio revealed his feelings for Desdemona in a dream. Othello's thoughts suddenly turn to revenge and he swears a terrible oath to kill his wife. He also orders Iago to murder Cassio.

- **Themes: Appearance and reality –** Iago's misinformation continues to distort reality. He pretends to Othello that he is reluctant to inform him about these unpleasant 'truths' while in reality he is glorying in his 'poisons', which 'Burn like the mines of sulphur'.
  Jealousy – aided by Iago's lies and innuendo, Othello's 'green-eyed monster' is born in this scene. The noble general abandons all reason and is degraded to the level of a roaring beast, 'I'll tear her all to pieces'.
- **Characters: Othello –** insecure and easily manipulated, transformed from noble general to dishonourable avenger.
  Iago – ingenious, evil, opportunist, gambler, hypocrite, vulgar.
  Desdemona – reassuring, reliable, honest, naive, kind.
  Cassio – impatient, self-centred, weak-willed.

Exam Focus

Act 3 Scene 3 can be used successfully in response to a range of examination questions about the play's central themes, characters, relationships and the playwright's dramatic style.

This **key scene** has significant dramatic functions:

- Presents the fateful meeting of Desdemona, Cassio and Emilia.
- Illustrates the opportunistic capabilities and villainy of Iago.
- Details the degradation of Othello.
- Develops themes of appearance and reality, jealousy, reputation/dishonour.
- Effectively uses animal imagery to inflame, cheating imagery to ridicule, hellish imagery to terrify.
- Appals the audience by Iago's clever conspiracies and the grains of truth contained in his cynical views of the world.
- Marks a turning point in the play.

Key Quotes

That I being absent, and my place supplied, My general will forget my love and service *(Cassio to Desdemona) l.19–20*	Cassio doubts the power of his friendship with Othello. He urges Desdemona to persuade her husband to reinstate him as lieutenant. This crucial development initiates the play's tragic outcome. Desdemona is about to put herself in great danger. Ironically, It was Iago who first suggested this course of action to Cassio.
O, beware, my lord, of jealousy; It is the green-eyed monster *(Iago to Othello) l.186–7*	Iago pretends to be a loyal friend. His vividly poetic advice both provokes and warns Othello about losing self-control. What he says is brutally effective and foreshadows the tragedy ahead for a husband consumed with jealousy.
Thou has set me on the rack *(Othello to Iago) l.372*	Othello complains that he is the victim of torture. He is intensely aware that he has sacrificed his peace of mind because he has believed Iago's rumours about Desdemona's apparent infidelity. Othello believes that he has lost his friend, his wife and his career because he has become a slave to suspicion and vengeance.
give me the ocular proof *(Othello to Iago) l.398*	This moment marks a key turning point in the play. Troubled and distraught, Othello demands proof of his wife's adultery. Iago is now under pressure to produce tangible evidence to support his accusations. The Moor is a professional soldier who has a simplistic view of the world. His desire for justice will have disastrous consequences.
I am your own for ever *(Iago to Othello) l.529*	Iago's deeply ironic statement uses the chilling language of love and marriage. Yet Othello has lost all trust in his young wife and the audience now understands that it is Othello who is tragically tied to Iago. Indeed, Othello will never be able to escape from his hypocritical ensign and his devious schemes.

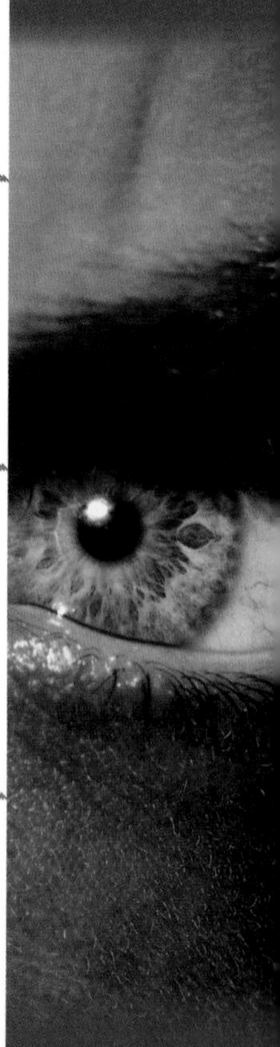

Act 3
Scene 4

INTRODUCTION

- The missing handkerchief causes confusion.
- More secrets and lies.
- Iago continues to control events.
- Couples at odds: Desdemona and Othello, Cassio and Bianca.

Outside the castle

Enter Desdemona, Emilia, and Clown

Desdemona	Do you know, sirrah, where Lieutenant Cassio lies?
Clown	I dare not say he lies any where.
Desdemona	Why, man?
Clown	He's a soldier, and for one to say a soldier lies, is stabbing.
Desdemona	Go to, where lodges he?
Clown	To tell you where he lodges, is to tell you where I lie.
Desdemona	Can any thing be made of this?
Clown	I know not where he lodges, and for me to devise a lodging and say he lies here or he lies there, were to lie in mine own throat.
Desdemona	Can you inquire him out, and be edified by report?
Clown	I will catechise the world for him; that is, make questions and by them answer.
Desdemona	Seek him, bid him come hither: tell him I have moved my lord on his behalf, and hope all will be well.
Clown	To do this is within the compass of man's wit, and therefore I will attempt the doing it.

Exit

Desdemona	Where should I lose that handkerchief, Emilia?
Emilia	I know not, madam.
Desdemona	Believe me, I had rather have lost my purse Full of crusadoes: and, but my noble Moor Is true of mind and made of no such baseness As jealous creatures are, it were enough To put him to ill thinking.
Emilia	Is he not jealous?
Desdemona	Who, he? I think the sun where he was born Drew all such humours from him.
Emilia	Look, where he comes.
Desdemona	I will not leave him now till Cassio Be called to him.

Enter Othello

	How is it with you, my lord?
Othello	Well, my good lady.

Line notes:
1 lies: *lodges*
2 lies: *tells a lie*
9 devise: *make up, invent*
12 edified: *instructed, enlightened*
13 catechise: *interrogate*
16 moved: *pleaded with*
17 compass: *scope*
22 crusadoes: *gold coins*
28 humours: *moods*

Line numbers: 5, 10, 15, 20, 25, 30

[*Aside*]

O, hardness to dissemble! –
How do you, Desdemona?

Desdemona Well, my good lord.

Othello Give me your hand: this hand is moist, my lady.

Desdemona It yet hath felt no age nor known no sorrow.

Othello This argues fruitfulness and liberal heart;
Hot, hot, and moist, this hand of yours requires
A sequester from liberty; fasting and prayer,
Much castigation, exercise devout;
For here's a young and sweating devil here,
That commonly rebels. 'Tis a good hand,
A frank one.

Desdemona You may indeed say so,
For 'twas that hand that gave away my heart.

Othello A liberal hand: the hearts of old gave hands,
But our new heraldry is hands, not hearts.

Desdemona I cannot speak of this. Come now, your promise.

Othello What promise, chuck?

Desdemona I have sent to bid Cassio come speak with you.

Othello I have a salt and sorry rheum offends me;
Lend me thy handkerchief.

Desdemona Here, my lord.

Othello That which I gave you.

Desdemona I have it not about me.

Othello Not?

Desdemona No, indeed, my lord.

Othello That is a fault. That handkerchief
Did an Egyptian to my mother give;
She was a charmer, and could almost read
The thoughts of people: she told her, while
she kept it,
'Twould make her amiable and subdue my father
Entirely to her love, but if she lost it
Or made gift of it, my father's eye
Should hold her loathed and his spirits should hunt
After new fancies: she, dying, gave it me,
And bid me, when my fate would have me wive,
To give it her. I did so: and take heed on it,
Make it a darling like your precious eye,

34 dissemble: *hide true feelings, pretend*
41 sequester: *break, retreat*
42 castigation: *discipline*
42 exercise devout: *prayer*
48 liberal: *giving*
49 heraldry: *custom*
51 chuck: *dear (term of endearment)*
53 salt and sorry rheum: *running cold*
62 charmer: *someone skilled in magic*
64 amiable: *loving, desirable*
68 new fancies: *other lovers*
69 wive: *marry*

72 perdition: *damnation*

76 sibyl: *prophetess*

80 mummy: *embalming fluid*

95 suit: *efforts to persuade you*

97 misgives: *is suspicious*

99 sufficient: *competent, suitable*

108 'Zounds!: *Damn!*

To lose it or give it away were such perdition
As nothing else could match.

Desdemona Is it possible?

Othello 'Tis true, there's magic in the web of it.
A sibyl, that had numbered in the world
The sun to course two hundred compasses,
In her prophetic fury sewed the work;
The worms were hallowed that did breed the silk,
And it was dyed in mummy which the skilful
Conserved of maidens' hearts.

Desdemona Indeed! Is it true?

Othello Most veritable, therefore look to it well.

Desdemona Then would to God that I had never seen it!

Othello Ha! wherefore?

Desdemona Why do you speak so startingly and rash?

Othello Is it lost? Is it gone? Speak, is it out of the way?

Desdemona Heaven bless us!

Othello Say you?

Desdemona It is not lost; but what and if it were?

Othello How!

Desdemona I say, it is not lost.

Othello Fetch it, let me see it.

Desdemona Why, so I can, sir, but I will not now.
This is a trick to put me from my suit,
Pray you, let Cassio be received again.

Othello Fetch me the handkerchief, my mind misgives.

Desdemona Come, come,
You'll never meet a more sufficient man.

Othello The handkerchief!

Desdemona I pray, talk me of Cassio.

Othello The handkerchief!

Desdemona A man that all his time
Hath founded his good fortunes on your love,
Shared dangers with you—

Othello The handkerchief!

Desdemona In faith, you are to blame.

Othello 'Zounds!

Exit

Emilia Is not this man jealous?

Desdemona I ne'er saw this before.
Sure, there's some wonder in this handkerchief:
I am most unhappy in the loss of it.

Emilia 'Tis not a year or two shows us a man:
They are all but stomachs, and we all but food;
To eat us hungerly, and when they are full,
They belch us. Look you, Cassio and my husband!

Enter Cassio and Iago

Iago There is no other way, 'tis she must do it,
And, lo, the happiness! Go, and importune her.

Desdemona How now, good Cassio! What's the news with you?

Cassio Madam, my former suit. I do beseech you
That by your virtuous means I may again
Exist, and be a member of his love
Whom I with all the office of my heart
Entirely honour: I would not be delayed.
If my offence be of such mortal kind
That nor my service past, nor present sorrows,
Nor purposed merit in futurity,
Can ransom me into his love again,
But to know so must be my benefit;
So shall I clothe me in a forced content,
And shut myself up in some other course,
To fortune's alms.

Desdemona Alas, thrice-gentle Cassio!
My advocation is not now in tune;
My lord is not my lord, nor should I know him,
Were he in favour as in humour altered.
So help me every spirit sanctified,
As I have spoken for you all my best
And stood within the blank of his displeasure
For my free speech! You must awhile be patient;
What I can do I will, and more I will
Than for myself I dare: let that suffice you.

Iago Is my lord angry?

Emilia He went hence but now,
And certainly in strange unquietness.

Iago Can he be angry? I have seen the cannon,
When it hath blown his ranks into the air,
And, like the devil, from his very arm
Puffed his own brother: – and can he be angry?

116 belch us: *throw us up*
118 importune: *ask*
123 office: *loyal service*
127 purposed merit: *pledges to serve*
128 ransom: *buy, restore*
131 shut myself up: *confine myself to*
132 fortune's alms: *whatever Fate offers*
134 advocation: *pleading*
136 favour: *appearance*
139 blank: *line of fire*
149 Puffed: *blown up*

150 moment: *importance*
154 unhatched: *developing*
155 demonstrable: *known*
156 puddled: *muddied, clouded*
157 wrangle: *find fault with*
159 endues: *infects*
162 observancy: *loving attention*
163 bridal: *wedding day*
163 Beshrew: *condemn*
164 unhandsome warrior: *unsuitable companion*
165 Arraigning: *accusing*
166 suborned the witness: *made the witness give false evidence*
167 indicted: *accused*
169 toy: *matter, suspicion*
182 Save you: *God save you*
188 Eight ... hours: *168 hours*

Something of moment then: I will go meet him,
There's matter in it indeed, if he be angry.

Desdemona I prithee, do so.

Exit Iago

Something, sure, of state,
Either from Venice, or some unhatched practice
Made demonstrable here in Cyprus to him,
Hath puddled his clear spirit: and in such cases
Men's natures wrangle with inferior things,
Though great ones are their object. 'Tis even so.
For let our finger ache, and it endues
Our other healthful members even to that sense
Of pain. Nay, we must think men are not gods,
Nor of them look for such observancy
As fit the bridal. Beshrew me much, Emilia,
I was, unhandsome warrior as I am,
Arraigning his unkindness with my soul;
But now I find I had suborned the witness,
And he's indicted falsely.

Emilia Pray heaven it be state-matters, as you think,
And no conception nor no jealous toy
Concerning you.

Desdemona Alas the day! I never gave him cause.

Emilia But jealous souls will not be answered so;
They are not ever jealous for the cause,
But jealous for they are jealous: 'tis a monster
Begot upon itself, born on itself.

Desdemona Heaven keep that monster from Othello's mind!

Emilia Lady, amen.

Desdemona I will go seek him. Cassio, walk hereabout:
If I do find him fit, I'll move your suit
And seek to effect it to my uttermost.

Cassio I humbly thank your ladyship.

Exeunt Desdemona and Emilia

Enter Bianca

Bianca Save you, friend Cassio!

Cassio What make you from home?
How is it with you, my most fair Bianca?
I' faith, sweet love, I was coming to your house.

Bianca And I was going to your lodging, Cassio.
What, keep a week away? Seven days and nights?
Eight score eight hours? And lovers' absent hours,

More tedious than the dial eight score times?
O weary reckoning!

Cassio Pardon me, Bianca:
I have this while with leaden thoughts been pressed:
But I shall, in a more continuate time,
Strike off this score of absence. Sweet Bianca,

Giving her Desdemona's handkerchief

Take me this work out.

Bianca O Cassio, whence came this?
This is some token from a newer friend:
To the felt absence now I feel a cause.
Is it come to this? Well, well.

Cassio Go to, woman!
Throw your vile guesses in the devil's teeth,
From whence you have them. You are jealous now
That this is from some mistress, some remembrance.
No, by my faith, Bianca.

Bianca Why, whose is it?

Cassio I know not, sweet. I found it in my chamber.
I like the work well: ere it be demanded –
As like enough it will – I'd have it copied.
Take it, and do it, and leave me for this time.

Bianca Leave you! wherefore?

Cassio I do attend here on the general;
And think it no addition, nor my wish,
To have him see me womaned.

Bianca Why, I pray you?

Cassio Not that I love you not.

Bianca But that you do not love me.
I pray you, bring me on the way a little,
And say if I shall see you soon at night.

Cassio 'Tis but a little way that I can bring you;
For I attend here: but I'll see you soon.

Bianca 'Tis very good; I must be circumstanced.

Exeunt

193 continuate: *uninterrupted*

195 Take me this work out: *copy this embroidery for me*

213 womaned: *with a woman*

221 be circumstanced: *ruled by circumstances*

Commentary

Comic interlude (lines 1–18)

Desdemona engages in light-hearted conversation with the clown (who was last seen mocking the musicians in Act 3 Scene 1). She is looking for Cassio to send him a message that she feels certain Othello will soon restore him to his former position and that 'all will be well'.

Lies and a lost handkerchief (lines 19–116)

Desdemona is also concerned that she has lost the handkerchief Othello gave her. She confides in Emilia, who lies to her mistress, denying that she knows where it is. Tragically for Desdemona, this small lie will allow Iago's plan to succeed, sealing her fate. When Othello arrives, Desdemona greets him warmly, but he takes her hand and comments on how 'hot, and moist' it is. He attaches a sinister significance to this, 'here's a young and sweating devil here'. Desdemona reminds her husband that it was 'that hand that gave away my heart'. She has no idea that he is obsessively trying to find evidence of her infidelity and – in good faith – mentions Cassio again.

Othello then pretends to have a cold and asks for her handkerchief. When Desdemona replies that she does not have it, he informs her of its magical powers and its significance as a symbol of their true love. Othello's traditional Moorish background, where belief in the supernatural is common, contrasts starkly with Desdemona's refined upbringing. Unsure of how to react, Desdemona resorts to lying, 'It is not lost'. She challenges him: 'but what and if it were?' A sharp exchange develops as Othello repeatedly demands the handkerchief. Desdemona insists on speaking about Cassio. She confronts Othello directly while Emilia fails to disclose what she knows. However, unlike her naive mistress, Emilia correctly judges that Othello's fitful behaviour is based on jealousy. She cynically remarks that men regard women solely in the context of satisfying their desires.

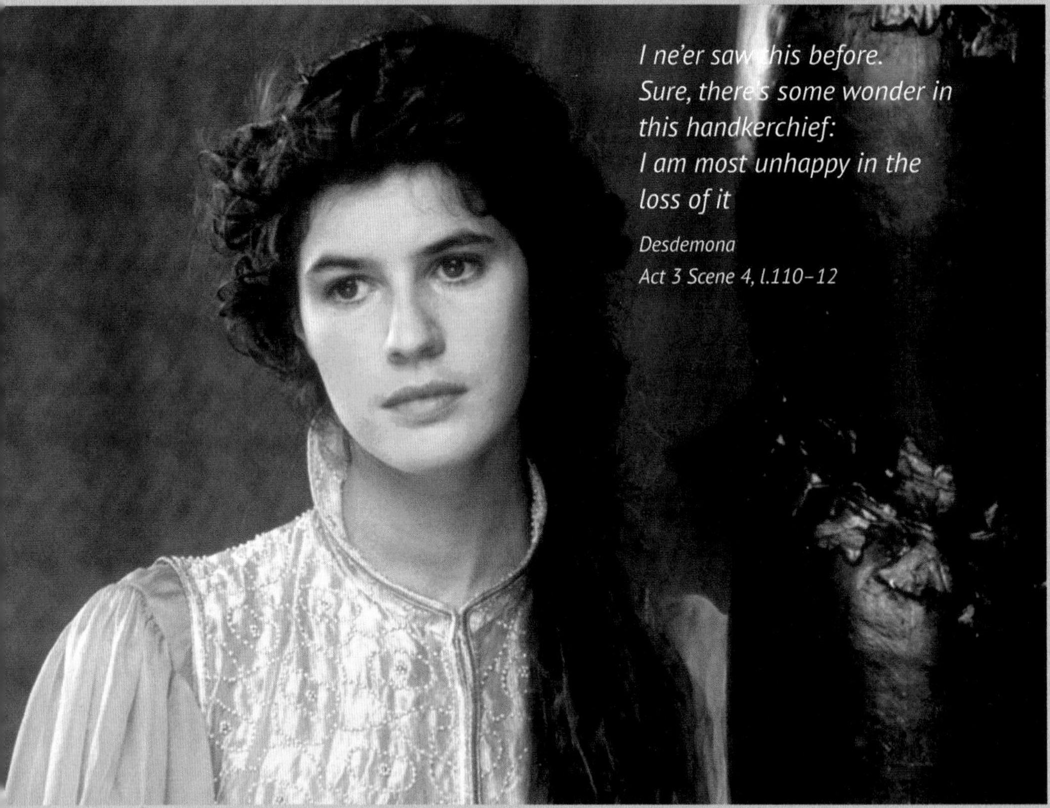

I ne'er saw this before.
Sure, there's some wonder in this handkerchief:
I am most unhappy in the loss of it

Desdemona
Act 3 Scene 4, l.110–12

The encircling web (lines 117–152)

Iago urges Cassio to ask Desdemona to intervene on his behalf again, 'Go, and importune her'. The courteous conversation between Cassio and Desdemona emphasises Othello's rude outburst. She confides that she fears her husband has changed, 'in humour altered'.

The cause (lines 153–181)

Iago speculates that the change in Othello has to be caused by something important, 'Something of moment'. Desdemona excuses her husband's bad behaviour by suggesting that it might be a matter 'of state' linked to his military duties on Cyprus. But again, the astute Emilia correctly suspects that it is another case of a husband distrusting his wife. The two women pray that it is not jealousy, 'Heaven keep that monster from Othello's mind!' Desdemona then promises Cassio that she will keep asking Othello to reinstate him as lieutenant.

Something of moment then: I will go meet him

Iago
Act 3 Scene 4, l.150

A new arrival (lines 182–221)

Another lovers' quarrel erupts when Cassio's mistress, Bianca, arrives. She complains bitterly about how he has been neglecting her, 'keep a week away'. Casually, he asks her to copy the embroidery from a handkerchief he has found in his lodging. Bianca immediately becomes suspicious that it is 'some token from a newer friend'. Like Othello, she is jealous, but she is willing to forgive Cassio when he promises to visit her soon.

Dramatic Significance

Beneath the opening witty comments exchanged between Desdemona and the clown, there is a sinister exploration concerning the **distortion of language** and how misunderstanding can so easily occur. Act 3 Scene 4 is filled with deception and self-deception. Desdemona is convinced that her husband trusts her, but still lies to him. Emilia is hiding the truth about the handkerchief.

The unseen handkerchief (a 'jealous toy') is an **important device** in the plot and dominates much of this scene. The treasured love-token has increasing symbolic meaning. Desdemona is afraid of its loss; Emilia uses the napkin to demonstrate her loyalty to Iago – and then keeps silent about it. Othello demands it and gives it a magical and emotional significance, using it as a test of Desdemona's fidelity. After finding the handkerchief in his lodgings, Cassio's request to have the embroidery copied by Bianca aids Iago's malicious plans. Indeed, the handkerchief becomes the ensign's most deadly weapon.

Shakespeare makes effective use of **irony** to increase the tension in this dramatic scene. Desdemona mistakenly believed Othello was 'made of no such baseness/ As jealous creatures are'. Desdemona assumes that her husband is preoccupied with some matter of state rather than a mere domestic concern. Cassio's desire to renew his friendship with

Othello and 'be a member of his love' now applies to Desdemona. Her innocent comment that 'My lord is not my lord' is alarmingly true. Iago has replaced Othello's identity with a new one – the wronged husband sworn to revenge.

The playwright has positioned the audience as **helpless witnesses** to an inevitable tragedy. This tense scene brings together Iago's twin plots – Cassio's efforts for reinstatement and Desdemona's supposed infidelity – in a violent collision. Othello and Desdemona attack each other with clashing word weapons, 'Cassio' and 'handkerchief'. Their high-minded love is breaking apart.

Class/Homework Exercise

'Shakespeare highlights the theme of deception through the use of contrasts in the play *Othello*.'

Discuss this statement with particular reference to Act 3 Scene 4. Write a paragraph (about 150–200 words), supporting your answer with reference to at least one contrast in Act 3 Scene 4.

Prompt!

- Iago's evil is brought into sharp focus by the innocence of Othello and Desdemona.
- Emilia's loyalty to her husband places Desdemona in a precarious position.
- Two cultures collide as the Moor's former world of magic and superstition meets Venetian refinement.
- The main characters all contribute to the play's catastrophic outcome by practising different kinds of deceit.
- Jealousy is contrasted in the distinctive attitudes of Othello and Bianca.

Revision Overview

Desdemona is now caught in a web where everything she does places her in danger. After she questions Emilia about the 'lost' handkerchief, Othello enters and makes confusing comments about her character. She reminds him of his promise to meet with Cassio. Immediately, Othello's mood changes and he demands her handkerchief. When she admits that she does not have it, he rushes off in anger.

Emilia wonders if the Moor is jealous, but Desdemona continues to believe in her husband. Cassio enters with Iago, who suggests he ask Desdemona to plead his case again with Othello. In response, Desdemona advises Cassio to have patience because her husband is acting strangely. She believes that Othello's behaviour is related to concerns about his duties of state. Emilia does not agree. She warns Desdemona that jealousy does not need a reason to exist. As the scene ends, Cassio is confronted by his mistress, Bianca, who complains that he has been neglecting her. He promises to change and asks her to copy the embroidery in a handkerchief that he found in his room. Although she suspects that the handkerchief belongs to another of Cassio's lovers, she calms down when he promises to visit her soon.

- **Themes: Jealousy –** conveyed through dramatic irony where the most jealous fury is expressed over offences that did not actually happen. Othello is jealous about Desdemona, Bianca is jealous about Cassio and Iago is jealous about Emilia.
  Deception – this tense scene is filled with lies and innuendo. Iago manipulates Cassio, Othello, Desdemona and Emilia. Othello deceives his wife, Desdemona lies to Othello, Emilia betrays both Desdemona and Othello through her silence about the handkerchief.

- **Characters: Desdemona –** naive, trusting, unaware, loving, troubled, submissive.
  Emilia – worldly-wise, realistic, cynical, secretive, submissive.
  Othello – confused, angry, superstitious, jealous, boorish, dominant.
  Cassio – impatient, self-obsessed, courteous, dominant.
  Iago – deceptive, manipulative, dominant.
  Bianca – impatient, angry, jealous, submissive.

Key Quotes

my noble Moor Is true of mind and made of no such baseness As jealous creatures are *(Desdemona to Emilia) l.22–4*	Desdemona is unaware of Othello's true character. She loves her husband so much that she cannot imagine he could possibly be jealous. However, the audience is acutely aware that Othello has been consumed by jealousy and now wants to kill her, giving the scene a powerful sense of dramatic irony.
Something, sure, of state … Hath puddled his clear spirit *(Desdemona to Emilia) l.153–6*	Oblivious to the real reason for her husband's strange behaviour, Desdemona thinks it is due to his stress over public matters of Cyprus. Again, this is evidence that the couple do not really know each other very well.
no jealous toy Concerning you *(Emilia to Desdemona) l.169–70*	The handkerchief is the trivial object that has become such an important element in Othello's suspicion of Desdemona. Emilia is the only one who is actually aware that Iago is in possession of the 'lost' handkerchief. She chooses to remain silent out of misguided loyalty – a decision that will have awful consequences.
'tis a monster Begot upon itself, born on itself *(Emilia to Desdemona) l.174–5*	The worldly-wise Emilia attempts to explain the true nature of jealousy to her innocent mistress. She understands the irrational element of distrust when there is no reason to be suspicious. This metaphor echoes Iago's earlier reference to the 'green-eyed monster'. The ugly alliterative 'b' underlines the foul aspect of this character trait.

Scene 1

INTRODUCTION

- Iago continues to control events.
- Othello's jealousy blinds him to reason.
- Desdemona is publicly humiliated.
- Lodovico is shocked by the Moor's behaviour.

Cyprus. Before the castle

Enter Othello and Iago

Iago Will you think so?

Othello Think so, Iago!

Iago What,
To kiss in private?

Othello An unauthorised kiss.

Iago Or to be naked with her friend in bed
An hour or more, not meaning any harm?

Othello Naked in bed, Iago, and not mean harm?
It is hypocrisy against the devil:
They that mean virtuously, and yet do so,
The devil their virtue tempts, and they tempt heaven.

Iago So they do nothing, 'tis a venial slip.
But if I give my wife a handkerchief—

Othello What then?

Iago Why, then, 'tis hers, my lord; and, being hers,
She may, I think, bestow it on any man.

Othello She is protectress of her honour too,
May she give that?

Iago Her honour is an essence that's not seen,
They have it very oft that have it not:
But, for the handkerchief—

Othello By heaven, I would most gladly have forgot it!
Thou said'st – it comes o'er my memory,
As doth the raven o'er the infected house,
Boding to all – he had my handkerchief.

Iago Ay, what of that?

Othello That's not so good now.

Iago What, if I had said I had seen him do you wrong?
Or heard him say – as knaves be such abroad,
Who having, by their own importunate suit,
Or voluntary dotage of some mistress,
Convinced or supplied them, cannot choose
But they must blab—

Othello Hath he said any thing?

Iago He hath, my lord, but be you well assured,
No more than he'll unswear.

Othello What hath he said?

2 Think so: *think what*
5 unauthorised: *inappropriate*
9 hypocrisy against the devil: *tricking the devil*
11 tempt: *provoke*
12 venial slip: *minor misdeed*
17 honour: *chastity*
19 essence: *quality*
24 raven: *bird bringing bad luck*
25 Boding: *threatening*
29 abroad: *in the world*
30 importunate suit: *flirting, courting*
31 dotage: *infatuation*
32 Convinced or supplied: *seduced*
33 blab: *brag*
36 unswear: *deny*

40 Lie: *tell an untruth, sleep with (two meanings)*

44 belie: *slander*
44 fulsome: *obscene, worst of all*

48 invest: *concern*
48 shadowing: *imagined*
49 instruction: *reason*

53 credulous: *gullible*
54 chaste dames: *decent women*
55 reproach: *punishment*

59 epilepsy: *seizure*

62 forbear: *wait*
63 lethargy: *fit*
63 have his quiet course: *run its course*

68 great occasion: *some important matter*

73 A horned man: *a man with an unfaithful wife*

75 civil: *civilised, unsupecting*

Iago 'Faith, that he did – I know not what he did.

Othello What? what?

Iago Lie–

Othello With her?

Iago With her, on her; what you will.

Othello Lie with her! lie on her! We say lie on her, when they belie her. Lie with her! That's fulsome. – Handkerchief – confessions – handkerchief! – To confess, and be hanged for his labour – first, to be hanged, and then to confess – I tremble at it. Nature would not invest herself in such shadowing passion without some instruction. It is not words that shake me thus. Pish! Noses, ears, and lips. – Is it possible? – Confess – handkerchief! – O devil!

Falls in a trance

Iago Work on,
My medicine, work! Thus credulous fools are caught,
And many worthy and chaste dames even thus,
All guiltless, meet reproach. What, ho! my lord!
My lord, I say! Othello!
How now, Cassio!

Cassio What's the matter?

Iago My lord is fallen into an epilepsy,
This is his second fit; he had one yesterday.

Cassio Rub him about the temples.

Iago No, forbear,
The lethargy must have his quiet course:
If not, he foams at mouth and by and by
Breaks out to savage madness. Look, he stirs:
Do you withdraw yourself a little while,
He will recover straight: when he is gone,
I would on great occasion speak with you.

Exit Cassio

How is it, general? Have you not hurt your head?

Othello Dost thou mock me?

Iago I mock you! No, by heaven.
Would you would bear your fortune like a man!

Othello A horned man's a monster and a beast.

Iago There's many a beast then in a populous city,
And many a civil monster.

Othello Did he confess it?

Iago
Good sir, be a man,
Think every bearded fellow that's but yoked
May draw with you: there's millions now alive
That nightly lie in those unproper beds
Which they dare swear peculiar: your case is better.
O, 'tis the spite of hell, the fiend's arch-mock,
To lip a wanton in a secure couch,
And to suppose her chaste! No, let me know,
And knowing what I am, I know what she shall be.

Othello
O, thou art wise, 'tis certain.

Iago
Stand you awhile apart;
Confine yourself but in a patient list.
Whilst you were here o'erwhelmed with your grief –
A passion most unsuiting such a man –
Cassio came hither: I shifted him away,
And laid good 'scuse upon your ecstasy,
Bade him anon return and here speak with me,
The which he promised. Do but encave yourself,
And mark the jeers, the gibes, and notable scorns,
That dwell in every region of his face;
For I will make him tell the tale anew,
Where, how, how oft, how long ago, and when
He hath, and is again to cope your wife:
I say, but mark his gesture. Marry, patience;
Or I shall say you are all in all in spleen,
And nothing of a man.

Othello
Dost thou hear, Iago?
I will be found most cunning in my patience;
But – dost thou hear? – most bloody.

Iago
That's not amiss;
But yet keep time in all. Will you withdraw?

Othello retires

Now will I question Cassio of Bianca,
A housewife that by selling her desires
Buys herself bread and clothes: it is a creature
That dotes on Cassio; as 'tis the strumpet's plague
To beguile many and be beguiled by one:
He, when he hears of her, cannot refrain
From the excess of laughter. Here he comes:

Re-enter Cassio

As he shall smile, Othello shall go mad,
And his unbookish jealousy must construe
Poor Cassio's smiles, gestures and light behaviour,
Quite in the wrong. How do you now, lieutenant?

78 yoked: *married*
79 draw with you: *join you*
80 unproper: *belonging to lovers*
81 peculiar: *their own*
82 arch-mock: *devilish joke*
83 lip: *kiss*
83 wanton: *cheating wife*
83 secure couch: *marriage bed*
88 Confine ... list: *be patient*
91 shifted him away: *fobbed him off*
92 ecstasy: *fit*
94 encave: *hide nearby*
99 cope: *sleep with*
101 spleen: *anger*
104 cunning: *skilful*
109 housewife: *hussy*
111 strumpet's plague: *prostitute's habit*
112 beguile: *attract*
116 unbookish: *uninformed*
116 construe: *interpret*

Cassio The worser that you give me the addition
Whose want even kills me.

Iago Ply Desdemona well, and you are sure on it.
Speaking lower
Now, if this suit lay in Bianca's power,
How quickly should you speed!

Cassio Alas, poor caitiff!

Othello Look, how he laughs already!

Iago I never knew woman love man so.

Cassio Alas, poor rogue! I think, in faith, she loves me.

Othello Now he denies it faintly, and laughs it out.

Iago Do you hear, Cassio?

Othello Now he importunes him
To tell it o'er. Go to, well said, well said.

Iago She gives it out that you shall marry her,
Do you intend it?

Cassio Ha, ha, ha!

Othello Do you triumph, Roman? Do you triumph?

Cassio I marry her! What? A customer!
Prithee, bear some charity to my wit,
Do not think it so unwholesome.
Ha, ha, ha!

Othello So, so, so, so: they laugh that win.

Iago 'Faith, the cry goes that you shall marry her.

Cassio Prithee, say true.

Iago I am a very villain else.

Othello Have you scored me? Well.

Cassio This is the monkey's own giving out: she is persuaded I will marry her, out of her own love and flattery, not out of my promise.

Othello Iago beckons me, now he begins the story.

Cassio She was here even now, she haunts me in every place. I was the other day talking on the sea-bank with certain Venetians; and thither comes the bauble, and, by this hand, she falls me thus about my neck—

Othello Crying 'O dear Cassio!' as it were; his gesture imports it.

119 addition: *title of lieutenant*
120 want: *lack of*
124 caitiff: *wretch*
135 Roman: *like a victorious Roman soldier*
136 customer: *prostitute*
137 bear some charity: *give some credit*
141 cry: *gossip*
144 scored: *wronged*
145 the monkey's own giving: *Bianca's version*
149 haunts: *follows*
151 bauble: *plaything*
152 falls: *caresses*

Cassio So hangs, and lolls, and weeps upon me; so hales, and pulls me. Ha, ha, ha!

Othello Now he tells how she plucked him to my chamber. O, I see that nose of yours, but not that dog I shall throw it to.

Cassio Well, I must leave her company.

Iago Before me! Look, where she comes.

Cassio 'Tis such another fitchew! Marry, a perfumed one.

Enter Bianca

What do you mean by this haunting of me?

Bianca Let the devil and his dam haunt you! What did you mean by that same handkerchief you gave me even now? I was a fine fool to take it. I must take out the work? – A likely piece of work, that you should find it in your chamber, and not know who left it there! This is some minx's token, and I must take out the work? There; give it your hobby-horse: wheresoever you had it, I'll take out no work on it.

Cassio How now, my sweet Bianca! How now! How now!

Othello By heaven, that should be my handkerchief!

Bianca An you'll come to supper to-night, you may; an you will not, come when you are next prepared for.

Exit

Iago After her, after her.

Cassio 'Faith, I must; she'll rail in the street else.

Iago Will you sup there?

Cassio 'Faith, I intend so.

Iago Well, I may chance to see you, for I would very fain speak with you.

Cassio Prithee, come; will you?

Iago Go to; say no more.

Exit Cassio

Othello [***Advancing***] How shall I murder him, Iago?

Iago Did you perceive how he laughed at his vice?

Othello O Iago!

Iago And did you see the handkerchief?

Othello Was that mine?

155 hales: *tugs*

161 Before me: *Goodness*

162 fitchew: *polecat*

164 dam: *mother*

166 take out: *copy*

169 minx's token: *other woman's gift*

170 hobby-horse: *prostitute*

174 An: *if*

177 rail: *shout*

180 very fain: *really would like to*

189 by this hand: *I swear it*
189 prizes: *values, cares about*
192 a-killing: *dying a slow death*
204 plenteous ... invention: *clever and intelligent*
211 fond over: *foolish about*
211 patent: *a chance*
212 offend: *cheat on you*
214 messes: *pieces*
219 expostulate: *discuss this*
220-1 unprovide my mind: *weaken my resolve*
223 contaminated: *dirtied*
225 undertaker: *killer*

Iago Yours by this hand: and to see how he prizes the foolish woman your wife! She gave it him, and he hath given it his whore.

Othello I would have him nine years a-killing.
A fine woman! A fair woman! A sweet woman!

Iago Nay, you must forget that.

Othello Ay, let her rot, and perish, and be damned to-night, for she shall not live: no, my heart is turned to stone; I strike it, and it hurts my hand. O, the world has not a sweeter creature: she might lie by an emperor's side and command him tasks.

Iago Nay, that's not your way.

Othello Hang her! I do but say what she is: so delicate with her needle, an admirable musician. O! She will sing the savageness out of a bear! Of so high and plenteous wit and invention!

Iago She's the worse for all this.

Othello A thousand thousand times: and then, of so gentle a condition!

Iago Ay, too gentle.

Othello Nay, that's certain: but yet the pity of it, Iago!
O Iago, the pity of it, Iago!

Iago If you are so fond over her iniquity, give her patent to offend; for, if it touch not you, it comes near nobody.

Othello I will chop her into messes. Cuckold me!

Iago O, 'tis foul in her.

Othello With mine officer!

Iago That's fouler.

Othello Get me some poison, Iago; this night: I'll not expostulate
with her, lest her body and beauty unprovide
my mind again, this night, Iago.

Iago Do it not with poison, strangle her in her bed, even the bed she hath contaminated.

Othello Good, good. The justice of it pleases; very good.

Iago And for Cassio, let me be his undertaker: you shall hear more by midnight.

Othello Excellent good.

A trumpet within

What trumpet is that same?

Iago Something from Venice, sure. 'Tis Lodovico
Come from the duke: and, see, your wife is with him.

Enter Lodovico, Desdemona, and Attendants

Lodovico Save you, worthy general!

Othello With all my heart, sir.

Lodovico The duke and senators of Venice greet you.

Gives him a letter

Othello I kiss the instrument of their pleasures.

234 pleasures: *wishes, commands*

Opens the letter, and reads

Desdemona And what's the news, good cousin Lodovico?

Iago I am very glad to see you, signior.
Welcome to Cyprus.

Lodovico I thank you. How does Lieutenant Cassio?

Iago Lives, sir.

Desdemona Cousin, there's fallen between him and my lord
An unkind breach, but you shall make all well.

Othello Are you sure of that?

Desdemona My lord?

Othello [*Reads*] 'This fail you not to do, as you will—'

Lodovico He did not call; he's busy in the paper.
Is there division between my lord and Cassio?

245 busy in the paper: *reading the letter*
246 division: *conflict*

Desdemona A most unhappy one: I would do much
To atone them, for the love I bear to Cassio.

248 atone: *reconcile*

Othello Fire and brimstone!

Desdemona My lord?

Othello Are you wise?

251 wise: *sane*

Desdemona What, is he angry?

Lodovico Maybe the letter moved him;
For, as I think, they do command him home,
Deputing Cassio in his government.

Desdemona Trust me, I am glad on it.

Othello Indeed!

Desdemona My lord?

Othello I am glad to see you mad.

259 mad: *moved, annoyed*

Desdemona Why, sweet Othello?

Othello [***Striking her***] Devil!

Desdemona I have not deserved this.

Lodovico My lord, this would not be believed in Venice,
Though I should swear I saw it: 'tis very much:
Make her amends, she weeps.

Othello O devil, devil!
If that the earth could teem with woman's tears,
Each drop she falls would prove a crocodile.
Out of my sight!

Desdemona I will not stay to offend you.

Going

Lodovico Truly, an obedient lady:
I do beseech your lordship, call her back.

Othello Mistress!

Desdemona My lord?

Othello What would you with her, sir?

Lodovico Who, I, my lord?

Othello Ay; you did wish that I would make her turn:
Sir, she can turn, and turn, and yet go on,
And turn again, and she can weep, sir, weep;
And she's obedient, as you say, obedient,
Very obedient. Proceed you in your tears.
Concerning this, sir – O well-painted passion!–
I am commanded home. Get you away!
I'll send for you anon. Sir, I obey the mandate,
And will return to Venice. Hence, avaunt!

Exit Desdemona

Cassio shall have my place. And, sir, tonight,
I do entreat that we may sup together:
You are welcome, sir, to Cyprus. – Goats and monkeys!

Exit

Lodovico Is this the noble Moor whom our full senate
Call all in all sufficient? Is this the nature
Whom passion could not shake? whose solid virtue
The shot of accident, nor dart of chance,
Could neither graze nor pierce?

Iago He is much changed.

Lodovico Are his wits safe? Is he not light of brain?

Iago He's that he is; I may not breathe my censure
What he might be. If what he might he is not,
I would to heaven he were!

264 much: *serious*

268 prove a crocodile: *be hypocritical*

273 Mistress: *derogatory term*

275 would you: *do you want*

277 turn: *turn around, be false*

282 well-painted: *false*

284 mandate: *order*

285 avaunt: *get out of my sight*

288 Goats and monkeys: *supposedly lecherous animals*

290 all in all sufficient: *fully competent and capable*

293 graze nor pierce: *hurt, affect*

295 safe: *stable, sane*

296 censure: *judgement*

Lodovico What, strike his wife!

Iago 'Faith, that was not so well; yet would I knew
That stroke would prove the worst!

Lodovico Is it his use?
Or did the letters work upon his blood,
And new-create this fault?

Iago Alas, alas!
It is not honesty in me to speak
What I have seen and known. You shall observe him,
And his own courses will denote him so
That I may save my speech: do but go after,
And mark how he continues.

Lodovico I am sorry that I am deceived in him.

Exeunt

302 use: *usual custom*
303 blood: *passions*
308 courses will denote: *actions will show*
310 mark: *watch closely*

Commentary

Psychological manipulation (lines 1–57)

Iago uses his conversation with Othello to fill the Moor's mind with suggestive descriptions of Desdemona's secret affair with Cassio. As the ensign pretends to make excuses for Desdemona, her helpless husband forlornly repeats Iago's words, 'Naked in bed'. Iago plays with Othello's jealous fixation and refers once more to the contentious 'handkerchief'. This has become a symbol to the Moor of his wife's fidelity and honour. Iago adopts his much practised pose of the one who does not want to tell what has been going on, but goads Othello to extract it from him, detail by painful detail. The excruciating torture reduces Othello to an illogical and incoherent wreck who mutters to himself, 'Nose, ears, and lips'. The mental strain causes him to collapse at his tormentor's feet. An exultant Iago towers in triumph over the once great general, sadistically gloating, 'Work on,/ My medicine, work!'

Glittering evil (lines 58–162)

Cassio quickly adopts an attitude of genuine concern for the stricken Othello, suggesting, 'Rub him about the temples'. Iago advises the unsuspecting lieutenant to stay away for the present. When Othello regains

It is not words that shake me thus
Othello
Act 4 Scene 1, l.49–50

consciousness, Iago forces him to confront the full implications of the alleged affair with the vivid image 'To lip a wanton in a secure couch'. The Moor is no longer capable of seeing with his own eyes, looking instead at events through the filter of Iago's insinuations. The ensign then arranges that Othello can observe an orchestrated conversation in which Cassio will appear to boast about his relationship with Desdemona.

Othello readily agrees to Iago's plan, unaware that he will be deceived and Cassio will speak about Bianca. Iago creates an image of the sexually triumphant Cassio before Othello, 'mark the jeers'. Once again Iago expresses his contempt for the gullible Moor, dismissing him as 'unbookish'. The 'eavesdropping scene' consists of Iago confiding to Cassio about a rumour being spread that he is to marry Bianca. As Cassio laughs at the idea ('she haunts me in every place'), Othello immediately descends into frantic jealousy.

Roles reversed (lines 163–230)

Bianca confronts Cassio with the strawberry-spotted handkerchief, believing that it is a gift from his latest lover, 'some minx's token'. Iago encourages Cassio to go after her. Meanwhile, Othello is still not fully convinced of Desdemona's guilt. He and Iago have now exchanged roles. Completely dependent on the ensign, he is increasingly pitiful, asking him for advice about dealing with Cassio, 'How shall I murder him, Iago?' The tragic scene reaches a heart-breaking moment when Othello alternates between loving thoughts for his wife, 'A sweet woman', and outright hatred, 'she shall not live'. His acceptance of Iago's warped view of Desdemona is highly ironic, 'the pity of it, Iago!' Almost immediately, however, it is replaced by the violent language of the battlefield, 'I will chop her into messes'. Iago soon persuades him to strangle Desdemona in 'the bed she hath contaminated'.

Public humiliation (lines 231–285)

A reminder of the civilised world of Venice occurs with the arrival of Desdemona's cousin, Lodovico. Desdemona recounts how Othello and Cassio have fallen out despite her best efforts to 'atone them'. Othello misunderstands her concern and becomes angry. Desdemona's delight at the prospect of returning to Venice is cut short by Othello calling her 'Devil!' and physically striking her. Lodovico is understandably outraged, 'this would not be believed in Venice' and calls on Othello to 'Make her amends'. A submissive Desdemona offers to leave so that she won't 'offend' her husband. At Lodovico's insistence, Othello calls her back, only to insult her again, 'Proceed you in your tears'.

I have not deserved this
Desdemona
Act 4 Scene 1, l.262

Volatile behaviour (lines 286–311)

For a brief moment, Othello turns his attention to business and agrees to obey the Senate's command, 'Cassio shall have my place'. But Iago's coarse language is echoed in the Moor's speech, 'Goats and monkeys!' Lodovico is appalled by the transformation in Othello's character. Iago continues to play his well-rehearsed role of the reluctant truth-teller, 'It is not honesty in me to speak/ What I have seen and known'. He knows that Othello has been ordered back to Venice and that the murders will have to be done immediately.

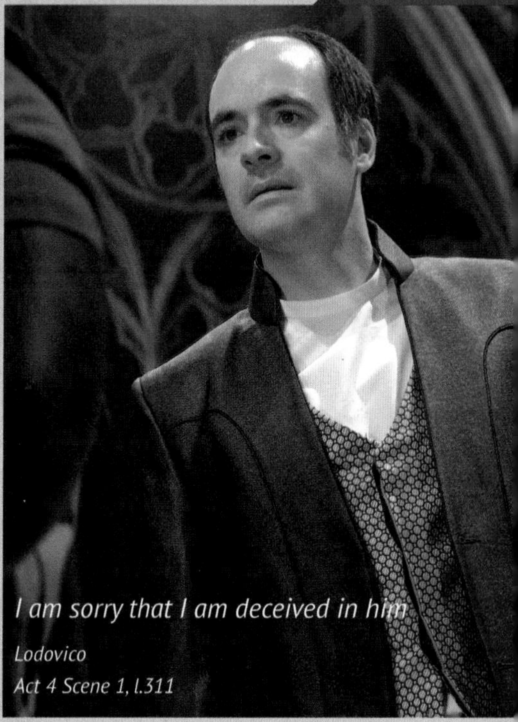

I am sorry that I am deceived in him

Lodovico

Act 4 Scene 1, l.311

Dramatic Significance

In this tense scene, Shakespeare unnerves the audience through the use of **effective contrasts**. Othello suffers severe mental distress while Iago remains detached. When Lodovico arrives, it becomes evident that the edgy world of uncontrolled passion in Cyprus is weighed against the cool, civilised standards of Venetian life. The audience hopes that normality will be restored, particularly when Lodovico urges Othello to apologise to his humiliated wife. But Othello is 'much changed', the obsessive outsider enraged by thoughts of Desdemona's infidelity. Contrast is also used to convey his unstable state of mind, which alternates between praise for his wife as one 'might lie by an emperor's side' and jealous frenzy, 'I will chop her into messes'.

Iago reigns as the puppet-master, never once leaving the stage and effortlessly combining the roles of tormentor, concerned friend and loyal aide. He **orchestrates every event to his advantage**. Iago uses Bianca's appearance with the handkerchief to intensify Othello's jealousy. Now that his power is at its peak, he chooses his words purposefully to further inflame the gullible general, 'To kiss in private?' Othello's epileptic fit robs him of the ability to speak and reduces him to the level of a gibbering animal while Iago delights in the Moor's degradation. Inventive as always, the vindictive ensign stages the misleading conversation with Cassio, carefully placing Othello to observe from a distance. Playing on Othello's perception of himself as a wronged victim, Iago succeeds in reducing the 'noble Moor' to a 'monster and a beast'.

Class/Homework Exercise

'Shakespeare's play *Othello* includes moments of riveting drama that provide thought-provoking insights into the human condition.'

Choose a moment which you consider dramatically riveting from Act 4 Scene 1 and describe a thought-provoking insight it provided. Write a paragraph (about 150–200 words), supporting your answer with reference to the text.

Prompt!

- Act 4 Scene 1 contains compelling insights into the different experiences of human suffering, mind control, mental anguish and public humiliation.
- Dramatic presentation of power and powerlessness through the deliberate dehumanising of Othello by Iago, who has a real understanding of Othello's weaknesses; outsider, race, age, lack of formal education.
- Shakespeare explores the fragile balance between sanity and madness through the Moor's struggle to judge reality.

Revision Overview

Iago provokes the Moor into a frenzied state of jealousy. Othello is caught between believing Iago's version of Desdemona's relationship with Cassio and his own knowledge of his wife's character. It does not take long for Iago to exploit Othello's insecurities and reduce him to a quivering wreck, writhing on the ground in a helpless state.

When Othello regains consciousness, he demands conclusive evidence of his wife's alleged affair. In response, Iago devises a plot to provide proof by placing Othello as an eavesdropper on a conversation between himself and Cassio. Othello then watches the lieutenant smiling and laughing as he discusses Bianca. He misjudges the conversation and loses control, convinced that it is about Desdemona.

Bianca herself enters and immediately argues with Cassio. Seeing his wife's handkerchief in the hands of Cassio's mistress is, for Othello, the 'ocular proof' he wanted. He is now convinced of his wife's infidelity and swears to kill both Cassio and Desdemona that very night.

Lodovico arrives with orders to recall Othello to Venice and make Cassio governor of Cyprus. Desdemona is glad to hear of Cassio's good fortune, but Othello misinterprets her reaction. He becomes violently angry and strikes her. Lodovico is shocked by Othello's transformation and seeks an explanation from Iago, who pretends to be concerned as well.

- **Themes: Power and powerlessness –** Iago controls the action, leaving his enemies defenceless. Power is obtained by exploiting the weaknesses of others.
  Appearance and reality – when someone gives up independent critical thought and relies on another's interpretation of events, perception of reality becomes blurred.
- **Characters: Iago –** diabolical manipulator, gloats at his own evil, destructive force.
  Othello – transformed, irrational, violent, degraded, vengeful.
  Desdemona – quiet, submissive, concerned.
  Cassio – self-obsessed, misogynistic, callous.
  Lodovico – stunned, symbol of civilised Venice.

I will chop her into messes. Cuckold me!

Othello
Act 4 Scene 1, l.214

Key Quotes

It is not words that shake me thus *(Othello to Iago) l.49–50*	This ironic statement clearly shows Othello's lack of self-knowledge. It is precisely Iago's clever manipulation of language that has ruined Othello's peace of mind by diminishing his trust in Desdemona.
Work on, *My medicine, work!* *(Iago to Othello) l.52–3*	As he towers above the stricken Othello, the vengeful ensign takes great pleasure from the hurt he is inflicting. In this powerfully dramatic moment, he continues to corrupt language by using the metaphor of medicine which is used for healing. Iago's 'medicine' infects like poison.
but yet the pity of it, Iago! *(Othello to Iago) l.209*	One of the play's most ironic moments. The gullible Moor is torn between thoughts of his wife's sweetness and the apparent 'evidence' of her guilt provided by Iago. Yet he still finds it hard to think ill of Desdemona. This is the exquisite torture that Iago has fashioned for him.
The justice of it pleases; very good *(Othello to Iago) l.224*	Iago suggests the 'just' punishment of strangling Desdemona in the bed where she committed the sin of adultery. He is pandering to Othello's self-righteous perception of himself as judge and executioner. At every opportunity, Iago exploits the Moor's lack of self-knowledge.
I am sorry that I am deceived in him *(Lodovico to Iago) l.311*	Much of the play centres on deception and the upheaval it can cause. Desdemona's cultured cousin is outraged at Othello's barbaric treatment of his wife. Lodovico cannot believe the transformation of the once-noble general in whom the Senate placed so much trust.

Act 4
Scene 2

INTRODUCTION

- Othello struggles with the thought of losing his wife's love.
- Emilia suspects that someone has been poisoning the Moor's mind.
- Iago reaches the height of his powers.
- Roderigo becomes more involved in the revenge plot.

A room in the castle

Enter Othello and Emilia

Othello You have seen nothing then?

Emilia Nor ever heard, nor ever did suspect.

Othello Yes, you have seen Cassio and she together.

Emilia But then I saw no harm, and then I heard
Each syllable that breath made up between them.

Othello What, did they never whisper?

Emilia Never, my lord.

Othello Nor send you out of the way?

Emilia Never.

Othello To fetch her fan, her gloves, her mask, nor nothing?

Emilia Never, my lord.

Othello That's strange.

Emilia I durst, my lord, to wager she is honest,
Lay down my soul at stake: if you think other,
Remove your thought; it doth abuse your bosom.
If any wretch have put this in your head,
Let heaven requite it with the serpent's curse!
For, if she be not honest, chaste, and true,
There's no man happy. The purest of their wives
Is foul as slander.

Othello Bid her come hither: go.

Exit Emilia

She says enough, yet she's a simple bawd
That cannot say as much. This is a subtle whore,
A closet lock and key of villainous secrets
And yet she'll kneel and pray; I have seen her do it.

Enter Desdemona with Emilia

Desdemona My lord, what is your will?

Othello Pray, chuck, come hither.

Desdemona What is your pleasure?

Othello Let me see your eyes;
Look in my face.

Desdemona What horrible fancy's this?

Othello [*To Emilia*] Some of your function, mistress;
Leave procreants alone and shut the door;
Cough, or cry 'hem,' if any body come:
Your mystery, your mystery: nay, dispatch.

5 that ... up: *was spoken*
13 durst: *dare*
15 abuse your bosom: *hurt you*
17 Let ... curse: *God curse him*
22 bawd: *fool*
23 subtle: *sneaky*
27 chuck: *dear*
32 function: *cheating*
33 procreants: *lovers like us*
35 your mystery: *do your job*
35 dispatch: *get going*

36 import: *mean*

42 one of heaven: *an angel*

51 haply: *perhaps*

52 An instrument of: *involved in*

54 lost: *fallen out with*

65 garnered ... heart: *stored my feelings*

69 cistern: *basin*

70 gender: *breed*

70 complexion: *face*

71 cherubin: *angel*

74 shambles: *slaughterhouse*

75 quicken: *reproduce*

Exit Emilia

Desdemona Upon my knees, what doth your speech import?
I understand a fury in your words.
But not the words.

Othello Why, what art thou?

Desdemona Your wife, my lord; your true and loyal wife.

Othello Come, swear it, damn thyself
Lest, being like one of heaven, the devils themselves
Should fear to seize thee: therefore be double damned:
Swear thou art honest.

Desdemona Heaven doth truly know it.

Othello Heaven truly knows that thou art false as hell.

Desdemona To whom, my lord? With whom? How am I false?

Othello O Desdemona! Away! Away! Away!

Desdemona Alas the heavy day! Why do you weep?
Am I the motive of these tears, my lord?
If haply you my father do suspect
An instrument of this your calling back,
Lay not your blame on me. If you have lost him,
Why, I have lost him too.

Othello Had it pleased heaven
To try me with affliction; had they rained
All kinds of sores and shames on my bare head.
Steeped me in poverty to the very lips,
Given to captivity me and my utmost hopes,
I should have found in some place of my soul
A drop of patience: but, alas, to make me
A fixed figure for the time of scorn
To point his slow unmoving finger at!
Yet could I bear that too; well, very well:
But there, where I have garnered up my heart,
Where either I must live, or bear no life;
The fountain from the which my current runs,
Or else dries up, to be discarded thence,
Or keep it as a cistern for foul toads
To knot and gender in! Turn thy complexion there,
Patience, thou young and rose-lipped cherubin –
Ay, there, look grim as hell!

Desdemona I hope my noble lord esteems me honest.

Othello O, ay, as summer flies are in the shambles,
That quicken even with blowing.
O thou weed,

Who art so lovely fair and smellest so sweet
That the sense aches at thee, would thou hadst never been born!

Desdemona Alas, what ignorant sin have I committed?

Othello Was this fair paper, this most goodly book,
Made to write 'whore' upon? What committed!
Committed! O thou public commoner!
I should make very forges of my cheeks,
That would to cinders burn up modesty,
Did I but speak thy deeds. What committed!
Heaven stops the nose at it and the moon winks,
The bawdy wind that kisses all it meets
Is hushed within the hollow mine of earth,
And will not hear it. What committed?
Impudent strumpet!

Desdemona By heaven, you do me wrong.

Othello Are you not a strumpet?

Desdemona No, as I am a Christian:
If to preserve this vessel for my lord
From any other foul unlawful touch
Be not to be a strumpet, I am none.

Othello What, not a whore?

Desdemona No, as I shall be saved.

Othello Is't possible?

Desdemona O, heaven forgive us!

Othello I cry you mercy, then:
I took you for that cunning whore of Venice
That married with Othello. You, mistress

Raising his voice

That have the office opposite to Saint Peter,
And keep the gate of hell!

Re-enter Emilia

You, you, ay, you!
We have done our course; there's money for your pains:
I pray you, turn the key and keep our counsel.

Exit

Emilia Alas, what does this gentleman conceive?
How do you, madam? How do you, my good lady?

Desdemona 'Faith, half asleep.

Emilia Good madam, what's the matter with my lord?

Desdemona With who?

79 ignorant: *unintentional*
80 fair paper: *Desdemona*
82 commoner: *prostitute*
83 make ... cheeks: *blush*
86 stops ... at: *smells*
87 bawdy: *promiscuous*
88 mine: *depths*
90 strumpet: *prostitute*
94 this vessel: *my body*
104 Saint Peter: *heaven's guard*
108 counsel: *secret*
109 conceive: *imagine*

Emilia Why, with my lord, madam.

Desdemona Who is thy lord?

Emilia He that is yours, sweet lady.

Desdemona I have none: do not talk to me, Emilia;
I cannot weep; nor answer have I none,
But what should go by water. Prithee, tonight
Lay on my bed my wedding sheets: remember;
And call thy husband hither.

Emilia Here's a change indeed!

Exit

Desdemona 'Tis meet I should be used so, very meet.
How have I been behaved, that he might stick
The smallest opinion on my least misuse?

Re-enter Emilia with Iago

Iago What is your pleasure, madam?
How is it with you?

Desdemona I cannot tell. Those that do teach young babes
Do it with gentle means and easy tasks:
He might have chid me so; for, in good faith,
I am a child to chiding.

Iago What's the matter, lady?

Emilia Alas, Iago, my lord hath so bewhored her.
Thrown such despite and heavy terms upon her,
As true hearts cannot bear.

Desdemona Am I that name, Iago?

Iago What name, fair lady?

Desdemona Such as she says my lord did say I was.

Emilia He called her whore: a beggar in his drink
Could not have laid such terms upon his callat.

Iago Why did he so?

Desdemona I do not know; I am sure I am none such.

Iago Do not weep, do not weep. Alas the day!

Emilia Hath she forsook so many noble matches,
Her father and her country and her friends,
To be called whore? Would it not make one weep?

Desdemona It is my wretched fortune.

Iago Beshrew him for it!
How comes this trick upon him?

Desdemona Nay, heaven doth know.

119 should … water: *be expressed by tears*

123 meet: *appropriate*

125 misuse: *fault*

130 chid: *scolded*

131 child to: *not used to*

133 bewhored: *insulted*

134 despite: *abuse*

140 callat: *slut*

Emilia I will be hanged, if some eternal villain,
Some busy and insinuating rogue,
Some cogging, cozening slave, to get some office,
Have not devised this slander; I'll be hanged else.

Iago Fie, there is no such man; it is impossible.

Desdemona If any such there be, heaven pardon him!

Emilia A halter pardon him! And hell gnaw his bones!
Why should he call her whore? Who keeps her company?
What place? What time? What form? What likelihood?
The Moor's abused by some most villainous knave,
Some base notorious knave, some scurvy fellow.
O heaven, that such companions thou'dst unfold,
And put in every honest hand a whip
To lash the rascals naked through the world
Even from the east to the west!

Iago Speak within doors.

Emilia O, fie upon them! Some such squire he was
That turned your wit the seamy side without,
And made you to suspect me with the Moor.

Iago You are a fool; go to.

Desdemona O good Iago,
What shall I do to win my lord again?
Good friend, go to him; for, by this light of heaven,
I know not how I lost him. Here I kneel:
If ever my will did trespass against his love,
Either in discourse of thought or actual deed,
Or that mine eyes, mine ears, or any sense,
Delighted them in any other form;
Or that I do not yet, and ever did.
And ever will – though he do shake me off
To beggarly divorcement – love him dearly,
Comfort forswear me! Unkindness may do much;
And his unkindness may defeat my life,
But never taint my love. I cannot say 'whore:'
It does abhor me now I speak the word;
To do the act that might the addition earn
Not the world's mass of vanity could make me.

Iago I pray you, be content, 'tis but his humour,
The business of the state does him offence,
And he does chide with you.

Desdemona If 'twere no other–

Iago 'Tis but so, I warrant.

152 insinuating: *two-faced*
153 cogging, cozening: *cheating, deceiving*
157 halter: *hangman's noose*
159 form: *opportunity*
162 companions: *villains*
166 within doors: *quietly*
168 turned ... side: *that confused*
170 go to: *be quiet*
176 discourse of thought: *thinking*
178 them: *themselves*
181 divorcement: *rejection*
182 Comfort ... me: *may I lose all happiness*
183 defeat: *destroy*
185 abhor: *horrify*
186 addition: *title*
188 humour: *mood*
189 does ... offence: *worries him*
190 he ... with: *takes out his anger on*
192 warrant: *promise*

194 stay the meat: *await dinner*
197 justly: *fairly*
199 daffest me: *fob me off*
201 conveniency: *opportunity*
207 no kin together: *don't match*
210 means: *money*
212 votarist: *nun*
214 respect: *affection*
217 scurvy: *horrible*
218 fopped: *fooled*
222 repent ... solicitation: *give up courting her*
223 satisfaction: *repayment*
225 intendment: *intention*
227 mettle: *spirit*

Trumpets within

Hark, how these instruments summon to supper!
The messengers of Venice stay the meat;
Go in, and weep not; all things shall be well.

Exeunt Desdemona and Emilia

Enter Roderigo

How now, Roderigo!

Roderigo I do not find that thou dealest justly with me.

Iago What in the contrary?

Roderigo Every day thou daffest me with some device, Iago; and rather, as it seems to me now, keepest from me all conveniency than suppliest me with the least advantage of hope. I will indeed no longer endure it, nor am I yet persuaded to put up in peace what already I have foolishly suffered.

Iago Will you hear me, Roderigo?

Roderigo Faith, I have heard too much, for your words and performances are no kin together.

Iago You charge me most unjustly.

Roderigo With nought but truth. I have wasted myself out of my means. The jewels you have had from me to deliver to Desdemona would half have corrupted a votarist: you have told me she hath received them and returned me expectations and comforts of sudden respect and acquaintance, but I find none.

Iago Well; go to; very well.

Roderigo Very well! Go to! I cannot go to, man; nor 'tis not very well: nay, I think it is scurvy, and begin to find myself fopped in it.

Iago Very well.

Roderigo I tell you 'tis not very well. I will make myself known to Desdemona: if she will return me my jewels, I will give over my suit and repent my unlawful solicitation; if not, assure yourself I will seek satisfaction of you.

Iago You have said now.

Roderigo Ay, and said nothing but what I protest intendment of doing.

Iago Why, now I see there's mettle in thee, and even from this instant to build on thee a better opinion than ever before. Give me thy hand, thou hast taken against me a most just exception; but yet, I protest, I have dealt most directly in thy affair.

Roderigo It hath not appeared.

Iago I grant indeed it hath not appeared, and your suspicion is not without wit and judgment. But, Roderigo, if thou hast that in thee indeed, which I have further reason to believe now than ever, I mean purpose, courage and valour, this night show it: if thou the next night following enjoy not Desdemona, take me from this world with treachery and devise engines for my life.

Roderigo Well, what is it? Is it within reason and compass?

Iago Sir, there is especial commission come from Venice to depute Cassio in Othello's place.

Roderigo Is that true? Why, then Othello and Desdemona return again to Venice.

Iago O, no, he goes into Mauritania and takes away with him the fair Desdemona, unless his abode be lingered here by some accident: wherein none can be so determinate as the removing of Cassio.

Roderigo How do you mean, removing of him?

Iago Why, by making him uncapable of Othello's place; knocking out his brains.

Roderigo And that you would have me to do?

Iago Ay, if you dare do yourself a profit and a right. He sups to-night with a harlot, and thither will I go to him: he knows not yet of his honourable fortune. If you will watch his going thence, which I will fashion to fall out between twelve and one, you may take him at your pleasure: I will be near to second your attempt, and he shall fall between us. Come, stand not amazed at it, but go along with me; I will show you such a necessity in his death that you shall think yourself bound to put it on him. It is now high suppertime, and the night grows to waste: about it.

Roderigo I will hear further reason for this.

Iago And you shall be satisfied.

Exeunt

230 exception: *complaint*
231 directly: *honestly*
234 wit: *good sense*
240 engines: *plots*
241 compass: *possibility*
246 Mauritania: *North African region*
247 abode be lingered: *stay is prolonged*
249 determinate: *desired*
255 harlot: *prostitute*
258 fashion ... out: *arrange that he is walking*
259 second: *support*
262 necessity in: *need for*
263 put it on: *kill*
263 high: *nearly*

Commentary

Questions (lines 1–25)

Othello interrogates Emilia about Desdemona's private life and is particularly keen to know if his wife has ever been alone with Cassio, 'Nor send you out of the way?' Emilia can say nothing against Desdemona. Instead, she lays 'down her soul' for her mistress's innocence. Othello instantly dismisses Emilia's testimony with a derisive comment, 'she's a simple bawd'. Echoing Iago's misogyny (hatred of women), he describes Desdemona as 'a subtle whore'. The Moor is unwilling to give up his belief that she is unfaithful. His thinking has been poisoned by Iago's manipulative influence.

Contempt (lines 26–108)

Desdemona recognises that her husband is angry, but she is at a loss to know why. Othello's questions alternate between tender terms of endearment, 'chuck', and treating her as a prostitute, 'Leave procreants alone'. He continues to mimic Iago in his violent language ('damn thyself'). Desdemona suggests that his sudden rage might be a response to the letter he received calling him back to Venice. She wonders if perhaps Othello thinks that Brabantio was behind the summons to leave Cyprus. Loyally, she swears allegiance to her husband rather than to her father, 'If you have lost him,/ Why, I have lost him too'.

Heaven truly knows that thou art false as hell

Othello
Act 4 Scene 2, l.46

Othello, however, remains fully engrossed in his own trauma. Although his suffering is deluded and self-inflicted, his agony is real enough. The Moor's love for Desdemona is the source of his life, 'where I have garnered up my heart'. Unfortunately, this has been diminished both by Iago's malicious insinuations and his own uncontrollable jealousy. He compares his wife to a wayward wind that 'kisses all it meets'. But Othello's imagination is overrun by the recurring image of her alleged affair – something that he keeps associating with prostitution. As he rushes away, he flings coarse insults at his wife, 'cunning whore of Venice' and coins at Emilia, 'there's money for your pains'.

Disbelief and resignation (lines 109–170)

Desdemona is dazed by Othello's vicious outburst. She is also worn out, 'I cannot weep', and requests that her wedding sheets be laid on her bed in a pitiful hope that she might reawaken the couple's love. Emilia is also astonished by what has been happening, 'Here's a change indeed!' Desdemona wonders what she could possibly have done to merit such abuse and recalls that she has never been treated so harshly, 'I am a child to chiding'.

Emilia is more cynical and suspects that an unknown villain ('Some busy and insinuating rogue') has used jealousy to turn Othello against his wife. Yet she still fails to connect this with her husband, despite his previous demand for the handkerchief. Iago attempts to keep her quiet, 'Speak within doors', but Emilia will not be so easily silenced.

False explanations
(lines 171–195)

Desdemona begs assistance from the very man who is intent on destroying her, 'What shall I do to win my lord again?' She is barely able to utter the word 'whore', let alone act like one. Iago's explanation for Othello's aggressive behaviour is a blatant lie, 'The business of the state does him offence'. As usual, Iago offers her false comfort, 'all things shall be well'.

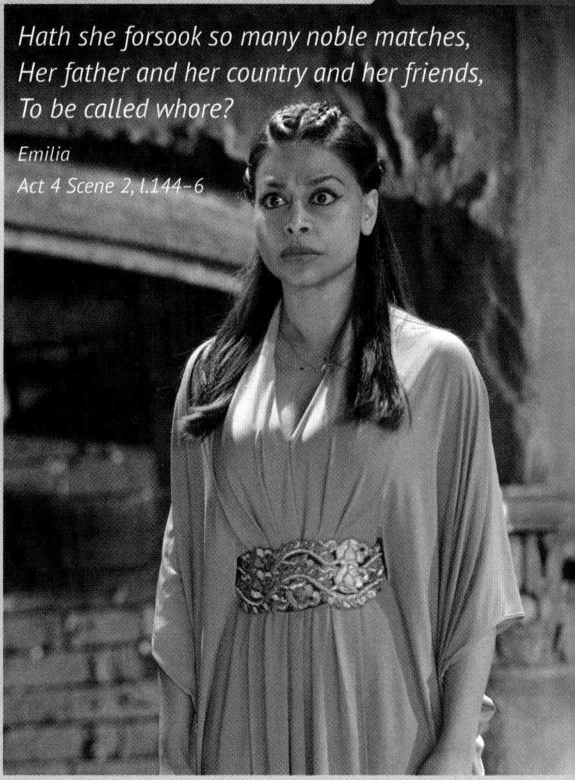

Hath she forsook so many noble matches,
Her father and her country and her friends,
To be called whore?

Emilia
Act 4 Scene 2, l.144–6

Turning the tables (lines 196–266)

In a rare moment of petulance, Roderigo confronts Iago because his attempts to win Desdemona's love have come to nothing, 'I have wasted myself out of my means'. Roderigo threatens to reveal the truth and even challenges the ensign to a duel. Ingeniously, Iago does not rise to the bait, but calms the young man's anger by flattery, complimenting him on his courage. Iago also holds out the promise that Desdemona is still within easy reach.

Mixing truth and lies, the ensign convinces Roderigo to kill the lieutenant that very night. He manipulates the easily duped nobleman with a mixture of indirectness ('the removing of Cassio') and harsh reality ('knocking out his brains'). Roderigo reacts with typical moral blindness, 'I will hear further reason for this'.

Dramatic Significance

Shakespeare uses **dramatic irony** in this scene to engage audiences while making them feel uneasy. Emilia unknowingly curses Iago for inciting Othello's jealousy. She also swears Desdemona's innocence, 'Let heaven requite it with the serpent's curse!' She knows precisely what has happened and informs her husband, the cause of all the turmoil, of her suspicion that 'some eternal villain ... Have not devised this slander'. Yet she is the only one – apart from Iago – who is aware of how the handkerchief got lost. If she had revealed this, the tragedy could be avoided. But the difference between Iago's private and public personas is known only to the audience. Both Emilia and Desdemona seek help from the person who is intent on causing ruin.

Throughout the scene, **imagery is used effectively** to highlight the devastating conflict between good and evil. The degradation of the once-noble general is seen in his obsessive references to brothels and prostitution. Othello calls Emilia a 'bawd' and Desdemona 'that cunning whore of Venice'. He resorts to bestial language to describe the vileness of her intimate relationship with Cassio, 'a cistern for foul toads'. It's clear that Othello's mind has been truly poisoned. Religious images further inflame the torrid atmosphere. Repeated mention of the 'devil', 'hell' and damnation intensify the deathly mood. The audience is left appalled by the transformation of Othello and Desdemona's loving relationship.

I pray you, be content, 'tis but his humour

Iago
Act 4 Scene 2, l.188

Class/Homework Exercise

'Iago plays a more significant role than Othello or Desdemona in the play *Othello*.'

Discuss the above statement with particular reference to Act 4 Scene 2. In your response, you should consider the roles played by the three main characters, Iago, Othello and Desdemona. Write a paragraph (about 150–200 words), supporting your answer with reference to the text.

Prompt!

Iago plays a more significant role than Othello or Desdemona:

- Dominates action and propels the plot.
- Catalyst for a series of disastrous events.
- Othello becomes totally controlled by Iago.
- Personifies evil throughout.
- Desdemona and Roderigo seek Iago's advice.

Iago does not play a more significant role than Othello or Desdemona:

- Iago operates in the background.
- Othello's powerful jealousy and tortured anguish advance the plot.
- Desdemona's submissive behaviour is compelling.
- The couple's broken relationship is central to the tragedy.

Revision Overview

Othello quizzes Emilia, trying to get her to confess that Desdemona and Cassio are having a secret affair. She tells the jealous Moor that Desdemona has done nothing suspicious. She also blames the 'wretch' who is spreading such rumours. Othello dismisses Emilia's testimony and has convinced himself that Desdemona is deceitful.

In a raging mood, he accuses his wife of cheating on him, but Desdemona denies it. She suggests that his anger might be the result of the letter he received recalling him to Venice. But Othello is filled with obsessive jealousy and even Emilia is worried by his erratic behaviour.

Desdemona is bewildered and seeks help from Iago, who pretends to be concerned. When Emilia explains her own suspicions, Iago tells her to be quiet and suggests that he does not fully understand why Othello is behaving so strangely.

After the women leave, a furious Roderigo arrives, threatening to expose Iago's villainy. But the ensign calms him and involves him in a plan to kill Cassio.

- **Theme: Appearance and reality –** the only person who is aware of the full truth of the situation is Iago. Everyone else is manipulated by him for his own diabolical purposes.
- **Characters: Othello –** the demanding, hysterical husband is now blinded by jealousy. This is in stark contrast to the honourable general who was so respected in Venice.
  Desdemona – bewildered, submissive wife, a contrast to the independent, spirited woman who defied family and society for love.
  Iago – manipulative, duplicitous instigator of events.
  Emilia – loyal defender of Desdemona; unwittingly pinpoints the source of the evil.

Key Quotes

If any wretch have put this in your head, Let heaven requite it with the serpent's curse! (Emilia to Othello) l.16–17	Emilia loyally defends her mistress's innocence. Biblical imagery strengthens her curse on the person who has poisoned Othello's mind against Desdemona. Ironically, Emilia is cursing her own husband. God put a curse on the serpent for deceiving Eve in the Garden of Eden.
This is a subtle whore (Othello aside) l.23	Othello disregards his own knowledge of his wife and is consumed by the false image Iago has planted in his mind. The sibilant 's' sounds suggest his gross perception of Desdemona.
as summer flies are in the shambles, That quicken even with blowing (Othello to Desdemona) l.74–5	A bitterly sarcastic aside from Othello shows the depth to which his mind has been polluted by Iago's devilish insinuations. A slaughterhouse in summer swarms with flies, which come to life as soon as the flies' eggs are laid. Othello believes Desdemona is dishonest – selfishly satisfyng her own needs like flies devouring rotting meat.
Hath she forsook so many noble matches, Her father and her country and her friends, To be called whore? (Emilia to Iago) l.144–6	Emilia lists her mistress's many sacrifices for love of Othello and is angry that Desdemona is now being abused by him in a way that is not acceptable anywhere. Ironically, Emilia is telling all this to Iago, the mastermind responsible for all the lies and unhappiness.
And his unkindness may defeat my life, But never taint my love (Desdemona to Emilia) l.183–4	Othello's naive wife is stunned by her husband's cruel and unwarranted behaviour towards her. She believes his treatment is so bad that it might possibly kill her, but she will never stop loving him. As on so many occasions that foreshadow the tragedy ahead, Desdemona is completely unaware of the irony of her statement.

Act 4
Scene 3

INTRODUCTION

- Othello continues his mistreatment of his wife.
- Desdemona defends her husband and is filled with morbid thoughts.
- Emilia tries to make her mistress see the ways of the real world.

Another room in the castle

Enter Othello, Lodovico, Desdemona, Emilia, and Attendants

Lodovico I do beseech you, sir, trouble yourself no further.

Othello O, pardon me, it shall do me good to walk.

Lodovico Madam, good night. I humbly thank your ladyship.

Desdemona Your honour is most welcome.

Othello Will you walk, sir?
O – Desdemona–

Desdemona My lord?

Othello Get you to bed on the instant. I will be returned
forthwith: dismiss your attendant there. Look it be done.

Desdemona I will, my lord.

Exeunt Othello, Lodovico, and Attendants

Emilia How goes it now? He looks gentler than he did.

Desdemona He says he will return incontinent:
He hath commanded me to go to bed,
And bade me to dismiss you.

Emilia Dismiss me?

Desdemona It was his bidding: therefore, good Emilia,
Give me my nightly wearing, and adieu:
We must not now displease him.

Emilia I would you had never seen him!

Desdemona So would not I my love doth so approve him,
That even his stubbornness, his checks, his frowns –
Prithee, unpin me – have grace and favour in them.

Emilia I have laid those sheets you bade me on the bed.

Desdemona All's one. Good faith, how foolish are our minds!
If I do die before thee prithee, shroud me
In one of those same sheets.

Emilia Come, come you talk.

Desdemona My mother had a maid called Barbary,
She was in love, and he she loved proved mad
And did forsake her: she had a song of 'willow',
An old thing 'twas, but it expressed her fortune,
And she died singing it: that song to-night
Will not go from my mind; I have much to do,
But to go hang my head all at one side,
And sing it like poor Barbary. Prithee, dispatch.

Emilia Shall I go fetch your night-gown?

8 returned: *coming back*
12 incontinent: *immediately*
20 approve: *admire*
21 checks: *insults*
22 favour: *attractiveness*
24 All's one: *all right*
27 talk: *speak foolishly*
30 willow: *tree symbolising unhappy love*
34 hang ... side: *be sad*
35 Prithee, dispatch: *please hurry*

38 proper: *honourable*

42 nether: *lower*

50 Lay by these: *put these (clothes) away*

52 hie: *hurry*

52 anon: *soon*

59 couch with moe: *sleep with more*

61 bode: *foretell*

64 in conscience: *honestly*

66 gross kind: *crudely*

74 price: *reward*

Desdemona No, unpin me here.
This Lodovico is a proper man.

Emilia A very handsome man.

Desdemona He speaks well.

Emilia I know a lady in Venice would have walked barefoot
to Palestine for a touch of his nether lip.

Desdemona [***Singing***] *The poor soul sat sighing by a sycamore tree,*
Sing all a green willow:
Her hand on her bosom, her head on her knee,
Sing willow, willow, willow:
The fresh streams ran by her, and murmured her moans;
Sing willow, willow, willow.
Her salt tears fell from her, and softened the stones;
Lay by these –
[***Singing***] *Sing willow, willow, willow.*
Prithee, hie thee; he'll come anon –
[***Singing***] *Sing all a green willow must be my garland.*
Let nobody blame him; his scorn I approve –
ay, that's not next – Hark! Who is it that knocks?

Emilia It's the wind.

Desdemona [***Singing***] *I called my love false love; but what said he then?*
Sing willow, willow, willow.
If I court moe women, you'll couch with moe men!
So, get thee gone; good night. Mine eyes do itch,
Doth that bode weeping?

Emilia 'Tis neither here nor there

Desdemona I have heard it said so. O, these men, these men!
Dost thou in conscience think – tell me, Emilia –
That there be women do abuse their husbands
In such gross kind?

Emilia There be some such, no question.

Desdemona Wouldst thou do such a deed for all the world?

Emilia Why, would not you?

Desdemona No, by this heavenly light!

Emilia Nor I neither by this heavenly light,
I might do it as well in the dark.

Desdemona Wouldst thou do such a deed for all the world?

Emilia The world's a huge thing: it is a great price.
For a small vice.

Desdemona In troth, I think thou wouldst not.

Emilia In troth, I think I should; and undo it when I had done. Marry, I would not do such a thing for a joint-ring, nor for measures of lawn, nor for gowns, petticoats, nor caps, nor any petty exhibition; but for the whole world – why, who would not make her husband a cuckold to make him a monarch? I should venture purgatory for it.

Desdemona Beshrew me, if I would do such a wrong
For the whole world.

Emilia Why the wrong is but a wrong in the world: and having the world for your labour, 'tis a wrong in your own world, and you might quickly make it right.

Desdemona I do not think there is any such woman.

Emilia Yes, a dozen; and as many to the vantage as would store the world they played for.
But I do think it is their husbands' faults
If wives do fall: say that they slack their duties,
And pour our treasures into foreign laps,
Or else break out in peevish jealousies,
Throwing restraint upon us; or say they strike us,
Or scant our former having in despite
Why, we have galls, and though we have some grace,
Yet have we some revenge. Let husbands know
Their wives have sense like them: they see, and smell
And have their palates both for sweet and sour,
As husbands have. What is it that they do
When they change us for others? Is it sport?
I think it is: and doth affection breed it?
I think it doth. Is it frailty that thus errs?
It is so too. And have not we affections,
Desires for sport, and frailty, as men have?
Then let them use us well: else let them know,
The ills we do, their ills instruct us so.

Desdemona Good night, good night. Heaven me such uses send,
Not to pick bad from bad, but by bad mend!

Exeunt

79 joint-ring: *ring that can be separated into two halves*
79 measures of lawn: *lengths of fine linen*
80–1 petty exhibition: *little gift*
82–3 make ... monarch: *increase his wealth and power*
83 venture: *risk*
84 Beshrew: *curse*
90 to the vantage: *in addition*
91 store: *populate*
93 slack their duties: *stop sleeping with us*
94 foreign laps: *other lovers*
95 peevish jealousies: *bad tempers*
97 scant ... despite: *cut our allowances in spite*
98 galls: *grudges*
100 sense: *feelings*
101 palates: *appetites*
103 sport: *fun*
109 The ills ... so: *we imitate their bad behaviour*
110 uses: *habits*
111 Not ... mend: *so that I don't imitate a bad example*

Commentary

Sharp contrasts (lines 1–10)

Lodovico's world of Venetian refinement, 'Madam, good night', is in dramatic contrast to the churlish behaviour of Othello who rudely orders his wife, 'Get you to bed'. He also instructs her to dismiss her maidservant, Emilia. An obedient Desdemona readily agrees, 'I will, my lord'.

Omens of doom (lines 11–61)

She had a song of 'willow',
And old thing 'twas, but it expressed her fortune

Desdemona
Act 4 Scene 3, l.30–1

Emilia's attempt to comfort her mistress, 'He looks gentler than he did', is of little consolation to the distracted Desdemona. Emilia is concerned by Othello's erratic behaviour and wishes that Desdemona 'had never seen him'. But Desdemona continues to be completely loyal to her husband, excusing even his 'stubbornness' and 'frowns', which, she says, have 'grace and favour in them'. Ominously, she asks Emilia to 'shroud' her in one of the wedding sheets and recalls how her mother's unhappy maid, Barbary, died singing a tragic song of rejected love. Desdemona has also lost her husband to jealousy and madness. She sings the poignant song of a disappointed lover, becoming so overwrought that she adds words of her own, referencing her husband, 'Let nobody blame him; his scorn I approve'.

The ways of the world (lines 62–111)

The two women discuss their differing attitudes to marriage and fidelity. Desdemona is rather naive and asks Emilia if there are women who would cheat on their husbands. Emilia replies unhesitatingly, 'There be some such, no question'. Unlike her mistress, Emilia is familiar with real life and has a down-to-earth approach to marriage. She regards an act of infidelity as a 'small vice' if it gained 'all the world'. She admits that she might be unfaithful if it would make her husband 'a monarch'. Desdemona is shocked by such an unromantic attitude.

Emilia offers excuses for women who are unfaithful, 'it is their husbands' faults/ If wives do fall'. She believes wives also have desires and that if men are unfaithful, then women will be too, 'The ills we do, their ills instruct us so'. Desdemona bids Emilia goodnight and declares that she would prefer to learn from her bad experiences than to seek revenge on a man who mistreated her, 'Not to pick bad from bad, but by bad mend!'

Dramatic Significance

An **ominous atmosphere** pervades the final scene of Act 4. It begins with Othello's menacing instructions to his wife, telling her to dismiss Emilia from her presence. Desdemona is filled with disquiet. She remembers a tragic 'willow' song that was sung by one of her mother's maids who was unfortunate in love. The drooping willow tree is associated with weeping and loss, but it also bends without breaking. Desdemona's plaintive singing and the subdued candlelit setting add to the sense of dread. The final line of the song, 'you'll couch with moe men' foreshadows Othello's words at the climax of the tragedy, 'she'll betray more men'.

Shakespeare uses **contrast to create suspense** and unease throughout the scene. We are reminded of the sophisticated world of Venice represented by the 'proper man' Lodovico, who 'speaks well', unlike Othello's coarse behaviour. The contrasting attitudes of the down-to-earth Emilia and the naive, romantic Desdemona are highlighted in their discussion about marriage. Through a series of sharp, rhetorical questions, Emilia illustrates society's double standards. While it is acceptable for men to have affairs, women are expected to be faithful. In contrast to the uncertainty of Desdemona and Emilia, the audience is already much more informed about the impending tragedy. The scene ends on a note of almost unbearable tension.

Class/Homework Exercise

'Throughout the play *Othello*, Shakespeare explores key aspects of the balance of power within male–female relationships.'

Discuss the above statement with particular reference to Act 4 Scene 3. Write a paragraph (about 150–200 words), supporting your answer with reference to the text.

Prompt!

- Conservative patriarchal society disempowers women.
- Othello and Iago both dominate women.
- Double standards regarding marriage and fidelity.
- Desdemona is naive, a subservient victim.
- Emilia is realistic and challenges traditional gender roles.

Revision Overview

The formal supper in honour of the Venetian ambassador, Lodovico, is concluded. As a mark of courtesy to the ambassador, Othello invites him for a walk, but continues treating Desdemona rudely. Emilia is critical of Othello but Desdemona defends her husband. Othello's cruel behaviour is having a detrimental effect on her mind. She speaks of death and recalls a song about lost love. As Desdemona prepares for bed, she asks Emilia about unfaithful wives and is genuinely baffled that some women could cheat like this. Emilia is of the opinion that wives' infidelity is a result of the weaknesses and misdeeds of their husbands. However, Desdemona believes that one evil deed should not be repaid by another. She resolves to learn to behave better from bad experiences.

- **Theme: Love and betrayal** – Desdemona and Emilia's conversation about marriage and fidelity is a cynical commentary on the double standard between the sexes.
- **Characters: Othello –** vacillates between courteous treatment of Lodovico and ill-mannered behaviour towards his wife.
  Desdemona – naive, submissive, morose, loyal and romantic.
  Emilia – worldly-wise, practical, spirited, witty.
  Lodovico – well-mannered, symbol of civilised Venice.

Key Quotes

If I do die before thee prithee, shroud me In one of those same sheets *(Desdemona to Emilia) l.25–6*	Desdemona is overwhelmed by dejected thoughts of death due to her husband's cruel treatment. She instructs her maid to dress her in one of her wedding sheets for burial. She has no idea that she is about to be killed, of course, which makes it all the more painful for the audience to watch her submit so meekly to Othello.
Nor I neither by this heavenly light, I might do it as well in the dark *(Emilia to Desdemona) l.71–2*	Emilia's sharp sense of humour is evident in this scene. She admits that she would never cheat on her husband anywhere she could be seen, but she would do so if she could conceal the act. Throughout the play, such images of light and darkness are associated with goodness and sin respectively.
And have not we affections, Desires for sport, and frailty, as men have? *(Emilia to Desdemona) l.106–7*	Emilia is less naive than Desdemona and believes that women have the same sexual needs as men. She points out the obvious double standard of behaviour that is accepted between the sexes in society. All the female characters are subjected to misogynistic abuse over the course of the story.
Heaven me such uses send, Not to pick bad from bad, but by bad mend! *(Emilia to Desdemona) l.110–1*	Desdemona is frequently associated with heavenly goodness. She herself does not want to behave badly because of the immoral actions of others. In contrast to Emilia, she refuses to sink to their low level, hoping instead to learn to be a better person from such a bad example.

Act 5
Scene 1

INTRODUCTION

- Roderigo and Iago lie in wait to kill Cassio.
- Both Cassio and Roderigo are wounded.
- Bianca is falsely blamed for the attack.
- Iago manages to take control of the situation.

1 bulk: *wall*
1 straight: *soon*
2 put it home: *stab him*
4 mars: *ruins*
6 miscarry in it: *fail*
11 young quat: *little pimple*
11 sense: *limit*
14 live Roderigo: *if Roderigo lives*
15 restitution: *repayment*
16 bobbed: *took*
21 unfold: *expose*
23 gait: *way of walking*
25 coat is better: *armour is stronger*

Cyprus: A street

Enter Iago and Roderigo

Iago
Here, stand behind this bulk; straight will he come:
Wear thy good rapier bare, and put it home:
Quick, quick; fear nothing; I'll be at thy elbow:
It makes us, or it mars us; think on that,
And fix most firm thy resolution.

Roderigo
Be near at hand, I may miscarry in it.

Iago
Here, at thy hand. Be bold, and take thy stand.

Retires

Roderigo
I have no great devotion to the deed;
And yet he hath given me satisfying reasons:
'Tis but a man gone. Forth, my sword: he dies.

Iago
I have rubbed this young quat almost to the sense,
And he grows angry. Now, whether he kill Cassio,
Or Cassio him, or each do kill the other,
Every way makes my gain: live Roderigo,
He calls me to a restitution large
Of gold and jewels that I bobbed from him,
As gifts to Desdemona;
It must not be: if Cassio do remain,
He hath a daily beauty in his life
That makes me ugly; and, besides, the Moor
May unfold me to him; there stand I in much peril.
No, he must die. But so, I hear him coming

Enter Cassio

Roderigo
I know his gait, 'tis he. – Villain, thou diest!

Makes a pass at Cassio

Cassio
That thrust had been mine enemy indeed,
But that my coat is better than thou knowest
I will make proof of thine.

Draws, and wounds Roderigo

Roderigo
O, I am slain!

Iago from behind wounds Cassio in the leg, and exit

Cassio
I am maimed for ever. Help, ho! Murder! Murder!

Falls

Enter Othello

Othello
The voice of Cassio; Iago keeps his word.

Roderigo
O, villain that I am!

Othello
It is even so.

Cassio
O, help, ho! Light! A surgeon!

Othello 'Tis he. – O brave Iago, honest and just,
That hast such noble sense of thy friend's wrong!
Thou teachest me. Minion, your dear lies dead,
And your unblest fate hies: strumpet, I come.
Forth of my heart those charms, thine eyes, are blotted.
Thy bed, lust-stained, shall with lust's blood be spotted.

Exit

Enter Lodovico and Gratiano

Cassio What, ho! No watch? No passage? Murder! Murder!

Gratiano 'Tis some mischance; the cry is very direful.

Cassio O, help!

Lodovico Hark!

Roderigo O wretched villain!

Lodovico Two or three groan: it is a heavy night:
These may be counterfeits: let's think it unsafe
To come in to the cry without more help.

Roderigo Nobody come? Then shall I bleed to death.

Lodovico Hark!

Re-enter Iago, with a light

Gratiano Here's one comes in his shirt, with light and weapons.

Iago Who's there? Whose noise is this that cries on murder?

Lodovico We do not know.

Iago Did not you hear a cry?

Cassio Here, here! For heaven's sake, help me!

Iago What's the matter?

Gratiano This is Othello's ancient, as I take it.

Lodovico The same indeed, a very valiant fellow.

Iago What are you here that cry so grievously?

Cassio Iago? O, I am spoiled, undone by villains!
Give me some help.

Iago O me, lieutenant! What villains have done this?

Cassio I think that one of them is hereabout,
And cannot make away.

Iago O treacherous villains!
What are you there? Come in, and give some help.

To Lodovico and Gratiano

Roderigo O, help me here!

35 Minion: *darling (spoken in contempt)*
36 hies: *approaches*
37 blotted: *wiped away*
39 watch: *guard*
39 passage: *passers-by*
40 direful: *dreadful*
44 heavy: *dark*
45 counterfeits: *traps*
49 shirt: *night-shirt*
57 What are you: *who are you*
58 spoiled: *wounded*
62 make away: *escape*

72 As ... praise us: *judge us by our actions*

75 cry you mercy: *beg your pardon*

85 notable: *notorious*

86 mangled: *attacked*

89 garter: *bandage*

89 chair: *stretcher*

92 this: *this piece of*

93 a party ... injury: *involved in this attack*

Cassio That's one of them.

Iago O murderous slave! O villain!

Stabs Roderigo

Roderigo O damned Iago! O inhuman dog!

Iago Kill men in the dark! – Where be these bloody thieves? –
How silent is this town! – Ho! Murder! Murder! –
What may you be? Are you of good or evil?

Lodovico As you shall prove us, praise us.

Iago Signior Lodovico?

Lodovico He, sir.

Iago I cry you mercy. Here's Cassio hurt by villains.

Gratiano Cassio!

Iago How is it, brother!

Cassio My leg is cut in two.

Iago Marry, heaven forbid!
Light, gentlemen; I'll bind it with my shirt.

Enter Bianca

Bianca What is the matter, ho? Who is it that cried?

Iago Who is it that cried!

Bianca O my dear Cassio! my sweet Cassio! O Cassio,
Cassio, Cassio!

Iago O notable strumpet! Cassio, may you suspect
Who they should be that have thus mangled you?

Cassio No.

Gratiano I am sorry to find you thus: I have been to seek you.

Iago Lend me a garter. So. – O, for a chair,
To bear him easily hence!

Bianca Alas, he faints! O Cassio, Cassio, Cassio!

Iago Gentlemen all, I do suspect this trash
To be a party in this injury.
Patience awhile, good Cassio. Come, come;
Lend me a light. Know we this face or no?
Alas my friend and my dear countryman
Roderigo! No: – yes, sure. O heaven! Roderigo.

Gratiano What, of Venice?

Iago Even he, sir; did you know him?

Gratiano Know him! Ay.

Iago Signior Gratiano? I cry you gentle pardon;
These bloody accidents must excuse my manners,
That so neglected you.

Gratiano I am glad to see you.

Iago How do you, Cassio? O, a chair, a chair!

Gratiano Roderigo!

Iago He, 'tis he.

A chair brought in

O, that's well said; the chair!

Gratiano Some good man bear him carefully from hence;
I'll fetch the general's surgeon.

To Bianca

For you, mistress,
Save you your labour. He that lies slain here, Cassio,
Was my dear friend: what malice was between you?

Cassio None in the world, nor do I know the man.

Iago [***To Bianca***] What, look you pale? O, bear him out
o' the air.

Cassio and Roderigo are borne off

Stay you, good gentlemen. Look you pale, mistress?
Do you perceive the gastness of her eye?
Nay, if you stare, we shall hear more anon.
Behold her well; I pray you, look upon her:
Do you see, gentlemen? Nay, guiltiness will speak,
Though tongues were out of use.

Enter Emilia

Emilia 'Las, what's the matter? What's the matter, husband?

Iago Cassio hath here been set on in the dark
By Roderigo and fellows that are scaped:
He's almost slain, and Roderigo dead.

Emilia Alas, good gentleman! Alas, good Cassio!

Iago This is the fruit of whoring. Prithee, Emilia,
Go know of Cassio where he supped tonight.

To Bianca

What, do you shake at that?

Bianca He supped at my house; but I therefore shake not.

Iago O, did he so? I charge you, go with me.

Emilia Fie, fie upon thee, strumpet!

101 cry: *beg*

102 accidents: *unfortunate events*

112 Save you your labour: *stop trying to help*

117 gastness: *terrified look*

127 fruit: *result*

130 I therefore shake not: *that's not why I'm shaking*

132 strumpet: *prostitute*

136 dressed: *gets his wounds treated*

138 citadel: *castle*

139 happed: *happened*

142 fordoes: *ruins*

Bianca
I am no strumpet; but of life as honest
As you that thus abuse me.

Emilia
As I! Foh! Fie upon thee!

Iago
Kind gentlemen, let's go see poor Cassio dressed.
Come, mistress, you must tell us another tale.
Emilia run you to the citadel,
And tell my lord and lady what hath happed.
Will you go on afore? I pray.

Aside

This is the night
That either makes me or fordoes me quite.

Exeunt

O brave Iago, honest and just ...
Thou teachest me

Othello
Act 5 Scene 1, l.33–4

Commentary

Continuing intrigue (lines 1–27)

Roderigo and Iago wait for Cassio under cover of darkness outside Bianca's lodgings. Roderigo is not enthusiastic about murdering Cassio. However, he accepts Iago's 'satisfying reasons'. Iago withdraws and chillingly considers killing the angry Roderigo. He is pragmatic, calculating that no matter how events turn out, 'Every way makes my gain'. Iago admits that he feels inferior to Cassio, who has a 'daily beauty' in his life that makes the ensign feel 'ugly'. Roderigo launches an unsuccessful attack on Cassio. Amid the confusion, Cassio retaliates and wounds Roderigo.

Vengeance (lines 28–38)

A passing Othello hears the cries and mistakenly thinks

that 'Iago keeps his word' and has carried out his promise to kill Cassio. He also believes that Iago's actions are teaching him what he must do, so he continues to exact a terrible vengeance on the innocent Desdemona, 'Thy bed, lust-stained, shall with lust's blood be spotted'. The Moor is no longer a free agent with an independent mind; he now does exactly what Iago wants him to do.

Unexpected arrivals (lines 39–64)

When Lodovico and Gratiano arrive, the chameleon-like Iago adopts yet another persona. He pretends to be the confused bystander, unaware of everything that has just happened. His urgent questions appear to show genuine concern, 'Whose noise is this that cries on murder?' Once again, everyone is fooled.

Masterly improvisation (lines 65–97)

Roderigo calls out for help. Immediately, the 'concerned' Iago jumps to Cassio's defence, seizing the moment to stab Roderigo. Only now, as he lies dying, does the foolish young Venetian realise that he has been tricked by Iago, the 'inhuman dog'. Continuing in his role of 'concerned friend', Iago attends to Cassio's wounds. When Bianca arrives, she becomes distraught at the sight of her wounded lover. Iago immediately casts doubt on her, 'I do suspect this trash/ To be a party in this injury'. He cleverly deflects attention away from himself by suggesting that Bianca is involved in the attack.

Director of proceedings (lines 98–142)

Iago now takes charge, courteously greeting Gratiano. He is attentive to Cassio and initiates an interrogation about what 'malice' might have existed between Cassio and his dear friend, Roderigo. He orders the wounded Cassio to be moved. Through clever suggestion, he blames Bianca, 'What, do you shake at that?' He even encourages Emilia to criticise the 'strumpet' to strengthen his accusations. While the two women argue,

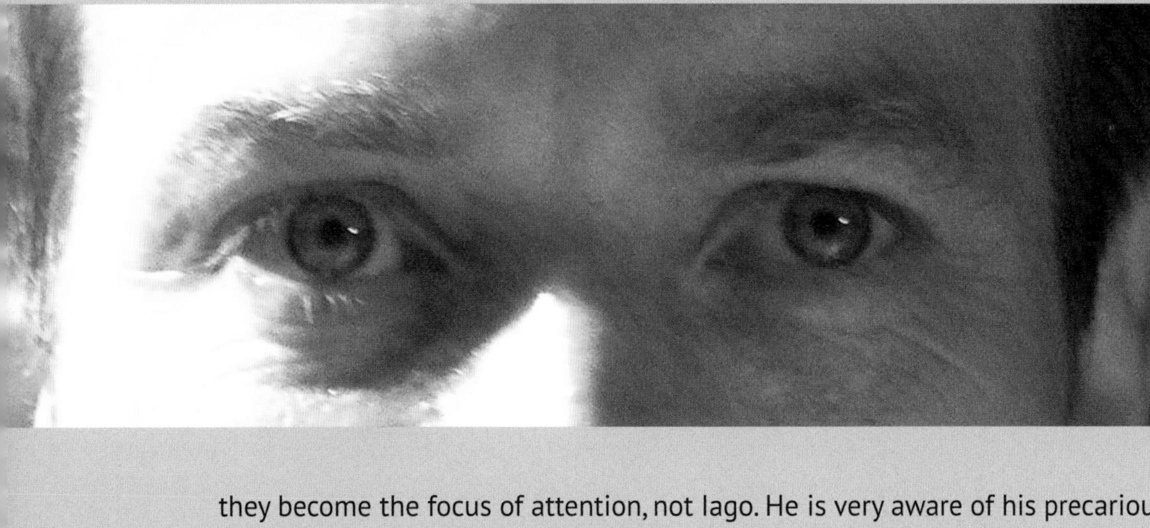

This is the night
That either makes me or
fordoes me quite

Iago
Act 5 Scene 1, l.141–3

they become the focus of attention, not Iago. He is very aware of his precarious position. Everything had been going his way, but Cassio is still alive. His diabolical schemes are now perched on the edge of success or failure.

Dramatic Significance

The scene is steeped in **dramatic treachery**. The quick rhythm is maintained by rapid cinematic 'cutting' between groups of characters. Roderigo and Cassio's encounter is interrupted by Iago. Othello appears on his way to murder Desdemona. Lodovico and Gratiano discover the wounded Cassio. Iago stabs Roderigo. Bianca's arrival gives Iago an opportunity to blame her for Cassio's wounds. As always, the action is directed by Iago and his incriminating insinuations, 'guiltiness will speak/ Though tongues were out of use'.

Iago continues to spin his intricate web with assured creativity, 'Cassio,/ Was my dear friend', 'Roderigo was 'my friend and my dear countryman'. All the main characters view events through the perspective Iago has crafted. As he takes more and more risks and his **character becomes increasingly reckless**, the audience is caught between an unwilling admiration for his inventiveness and disgust at his cynical calculation, 'This is the night/ That either makes me or fordoes me quite'. Is he really delighting in his life-and-death risk-taking?

Class/Homework Exercise

'Iago's relationships with other central characters can be seen primarily as power struggles which prove crucial to the unfolding tragedy.'

Discuss the above statement with particular reference to Act 5 Scene 1. Write a paragraph (about 150–200 words), supporting your answer with reference to the text.

Prompt!

All of Iago's manipulative relationships propel the play's tragic outcome:

- Control of Othello and Desdemona is central to the inevitable tragedy.
- Dominance of Roderigo has catastrophic consequences.
- Iago/Cassio power struggle leads to attempted murder.
- Domineering influence on Bianca contributes to the tragic conclusion.
- Iago's macho scheming involves his wife Emilia in his diabolical plans.

Revision Overview

Roderigo and Iago lurk in the shadows outside Bianca's lodgings with the intention of murdering Cassio. Iago has become aware that he is losing control of Roderigo and that Cassio might soon undermine his plot against Othello. The ensign almost succeeds in his evil plan. During the chaotic skirmish, both Roderigo and Cassio are wounded. When Iago is presented with the opportunity to stab Roderigo, he acts swiftly. Othello overhears the disturbance and mistakenly believes that Iago is carrying out his part of their murderous agreement.

As he lies dying, Roderigo finally realises Iago's true evil nature. When Bianca appears, Iago seizes another chance to wreak havoc by blaming her for the assault on Cassio. He also enlists Emilia to support his accusations against Bianca. However, although Iago resumes control of the situation, all has not gone perfectly for him – and Cassio still lives.

- **Theme: Love and hate** – ironically it is the prostitute Bianca who shows genuine concern. Iago, Roderigo and Othello are all consumed with hatred.
- **Characters: Iago –** puppet-master, coward, full of self-contempt, a man of many roles – conspirator, concerned friend, outraged avenger, sanctimonious judge, controlling husband. Beginning to be unsure of the success of his plans.
  Othello – degraded avenger, sadistic tendencies.
  Roderigo – sad victim of Iago's manipulations, aware of the truth too late.
  Emilia – shrewish and streetwise, but blind to Iago's manipulations.

Key Quotes

I have no great devotion to the deed *(Roderigo to Iago) l.8*	Roderigo is not enthusiastic about killing Cassio. He lacks physical courage and knows that murder is wrong, but he doesn't have the intellect to see through Iago's arguments. Roderigo has always been a weak-willed character without the moral strength to follow his own conscience.
He hath a daily beauty in his life *That makes me ugly* *(Iago) l.19–20*	Iago's haunting comment is a chilling and precise expression of the bitterness that typifies him. He suffers from an inferiority complex and is keenly aware that – unlike himself – Michael Cassio is effortlessly attractive. Cassio is also a popular man while Iago is unfulfilled and deeply unhappy.
Thou teachest me *(Othello) l.35*	Ironically, Othello mistakenly assumes that Iago has killed Cassio as he promised. The Moor is now entirely controlled by his vindictive ensign and hurries to carry out his part of their pact by murdering his own innocent wife.
Do you see, gentlemen? Nay, guiltiness will speak, *Though tongues were out of use* *(Iago to Gratiano and Lodovico) l.120–1*	Iago shapes reality for his own purposes through vague but clever insinuations. He skilfully deflects any suspicion from himself by casting doubt on Bianca, pretending to see guilt written across her face. He uses her silence as proof of her 'guilt', so that Lodovico and Gratiano won't need to question her.
This is the night *That either makes me or fordoes me quite* *(Iago) l.141–2*	This rhyming couplet creates anticipation about how events will turn out. Iago is always conscious of the risks he takes. For the first time, he now admits that his vengeful schemes are slipping out of his control. Iago is nervous that he has failed to have Cassio killed. Will evil or good triumph?

Act 5
Scene 2*

INTRODUCTION

- Othello interrogates his wife.
- Desdemona pleads her innocence.
- Emilia confronts the Moor.
- Iago maintains his silence.
- Establishment of a new order.

* Key scene requiring close, detailed study

A bedchamber in the castle

Enter Othello

Othello It is the cause, it is the cause, my soul –
Let me not name it to you, you chaste stars! –
It is the cause. Yet I'll not shed her blood;
Nor scar that whiter skin of hers than snow,
And smooth as monumental alabaster.
Yet she must die, else she'll betray more men.
Put out the light, and then put out the light:
If I quench thee, thou flaming minister,
I can again thy former light restore,
Should I repent me: but once put out thy light,
Thou cunning pattern of excelling nature,
I know not where is that Promethean heat
That can thy light relume. When I have plucked the rose,
I cannot give it vital growth again.
It must needs wither; I'll smell it on the tree.

Kissing her

Oh balmy breath, that dost almost persuade
Justice to break her sword! One more, one more.
Be thus when thou art dead, and I will kill thee,
And love thee after. One more, and this the last:
So sweet was ne'er so fatal. I must weep,
But they are cruel tears. This sorrow's heavenly,
It strikes where it doth love. She wakes.

Desdemona Who's there? Othello?

Othello Ay, Desdemona.

Desdemona Will you come to bed, my lord?

Othello Have you prayed to-night, Desdemona?

Desdemona Ay, my lord.

Othello If you bethink yourself of any crime
Unreconciled as yet to heaven and grace,
Solicit for it straight.

Desdemona Alas, my lord, what do you mean by that?

Othello Well, do it, and be brief. I will walk by.
I would not kill thy unprepared spirit.
No, heaven forfend! I would not kill thy soul.

Desdemona Talk you of killing?

Othello Ay, I do.

Desdemona Then heaven
Have mercy on me!

1 cause: *adultery (his reason to justify murder)*

5 monumental alabaster: *translucent stone*

7 put out the light: *he will extinguish both the torch and his wife's life*

8 flaming minister: *burning candle*

12 Promethean heat: *Prometheus used fire to create human life (Greek myth)*

13 relume: *rekindle*

17 sword: *justice is often depicted as a woman holding a sword*

30 Solicit for it straight: *ask pardon immediately*

34 forfend: *forbid*

Othello Amen, with all my heart!

Desdemona If you say so, I hope you will not kill me.

Othello Hum!

Desdemona And yet I fear you, for you are fatal then
When your eyes roll so; why I should fear I know not,
Since guiltiness I know not; but yet I feel I fear.

Othello Think on thy sins.

Desdemona They are loves I bear to you.

Othello Ay, and for that thou diest.

Desdemona That death's unnatural that kills for loving.
Alas, why gnaw you so your nether lip?
Some bloody passion shakes your very frame:
These are portents; but yet I hope, I hope,
They do not point on me.

Othello Peace, and be still!

Desdemona I will so. What's the matter?

Othello That handkerchief which I so loved and gave thee,
Thou gavest to Cassio.

Desdemona No, by my life and soul!
Send for the man, and ask him.

Othello Sweet soul, take heed,
Take heed of perjury; thou art on thy deathbed.

Desdemona Ay, but not yet to die.

Othello Yes, presently:
Therefore confess thee freely of thy sin;
For to deny each article with oath
Cannot remove nor choke the strong conception
That I do groan withal. Thou art to die.

Desdemona Then Lord have mercy on me!

Othello I say, Amen.

Desdemona And have you mercy too! I never did
Offend you in my life; never loved Cassio
But with such general warranty of heaven
As I might love: I never gave him token.

Othello By heaven, I saw my handkerchief in his hand.
O perjured woman! Thou dost stone my heart,
And makest me call what I intend to do
A murder, which I thought a sacrifice:
I saw the handkerchief.

49 nether: *lower*
51 portents: *bad signs*
60 perjury: *untruthfulness*
62 presently: *at once*
64 article: *accusation*
65 choke the strong conception: *block out the deep suspicion*
66 do groan withal: *am pained by*
71 with … heaven: *as a good friend*
76 sacrifice: *ritualistic punishment*

Desdemona He found it then;
I never gave it him: send for him hither;
Let him confess a truth.

Othello He hath confessed.

Desdemona What, my lord?

Othello That he hath used thee.

83 used: *had sex with*

Desdemona How? Unlawfully?

Othello Ay.

Desdemona He will not say so.

Othello No, his mouth is stopped;
Honest Iago hath taken order for it.

Desdemona O, my fear interprets: what, is he dead?

Othello Had all his hairs been lives, my great revenge
Had stomach for them all.

91 stomach: *appetite*

Desdemona Alas! He is betrayed and I undone.

92 undone: *ruined*

Othello Out, strumpet! Weepest thou for him to my face?

93 strumpet: *whore*

Desdemona O, banish me, my lord, but kill me not!

Othello Down, strumpet!

Desdemona Kill me tomorrow: let me live tonight!

Othello Nay, if you strive—

97 strive: *struggle*

Desdemona But half an hour!

Othello Being done, there is no pause.

99 Being ... pause: *I can't stop now*

Desdemona But while I say one prayer!

Othello It is too late.

He smothers her

Emilia [***Within***] My lord, my lord! What, ho! My lord, my lord!

Othello What noise is this? Not dead? Not yet quite dead?
I that am cruel am yet merciful;
I would not have thee linger in thy pain.
So, so.

Emilia [***Within***] What, ho! My lord, my lord!

Othello Who's there?

Emilia [***Within***] O, good my lord, I would speak a word with you!

Othello Yes: 'tis Emilia. By and by. She's dead.
'Tis like she comes to speak of Cassio's death.
The noise was high. Ha! No more moving?
Still as the grave. Shall she come in? Were it good?

112 high: *loud*

117 insupportable: *unbearable*

119–120 affrighted ... alteration: *terrified world should erupt at what has occurred*

130 error: *deviation*

131 she ... wont: *usual*

138 out of tune: *gone wrong*

149 Commend: *speak well of*

I think she stirs again – no. What's best to do?
If she come in, she'll sure speak to my wife:
My wife! My wife! What wife? I have no wife.
O insupportable! O heavy hour!
Methinks it should be now a huge eclipse
Of sun and moon, and that the affrighted globe
Should yawn at alteration.

Emilia [***Within***] I do beseech you
That I may speak with you, O, good my lord!

Othello I had forgot thee: O, come in, Emilia.
Soft, by and by. Let me the curtains draw.
Where art thou?

Unlocks the door

Enter Emilia

What's the matter with thee now?

Emilia O, my good lord, yonder's foul murders done!

Othello What, now?

Emilia But now, my lord.

Othello It is the very error of the moon,
She comes more nearer earth than she was wont,
And makes men mad.

Emilia Cassio, my lord, hath killed a young Venetian
Called Roderigo.

Othello Roderigo killed!
And Cassio killed!

Emilia No, Cassio is not killed.

Othello Not Cassio killed! Then murder's out of tune,
And sweet revenge grows harsh.

Desdemona O, falsely falsely murdered!

Emilia Alas, what cry is that?

Othello That! What?

Emilia Out, and alas! That was my lady's voice.
Help! Help, ho! Help! O lady, speak again!
Sweet Desdemona! O sweet mistress, speak!

Desdemona A guiltless death I die.

Emilia O, who hath done this deed?

Desdemona Nobody; I myself. Farewell:
Commend me to my kind lord: O, farewell!

Dies

Othello Why, how should she be murdered?

Emilia Alas, who knows?

Othello You heard her say herself, it was not I.

Emilia She said so: I must needs report the truth.

Othello She's like a liar gone to burning hell,
'Twas I that killed her.

Emilia O, the more angel she,
And you the blacker devil!

Othello She turned to folly, and she was a whore.

158 folly: *sin*

Emilia Thou dost belie her, and thou art a devil.

159 belie: *falsely accuse*

Othello She was false as water.

Emilia Thou art rash as fire, to say
That she was false: O, she was heavenly true!

Othello Cassio did top her; ask thy husband else.
O, I were damned beneath all depth in hell,
But that I did proceed upon just grounds
To this extremity. Thy husband knew it all.

163 top: *make love to*
163 else: *if it was otherwise*
166 extremity: *final punishment*

Emilia My husband!

Othello Thy husband.

Emilia That she was false to wedlock?

Othello Ay, with Cassio. Nay, had she been true,
If heaven would make me such another world
Of one entire and perfect chrysolite,
I would not have sold her for it.

172 chrysolite: *jewel*

Emilia My husband!

Othello Ay, 'twas he that told me first:
An honest man he is, and hates the slime
That sticks on filthy deeds.

Emilia My husband!

Othello What needs this iteration, woman? I say thy husband.

179 iteration: *repetition*

Emilia O mistress, villainy hath made mocks with love,
My husband say that she was false!

180 made mocks with: *mocked*

Othello He, woman;
I say thy husband: dost understand the word?
My friend, thy husband, honest, honest Iago.

Emilia If he say so, may his pernicious soul
Rot half a grain a day! He lies to the heart:
She was too fond of her most filthy bargain.

185 pernicious: *villainous*

192 Peace ... best: *you had better keep quiet*

194 gull, dolt: *fool, idiot*

206 full: *filled with anger*

211 odious: *hateful*

214 charm: *hold*

217 forfend: *forbid*

218 set ... on: *caused the murder*

226 charge: *order*

Othello Ha!

Emilia Do thy worst.
This deed of thine is no more worthy heaven
Than thou wast worthy her.

Othello Peace, you were best.

Emilia Thou hast not half that power to do me harm
As I have to be hurt. O gull! O dolt!
As ignorant as dirt! Thou hast done a deed –
I care not for thy sword; I'll make thee known,
Though I lost twenty lives. – Help! Help, ho! Help!
The Moor hath killed my mistress! Murder! Murder!

Enter Montano, Gratiano, Iago, and others

Montano What is the matter? How now, general!

Emilia O, are you come, Iago? You have done well,
That men must lay their murders on your neck.

Gratiano What is the matter?

Emilia Disprove this villain, if thou be'st a man:
He says thou toldest him that his wife was false.
I know thou didst not, thou art not such a villain.
Speak, for my heart is full.

Iago I told him what I thought, and told no more
Than what he found himself was apt and true.

Emilia But did you ever tell him she was false?

Iago I did.

Emilia You told a lie, an odious, damned lie;
Upon my soul, a lie, a wicked lie.
She false with Cassio! Did you say with Cassio?

Iago With Cassio, mistress. Go to, charm your tongue.

Emilia I will not charm my tongue; I am bound to speak.
My mistress here lies murdered in her bed—

All O heavens forfend!

Emilia And your reports have set the murder on.

Othello Nay, stare not, masters: it is true, indeed.

Gratiano 'Tis a strange truth.

Montano O monstrous act!

Emilia Villainy, villainy, villainy!
I think upon it, I think: I smell it: O villainy!
I thought so then – I'll kill myself for grief –
O villainy, villainy!

Iago What, are you mad? I charge you, get you home.

Emilia Good gentlemen, let me have leave to speak:
'Tis proper I obey him, but not now.
Perchance, Iago, I will never go home.

Othello O! O! O!

He falls on the bed

Emilia Nay, lay thee down and roar;
For thou hast killed the sweetest innocent
That ever did lift up eye.

Othello [***Rising***] O, she was foul!
I scarce did know you, uncle: there lies your niece,
Whose breath, indeed, these hands have newly stopped.
I know this act shows horrible and grim.

Gratiano Poor Desdemona! I am glad thy father's dead.
Thy match was mortal to him, and pure grief
Shore his old thread in twain: did he live now,
This sight would make him do a desperate turn,
Yea, curse his better angel from his side,
And fall to reprobation.

Othello 'Tis pitiful; but yet Iago knows
That she with Cassio hath the act of shame
A thousand times committed; Cassio confessed it:
And she did gratify his amorous works
With that recognisance and pledge of love
Which I first gave her I saw it in his hand:
It was a handkerchief, an antique token
My father gave my mother.

Emilia O heaven! O heavenly powers.

Iago Come, hold your peace.

Emilia 'Twill out, 'twill out: I hold my peace, sir? No!
No, I will speak as liberal as the north:
Let heaven and men and devils, let them all,
All, all, cry shame against me, yet I'll speak.

Iago Be wise, and get you home.

Emilia I will not.

Iago threatens to stab Emilia

Gratiano Fie!
Your sword upon a woman?

Emilia O thou dull Moor, that handkerchief thou speakest of
I found by fortune and did give my husband;
For often, with a solemn earnestness,
More than indeed belonged to such a trifle,
He begged of me to steal it.

229 Perchance: *perhaps*

237 shows: *appears*

239 Thy match ... him: *your marriage pained hm*

240 Shore ... twain: *cut his life short*

243 reprobation: *damnation*

245 shame: *adultery*

247 amorous works: *love-making*

248 recognizance: *keepsake*

254 'twill out: *truth will come out*

255 liberal: *freely*

263 fortune: *chance*

264 solemn earnestness: *extreme seriousness*

265 belonged: *was appropriate*

Iago Villainous whore!

Emilia She give it Cassio! No, alas! I found it,
And I did give it my husband.

Iago Filth, thou liest!

272 coxcomb: *clown*

Emilia By heaven, I do not, I do not, gentlemen.
O murderous coxcomb! What should such a fool
Do with so good a woman?

274 stones: *thunderbolts*

Othello Are there no stones in heaven
But what serve for the thunder? Precious villain!

He runs at Iago. Iago, from behind, stabs Emilia, and exit

Gratiano The woman falls; sure he hath killed his wife.

Emilia Ay, ay. O, lay me by my mistress' side.

Gratiano He's gone, but his wife's killed.

280 recovered: *taken*

Montano 'Tis a notorious villain. Take you this weapon,
Which I have here recovered from the Moor:
Come, guard the door without. Let him not pass,
But kill him rather. I'll after that same villain,
For 'tis a damned slave.

Exeunt Montano and Gratiano

285 puny whipster: *weak upstart*

Othello I am not valiant neither,
But ever puny whipster gets my sword:
But why should honour outlive honesty?
Let it go all.

288 bode: *foretell*
289 play the swan: *sing before death*

Emilia What did thy song bode, lady?
Hark, canst thou hear me? I will play the swan
And die in music.

Singing

Willow, willow, willow –
Moor, she was chaste, she loved thee, cruel Moor.
So come my soul to bliss, as I speak true;
So speaking as I think, I die, I die.

Dies

296 ice-brook's temper: *hardened in icy water*

Othello I have another weapon in this chamber;
It is a sword of Spain, the ice-brook's temper –
O, here it is. Uncle, I must come forth.

Gratiano [***Within***] If thou attempt it, it will cost thee dear:
Thou hast no weapon, and perforce must suffer.

301 naked: *unarmed*

Othello Look in upon me then and speak with me,
Or, naked as I am, I will assault thee.

Re-enter Gratiano

Gratiano What is the matter?

Othello Behold, I have a weapon;
A better never did itself sustain
Upon a soldier's thigh: I have seen the day,
That, with this little arm and this good sword,
I have made my way through more impediments
Than twenty times your stop: but, O vain boast!
Who can control his fate? 'Tis not so now.
Be not afraid, though you do see me weaponed;
Here is my journey's end, here is my butt,
And very sea-mark of my utmost sail.
Do you go back dismayed? 'Tis a lost fear;
Man but a rush against Othello's breast,
And he retires. Where should Othello go?
Now, how dost thou look now? O ill-starred wench!
Pale as thy smock! When we shall meet at compt,
This look of thine will hurl my soul from heaven,
And fiends will snatch at it. Cold, cold, my girl!
Even like thy chastity. O cursed slave!
Whip me, ye devils,
From the possession of this heavenly sight!
Blow me about in winds! Roast me in sulphur!
Wash me in steep-down gulfs of liquid fire!
O Desdemona! Desdemona! Dead!
Oh! Oh! Oh!

Enter Lodovico, Montano, Cassio carried in a chair, and Officers with Iago, prisoner

Lodovico Where is this rash and most unfortunate man?

Othello That's he that was Othello: here I am.

Lodovico Where is that viper? Bring the villain forth.

Othello I look down towards his feet; but that's a fable.
If that thou be'st a devil, I cannot kill thee.

Wounds Iago

Lodovico Wrench his sword from him.

Iago I bleed, sir; but not killed.

Othello I am not sorry neither: I would have thee live;
For, in my sense, 'tis happiness to die.

Lodovico O thou Othello, thou wert once so good,
Fallen in the practice of a damned slave,
What shall be said to thee?

Othello Why, any thing:
An honourable murderer, if you will;
For nought I did in hate, but all in honour.

308 stop: *strength*

311 butt: *aim, goal*

312 sea-mark ... sail: *sign of my final journey*

314 Man but a rush: *use only a reed*

316 ill-starred: *unfortunate*

317 smock: *nightgown*

317 compt: *day of judgement*

329 viper: *snake*

330 fable: *myth that a devil has hooves*

337 practice: *schemes*

347 demi-devil: *half-devil*
348 ensnared: *trapped*
352 Torments ... ope: *torture will make you talk*
353 thou dost best: *do your best*
354 befallen: *occurred*
357 imports: *suggests*
361 heathenish ... gross: *savage and terrible*
362 discontented: *incriminating*
365 belike: *it is likely*
366 satisfied him: *stopped him complaining*
367 pernicious caitiff: *evil wretch*
376 upbraids: *criticises*
377 Brave: *insult*
378 cast: *dismissed*
382 taken off: *removed*

Lodovico This wretch hath part confessed his villainy:
Did you and he consent in Cassio's death?

Othello Ay.

Cassio Dear general, I never gave you cause.

Othello I do believe it, and I ask your pardon.
Will you, I pray, demand that demi-devil
Why he hath thus ensnared my soul and body?

Iago Demand me nothing: what you know, you know:
From this time forth I never will speak word.

Lodovico What, not to pray?

Gratiano Torments will ope your lips.

Othello Well, thou dost best.

Lodovico Sir, you shall understand what hath befallen,
Which, as I think, you know not. Here is a letter
Found in the pocket of the slain Roderigo;
And here another: the one of them imports
The death of Cassio to be undertook
By Roderigo.

Othello O villain!

Cassio Most heathenish and most gross!

Lodovico Now here's another discontented paper,
Found in his pocket too; and this, it seems,
Roderigo meant to have sent this damned villain;
But that, belike, Iago in the interim
Came in and satisfied him.

Othello O the pernicious caitiff!
How came you, Cassio, by that handkerchief
That was my wife's?

Cassio I found it in my chamber:
And he himself confessed but even now
That there he dropped it for a special purpose
Which wrought to his desire.

Othello O fool! Fool! Fool!

Cassio There is besides in Roderigo's letter,
How he upbraids Iago, that he made him
Brave me upon the watch; whereon it came
That I was cast: and even but now he spake,
After long seeming dead, Iago hurt him,
Iago set him on.

Lodovico You must forsake this room, and go with us.
Your power and your command is taken off,

And Cassio rules in Cyprus. For this slave,
If there be any cunning cruelty
That can torment him much and hold him long,
It shall be his. You shall close prisoner rest,
Till that the nature of your fault be known
To the Venetian state. Come, bring him away.

Othello Soft you; a word or two before you go.
I have done the state some service, and they know it.
No more of that. I pray you, in your letters,
When you shall these unlucky deeds relate,
Speak of me as I am; nothing extenuate,
Nor set down aught in malice: then must you speak
Of one that loved not wisely but too well;
Of one not easily jealous, but being wrought
Perplexed in the extreme; of one whose hand,
Like the base Indian, threw a pearl away
Richer than all his tribe; of one whose subdued eyes,
Albeit unused to the melting mood,
Drop tears as fast as the Arabian trees
Their medicinal gum. Set you down this.
And say besides, that in Aleppo once,
Where a malignant and a turbaned Turk
Beat a Venetian and traduced the state,
I took by the throat the circumcised dog,
And smote him, thus.

Stabs himself

Lodovico O bloody period!

Gratiano All that's spoke is marred.

Othello I kissed thee ere I killed thee: no way but this;
Killing myself, to die upon a kiss.

Falls on the bed, and dies

Cassio This did I fear, but thought he had no weapon;
For he was great of heart.

Lodovico [*To Iago*] O Spartan dog,
More fell than anguish, hunger, or the sea!
Look on the tragic loading of this bed.
This is thy work. The object poisons sight,
Let it be hid. Gratiano, keep the house
And seize upon the fortunes of the Moor,
For they succeed to you. To you, lord governor,
Remains the censure of this hellish villain;
The time, the place, the torture: O, enforce it!
Myself will straight aboard: and to the state
This heavy act with heavy heart relate.

Exeunt

386 close ... rest: *be well guarded*
389 Soft you: *wait*
390 service: *military service*
393 nothing extenuate: *do not make excuses*
394 set ... malice: *exaggerate maliciously*
396 wrought: *manipulated and provoked*
398 base: *ignorant and foolish*
399 subdued: *grief-stricken*
400 melting mood: *weeping*
402 gum: *sap*
403 Aleppo: *Syrian city*
405 traduced: *betrayed*
406 took ... dog: *killed the Muslim*
408 period: *ending*
409 marred: *ruined*
410 ere: *before*
414 Spartan: *savage*
415 fell: *cruel*
419 fortunes: *possessions*
421 censure: *punishment*
424 heavy: *sorrowful*

Key Scene Extended Commentary

Deluded justice (lines 1–101)

In the couple's bedroom, Othello observes his sleeping wife. He has persuaded himself that by avenging Desdemona's infidelity, he is acting honourably. The Moor now believes that 'she'll betray more men' if he does not kill her. He is also aware that he can never bring Desdemona back to life again, 'When I have plucked the rose,/ I cannot give it vital growth again'. Desdemona wakes.

Using legal terms, Othello interrogates his disoriented wife, asking her if she wishes to repent any sins she might have committed before he kills her. Desdemona is terrified by the spectacle of her impassioned husband. She confesses that her only sins are the 'loves I bear to you'. Othello is fixated on the 'ocular proof' of the handkerchief, accusing his wife of giving it to Cassio. She urges him to send for Cassio, who can explain that she 'never gave him token'. But Othello insists, 'I saw my handkerchief in his hand'. He accuses his helpless wife of perjury and informs her that Cassio is dead. Desdemona begins to weep, fearing that 'he is betrayed and I am undone'. Blinded by paranoia, Othello interprets her tears as proof of her love for Cassio. This seals her fate. Now, he will not even give her time to pray, but smothers her.

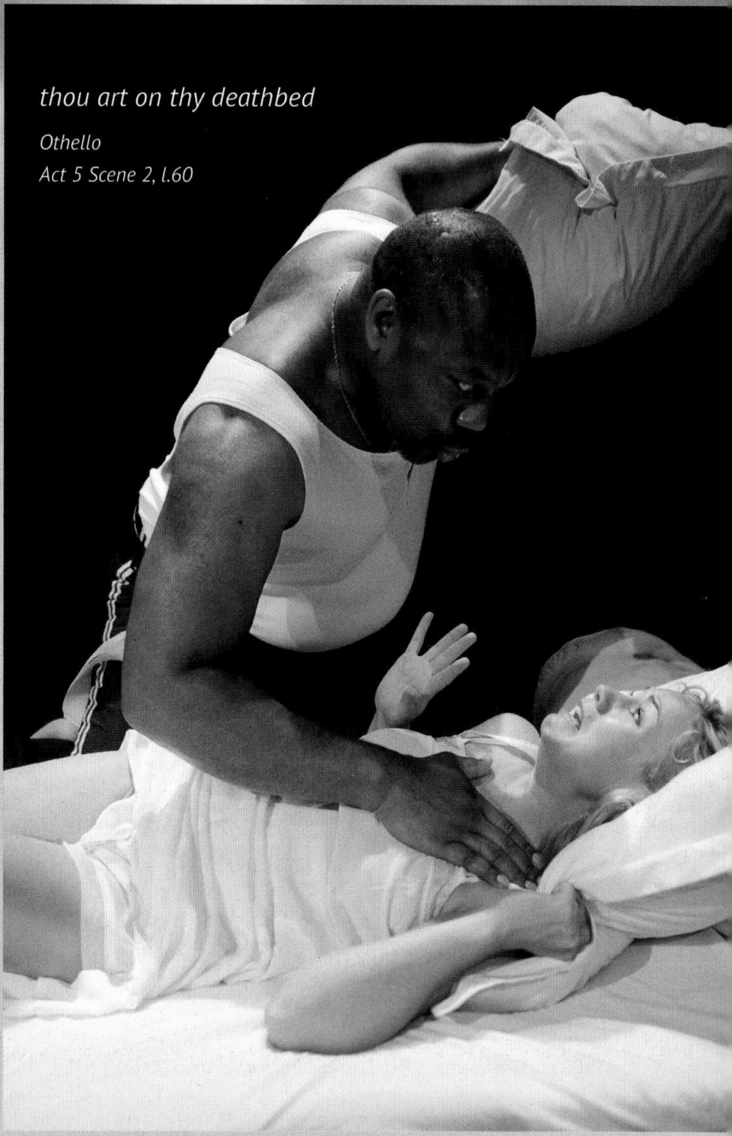

thou art on thy deathbed

Othello
Act 5 Scene 2, l.60

Murder (lines 102–155)

Emilia knocks at the bedroom door, demanding to speak to Othello. He imagines that she has heard news of Cassio's death and will want to speak to Desdemona. Realising the enormity of what he has done, Othello suddenly laments his loss, 'I have no wife'. Everything has changed. He draws the curtains around the bed to hide Desdemona's body from view and unlocks the door. Emilia bursts in with news of 'foul murders' and tells him that Cassio has killed Roderigo. But Othello mishears her and thinks that both Cassio and Roderigo are dead. He is shocked when she corrects him and explains that Cassio is still alive.

From behind the curtain, Desdemona's weak voice calls out, 'falsely falsely murdered!' Can Iago's evil plan be thwarted even at this late stage? Emilia demands to know, 'who hath done this deed?' With her dying breath, Desdemona tries to exonerate Othello from any blame, 'Nobody; I myself'. The Moor immediately uses his wife's dying words to deny responsibility for her murder, 'You heard her say herself, it was not I'. But Othello's denial is short-lived and he then admits that he killed her because she betrayed his love, 'She's like a liar gone to burning hell'.

More accusations (lines 156–208)

Emilia defies the Moor's accusation, 'Thou dost belie her, and thou art a devil'. In a dramatic exchange, she defends Desdemona's honour. Othello intimidates her, as he did his wife, 'Thy husband knew it all'. Like everyone else, Emilia has been completely unaware of Iago's true character up until this moment. She condemns him immediately, 'He lies to the heart'. Outraged by the murder of her mistress, Emilia continues to confront Othello, telling him that Desdemona was 'too fond of her most filthy bargain'. Her emotional attack echoes the simple, clear voice of the real world, 'O gull! O dolt!/ As ignorant as dirt!' Othello threatens her again, but Emilia has finally found her voice and declares, 'I care not for thy sword'. She shouts for help once more, determined to reveal Othello's guilt, 'I'll make thee known/ Though I lost twenty lives'.

O, she was heavenly true!

Emilia
Act 5 Scene 2, l.162

The truth emerges (lines 209–284)

When Iago arrives, Emilia refutes all the charges against Desdemona as an 'odious, damned lie'. She insists on being heard, 'let me have leave to speak'. Othello still accuses his wife, 'she was foul', and clings desperately to the flimsy 'evidence' of the handkerchief. Emilia, despite Iago's attempt to stop her, reveals the full truth about what has happened, 'that handkerchief thou speakest of/ I found by fortune and did give my husband'. She continues, 'He begged of me to steal it'. Iago calls her a liar. Emilia rounds on the Moor again, calling him a 'murderous coxcomb'. For the first time, Othello accepts that he was deceived and attempts to attack Iago, who manages to escape – but not before stabbing his wife. Montano and Gratiano go after the 'notorious villain'.

Inevitable tragedy (lines 284–424)

With her dying breath, Emilia sings Desdemona's 'willow' song, defending her mistress to the end, 'Moor, she was chaste, she loved thee, cruel Moor'. As he looks at Desdemona's lifeless body, Othello is filled with guilt and fears Judgement Day, 'This look of thine will hurl my soul from heaven'. He is petrified that he will be condemned to

If that thou be'st a devil, I cannot kill thee

Othello
Act 5 Scene 2, l.331

hell for killing an innocent woman. When Iago is brought in as a prisoner, Othello lunges at him, but the ensign survives and the Moor is disarmed. Lodovico is appalled at the change in Othello, 'thou wert once so good'.

Despite everything he has done, Othello still regards himself as 'someone who did nothing in hate, but all in honour'. He is desperate to know why Iago has 'ensnared' him. However, the ensign refuses to give Othello the satisfaction of an explanation, 'From this time forth I never will speak word'. The enigmatic villain attempts to maintain control to the bitter end.

Two letters have been found in Roderigo's pocket. One explains the part he played in Cassio's attempted murder. The other is to Iago. Cassio explains how he found the handkerchief in his lodgings and that Iago had confessed to placing it there. Othello now acknowledges his terrible recklessness, 'O fool!' and realises that he has been completely deceived by Iago. The Moor has gained insight – but it is much too late. He is stripped of his official position and is to be imprisoned, while Cassio is promoted to governor of Cyprus.

Othello's final speech is dignified and reflective. He sees himself as both killer and victim, 'one that loved not wisely but too well'. He recognises his guilt and how he 'threw a pearl away' by killing Desdemona. His primary concern, however, is his reputation. Othello retreats into his heroic military past and tells a story about a time when he once overpowered a Muslim Turk who had killed a Venetian. As he describes their fierce struggle, he takes out a hidden dagger and stabs himself. He falls onto the bed next to Desdemona and dies while giving her a final kiss.

Killing myself, to die upon a kiss

Othello
Act 5 Scene 2, l.411

The Moor's last words reflect the complexity of his character. They could suggest that he is still delusional and self-centred – or they might indicate a return to his former nobility. Is his suicide cowardly or heroic? Cassio pays tribute to Othello, calling him a man who was 'great of heart'. The audience is left to make its own judgement. The stage is now filled with the 'tragic loading' of Iago's victims. Lodovico asks Cassio, the island's new commander, to decide on the ensign's punishment. For the present, order has been restored. But has the force of evil been completely defeated?

Shakespeare's Dramatic Style

The troubled stillness of this concluding scene contrasts sharply with the earlier activity. Othello's hypnotic repetition, 'It is the cause', establishes the **dreadful tone**. There are two possible meanings of the word 'cause'. First, Desdemona's alleged infidelity is the source of the Moor's action. Second, he believes that he has a mission to dispense justice. He uses formal legal terms, such as 'perjury' and 'article', while merging the self-appointed roles of judge, jury and executioner. Caught between deluded superiority and pity, Othello becomes incensed at Desdemona's tears for Cassio and, despite his previous concerns about sending her unprepared to the next world, he does precisely that.

The slow pace of Desdemona's death stretches out its brutality, adding to the suspense and heightening the play's tragedy. Emilia's sudden entrance changes the mood. Her energy represents the voice of human decency and her independent spirit illustrates the playwright's **perspective on gender issues** the play. Emilia challenges traditional social attitudes. She tells the Moor that he knows nothing about justice, but is indeed a 'blacker devil', a 'fool'. Emilia is also shocked by Iago's deception and condemns him unreservedly. In the end, her female realism momentarily defies the power of men – until male violence again prevails. All three female characters, Desdemona, Emilia and Bianca, unlike the men, display loyalty, courage and solidarity. Emilia's poignant death shows the tragedy from the viewpoint of the victims of routine misogyny in a patriarchal society.

Shakespeare presents the audience with several **unanswered questions**. Othello's final speech, with its deliberate opening understatement, 'I have done the state some service, and they know it', reminds us of his former nobility. He speaks of himself in the third person, thereby still distancing himself from the heinous crime he has just committed. Maintaining that he was never 'easily jealous', he then takes his own life, therefore becoming both killer and victim. Is his suicide a cowardly escape? Or is it an honourable act of atonement for the murder of his innocent wife? Shakespeare leaves us with one final lesson. No matter how catastrophic the hero's downfall, or what awful tragedy occurs, life still goes on. In Lodovico's concluding words, the 'tragic loading' of the violent scene 'poisons sight'. However, despite the 'heavy act', order will be restored – for the moment at least.

Critical Analysis

'The values and societal attitudes evident in *Othello* have a profound effect on the tragic outcome of the play.'

Discuss this view in relation to Act 5 Scene 2 with reference to at least one value or societal attitude evident in the scene. Write a paragraph (about 150–200 words), supporting your answer with suitable reference to the text.

Prompt!

- Characters represent/reflect/reject the principles/standards/values/attitudes of society influencing the catastrophic conclusion.
- Unfortunate events/conclusion shaped by Venetian values/norms: status, reputation, patriarchy, misogyny, racism, duty, honour.
- Values of loyalty/disloyalty and morality/immorality have consequences throughout, determine the play's tragic outcome.

Sample Paragraph 1

The last scene is very voilent. All the characters is dead on Othello's bed. It is very tragic. Iago won't tell why he plotted, but Emilia wasn't exactly afraid of him. She spoke up so that everyone knew he was guilty. Which is why he killed her. But it was too late. The two Venetians Lodivoco and Montano put things back on track by hiding the dead corpses behind a curtain and telling Cassio to beat Iago until he cracks. Iago values his life and runs. Both good and bad die. Desdemona was pure but she died. Emilia was kilt for telling the truth and she died too. Othello had been a great general in the army but he was made jealous by Iago's lies about Desdemona. He then does away with himself with a hidden spear when he finds out the true value of knowing who your'e friends are. Iago who is the villain is still alive. Good isn't exactly rewarded at the end. *(165 words)*

Examiner's Comment

- Basic response that fails to take on the idea of values contributing to tragedy.
- Occasional references to violence and failure.
- Slight narrative details lack focus and relevance.
- Weak expression and some spelling errors ('voilent', 'Lodivoco', 'kilt', 'your'e').

Sample Paragraph 2

Iago's given up the laws of Venice society because he thinks he's been rejected by Venice because he missed promotion from the moor. He works hard to get his evil vengeance. He goes in for schemes and plots against Othello and Cassio. And he treats women very badly. Basically he's not acting properly in line with what's expected of a decent citizen. He exploits peoples weaknesses. Cassio couldnt hold his drink and Othello is an outsider whose easily made jealous. All this causes the tragedy. He convinces Othello to kill his 'foul' wife because she was 'false'. But when Othello learns she's true he kills himself. Iago's got what he wants by lies and secrecy – the very things he valued most. But Cassio still lives on and he's even promoted more by being made a governor. He'll actually be in charge of punishing Iago. So Iago hasn't fully succeeded in getting vengeance against Cassio. By not having the values of his native society in Venice, Iago causes a lot of trouble but only influences the story in part. *(180 words)*

Examiner's Comment

- Mid-grade response makes an attempt to address the question.
- Reasonably focused discussion on the impact of Iago's warped values.
- The point about the treatment of women deserves further development.
- More supportive reference and quotation would have improved the answer.
- Expression flawed by overuse of contractions (it's) and punctuation errors.

To you, lord governor,
Remains the censure of this hellish villain

Lodovico
Act 5 Scene 2, l.420–21

Sample Paragraph 3

Desdemona is strong-willed and chooses Othello. She has spurned family and society for her only 'sin', the 'loves' she bears her husband. Shakespeare presents us with the terrible truth that innocence is no match for corruption. Desdemona discards the Christian values of her society by dying on a lie, trying to remove any suspicion about her death from her husband. She places herself beyond redemption because of her passionate feelings for Othello. In contrast, Emilia embraces the attitudes of Venetian society. She puts her trust in its civilised principles of truth and justice when she heroically demands to speak on behalf of her maligned mistress, 'I will speak as liberal as the north'. She defies her husband, 'I will not charm my tongue'. Not only does she reveal her husband's guilt, she also teaches Othello about reality, 'she loved thee, cruel Moor'. True to the Christian belief of Venetian society she will go to heaven, 'bliss' because she dies speaking 'true'. Tragically, both women die. Yet Emilia is a heroine and Desdemona a victim because one accepted society's values and the other revolted against them. These values of justice and truth profoundly affected the play's outcome. *(195 words)*

Examiner's Comment

- Clearly illustrated arguments focusing on different sets of social attitudes and their significance in the drama.
- Supported development of nuanced points on Christian values, civilised standards – and their tragic effects.
- Impressive vocabulary ('beyond redemption', 'civilised principles', 'maligned mistress').
- A well-written top-grade standard.

Class/Homework Exercise

'Desdemona and Emilia are weak characters who fail to gain our sympathy.'

To what extent do you agree or disagree with the statement on Desdemona and Emilia as presented in Act 5 of *Othello*? Write a paragraph (about 150–200 words), giving reasons for your views and supporting your response with suitable reference to the text.

Prompt!

- Desdemona is a sympathetic figure, strong-willed, loving, dignified, idealistic, loyal, but she is also naive, passive and a pitiful victim.
- Emilia is worldly, dutiful, pragmatic and ultimately heroic, yet she is also cynical and submissive.
- The audience fluctuates in its sympathy for each character, at times understanding their motives and at other times condemning their actions.

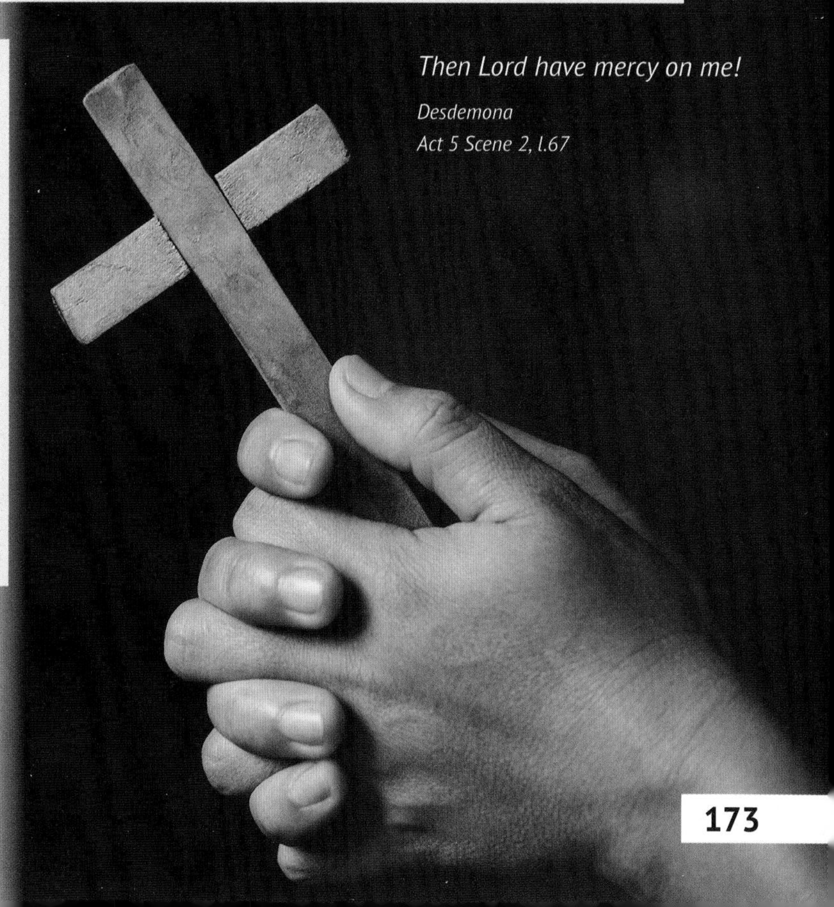

Then Lord have mercy on me!

Desdemona
Act 5 Scene 2, l.67

Revision Overview

Othello enters his wife's bedroom, where she is sleeping. He regards himself as a moral judge who has a duty to dispense justice. Desdemona awakes and he accuses her of being Cassio's lover. She pleads her innocence, but he refuses to listen and smothers her. Emilia discovers the dying Desdemona, who attempts to protect Othello by taking the blame for her own death. Othello finally discovers the tragic truth that he has misjudged his wife. He attacks Iago, who manages to escape after fatally stabbing Emilia. Othello speaks of the service he has done the state of Venice and then commits suicide. Although Iago is recaptured, he refuses to give any explanation for his actions. Cassio is made governor of Cyprus and Lodovico leaves for Venice.

- **Theme: Justice and injustice** – Othello mistakenly views himself as the agent of justice. Is his suicide a just price for his actions? Roderigo, the dupe of Iago, has died and his letters expose Iago. The innocent victims, Emilia and Desdemona, pay with their lives. By refusing to co-operate, Iago seeks to obstruct justice. Lodovico attempts to restore order in this turbulent island. Based on the events of the play, what is Shakespeare's view of justice?
- **Characters: Othello –** diminished, deluded, out-of-control murderer – gains insight too late, seeks to regain redemption by suicide.
  Desdemona – tragic, innocent, loving, loyal, dies excusing her husband.
  Emilia – loyal, shocked by her husband's duplicity, brave, sincere, admirable.
  Iago – devious, murderer – resilient, enigmatic.
  Cassio – generous – praises Othello's greatness of heart.
  Lodovico – restores order after tremendous turmoil and tragedy.

Exam Focus

Act 5 Scene 2 can be used successfully in response to a range of examination questions about the play's central themes, characters, relationships and the playwright's dramatic style.

This **key scene** has significant dramatic functions:

- Shakespearean tragedy concludes with the death of the protagonist, who has gained insight despite falling foul of a tragic character flaw – in Othello's case, jealousy.
- The setting in the couple's bedroom is significant. In their private space, public events occur. Their relationship has been under public scrutiny from the beginning.
- Despite one brief moment of recognising the truth, Desdemona dies loving the husband who killed her. Innocence does not necessarily survive in a corrupt world.
- Emilia redeems herself as her mistress's defender, courageously speaking out against both Othello and her own husband. Her goodness is unrewarded. She is fatally stabbed by Iago.
- Othello adopts the role of righteous avenger but behaves contemptibly. He tries to regain some of his former greatness, but his suicide raises questions. Is he the evil man Iago created?
- Act 5 Scene 2 also develops key themes of love/hatred, jealousy, heroism/dishonour, feminism/misogyny, justice/injustice.
- Uses religious imagery to focus attention on the fate of each character's soul.
- A new order is established, but at the cost of many lives. Is the audience satisfied or disturbed by Iago's vow of silence? What lessons about life is Shakespeare teaching us in this play?

Key Quotes

Yet she must die, else she'll betray more men *(Othello) l.6*	The resolute rhythm suggests that Othello believes he is absolutely justified in doing what he is about to do. He sees himself as an honourable avenger dispensing justice on a sinful woman. Corrupted by the poisonous lies of Iago, he is consumed by jealousy. The noble general is no more.
She's like a liar gone to burning hell, *'Twas I that killed her* *(Othello to Emilia) l.154–5*	Desdemona's dying defence of her husband sought to protect him by blaming herself for her own death. Othello continues to accuse her of wrongdoing even though he knows this. He focuses on her duplicity and the terrible punishment she will receive in the next world for her sin. His proud declaration that he killed her contradicts his previous denial, showing his confused state of mind.
Demand me nothing: what you know, you know: *From this time forth I never will speak word* *(Iago) l.349–50*	The last defiant lines of the enigmatic villain highlight the ambiguity of his character. He refuses to give anyone the satisfaction of a full explanation for his evil behaviour. Is he still attempting to manipulate and control? The final irony is that after spending so long deceiving others through persuasive speech, Iago now uses silence.
then must you speak *Of one that loved not wisely but too well* *(Othello) l.394–5*	Othello tries to justify himself after killing Desdemona. He is composed and appears to have recovered from the jealous passion that drove him to murder. Yet he gave his wife little opportunity to prove her innocence. Although the Moor was certainly fooled by Iago, can he really claim that he was not 'easily jealous'? Was it actually Desdemona who 'loved not wisely but too well'?
Look on the tragic loading of this bed. *This is thy work.* *(Lodovico to Iago) l.416–7*	Observing the lifeless bodies of Othello, Desdemona and Emilia laid out together, Lodovico reminds Iago and the audience of the sheer enormity of the tragedy. But what does Iago himself feel? Is he delighted or remorseful at the horrific consequences of his web of deceit?

Character Studies

Othello

First Impressions

- The play's protagonist is an unusual tragic hero. Othello seems to be **a combination of contradictions**. In the beginning, he is proud, patient and self-confident, but once he falls victim to Iago's influence, he behaves in a most inhuman manner. From the outset, there are significant tensions underlying Othello's twin roles as dutiful military commander and loving husband.
- Our initial impression of Othello's character comes from his enemies, Iago and Roderigo, who depict him in a completely hostile way. Throughout the opening scenes, their obvious hatred and prejudice suggest that because of his Moorish background, Othello is viewed as a black man in a white world, **a cultural and racial outsider**. Iago describes him as 'an old black ram' and the 'lascivious Moor', a vile figure who has used witchcraft to seduce the innocent Desdemona.
- When Othello first appears, however, this negative viewpoint is immediately challenged. Responding to Brabantio, his irate father-in-law, he is self-controlled and diplomatic: 'Good signior, you shall more command with years/ Than with your weapons'. Audiences are already likely to feel a certain amount of **sympathy for Othello** because of the discipline he displays in reaction to the offensive treatment he receives.
- We do not even hear the central character's actual name until well into Act I Scene 3 when the Duke of Venice acknowledges his military leadership. 'Valiant Othello' is clearly **a highly regarded and valued servant of the Venetian empire**. It's in the Duke's interest, of course, to show full support for the commander of the state's armed forces. Indeed, even Othello's enemies publicly pretend to respect him since he holds such a vital position as general.
- The fact that Othello is distinguished and widely admired could also account for the resentment some characters feel towards him. Iago's insightful comment that 'The Moor is of a free and open nature' can be seen as both a strength and a weakness. **Othello himself is understandably proud of his military reputation.** He is undoubtedly a fearless and experienced soldier. He is used to military life and the need to act quickly and decisively. In his role as army leader, he is indispensable to the defence of Venice. For this reason, he is sent to fight the Turks and protect Cyprus.

Before we are even introduced to Othello in person, his character is being mocked and ridiculed by Iago, who declares the Moor as 'loving his own pride and purposes'. When Othello does appear, however, his loyalty to the state of Venice is evident. Ironically, his lengthy military service has made him an outsider from Venetian society.

- But having spent so much of his life on the battlefield, the Moor is unfamiliar with Venetian culture and the norms of civil society. Although Othello claims that he is 'Rude' and inarticulate in his own use of language ('little blessed with the soft phrase of peace'), his seemingly rehearsed explanation for winning his 'fair lady's love' is polished and persuasive. Is this false modesty? Does it suggest that Othello is really trying to impress? We can only wonder about his egotism and whether it reflects an **underlying insecurity**.

I fetch my life and being
From men of royal siege

Othello
Act 1 Scene 2, l.23–24

- Audiences will also question **Othello's understanding of romantic love**. He says that Desdemona loved him 'for the dangers' he had experienced and that he, in turn, loved her because 'she did pity them'. Throughout the play's opening scenes, Shakespeare has created an aura of romance and mystery around the dark Moor, and Othello's poetic expression and thoughts strengthen this image.
- In a revealing reference to his own social background, Othello boasts: 'I fetch my life and being/ From men of royal siege'. His family is just as important as Brabantio's and he believes that he fully deserves to marry Desdemona. However, there is no denying Othello's status as a foreigner and hired army commander, his unfamiliarity with the refinements of Venetian life and his inexperience in love. Is he someone who needs appreciation and affirmation? **Will self-doubt prove to be his fatal flaw?**
- But although Othello first inspires confidence in his character, **the question of his elopement causes unease**. The circumstances surrounding his secret marriage to Desdemona are never explained, but it is Othello who is primarily blamed for the deception. Once again, the fact that the couple challenged social conventions raises doubts about both their characters.
- Questions have often been asked about Othello's love for Desdemona. Does he use her to flatter his own ego or is he simply infatuated with this beautiful Venetian woman? Yet he repeatedly expresses intense feelings. In response to **Brabantio's harsh warning** ('She has deceived her father, and may thee'), Othello confidently proclaims his absolute trust in his wife – 'My life upon her faith!' – as he leaves the care of Desdemona to 'Honest Iago'.

Othello's Character Development

> *'I'll see before I doubt'*
>
> ***(Act 3 Scene 3, l.212)***

- At the start of Act 2, Othello has triumphed over tremendous obstacles: cultural prejudice, Brabantio's hostility and the threat of the Turkish fleet. When he and Desdemona are reunited in Cyprus, Othello can barely express his happiness – 'it is too much of joy'. But less than two days later, the marriage is utterly destroyed and with it the lovers themselves. The fact that **Othello is unable to control his powerful emotions** is ominous. Some critics have argued that the hero's tragic downfall results primarily from his failure as a husband.
- From Act 3 Scene 3 onwards, Othello's suffering is intense. Over and over again he struggles with raging anger, confusion and jealousy. He is acutely aware of the precarious nature of success and contentment – particularly regarding his feelings for his wife. 'But I do love thee! And when I love thee not,/ Chaos is come again'. These are the words of **someone who fears uncertainty** and believes himself to have been rescued from it by true love.
- Yet he is soon tortured by fears about Desdemona, making him **vulnerable to manipulation** – particularly by his 'demi-devil' ensign. While audiences may view Othello as naive, it is important to remember that Iago is so plausible and cunning that he is able to deceive almost everyone else in the play.

The ferocity with which the Moor falls under Iago's control has long fascinated audiences. Questions remain about Othello's inherent savagery. Once he decides to punish Desdemona, a monster is unleashed. Was this aspect of his character always present?

- Although Othello is being transformed by jealousy, he tries to resist his suspicions: 'I'll see before I doubt'. After Desdemona's passionate speech on behalf of Cassio, Othello begins to suspect her underlying motives. He refers to her affectionately, 'Excellent wretch', but also admits, 'Perdition catch my soul, But I do love thee'. Othello is prepared to lose his eternal salvation just to love Desdemona, but then ironically **prophesies his own doom** if his love should fail, 'Chaos is come again'.

Pride is one of Othello's great weaknesses. His wife's alleged affair confirms his belief that he is a lesser man, that he cannot live up to her expectations and her position in society. Desdemona's apparent need for a more suitable Venetian husband is a critical blow to his social position, 'For nought, I did in hate, but all in honour'.

- Throughout the second half of the drama, **Othello's noble character is transformed for the worse** as he becomes more and more 'ensnar'd' by Iago. Why Othello should trust his ensign rather than his own wife has always intrigued audiences. That his enormous pride has been hurt is certain – 'Othello's occupation's gone!' Convinced that Desdemona has cheated on him, he now feels that he has lost his manly military identity.
- It is unclear why Iago's loyalty is trusted before Desdemona can prove her own. One possible explanation is the relative longevity of Iago and Othello's relationship. The thought of being betrayed by his young wife enrages Othello, sending him into a fit and persuading him to commit murder. He becomes almost incoherent, humiliating and striking Desdemona in public, either not knowing or **not caring what harm he is doing to his image**.
- While the Moor's cruel behaviour is crude and irrational, his obsession with trust and honour suggests that he is also **an idealistic character**. Central to Othello's downfall is an overwhelming desire for revenge, which brings together his crucial roles as soldier and husband. Tragically, his misplaced insistence on honour can be seen as both his redemption and downfall.

I know thou art full of love and honesty
Othello
Act 3 Scene 3, l.133

Overview

> *'Who can control his fate?'*
> ***(Act 5 Scene 2, l.309)***

- Othello remains an enigmatic figure who continues to divide opinion. We are left considering the extent to which he is a vulnerable victim or a pompous villain. He describes himself as an 'honourable murderer' who has acted out of love. His numerous **dying claims infuriate and fascinate** – particularly his self-assessment as 'one that loved not wisely, but too well'. Othello's assertion that he was 'not easily jealous' must leave many people asking if he ever really knew himself.
- However, it is possible to feel some sympathy for the Moor although we can never condone his actions. In his final moments, he appears to be almost entirely self-centred and **concerned with his reputation**. Is he essentially narcissistic and self-dramatising? It is characteristic that Othello judges himself before carrying out his own execution and dying alongside the woman he loved?

Whatever about his heroic qualities on the battlefield, Othello is a poor judge of character, particularly of the deceitful Iago. As a result, he falls from a position of power and authority to a debased shadow of his former self. By Act 5, he is hardly recognisable even to himself.

- Over the course of the story, Othello shows that he is not just capable of admirable restraint ('Keep up your bright swords, for the dew will rust them'), but also of great ferocity. He is prepared to chop Desdemona 'into messes'. In contrast to Iago, he has little inner life and is given no revealing soliloquies. Unlike his multi-layered arch-enemy, Othello's **character lacks complexity**.
- The Moor's death could be seen as an attempt to regain his distinguished military identity. Whether his suicide is an act of redemption or an effort to restore his good name is open to debate. Some critics view Othello's violent death as **a cowardly escape** from taking responsibility for his actions. For others, his decision to die 'no way but this' is an acceptance of his inevitable fate as a wretched hero.
- On the surface at least, Iago is the undeniable architect of Othello's downfall. Yet it could be argued that it is the tension between Othello's experience as an outsider adopting to a foreign culture and his own personal trauma that makes him a **truly tragic figure**. At any rate, the protagonist's story forces audiences to consider the nature of his character flaws as well as his difficulty in acknowledging his own destructiveness.
- Significantly, Othello's last words focus on his own failings, not on Iago's deceptive plot. **He does not deflect the blame** but maintains that he was blinded by his own passion. His final plea before taking his own life is for his memory to be preserved and his name to retain the quality of heroism he fought so hard to establish throughout his life.
- In the end, fate is cruel to Othello. But in his ultimate speeches, there are some glimpses of the protagonist's former greatness: his military achievements, loyalty to Venice, the intensity of his love and **his terrible realisation** that, by killing Desdemona, he has destroyed the best in himself.

Othello – Key Characteristics

- **Honourable, dignified, calm, accomplished, idealistic.**
- **Insecure, naive, jealous, paranoid, uncontrolled.**
- **Violent, self-obsessed, heroic, delusional, tragic.**

Iago

First Impressions

- Iago is one of the most notorious and compelling villains in all of literature. His capacity for cruelty seems limitless, and none of the reasons he gives for his actions seems enough to explain the incredible destruction he wreaks on the lives of those around him. At first, Iago is portrayed in **stark contrast to Othello**. The audience is presented with a false and unscrupulous character who promises the gullible Roderigo that he will help him win Desdemona's love. He even brings Roderigo into his confidence by admitting, 'I am not what I am'.
- Although Iago says, 'I will wear my heart upon my sleeve', he is inherently deceitful, plotting relentlessly against Othello, Cassio and Roderigo. His malicious nature is evident from the start of the play when he informs Brabantio of Desdemona's elopement with Othello. We also get the clear impression that he is so **spiteful and racist** that he is almost unable to contain the deep resentment and jealousy he feels towards Othello, 'I hate the Moor'.
- Iago's manipulation of others leads directly to the play's tragic climax, Desdemona's death and the downfall of many central characters. However, critics disagree about why he acts as he does. Some argue that **Iago doesn't have a motivation** and doesn't need one. Because he presents several different aspects of his personality to the other characters, audiences are often left wondering if they ever get to know the real Iago.
- As Othello's 'ancient' or 'ensign', Iago has worked his way through the ranks to become a junior army officer, a flag-bearer. His resentment towards Othello for choosing Michael Cassio as his lieutenant provides an obvious motive for his revenge. The entrenched hostility at being **overlooked for promotion** is apparent in his egotistical comment 'I know my price'. Another possible reason for Iago's hatred is his suspicion that his wife, Emilia, has cheated on him with both Othello and Cassio. It seems that Iago's unhappy life is filled with envy and jealousy, feelings that he will soon use to ruin others.

Iago's evil character is revealed in his soliloquies and in his dialogues with others. He manipulates his allies cunningly to fulfil his selfish and cruel intentions. As the play's arch-villain, he is not only secretive and hypocritical, but also ambitious and intelligent. He can be charming when he wishes, convincing others that he is an honourable man, 'honest Iago'.

- Iago dominates much of the play. The language he uses repeatedly demonstrates his vulgar, sinister nature. He is frequently **racist and misogynistic**. Iago delights in telling Desdemona's father: 'an old black ram/ Is tupping your white ewe', reducing the love between two human beings to the level of animals. Iago frequently expresses his misogyny, degrading women at every turn. He shows no regard for the feelings of female characters, seeing them as mere objects to fulfil male desires. His coarse language – which is mainly in prose as opposed to verse – is in keeping with his role as a plain-speaking soldier.
- Consumed by a warped sense of sexual jealousy and self-interest, the embittered ensign devises a plan to destroy Othello by making him believe that his wife is having an affair with Cassio. For Iago, the destruction of his enemy soon turns into **an obsessive game** in which the Machiavellian schemer delights in his skills at deception. 'Let us be conjunctive in our revenge against him,' he tells Roderigo. 'If thou canst cuckold him, thou dost thyself a pleasure, me a sport'.
- While it might well appear that Iago is entirely evil, Shakespeare adds depth to his character, at times portraying him as amoral (beyond any sense of right and wrong), unlike the typical immoral villain. Yet the fixated ensign always believes that his actions against the Moor are justified: 'nothing can or shall content my soul/

I am not what I am

Iago
Act 1 Scene 1, l.66

Till I am evened with him'. In his insatiable desire for vengeance, **he manages to fool everyone**, especially Othello who constantly refers to him as 'honest Iago'. He is also trusted by Desdemona and soon takes advantage of her basic good nature to 'enmesh them all' in his paranoid scheme of revenge.

Iago's Character Development

> *'Work on,*
> *My medicine, work!'*
>
> ***(Act 4 Scene 1, l.52–3)***

- As the story develops, Iago gains the confidence of all the main characters and manages to keep controlling them by taking advantage of their failings. He continues to delight in manipulating his enemies, in being **the one who is truly in command**. Iago is extremely astute and clearly enjoys ruining people's lives. Always pragmatic and plausible, he does it with a sense of craftsmanship, appreciating his own clever ingenuity and the thrill of the risks he takes.

The vengeful hatred Iago feels for Othello is powerful in its determination to wreck and ruin. He controls Roderigo as a pawn and exploits Cassio's every innocent move – single-mindedly motivated to cause chaos that will result in tragic consequences.

- **Ruthless versatility is another of Iago's most notable characteristics.** He constantly improvises in unexpected situations and adapts his language to suit whoever he is speaking to. He flatters Roderigo ('Why, now I see there's mettle in thee') simply to gain his trust. When Iago is with Desdemona, his words are tenderly supportive: 'do not weep. Alas the day!' With Othello, he resorts to giving graphic details about Desdemona's infidelity that reflect the jealous Moor's worst fears. Iago understands that Othello is compassionate and naive, 'of a free and open nature', and he takes full advantage of this at every opportunity.
- Cassio's weakness for drink makes him a very easy target. While appearing to offer seemingly practical advice, Iago exploits this character flaw to have the lieutenant demoted. As his influence increases, he displays a contempt for women, suggesting that they are all promiscuous. His attitude to Emilia typifies his **innate disrespect** for people in general. Knowing that she is desperate to please him, he uses her to steal Desdemona's handkerchief and then dismisses her as 'a foolish wife'.
- However, it is in Act 3 Scene 3 (often referred to as the 'jealousy' or 'temptation' scene) that we see the ensign in his true element. **His relationship with Othello is complex**, veering at times between hatred and love. Iago pretends to be an honest – but reluctant – witness. His apparently casual remarks are carefully rehearsed. 'Ha! I like not that' is a particularly subtle indication that he is genuinely concerned about Othello's marriage.

Most of Iago's success comes from his extraordinary resourcefulness in taking opportunities and turning circumstances to his advantage. He is also helped by luck (as when Emilia finds Desdemona's handkerchief) and by the way all the major characters play into his hands so easily.

- Having planted doubts about Desdemona in Othello's mind, the ensign becomes **more confident**, specifically reminding the Moor of how she has already deceived her father. As Othello increasingly falls under his control, Iago presents him with further 'evidence' of Cassio's dream and introduces the sensitive matter of the handkerchief. In convincing the Moor that he has made a dreadful mistake in trusting Desdemona, Iago has his greatest triumph. His pride is satisfied when he is appointed lieutenant, but his duplicity still knows no bounds.

- When Othello becomes so distraught by jealousy that he falls into a trance, Iago derives pleasure and excitement from seeing his enemy reduced to such a pitiful state. He is almost **overwhelmed at the triumph of all his poisonous deceptions** and he states: 'Work on,/ My medicine, work!' Now that the Moor has lost all control, he lies helplessly at Iago's feet. It is a moment of great victory for the vindictive ensign.
- Despite – or perhaps because of – his obvious villainy, Iago fascinates audiences, who are **always aware of the irony surrounding him**. He also appeals (both to the audience and other characters) because of his macho sense of humour, entertaining others with his crude stories, often joking about his own 'honesty' and denying brazenly that he is playing 'the villain'.

Overview

> *'what you know, you know'*
>
> ***(Act 5 Scene 2, l.349)***

- Iago plays a crucial role as the play's antagonist, and without him there would be almost no conflict. He cares for nobody, yet he devotes his whole life to revenge. Towards the end of the drama, he takes greater chances as **his scheming** grows more and more elaborate. Fearing that Roderigo is becoming unreliable, he plots to have him kill Cassio. Both men are equally expendable. So too is Emilia, who eventually exposes the shocking truth about her husband's crucial part in Desdemona's death.
- It would be out of character for Iago to show any remorse and **he remains unrepentant** to the end. There is no regret, no seeking of redemption, no gloating or jubilation. His concluding words ('what you know, you know') are enigmatic. We may have some knowledge, but we understand little. And so the tragic potential for evil continues, uncontained and uncontainable. Does Iago's final silence suggest that it isn't possible to ever fully understand his inhumanity?

> **Iago has always loathed Othello, manipulating him for selfish purposes, masking his hatred with superficial loyalty and pretence. Right up to the end, he refuses to give his enemy the satisfaction of knowing the truth. His vengeful behaviour has been described as 'motiveless malignancy', a self-propelling obsession based loosely on rumour that is out of proportion to his stated reasons for revenge.**

- As a result, Iago's true nature and motives continue to intrigue. It has often been suggested that he is simply the embodiment of evil. Even his numerous asides and soliloquies are never quite enough to fully reveal his complex multi-layered personality. Iago's refusal to explain himself to the Moor illustrates his **ultimate victory** and highlights Othello's tragic failure.
- Perhaps the merciless ensign has no explanation for what happened. Is Iago an evil genius? A self-absorbed psychotic? His final statement, 'From this time forth I never will speak word', presents audiences with **a powerful mystery**. As always, Shakespeare leaves us with more questions than answers about human behaviour.

> **Iago – Key Characteristics**
>
> - **Vengeful, sadistic, racist, misogynistic.**
> - **Manipulative, resourceful, insecure, paranoid, cynical.**
> - **Obsessive, malevolent, defiant, inscrutable.**

Desdemona

First Impressions

> *'A maiden never bold'*
>
> ***(Act 1 Scene 3, l.104)***

- Desdemona is Senator Brabantio's beautiful young daughter. Like so many others in the play, she is a **contradictory character**. Initially, she appears strong-willed and independent, but becomes increasingly submissive as the story develops. Desdemona refuses to choose any of the rich, handsome Venetian men that everyone expects her to marry. Instead, she elopes with Othello – an older black man and an outsider in Venetian society.
- When we first hear of Desdemona, she is at the centre of a major social scandal. Iago takes great delight in spreading sensational gossip about this wealthy upper-class socialite marrying outside her race. He suggests that she is a victim of Othello's lust. But while Desdemona's act of rebellion seems to reflect her **unconditional love for her husband** (something that is never in any doubt), it raises questions about her attitude to all those whom she deceives. She herself is fully aware that because of her marriage, she now has a 'divided duty' to her father and the Moor.

> **Ironically, Brabantio's view of his daughter is of a dutiful girl 'so still and quiet', but Desdemona's secret marriage initially challenges her father and his traditional values. It seems that neither of them understands each other as well as they think they do.**

- For his part, Brabantio thinks of his only daughter as a 'jewel'. She is his pride and joy, 'A maiden never bold'. This description of an innocent young girl is in sharp contrast to the confident Desdemona we meet in the Senate council scene. With dignity and quiet intelligence, **she asserts her independence as a newly married woman**. At no point does she excuse her elopement but focuses primarily on her deep romantic feelings and loyalty towards Othello.
- However, the exact nature of Desdemona's relationship with Othello is of crucial interest. For her, he is the hero of many exciting and dangerous adventures. In addition, Othello is an important figure in Venice, and his heroic past would presumably make him attractive to young aristocratic women. After hearing about Othello's experiences as a soldier, the Duke says, 'I think this tale would win my daughter too'. In light of the tragedy ahead, audiences will wonder about Desdemona's impetuous judgement in marrying the Moor. Is she blinded by infatuation? **Does she really know her husband?** Or has she fallen in love with an idealised image of Othello – perhaps because he was different from all the other men she knew?
- Yet although Desdemona was 'half the wooer', she fully accepts her husband's authority, 'my heart's subdued/ Even to the very quality of my lord'. She is keen to support him by leaving the familiar comforts of Venice for Cyprus, happy to play the role of his 'fair warrior'. Unfortunately for her, all her good qualities will soon work against her as **she becomes central to Iago's devious plans** to destroy his enemies. It does not take long for the disaffected ensign to exploit Desdemona's natural decency, and 'out of her own goodness make the net/ That shall enmesh them all'.

Desdemona's Character Development

> *'his unkindness may defeat my life'*
>
> ***(Act 4 Scene 2, l.183)***

- Like Othello, Desdemona **undergoes a dramatic transformation over the course of the play**. For the most part, she is portrayed as a chaste and virtuous young woman – although she seems happy enough to join in with Iago's crude conversation at the beginning of Act 2. As the story develops, however, Desdemona begins to display just how naive she is about human behaviour. Trusting everyone around her, she takes up Cassio's cause and does all she can to persuade her husband of his lieutenant's qualities: 'I'll intermingle every thing he does/ With Cassio's suit'. She genuinely believes that a reconciliation will benefit both men.

- However, Desdemona soon becomes **vulnerable to Othello's increasingly uncontrollable jealousy**. She is understandably shocked when he insults her publicly, striking her and calling her 'Devil!' Despite such abuse, Desdemona remains as dignified as she can ('I have not deserved this') before defending her husband's behaviour: 'we must think men are not gods'. She blames herself for Othello's anger, promising to be even more dutiful as a devoted wife who 'must not now displease him'. Ironically, Iago persuades Othello of his wife's apparent infidelity partly because she betrayed her father by marrying in secret.

It has been argued that Desdemona is yet another victim of a misogynistic society. In contrast to her early assertiveness, she becomes weaker as a character and retreats into childlike behaviour to escape reality. Her individual identity disappears as Othello's jealousy becomes more defined. Throughout her short life, she is essentially controlled by men.

- During yet another ironic exchange, Desdemona implores Iago to intervene on her behalf with Othello. She swears that she has never loved another man and that **she will always love her husband**, even if he rejects her. She admits that, 'Unkindness may do much; / And his unkindness may defeat my life, / But never taint my love'. The fact that Othello has humiliated Desdemona in public and in front of family members has reduced her to a state of near despair.
- Confused and demeaned by her husband's jealous accusations, Desdemona is helpless: 'I am a child to chiding'. Her **unworldly nature** seems strangely out of touch with reality, particularly when she discusses with Emilia the subject of what it means to be an unfaithful wife: 'I do not think there is any such woman'. Once again, audiences will wonder about the extent to which Desdemona is a victim of her own gullible nature.

Overview

- By the end of Act 4, Desdemona seems **resigned to her 'wretched fortune'** and is prepared for the worst. The haunting song she sings reflects her own misfortune and foreshadows her eventual fate. Not once does she blame Othello for her unhappiness; indeed, she forgives all his failings: 'even his stubbornness, his checks and frowns ... have grace and favour in them'. Throughout the play, Shakespeare has emphasised her essential Christian virtues by associating the 'divine Desdemona' with heaven and light.
- Desdemona has absolutely nothing to hide from her husband. She struggles to understand why he is so angry and can only state the simple truth that she is a 'true and loyal wife'. Her violent death – smothered by her husband on their marriage bed – could hardly be more ironic. She proclaims her innocence to the end, insisting that the only sins she has committed are 'loves I bear'. **She dies bravely**, asserting the right to defend her honour: 'I never did/ Offend you in my life'.
- As she faces a 'guiltless death', **Desdemona's final words are ambiguous and intriguing**. Responding to Emilia's desperate question 'who hath done this deed?', she replies, 'Nobody; I myself'. Is she simply protecting the man she loves? Does her passivity reflect her innate naivety and powerlessness? Or is she taking responsibility at last for her own part in her tragic downfall?
- It is obvious that Desdemona is the **victim of a patriarchal society**. In one way or another, she is abused by the men in her life. She is ridiculed

your true and loyal wife

Desdemona
Act 4 Scene 2, l.40

and hurt by Brabantio, cruelly used by Iago and finally misjudged and murdered by Othello. As one of Shakespeare's best-known heroines, Desdemona has been the subject of much critical attention. For some, she is a saintly goddess, often described as goodness personified.

Desdemona is an innocent character, frequently portrayed as a Christ-like symbol of goodness in contrast to Iago's demonic evil. Although she is betrayed by those she loves, her love is unqualified and does not die in death.

- Other critics argue that she is too good to be true and too trusting to ever be convincing. Yet the playwright has presented her devotion to her husband in a sympathetic way. In contrast to Othello, who alternately idolises and then demonises Desdemona, she herself **remains deferentially loyal and forgiving** to the end. Does this make her a stereotype of female passivity?
- At any rate, few would deny the **enduring sense of pathos associated with Desdemona's downfall**. She remains a highly compelling figure, whether we regard her well-meaning intentions as admirable or foolish. It is not surprising, therefore, that audiences continue to see Desdemona as the sacrificial victim of this tragic play.

Desdemona – Key Characteristics

- **Romantic, beautiful, virtuous, strong-willed.**
- **Naive, obedient, passive, innocent.**
- **Dignified, weak, loyal, tragic, selfless.**

The heavens forbid
But that our loves and
comforts should increase

Desdemona
Act 2 Scene 1, l.208–9

Cassio

First Impressions

- Like many of the other central characters in the play, Michael Cassio is introduced to us by Iago. It is a typically unflattering portrayal based entirely on envy and prejudice. From the spiteful ensign's viewpoint, Cassio is a shallow character and an outsider, a native of Florence. Iago repeatedly sneers at this privileged **ladies' man**, 'a great arithmetician', who has been appointed to the rank of lieutenant despite his inexperience in warfare.
- Iago views Cassio as a somewhat pampered, ineffectual character, comparing him to a 'spinster' and mocking his unimpressive military record as 'mere prattle, without practice'. How such a man has become the general's second-in-command is beyond Iago's understanding. However, when we first meet the lieutenant, **he seems chivalrous and sincere**. Othello considers him a close friend who was aware of his courtship of Desdemona. Cassio's loyalty towards the general is never in doubt and he expresses his concern for his safety as he awaits Othello's arrival in Cyprus: 'O! let the heavens/ Give him defence against the elements'.

Shakespeare presents Cassio as a dramatic contrast to Othello. Though both of them are soldiers, Cassio is a well-spoken and well-educated man. He sometimes displays a complacent self-regard and attention-grabbing charm.

- From the outset, it is clear that Cassio's easy manner and good looks make him very attractive to women: 'A fellow almost damned in a fair wife'. His **polished language** and gracious behaviour are certainly in keeping with Iago's description, 'A proper man'. The lieutenant is obviously eager to display his refinement and shows every courtesy to Desdemona, as well as greeting Emilia with a kiss. Keen to promote this cultured image to the world, Cassio frequently uses exaggerated language to flatter women, comparing the 'divine' Desdemona to a chaste goddess. Unfortunately, this will soon be used by Iago to convince Othello that Cassio is having a secret love affair with his wife.

Cassio's Character Development

> *'I have lost my reputation!'*
>
> ***(Act 2 Scene 3, l.264–5)***

- Cassio's high regard for Desdemona is genuine and he is always **extremely respectful** of her. He resists all Iago's attempts to discuss her relationship with Othello in crude terms. Naturally amiable and polite, he describes her as 'a most exquisite lady'. However, while Cassio has some distinctively attractive traits, there are obvious questions about his maturity and sense of responsibility.
- The young lieutenant freely admits to having personal failings – and a particularly low tolerance of alcohol: 'I have very poor and unhappy brains for drinking'. Yet he lacks the strength of character to change his behaviour. His response to getting drunk with Iago is decidedly half-hearted: 'I'll do it; but it dislikes me'. This is a failing that the devious ensign fully exploits. The fact that Cassio falls so easily into Iago's trap is likely to make audiences view him as a somewhat **ludicrous figure**.
- Following his drunken brawl with Roderigo and Montano, it is not surprising that Cassio loses his important position as Othello's officer. He is thoroughly ashamed of his uncontrolled behaviour and immediately asks for the general's forgiveness: 'I pray you, pardon me; I cannot speak'. He is very greatly **concerned about his public image**. Indeed, his recurring use of the word 'reputation' highlights just how important it is to him. Desperate to rectify his error of judgement, Cassio is quick to accept Iago's support to help him regain his military rank.

- **Reduced to self-pity** about his loss of military honour, Cassio also resorts to relying on Desdemona to take up his cause of reinstatement. His characteristic pride – a trait that he shares with most of the other men in the play – exposes additional personality flaws. Anxious to regain Othello's confidence, he admits that he is too self-conscious to confront the general again, directly: 'I am very ill at ease,/ Unfit for mine own purposes'.
- Some critics have argued that Casio's use of women is cowardly, revealing a petulant self-interest that is far from admirable. Rather than face the truth about his obvious indiscipline, he **feels increasingly sorry for himself**, maintaining that he is 'past all surgery'. He constantly exaggerates his feelings over his demotion: 'I have lost the immortal part of myself, and what remains is bestial'.

Cassio's a proper man
Iago
Act 1 Scene 3, l.412

Cassio's frantic pleading to be re-instated in Othello's favour, and the fact that he repeatedly asks Desdemona to mediate on his behalf, can come across to audiences as melodramatic and pathetic.

- However, it is the lieutenant's relationship with his lover that is most unsettling. When they are together in private, Cassio is his usual charming self. He calls her his 'most fair Bianca' and 'sweet love'. At other times, **Cassio treats Bianca with complete contempt**, dismissing her cruelly because he does not want to be found 'womaned'. Ironically, she is much more honest than he is.
- Cassio is quite happy to use the relatively lower-class Bianca when it suits him, but he will also mock his courtesan mistress behind her back when he 'cannot refrain/ From the excess of laughter'. Whether this makes Cassio a plausible hypocrite or just another selfish 'customer' is debatable, but it certainly suggests that he is much more **concerned with keeping up appearances** than treating people with genuine regard.
- Nearly all of Shakespeare's characters mirror one another in certain ways. Just as Othello categorises his own wife at different times, Cassio also tends to view women either as pious virgins or shameless whores. When the lieutenant talks about Desdemona, it's clear that **he sees her as a kind of goddess**. On the day she arrives in Cyprus, he uses reverential imagery to elevate her to a seemingly divine level: 'Ye men of Cyprus, let her have your knees'. By contrast, he demeans the vulnerable Bianca and doesn't even want to be seen in public with her.

Overview

'He hath a daily beauty in his life'

(Act 5 Scene 1, l.19)

- Notwithstanding his various faults, it is important to remember that Cassio is yet another unsuspecting **victim of Iago's villainy**. Like everyone else, he is unable to resist the ensign's persuasive scheming. As the object of Iago's reckless jealousy, Cassio is soon caught up in this tragic revenge story. Overall, he is an innocent bystander. Indeed, Iago simply despises the 'daily beauty' of Cassio's easy life and punishes him severely for his happy disposition and flirtatious behaviour.
- In the play's final violent scene, Cassio is wounded. He reveals important evidence against the 'heathenish' Iago, renews his friendship with Othello and pays generous tribute to the Moor: 'For he was great of heart'. He is appointed as the new governor of Cyprus to replace Othello, a final indication, perhaps, that his many **qualities outweigh his occasional failings**.

It is ironic that Iago's plans to destroy Cassio eventually lead to even greater promotion and status. As the story concludes, he becomes Cyprus's new leader and is given the task of deciding Iago's fate. Will Cassio be cruel or forgiving?

- In the end, audiences are left with a relatively **lightweight figure** who is primarily concerned with his own popularity and the idea of his shallow self-image as a respected gentleman. However, he remains an interesting dramatic foil to Othello throughout the play. Furthermore, in a tragedy where more complex characters – particularly Iago – are so flawed, it seems appropriate that Cassio is given final responsibility for 'the censure of this hellish villain'.

Cassio – Key Characteristics

- **Mannerly, suave, scholarly, well-intentioned.**
- **Weak-willed, self-centred, vain, thoughtless.**
- **Popular, decent, loyal, honourable.**

Emilia

- Emilia is married to Iago and serves as a personal maid to Desdemona. Older and more worldly than her mistress, she develops **a close relationship with Desdemona** during the course of the story. Despite their different social backgrounds, they have much in common, particularly their troubled marriages. While both women are eager to please their military husbands, Emilia is much more spirited. She responds to Iago's vulgar criticisms of Venetian women with the sarcastic comment, 'You shall not write my praise'.
- Shakespeare's characterisation of Emilia creates an interesting comparison with Desdemona. Her cynical views on married life with Iago contrast with Desdemona's more romantic idealism. Discussing the subject of married men, Emilia says, 'They ... eat us hungerly, and when they are full/ They belch us'. It is evident that she has an unsatisfactory relationship with Iago, who rarely shows her any genuine affection. **Yet she remains loyal to him until she discovers the true extent of his treachery.**

I have a thing for you

Emilia
Act 3 Scene 3, l.333

- Emilia **desperately desires some appreciation from her husband**, openly admitting, 'I nothing but to please his fantasy'. But she remains disappointed, even when she presents Iago with Desdemona's special handkerchief. He snatches it from her, saying 'Go, leave me'. Later on, it seems as though Emilia has been considering Iago's hunger for power and wishes she could gratify it – even if it meant cheating on him with another man. At one stage, she asks her mistress, 'who would not make her husband a cuckold to make him a monarch?'
- As Desdemona's attendant, her one dishonest act of stealing the handkerchief turns out to have devastating consequences. This is what ultimately convinces Othello that Desdemona is guilty of infidelity, and so Emilia's **seemingly harmless theft** contributes greatly to the play's tragic outcome.
- Throughout the second half of the drama, Emilia plays a more significant role by supporting the increasingly submissive Desdemona. She **repeatedly defends her mistress's honour**, vowing to lay down her own soul 'to wager she is honest'. Although she is deceived by Iago, Emilia comes close to understanding Othello's obsessive jealousy, and suspects that 'The Moor's abused by some most villainous knave'.
- In the end, she **eventually exposes her husband's evil** and verifies Desdemona's innocence: 'she was chaste; she loved thee, cruel Moor'. Emilia's condemnation of Othello ('such a fool') is likely to echo the views of most audiences. However, although her dying words appear to reflect her basic honesty ('So come my soul to bliss, as I speak true'), Emilia herself feels guilty that she was unaware of Iago's evil behaviour for so long: 'I think: I smell it: O villainy!/ I thought so then – I'll kill myself for grief'.
- There is no denying Emilia's sense of outrage when she finally confronts Othello and defies Iago. Whether or not she can be taken altogether seriously as a reliable judge of character is less certain. Yet she is essentially loyal to her mistress and sacrifices her own life

to clear Desdemona's good name. To a great extent, Emilia is a woman of her time who **tries hard to make the most of life in a man's world**. It is also an interesting irony that Iago – who is so good at controlling most people's behaviour – underestimates the one person he should have known best.

Emilia's final words confirm her own (and Desdemona's) essential honesty. However, it has been argued that she has suppressed her suspicions about Iago and that her decision to reveal the truth comes too late. Other critics refer to her horrified repeated question 'My husband?' in the concluding scene as evidence that she is guiltless.

Overview

- While Emilia is a comparatively minor character for much of the play, she provides a strong contrast to Desdemona. Unromantic and cynical – particularly about men and marriage – she is realistic enough to admit that women also have 'frailty, as men have'. **Shakespeare uses Emilia mainly for dramatic purposes.** She and Desdemona have a close relationship. They exchange ideas and confidences, all of which enhance the audience's engagement with their tragic story.
- Overall, Emilia is a lively, engaging character whose good-humoured nature adds vitality to the play. The image of women she presents **challenges the patriarchal society** of her times. However, while neither silence nor speech can save her, audiences generally have sympathy for this ordinary maidservant who eventually acts so heroically.

Let husbands know
Their wives have sense like them

Emilia
Act 4 Scene 3, l.99–100

Roderigo

- Throughout most of the play, Shakespeare presents Roderigo as **an extremely foolish character** with no saving graces. To a great extent, this rich Venetian nobleman is a figure of ridicule, an easy target for Iago's manipulation. From the outset, the ensign's merciless control of 'this poor trash of Venice' reveals much about both their characters. Roderigo is infatuated with Desdemona and Iago exploits these unrealistic feelings to the utmost.
- Even though he is sometimes aware that the quick-witted ensign is controlling him, Roderigo continues to look up to Iago and is seemingly incapable of thinking for himself. At the start of the play, his racist comments about Othello echo Iago's vulgar abuse. He has no hesitation in provoking Brabantio's anger, telling him that his daughter has been reduced to 'the gross clasps of a lascivious Moor'. At other times, Roderigo is simply overcome by Desdemona's 'most blessed condition' and displays more **gentlemanly qualities**.

Shakespeare uses Roderigo's character to underline the themes of manipulation, deception and thwarted love throughout the play. His weak personality is summed up by his pitiful reliance on Iago and his inability to make decisions for himself: 'What will I do, thinkest thou?'

- But he is essentially gullible and prone to self-delusion. Roderigo may have **little or no moral sense**, but he does have money – something that makes him particularly appealing to Iago, who boasts, 'Thus do I ever make my fool my purse'. Roderigo is also convinced that he can buy Desdemona's love – even after her marriage to Othello. The fact that she has no feelings whatsoever for him further emphasises his image as an impulsive fantasist. Indeed, if

What will I do, thinkest thou?

Roderigo
Act 1 Scene 3, l.325

Roderigo is typical of the 'curled darlings' who wished to marry Desdemona, it is understandable that she decided to elope with Othello.

- Characteristically, Iago takes full advantage of his rich friend's stupidity and uses him to attempt to destroy Michael Cassio. But while Roderigo is a very **willing accomplice**, he is not a particularly competent one. Although he admits to having 'no great devotion to the deed', he agrees to kill Cassio. The murder attempt is a complete fiasco, leaving Roderigo himself wounded by Cassio.
- Some critics maintain that Roderigo does not deserve such a violent fate. Unable to control his feelings and **lacking any real strength of character**, he stands no chance against the opportunistic ensign. Shortly before he is fatally stabbed in public, Roderigo eventually acknowledges his own wrongdoing: 'O, villain that I am!' and tries to expose Iago's true evil ('O inhuman dog!') with his dying breath.

Overview

- It could be argued that his ludicrous antics make Roderigo more a **comic caricature**, a one-dimensional love-sick failure, than a fully rounded character. He is so weak and inept that Iago sees him simply as a pathetic figure of fun, 'my sick fool'. Occasionally, Roderigo is even aware of his own overwhelming hopelessness, complaining at one point about being 'exceedingly well cudgelled'. Predictably, as soon as he has outlived his usefulness, Roderigo is literally stabbed in the back by Iago, who tries to blame everything on the hapless young nobleman.
- As much a villain as a victim, Roderigo's major dramatic function is to highlight the true character of his devious mentor, Iago. He also provides an interesting parallel to Othello. Both men are subject to irrational jealousy while being completely unaware of Iago's deception. However, despite Roderigo's **miserable life and unfortunate death**, it is hardly surprising that audiences tend to have little sympathy for him.

I do not find that thou dealest justly with me

Roderigo
Act 4 Scene 2, l.197

Brabantio

- Brabantio is largely defined by his twin roles as **respectable Venetian senator and dutiful father** to Desdemona. He is highly regarded by his fellow senators – and also by himself. The Duke admits to relying on his 'counsel' in moments of political crisis. His relationship with Desdemona is not quite as clear-cut, however, and her elopement with Othello raises questions about how well Brabantio and his daughter know each other.
- Unaware that he is being intentionally manipulated by Iago and Roderigo, the elderly senator is genuinely hurt by their graphic account of the secret marriage. He seems to blame himself for trusting Desdemona too much and the enduring sorrow over her marriage eventually contributes to his early death. Audiences are likely to have **some initial sympathy for Brabantio**, but this is short-lived.
- The senator appears to have been **slightly more liberal than most fathers** during Elizabethan times. We learn that he has already allowed Desdemona herself to reject various suitors from the 'wealthy curled darlings of our nation'. He has always thought of his only daughter as shy and nervous, 'A maiden never bold', and is shocked to learn that she has deceived him by marrying outside her race. For someone in his important position, her shameful behaviour is simply unacceptable, 'gross in sense'.
- Brabantio reacts emotionally to the scandal, accusing the 'foul thief' Othello of stealing his 'jewel'. He lapses into **self-pity** ('Who would be a father!') and selfish anger ('I had rather to adopt a child than get it'). While it is possible to have some understanding for his furious response as

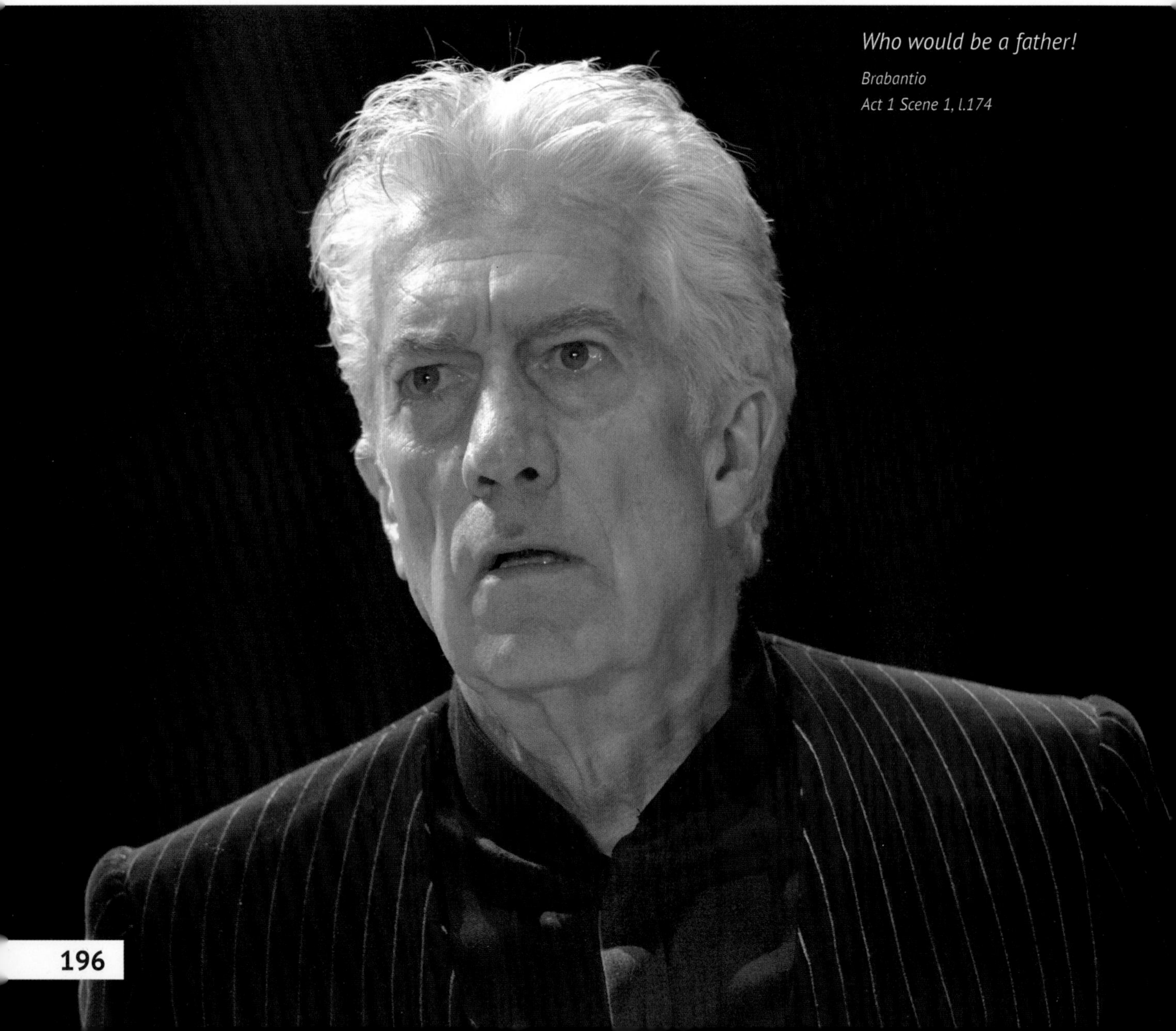

Who would be a father!

Brabantio
Act 1 Scene 1, l.174

the deceived father, Brabantio's racist insults about Othello ('such a thing') only highlight his hypocrisy.

- It's clear that he **represents the double standard** prevalent in Venetian society. According to Othello, Brabantio had been quite welcoming and friendly towards him before the elopement occurred. Brabantio admires Othello's bravery and is happy to socialise with the Moor. Yet he is appalled at the thought of having an unrefined black soldier as his son-in-law.

Brabantio's possessiveness and bigotry set the edgy tone for the play and reinforce key themes, such as jealousy and racism. His character is used to advance the story's tragic outcome.

- Brabantio's prejudiced views also lead to crude accusations of witchcraft ('foul charms') against the Moor. For the proud senator, inter-racial marriage is 'Against all rules of nature'. His **hysterical outburst** is in sharp contrast to Othello's controlled explanation of falling in love with Desdemona.
- To some extent, Brabantio fails to understand the realities of Venetian political affairs where he is of less use to the state than he imagines – particularly in times of war, when military leaders are more important. When Desdemona reveals that she has married freely and confirms that Othello is innocent of using magic spells to steal her away, he disowns her. Realising that his daughter is more faithful to Othello than to him, he **resorts to bitterness**: 'I am glad at soul I have no other child'.
- Yet although he misjudges Desdemona and treats her unkindly, Brabantio is **the first person to foreshadow the awful tragedy** that awaits the newlyweds: 'She has deceived her father, and may thee'. This ironic advice warns Othello to be wary of Desdemona, who might not be as honest as she appears. Brabantio advises the Moor to use his 'eyes to see', which is exactly how Othello judges people and situations.

Overview

- Twisted by Iago's lies and his own racist outlook, Brabantio's overprotective fatherly feelings are thrown into turmoil by Desdemona's marriage. It can be argued that he is both a victim of unfortunate circumstances and **the product of narrow-minded cultural attitudes**. Like so many others in the play, Brabantio is blinded by appearances, failing to recognise his daughter's true nature and unable to accept Othello as an equal.

I am glad at soul I have no other child

Brabantio

Act 1 Scene 3, l.210

Bianca

- Like Desdemona and Emilia, Bianca is abused by the male characters in the play. She is largely defined by her profession as a courtesan – although this is never explicitly stated. Critics disagree about whether or not she is a prostitute, but Cassio describes himself as her 'customer'. **Bianca's love for Cassio is evident from the start** and she always behaves affectionately towards him. Unfortunately, he does not take her very seriously and she fares badly as his mistress.
- Bianca is generally seen as a promiscuous and dishonest woman. All through the play, Shakespeare uses Bianca as **a foil to the chaste Desdemona**. In his vengeful jealousy, Othello mirrors Iago's misogyny, eventually seeing no difference between the two women.
- Bianca also shares many **similarities with Othello**. They are both outsiders who are paid for their services. The two of them become extremely jealous about their respective lovers – mainly because of the misunderstanding over Desdemona's handkerchief. But Bianca reacts more realistically and invites Cassio to explain himself: 'you'll come to supper to-night'.

I must be circumstanced

Bianca
Act 3 Scene 4, l.221

- Bianca's attitude to her selfish lover ('I must be circumstanced') reveals a reluctant acknowledgment that **she does not have equal power in the relationship**. However, she has little choice but to endure Cassio's dismissive treatment. This acceptance of his authority over her foreshadows Desdemona's words and actions in Act 4 Scene 2.

Bianca plays a crucial role in the tragic plot even though she appears in only three scenes. When Othello sees her with the handkerchief, he takes it as proof that Cassio and Desdemona are lovers. It is a pivotal moment in the story.

Overview

- There is never any question about the extent of Bianca's regard for Cassio. When he is attacked in Act 5 Scene 1, she rushes to help him, even though Iago accuses her of being involved in the assault to divert suspicion from himself. Despite this, **she shows true spirit**, defending herself against his accusations of treachery: 'I am no strumpet; but of life as honest/ As you that thus abuse me'.
- Her **genuine love for Cassio** allows her to affirm that, regardless of her reputation, she is a woman of some honour. Ironically, such strength of character contrasts with all the hypocrisy around her. It also highlights Cassio's shallowness and casts further doubt on his credibility.
- Despite her low status and vulnerability, Bianca is the only female character to survive. She is primarily defined by her relationships with men and must work hard to maintain whatever rights she can establish as Cassio's mistress. Her sincere feelings for her lover and her efforts to live in a predominately patriarchal society usually make her **a sympathetic figure** for modern audiences.

Key Themes in *Othello*

Introduction

Themes are **issues or ideas that are central to the drama**. Shakespeare explores a range of fascinating subjects in *Othello*, including jealousy, revenge, race, identity, gender and deception. All these themes – and many others – are closely interlinked. When studying the playwright's presentation of key themes, the prevailing culture of Elizabethan times should also be considered. Key themes are all closely associated with the main characters and are reflected in the play's language and imagery.

Leaving Certificate exam questions usually include **several elements**. It is unlikely that candidates will be asked to write about a single theme on its own. Instead, questions tend to focus on multiple themes or linking themes to characters and what they represent, for example:

> 'Over the course of the play, various forms of deception are responsible for Othello's tragic downfall.' To what extent do you agree with this view? Develop your answer with reference to the play *Othello*.

Another typical question might address aspects of the playwright's style, such as:

> 'In the play *Othello*, Shakespeare makes effective use of a variety of dramatic devices to explore the tragic consequences of secrets and lies.' Discuss this statement, developing your answer with reference to the play.

It is essential, therefore, to **study the wording of questions closely** and to identify the key aspects that are to be tackled. When planning and writing the 60-minute essay, follow the Exam Technique guidelines on page 214.

Always use your **critical thinking skills** and respond to the question by organising relevant discussion points supported by suitable reference or quotation from the play.

Remember!

Leaving Cert questions test your understanding of texts. Answers should demonstrate your ability to analyse rather than merely summarise the story. Avoid unfocused narrative.

Ay, let her rot, and perish, and be damned to-night

Othello
Act 4 Scene 1, l.195

Jealousy

Shakespeare presents jealousy as a powerful and devastatingly negative emotion. Several of the main characters in *Othello* experience jealousy, although none of them has any real cause. Nevertheless, **jealousy and envy are destructive elements throughout this tragic story**. Both Iago and Othello are filled with feelings of bitter resentment that they cannot control. Even minor characters, such as Roderigo and Bianca, are also affected adversely by longing and suspicion. However, audiences are most likely to remember this great tragedy for the central character's descent into an obsessive jealousy that overpowers his potential for greatness.

Iago's indignant attitude towards Cassio (who has been chosen as Othello's lieutenant) clearly shows that his ego has been undermined, which encourages him to take revenge. Iago is convinced that he himself deserved promotion and reveals his **deep sense of envious outrage**: 'I know my price, I am worth no worse a place'. He is furious that careers in the Venetian army appear to be based on favouritism and complains that 'Preferment goes by letter and affection'. As Othello's 'ancient', the relatively low-ranking ensign is determined to regain what he considers his rightful military rank by plotting against Cassio.

Iago's spiteful hatred for the young lieutenant is not only professional; he also despises Cassio's 'daily beauty' and engaging charm. In addition, the aggrieved flag-bearer is suspicious that his wife Emilia and Cassio might possibly be lovers. This deep-rooted **sexual jealousy** – which is directly linked to feelings of masculine insecurity – provides the idea for Iago's eventual plan to destroy Othello.

Ironically, the Moor's neurotic jealousy appears to be as extreme as his initial devotion to Desdemona. In Act 3 Scene 3 (the play's crucial turning point), Othello admits his anxieties about his age and racial background. Prompted by Iago, he soon loses his capacity for rational behaviour and is prepared to accept the handkerchief as proof of Desdemona's infidelity. Caught between frustrated anger and self-pitying shame, the military side of his personality takes over and he sees his young wife as the enemy he must destroy. Like Iago, he feels that he has lost something that is extremely important to him. The resulting **jealousy transforms both men into ruthless killers**.

Othello's increasingly vulgar language reflects his loss of judgement. Abrupt outbursts – 'I'll tear her all to pieces' – illustrate his desperation. Iago has always associated jealousy with poison ('pestilence') and observes that the Moor is 'eaten up with passion'. He even pretends to warn Othello of 'the green-eyed monster which doth mock/ The meat it feeds on'. His wife, Emilia, also describes jealousy as a 'monster/Begot upon itself'.

O, beware, my lord, of jealousy;
It is the green-eyed monster which doth mock
The meat it feeds on
Iago
Act 3 Scene 3, l.186–8

Shakespeare uses such disturbing imagery to suggest the horrendous effects of envy and jealousy. In his half-deranged state, Othello becomes preoccupied with blood revenge: 'Arise, black vengeance, from thy hollow cell!' The playwright develops and emphasises the central **metaphor of jealousy as a monster that devours itself**. In a sense, Iago personifies this consuming force, delighting in mocking his unfortunate victims.

Critics disagree about Othello's final assessment of himself as 'one not easily jealous'. It can be argued that the Moor's sexual **jealousy emerges from excessive affection** and that he truly was a man who 'loved not wisely but too well'. At the end of the play, he claims that Iago created such extraordinary circumstances that it was impossible to avoid becoming jealous. This view is supported by the fact that Othello initially defended his wife's honour, trusting Desdemona who 'had eyes, and chose me'. He also insisted on 'ocular proof' of her guilt.

Of course, the Moor's defence that he was 'Perplexed in the extreme' can also be challenged. Iago's allegations about Desdemona – including his report about Cassio's apparent dream – are not particularly credible. That such insubstantial evidence could convince a loving husband of his wife's betrayal highlights just how compulsive and **irrational jealousy** can be. It is rooted in fear and anger, causing desperate individuals to act foolishly. Unlike Bianca, who allowed her lover Cassio to explain how he found Desdemona's handkerchief, Othello chose to **presume that his wife was unfaithful** without giving her a fair opportunity to defend herself.

Iago's vengeful behaviour is both personal and professional. His intense envy of Cassio and

And on the proof ... Away at once with love or jealousy!

Othello
Act 3 Scene 3, l.213–4

Othello propels the narrative to its catastrophic conclusion.

What is clear to audiences is that **jealousy corrupted love and honour**, causing the Moor's self-inflicted downfall. Along the way, other characters are also innocent victims of this wildly destructive force, which is repeatedly and aptly described as a 'monster'. In *Othello*, Shakespeare has presented us with a terrifyingly evil emotion that is central to this unhappy story.

Overview: jealousy in *Othello*

- Seen as corrupting and damaging throughout.
- Motivates the central characters' actions.
- Reveals major flaws in Iago and Othello.
- Contrasts with Desdemona's generous qualities.
- Provides compelling moments of dramatic irony.
- Intensifies the theatrical experience for audiences.

Gender

Shakespeare's audience would have sympathised with Brabantio's outraged reaction to Desdemona's elopement and secret marriage. Elizabethan **society was largely patriarchal** and the play reflects the gender discrimination that was common at the time; men were generally considered to be superior to women. Daughters depended on their fathers, who had responsibility for finding them appropriate husbands. Brabantio expects complete 'obedience' and Desdemona acknowledges that she has a 'divided duty' to both her father and Othello. Tensions resulting from gender, sexuality and male–female relationships are crucial to much of the conflict throughout this tragic drama.

The 'masculine world' of *Othello* is dominated by men of action who put great emphasis on military honour. It is Othello's daring heroism that first attracts Desdemona. The 'warlike Moor' defines himself by his 'dearest action' and views his wife's infidelity as a failure of his masculinity. Iago boasts of being a seasoned soldier – unlike the inexperienced Cassio, whom he describes as a 'spinster'. But the young lieutenant also becomes obsessed with his professional status and is devastated after losing his position as Othello's second-in-command. When the male characters find that their pride and ego are being undermined, their **usual reaction is to resort to violence**.

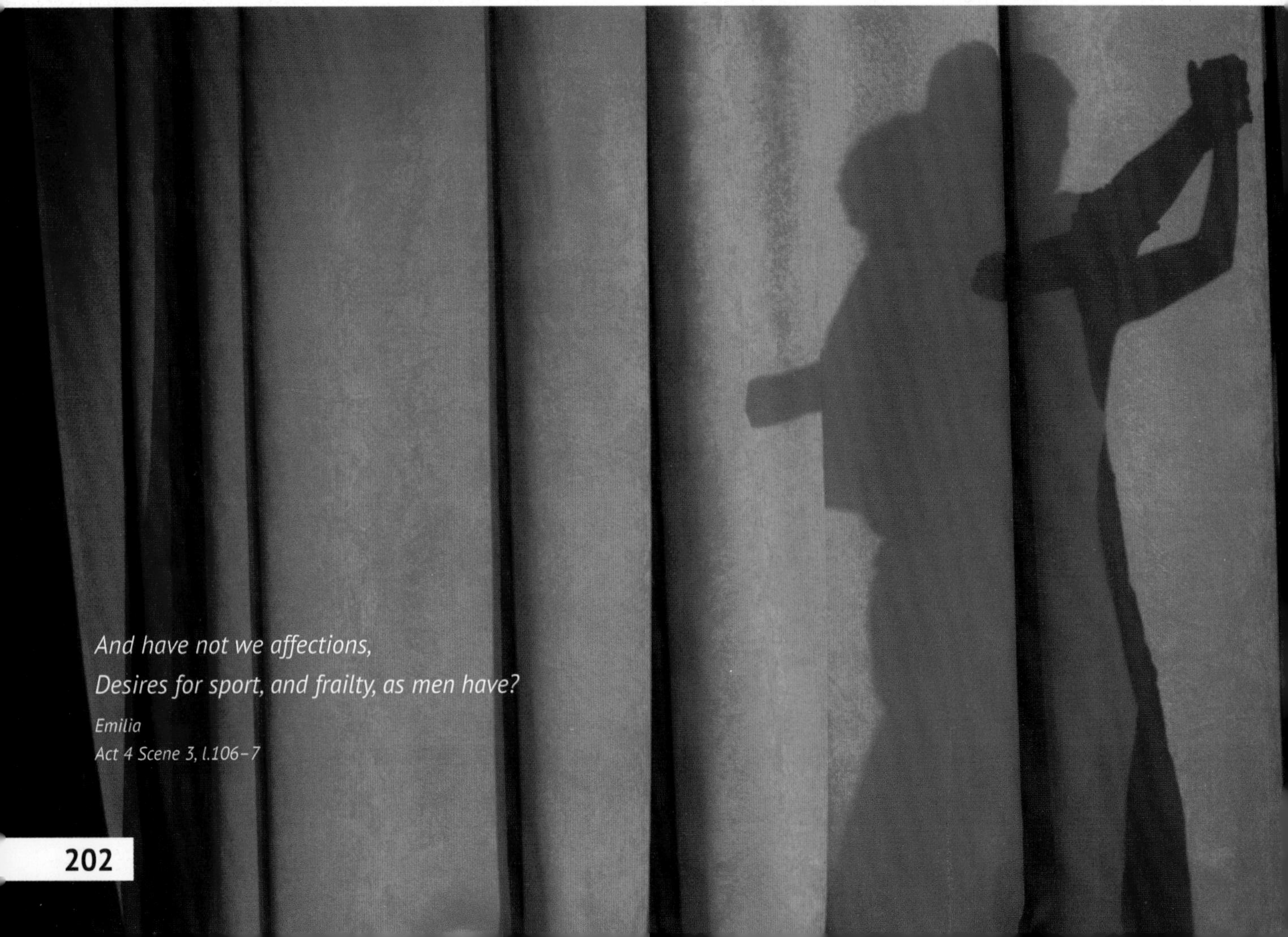

And have not we affections,
Desires for sport, and frailty, as men have?

Emilia
Act 4 Scene 3, l.106–7

At the start of the play, **Desdemona confronts patriarchal attitudes** by asserting her independence. She chooses her own husband and defies her father by marrying someone from outside her own race. She is also rebellious in her desire to accompany Othello to Cyprus. The reaction to her unconventional behaviour clearly highlights how men constantly try to control women. Brabantio speaks of losing his 'jewel'. Iago refers to Desdemona as if she were one of her father's possessions, similar to his 'house' and 'bags'. In his jealous rages, Othello continually reasserts his authority over his wife – both physically and verbally: 'we can call these delicate creatures ours,/ And not their appetites!'

During the 16th century, Venice was known not only for its wealth and sophistication, but also for its casual morals. There were many courtesans in the city and Venetian women were often seen as immoral, something that Iago uses effectively to suggest that Desdemona is unfaithful. Only half-jokingly does he accuse all women of being prostitutes who 'go to bed to work'. It's evident that **Iago resents Desdemona** (the general's 'general') since she is beginning to have more influence than him over Othello.

Iago's apparent misogyny typifies his warped personality and his contemptuous view of human relations. Overall, Shakespeare does not present female sexuality in a negative light. Bianca expresses genuine feelings for Cassio and is determined to resist their divisive social backgrounds. Initially, Othello loves Desdemona very dearly. However, his outward devotion to his 'soul's joy' is a reminder that women were generally regarded as **either innocent and virtuous or shameless and promiscuous**.

As a courtesan, Bianca is presumed to be untrustworthy and opportunistic, but she challenges these assumptions by being much more honourable than her lover Cassio, who treats her with little respect, seeing her as a mere 'bauble'. **Emilia also struggles to gain any happiness from her loveless marriage.** In questioning the hypocrisy about marital infidelity, she is certain that the blame lies with men who 'change us for others'.

Emilia's cynical outlook is understandable, considering the years she has spent being controlled by Iago. Her disastrous decision to steal Desdemona's handkerchief results from fear of displeasing him, even though this clashes with her loyalty to her mistress. Like the other female characters who try to assert themselves, Emilia is viewed as a troublemaker, simply because she **dares to defy the balance of power** in a predominantly masculine hierarchy. A good example of this occurs in Act 5 Scene 2, when she says, 'I will not charm my tongue; I am bound to speak'.

To a great extent, the playwright presents **traditional stereotypes** about gender. Ironically, while Othello and Iago see themselves as powerful men, they are subject to petty insecurities that largely explain their severely dysfunctional relationships. Indeed, the play's two marriages are marked by male envy and cruelty (both wives are murdered by their own husbands). In the end, cultural values ensure the victimisation of women in a male-dominated society.

Othello clearly highlights the destructive effects of patriarchy during Elizabethan times. However, Shakespeare leaves modern audiences with **much to consider about gender and sexuality** in the play. Some critics continue to view Desdemona as weak-willed and passive, while others admire her independent spirit. In the end, we are left to consider a fascinating world where public honour

she shall not live: no, my heart is turned to stone
Othello
Act 4 Scene 1, l.196

is very highly rated, and to make up our own minds about the many issues explored through same-sex and male–female relationships.

If virtue no delighted beauty lack,
Your son-in-law is far more fair than black
Duke of Venice
Act 1 Scene 3, l.310–11

Overview: gender in *Othello*

- Leads to male–female power struggles.
- Women's sexuality seen as a huge threat to men.
- Reveals major flaws in Iago and Othello.
- Contrasts male and female characters' qualities.
- Propels the plot to its tragic conclusion.
- Gender conflicts intensify the theatrical experience.

Race and Identity

Since the earliest stage productions of *Othello*, critics have disagreed about Shakespeare's presentation of the protagonist. Although Othello's actual race is never precisely defined, there is broad consensus that the playwright introduced a black hero to address the idea of difference and to explore the experience of **the outsider** in a white patriarchal society.

Othello's Moorish identity places him in a precarious position. Iago and Cassio also struggle with their own personal sense of identity, and this motivates their decisions throughout the play. However, most of the focus is on Othello, whose high-ranking military status makes him part of Venetian society while his racial background gives him a confused sense of identity.

Othello's ethnicity is **a cause of underlying tension** throughout the story. The term 'Moor' generally refers to people of North African origin, but is sometimes thought to include those of all Arab civilisations. Othello's race is the source of one of the play's dominant metaphors. For Othello's enemies, black is often associated with wickedness or dishonesty.

This negative view of black people prevalent in Shakespeare's time is particularly evident in the opening scene when Iago expresses overtly racist opposition to Desdemona's elopement with Othello. The flag-bearer's first soliloquy clearly shows that **his true identity is self-serving and vengeful**. Nevertheless, we are never in doubt that it's not just Iago the newlyweds are up against, but the prejudiced status quo that Iago merely embodies in its most offensive form.

Inter-racial marriage is said to be 'Against all rules of nature'. Bestial images of the 'lascivious' Moor as 'a Barbary horse' and 'an old black ram' depict Othello as a savage creature. Brabantio refers to his son-in-law as a 'thing', and there are recurring references to evil and witchcraft. To Iago, Roderigo and Brabantio, the Moor's **colour offers a basis for expressing their personal hatred**. Ironically, such intolerance is likely to make audiences feel greater sympathy for Othello.

In his earliest comments, **Othello uses his race positively**. Indeed, he seems proud – almost boastful at times – about his exotic origins: 'I fetch my life and being/ From men of royal siege'. His eloquent speech to the senators stresses the fact that his unique Moorish history attracted Desdemona, who acted freely in selecting a husband for herself: 'she had eyes, and chose me'.

Desdemona defends her husband at every opportunity, saying, 'I saw Othello's visage in his mind'. Her attitude is exceptional, of course, and reflects her unconditional – and possibly naive – feelings of love. Almost every other character in the play sees Othello's race as problematic.

On some occasions, the protagonist's colour is less of an issue, especially when Venice itself is under threat. The Moor seems be held in high esteem as a 'valiant' army general, recognised by the Duke as 'more fair than black'. Whether this is a genuine compliment or mere flattery designed to encourage Othello's military efforts is uncertain. It is yet another reminder that in Elizabethan times, fairness and whiteness were associated with goodness.

Othello's sense of self is shaped by others throughout the story. He displays some of the negative racial characteristics of which he was first accused, including his superstitious beliefs about Desdemona's handkerchief and his increasingly frenzied outbursts. Iago's persuasive expertise certainly infects Othello's view of himself towards the end of Act 3 Scene 3, where he seems horrified to think of Desdemona's name as 'begrimed and black/ As mine own face'. He soon turns to 'savage madness', for instance when he strikes his distressed wife in public.

Negative references to the protagonist's race are a recurring feature of the play. It is interesting that moments before the murder, Othello focuses on his sleeping wife's colour, seemingly obsessed with the 'monumental alabaster' of her skin, and once again challenging his own preconception of whiteness representing virtue. It is not surprising that some critics define Othello's downfall in terms of his essentially unsustainable position as a black mercenary who is hopelessly ill at ease in an unsympathetic white Christian culture.

Nevertheless, Othello's successful army career means that he is confident in his role as a soldier. He is uncomfortable, however, with his identity as a husband. By Act 5, he is barely recognisable, yet he still **clings to the noble image** he tried so hard to establish. Faced with the tragic reality of his personal choices, his final words suggest the sense of disconnect he feels between the man he imagined himself to be and the deeply flawed character he eventually became.

Ultimately, audiences are likely to view the tragic drama in relation to Othello's exclusion from Venice. Whether or not he ever fully knows himself or understands the part played by race in his demise remains doubtful. It is yet another irony that his **honour and heroism are confined mainly to the battlefield**. As a husband, his actions become barbarous. Yet many critics continue to argue that – regardless of race – Othello is simply an unfortunate human being who found himself caught in a complex web of deceit.

Overview: race and identity in *Othello*

- Racist attitudes in the play reflect the culture of Elizabethan times.
- Overlaps with other key issues, such as gender and social class.
- Race is just one aspect of Othello's multi-layered identity.
- Creates much of the play's most compelling drama.
- Propels the tragic narrative to its horrific conclusion.

How shall I murder him, Iago?

Othello
Act 4 Scene 1, l.184

Dramatic Techniques in *Othello*

Irony

As in many of Shakespeare's plays, Othello contains **a great deal of irony** – most of it centred on Iago's lies and deception. All of the many characters who are betrayed and destroyed by him trust him implicitly. While the Moor refers repeatedly to 'honest Iago', the audience is acutely aware of the vengeful ensign's villainy. It is only at the end of the play that Othello realises the awful truth.

Irony involves collusion between the playwright and the audience. We know more than the characters onstage. **Dramatic irony creates suspense and involves the audience**, often by creating reactions of sympathy, anger or disbelief. Iago communicates directly with the audience through his many soliloquies, 'I hate the Moor'. The ensign's true intentions are never disclosed to other characters. It is only through his short asides and hate-filled soliloquies that he reveals himself as an embittered man who is completely devoid of a conscience.

From the play's opening scene, we realise that Iago is corrupt and Desdemona is innocent – and that Othello knows neither of these facts. Indeed, he describes Iago as a man 'of honest and trust' and his own wife as a 'strumpet'. This is a **powerful irony**. As an outsider in Venice, Othello suffers from a lack of self-confidence connected to his background and social position. In contrast, Iago is a perfect model of a civilised man who appears to be very good at hiding his warped nature.

As the tragic story unfolds, **dramatic irony adds to the audience's engagement**. During Act 4 Scene 1, for example, where Othello is tricked into watching Iago and Cassio talking about Bianca, we have already been informed of the likely outcome. Iago has signalled earlier what will happen when the suspicious Moor observes the lieutenant apparently boasting about his success with women, 'As he shall smile, Othello shall go mad'.

So when Cassio makes fun of his mistress, we understand that Othello thinks that it is his young wife who is being discussed. Characteristically, Iago spins his web of lies around Desdemona, turning her innocence into a fatal weakness. By presenting a multi-faceted view of events like this, Shakespeare heightens tension and **enhances the audience's experience** of the tragic story.

Iago has many selves. He can be friend and adviser, but also betrayer and murderer. Roderigo believes that Iago is his true friend ('Thou art sure of me') when he hands over a fortune in jewels to pass on to Desdemona in his desperate efforts to win her love. Yet the ensign contemptuously regards Roderigo as a 'fool' whom he has made his 'purse'. Iago is the perfect actor. He is only honest with the audience; the rest of the time, he is 'seeming so'.

On numerous occasions, the ruthless ensign **masterminds situations ingeniously**, such as when he instructs Roderigo, 'Here, stand behind this bulk: straight will he come'. Then when the scuffle breaks out between Roderigo and Cassio, he emerges as if only discovering the fracas, asking, 'Whose noise is

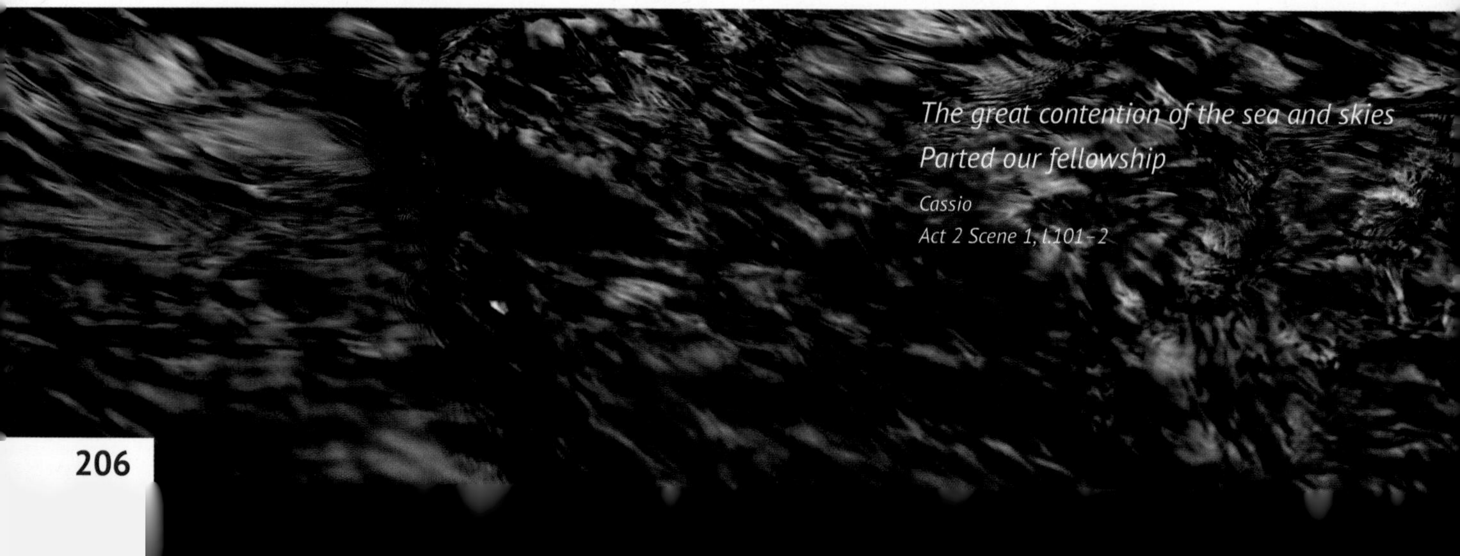
The great contention of the sea and skies
Parted our fellowship
Cassio
Act 2 Scene 1, l.101–2

this that cries murder?' Iago cares nothing about who is killed; it would actually suit him best if both men lost their lives as it would ensure that he would not be blamed for their deaths.

Perhaps the **greatest irony** of the play is that Othello eventually learns the truth that Desdemona is blameless, 'Cold, cold, my girl; Ever like thy chastity', but only after murdering her. He cannot comprehend why Iago had manipulated him into believing otherwise, 'Why he hath thus ensnared my soul and body?'

But the audience has known all along of Iago's seething resentment at being passed over for promotion and his suspicion that the Moor has been Emilia's lover. We know the real Iago ('I am not what I am') who chillingly declared to Roderigo, 'In following him, I follow but myself … for my peculiar end'. Right to the end, we feel **intimately connected with Iago's villainy**.

Both situational and verbal irony are also used to propel the action forward and to intensify the drama. **Situational irony** is when the result of an action is different from what was expected. An obvious example occurs when Cassio not only survives the best efforts of his rival Iago to have him murdered, but is also reinstated as lieutenant. Ironically, it is Iago's reputation that is destroyed. Equally ironic is the scene in which Desdemona kneels before a secretly delighted Iago and pitifully asks for help from the man who is poisoning her husband's mind against her, 'What shall I do to win my lord again?'

Another case of situational irony is that both wives, **Desdemona and Emilia, are murdered even though both are guiltless**. In tragedy, events often turn out to have the opposite result from what was originally intended. Desdemona is killed by her husband on their marital bed. For the audience, this accentuates the atmosphere of misfortune as reality seems to conspire against the innocent characters.

Verbal irony is when the opposite of what is spoken turns out to be true. Othello has absolute trust in Iago. He refers many times to Iago's qualities. He calls him 'brave Iago, honest and just'; he even considers him 'wise'. The Moor asks him for advice regarding his suspicions about Desdemona, fearing that Iago is so good that he won't want to tell him the horrible truth, that he is 'full of love and honesty'.

Yet the audience is in no doubt that Iago is inflaming Othello's concerns and systematically dismantling his relationship with Desdemona for his own diabolical ends. **Iago's duplicity constantly creates verbal irony.** He lies brazenly to the Moor, 'My lord, you know I love you'. He also issues a bogus warning to Othello – something that turns out to be tragically true – 'O, beware, my lord, of

What shall I do to win my lord again?

Desdemona
Act 4 Scene 2, l.172

jealousy'. This fatal comment relies heavily on irony as a means of helping the audience to grasp all its hidden nuances.

Irony plays an important part in *Othello*. For example, the Moor is initially a good man who commits a terrible crime. Meanwhile, the evil Iago masquerades as an honourable man throughout. Irony is a powerful technique that takes advantage of the difference between what is said and what is meant, or what is supposed to happen and what actually happens. It **increases the audience's involvement** in the play and heightens the sense of inevitable tragedy.

Soliloquies

The **soliloquy** originated in Greek tragedy as a speech delivered by a single character onstage. The term comes from two Latin words, *solo* ('to oneself') and *loquor* ('I talk'). The character who is alone onstage appears to be thinking aloud. Shakespeare's soliloquies are modern in that they break what is often referred to as the 'fourth wall' separating audience from stage.

An **aside** is a similar dramatic device, except that the character is not alone. However, when a character makes an aside, it is the accepted convention that while the audience can hear every word, other characters onstage are completely unaware of what is being said.

Soliloquies and asides are central for advancing the plot and for revealing a character's true state of mind. The most important soliloquies are delivered by Iago, who informs the audience of his plans and motives on several occasions. These speeches contain some of the play's most memorable language. Because they let us know the true state of the ensign's complex mind, **we understand his obsession with taking revenge** on Othello. This intensifies the play's tragic quality and adds to our experience of the drama.

Iago never hides his intentions from the audience while all the time deceiving everyone onstage. He clearly **enjoys his own evil scheming**. This makes the audience appreciate his delight in controlling others while condemning its horrific outcomes.

Othello has only one soliloquy (Act 5 Scene 2), which indicates how open he is compared with Iago. As he prepares to kill Desdemona, he **convinces himself that he is acting out of justice**, not revenge, finally justifying it with the belief that it will prevent her from betraying more men. The soliloquy enables us to see both Othello's personal trauma and his flawed reasoning.

Knavery's plain face is never seen, till used

Iago
Act 2 Scene 1, l.328

Shakespeare's Language

Throughout the play *Othello,* Shakespeare demonstrates the power of language. **The playwright skilfully develops central characters through the words they speak.** In his opening speeches, Othello's expression is dignified, 'She loved me for the dangers I had passed'. He speaks slowly in restrained blank verse (each line has an internal rhythm and a regular rhythmic pattern). The Moor's formal tone reflects his heroic background and natural sense of authority.

Othello's language changes dramatically in the play's concluding scene. His emotional turmoil is mirrored by the increasing irregularity of the rhythm, 'My wife! My wife! What wife? I have no wife'. The repetition further emphasises his inability to control his thoughts. It is only in his final speech ('Soft you ...') when he chooses what he believes is noble self-sacrifice that he speaks calmly and reflectively, 'I have done the state some service, and they know it'. The Moor dies, reflecting on his former life on the battlefield when men killed and were killed – and acted out of necessity without regret.

In contrast, Iago's conversational dialogue convinces Roderigo of the benefits of spending money to attract Desdemona. **By speaking in prose, Iago sounds honest and open**, 'Thou art sure of me. Go, make money'. Later, he tells the audience of his true plans. We can sense his clever, devious nature through his stylish verse and subtle rhymes, 'Hell and night/ Must bring this monstrous birth to the world's light'.

For the most part, however, Iago's crude diction is that of a straightforward soldier. Cassio comments on the ensign's plain style, 'He speaks home, madam: You may relish him more in the soldier than in the scholar'. When Iago is not with his superiors, his **conversation often becomes obsessively vulgar** and suggestive. He reduces love and sexual attraction to a hunger, 'Her eye must be fed'.

Iago's facility with words illustrates just how powerful and dangerous language can be. He is so good at lying that he manipulates all his victims

Rude am I in my speech,
And little blessed with the soft phrase of peace
Othello
Act 1 Scene 3, l.90–1

with ease. In his **persuasive dialogue**, he excels in concealing the truth through his use of vivid metaphors, provocative imagery, sly suggestions, emotional appeals, well-placed silences, leading questions and meaningful repetition.

The **contrasting 'voices' in *Othello* are an important part of the play's power** to engage and move the audience. Cassio's speech is refined and slightly pretentious while Emilia's is down to earth. Desdemona's tone reflects her Christian values. Discussing the subject of jealousy in marriage with her maid, she remarks, 'Heaven keep that monster from Othello's mind!' When Emilia suggests hanging the man who has been spreading lies about her mistress, Desdemona is characteristically forgiving, 'If any such there be, heaven pardon him!'

Characters exert power through both what they say and how they speak. Their **silence can also be powerful**. Immediately after his villainy is finally exposed, Iago's deliberate silence suggests that he still retains some power by refusing to disclose the reasons for all his wrongdoing, 'From this time forth I never will speak word'. It seems an appropriate ending to a story that is propelled largely by his twisted use of words.

Imagery

Shakespeare makes **effective use of imagery and symbolism as dramatic devices** in *Othello*. The playwright engages audiences through words and phrases, which create vivid pictures in our mind. The extensive use of descriptive language – particularly powerful metaphors and similes – appeals to the audience's senses and conveys meaning in an imaginative way.

Patterns of imagery help to **heighten evocative moods** in the drama. We learn about Iago's vindictive personality through a series of rich images and symbols, often associated with poison, animals and hell. Othello's character is also shaped by imagery, including water, wild beasts, entrapment, light and darkness.

Shakespeare often **personifies abstract ideas** to stir our imagination, for example suggesting the power of jealousy by memorable images, such as the green-eyed monster. References to infidelity and cuckolding are prominent throughout the story. Other recurring images (particularly the moon, Desdemona's handkerchief, the candle, the sea and storms) sharpen our appreciation of important aspects of the tragedy and intensify the audience's theatrical experience.

It's important to understand the significance of key images that Shakespeare uses in *Othello* since they **reveal additional layers of meaning** in the play. Symbols enrich our understanding of the effect particular events have on the characters. Vivid symbolic imagery can provide 'imaginary visuals' that enhance the play's emotional impact. Some of the central imagery patterns are discussed below.

Poison

References to poison are especially **appropriate to Iago's venomous character**. From the outset, he is depicted through his sadistic plans to wake Brabantio and 'poison his delight' with lurid gossip about Desdemona's elopement. Later on, he outlines his malicious plans to make Othello jealous by pouring 'pestilence' into his ear. Such figurative language continues throughout the play as the malicious ensign revels in his revenge, 'The Moor already changes with my poison', 'Work on,/ My medicine'.

Iago cultivates his evil schemes so that they become deadly poisons. He then plants their seeds in the minds of others. When Othello is considering how he will kill his young wife, Iago advises him, 'Do it not with poison, strangle her in her bed'. The audience will be well aware of the **cruel irony** that the real poisoner has already contaminated the Moor's mind.

Animals

References to animals permeate the play, conveying a sense that the laws of nature, rather than those of society, are the primary forces

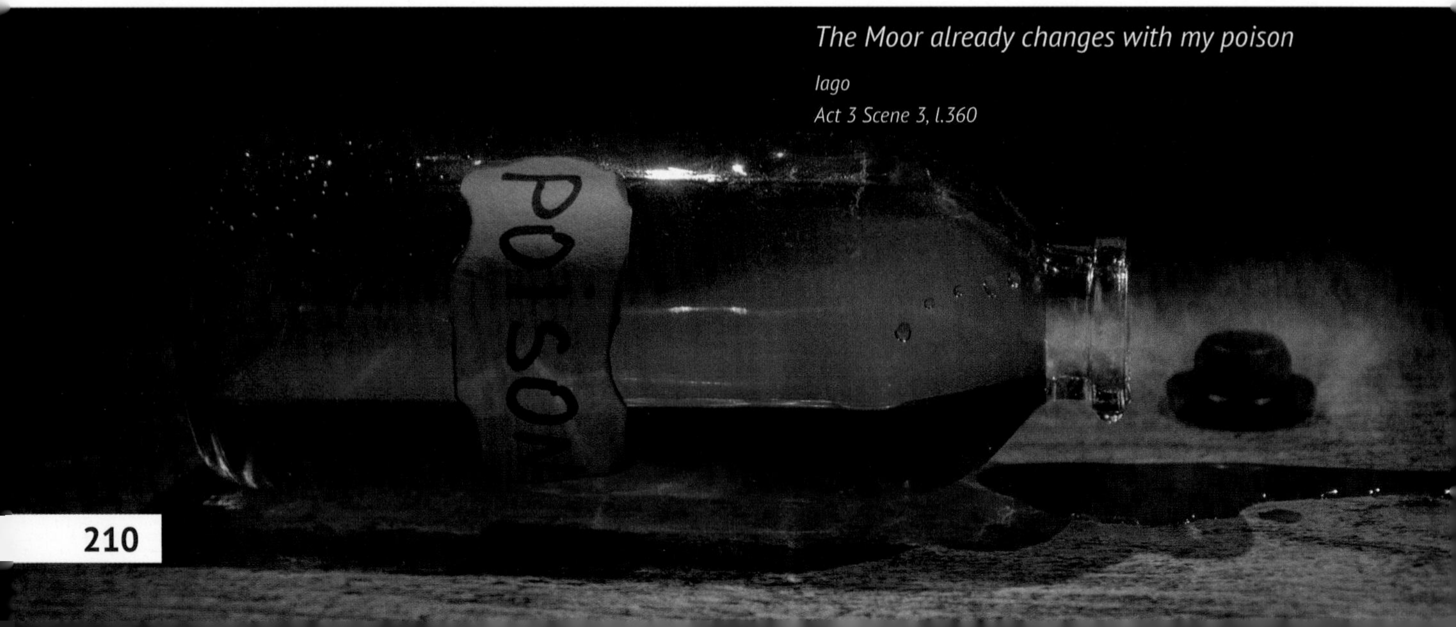

The Moor already changes with my poison

Iago

Act 3 Scene 3, l.360

O, I were damned beneath all depth in hell

Othello
Act 5 Scene 2, l.164

governing the characters. Iago routinely expresses his hatred of Othello in racist abuse, calling him a 'Barbary horse' and 'an old black ram'. Such images reflect the prejudice in Venetian culture and of Shakespeare's contemporary audience. Iago also **debases human relationships** to their lowest level, depicting Desdemona and Cassio's friendship on animalistic terms, 'hot as monkeys'.

The ensign's choice of words frequently suggests his warped loathing for others. He is confident that Othello can be 'led by the nose/ As asses are' and predicts that 'with as little a web as this will I ensnare as great a fly as Cassio'. Over time, as the exasperated Moor becomes increasingly obsessed with jealousy, echoes of Iago's animal imagery are found in his speech. 'I had rather be a toad ... ' he cries, 'Than keep a corner in the thing I love/ For others' uses'. After publicly humiliating his wife, Othello retreats in rage, shouting, 'Goats and monkeys!' Indeed, by the start of Act 4, the once-noble general has been reduced to a 'a monster and a beast'.

Hell and heaven

Images of hell and damnation recur throughout the play. Iago is frequently referred to in devilish terms and **identifies himself with the forces of evil vengeance**. He ends his Act 1 Scene 3 soliloquy with the chilling promise 'Hell and night/ Must bring this monstrous birth to the world's light'. The audience is never left in doubt that Iago delights in the 'Divinity of hell'.

As his jealousy grows, **the Moor's language becomes preoccupied with damnation**. In one of his many outbursts, he strikes Desdemona in public, calling her 'Devil'. Towards the end of the story, Othello is preoccupied with the religious and moral judgement of Desdemona and himself. After he has learned the awful truth about Iago's scheming, Othello calls him a devil several times. Shortly before he kills himself, the Moor cries out for eternal spiritual and physical torment in hell, 'Whip me, ye devils ... Roast me in sulphur!'

Shakespeare makes effective use of **contrasting imagery** to highlight Desdemona's innocence. Her essential goodness is reflected in Cassio's description of her as the 'divine Desdemona' and Roderigo also idolises her 'most blessed condition'. Emilia echoes these words, referring to her mistress as an 'angel' who has been cruelly murdered by Othello, 'the blacker devil'.

In his final moments of **traumatic despair**, Othello tries to make sense of Iago's evil and wonders, 'If that thou be'est a devil, I cannot kill thee'. The Moor's overwhelming awareness of failure is clearly evident at the close of this tragic story when he remains mesmerised by the 'hellish villain' who still refuses to explain his actions.

Sea and storms

Patterns of imagery create atmosphere and emphasise major themes in the play. The initial feelings of mutual love between Othello and Desdemona reflect the calm before the storm. The Moor swears his devotion to 'the gentle Desdemona' and he uses the vastness of the sea as an appropriate metaphor for the extent of his love: 'I would not my unhoused free condition/ Put into circumscription and confine/ For the sea's worth'.

As the tragedy unfolds, however, sea images are increasingly used to signify danger and to **foreshadow disaster**. Throughout Act 2, storm and flood imagery represent Iago's deceitful plans to bring about Othello's demise. All the main characters make the perilous journey to Cyprus during a great tempest, clearly symbolising the disorder that is about to engulf them on the island.

The disharmony that affects the Moor's unhappy marriage leads him to take revenge, 'Like to the Pontic sea,/ Whose icy current and compulsive course/ Never feels retiring ebb'. In comparing the unrelenting force of his hatred to a torrential flow of water, Othello confirms that his relationship with Desdemona is already doomed. Once again, the **threatening sea image** expresses his intention of violent revenge.

Shortly before his death, Othello reflects on his 'journey's end' and acknowledges the agonising moment as the 'very sea-mark of my utmost sail'. This final glimpse of his former heroism is all the more tragic as we witness the full extent of his downfall and the unbearable loss of his devoted wife.

Symbols

Some images have special symbolic significance. For example, the candle in *Othello* signifies the vulnerability of human life. Symbols appeal to the intellect, representing abstract ideas or qualities. Symbolism onstage can be achieved through characters, colour, actions, costume and props. Imagery and symbolism are often used together. For example, a storm at sea that has been described in great detail using imagery could also symbolise chaos or discontent among characters.

Shakespeare makes use of **motifs (recurring symbols) to reinforce key themes**. For instance, there are many references to the word 'monster' in the play. Othello also calls Desdemona's apparent betrayal 'monstrous! Monstrous!' while he refers to Iago as 'some monster in his thought'. The playwright's choice of locations is also symbolic. To a great extent, Venice represents civilisation, while Cyprus symbolises the wilderness. Other key symbols are discussed below.

The handkerchief

We first see the embroidered handkerchief just after Othello begins to suspect his wife of being unfaithful. For the Moor, the love-token he gave Desdemona is a treasured family heirloom – **a powerful symbol of the couple's enduring relationship**. Iago, of course, sees it as an opportunity to execute his vengeance. The handkerchief also signifies Othello's mysterious

If after every tempest come such calms,
May the winds blow till they have wakened death!

Othello
Act 2 Scene 1, l.199–200

that song to-night
Will not go from my mind

Desdemona
Act 4 Scene 3, l.32–3

past and exotic background. Emilia sees the handkerchief as a chance to please Iago, while Bianca makes the mistake of associating it with another of Cassio's lovers.

What begins as a **symbol of fidelity is soon transformed into one of unfaithfulness and betrayal**. Indeed, the handkerchief becomes the most crucial evidence to prove Iago's claim that Desdemona and Cassio are secret lovers. Had it not been for the handkerchief, the Moor would not have been as easily convinced of his wife's adultery. In *Othello*, Shakespeare explores numerous themes, including the fragility of marriage – something that is highlighted by the 'light as air' symbol of Desdemona's handkerchief.

The willow tree

In Shakespeare's plays, willow trees are often associated with unhappy love stories and the deaths of young women. As Desdemona prepares for bed, she sings a song of 'willow'. The tree is **a poignant symbol of her unhappiness** and sense of rejection. It foreshadows her impending death. Abandoned by Othello, Desdemona sings, *'Let nobody blame him; his scorn I approve'.* Although she is entirely innocent, she refuses to condemn her jealous husband. The willow tree song enhances our understanding of Desdemona's selfless character. Her love for Othello is unconditional.

The candle

An equally poignant symbol is the candle, which **epitomises Desdemona's fragile life**. Othello blows out the flickering light just moments before he strangles his innocent wife, and he himself is aware of the tragic symbolism, 'Put out the light, and then put out the light'. In his deluded state, he acknowledges her beauty and his love for her, but is convinced that he must kill her to cleanse her of her sins. Othello also understands the irreversibility of his desperate decision, 'If I quench thee, thou flaming minister,/ I can again thy former light restore'. He knows that he can easily light the candle again, but Desdemona's life will be lost for ever.

Put out the light, and then put out the light

Othello
Act 5 Scene 2, l.7

Exam Technique

Purposeful Use of Key Scenes

Successful *Othello* Leaving Cert answers will be assessed on four basic criteria:

- knowledge and understanding of the play
- developing relevant arguments
- effective use of suitable reference and quotation
- quality of the written expression

'Reading' Questions

You should read and study the wording of the question very carefully to identify the various elements that you are being asked to discuss. The three key terms (in bold) in the following exam question all need to be addressed over the course of an answer.

Q. 'Othello may be a **cruel character**, but he is **essentially a troubled figure** who **compels our sympathy**.'

Discuss this view, developing your answer with reference to Shakespeare's play *Othello*.

Planning Answers

- Take time (at least 5 minutes) to plan your main essay points, so that you construct a succinct, cogent response based on revealing scenes from the play. Your essay should have a clear sense of purpose, starting with a simple, coherent viewpoint, rather than an imprecise, rambling approach. **Every paragraph should be a step in a developing argument.** Effective critical literacy skills and incisive analysis will be well rewarded.
- **Avoid unfocused narrative** or general summary. You will need to be selective and refer to specific moments from the play that are relevant to the question.
- The examination questions are framed to invite candidates to engage with them but not necessarily to agree with the premise (or viewpoint) put forward in the question. Always **be prepared to challenge aspects of a question**, perhaps disagreeing with some part(s) or the entire premise outlined.

Paragraphing Guide

- A paragraph is a unit of writing that usually focuses on **one main idea**. This central idea (or point) is simply what the paragraph is about.
- It may be stated in a topic sentence (often early in the paragraph), or it may be so obvious that it is implied. **An effective paragraph develops the main idea** with enough relevant detail to maintain the examiner's attention while clearly conveying your own views. A paragraph is much more than a collection of connected sentences. It is a building block of essay development.
- Most paragraphs consist of at least five or six sentences; therefore, several supporting details (illustrated by suitable reference or quotation) are needed to build on the topic sentence and **develop the analysis**.
- The examiner needs to understand your train of thought, so what you write should be clear and **coherent**.

- Since most Single Text examination essays are at least 800 words in length, it makes sense to plan five or six key points (paragraphs) as the basis of your response. Main paragraphs would be around 150 words on average. Introductions and conclusions tend to be shorter. Of course, **a paragraph can be any length**, depending on its purpose.
- Your own language skills are crucial to success. Aim for **controlled expression** that is fresh, varied and assured. A common flaw is repetition of key words from the question in an attempt to maintain a relevant approach. Look for alternatives to invigorate your discussion, e.g. a character's 'admirable qualities' can also be described as 'personal attributes', 'attractive features', 'appealing traits', etc.
- You usually start **a new paragraph**:
  - after ending your introduction
  - to begin a new discussion point
  - when contrasting ideas
  - to begin your conclusion
- Aim to **structure your paragraphs** in the same way as a full essay, with a short introduction, main body and brief conclusion:
  - introduce the main point of the paragraph
  - develop and support the point
  - show the significance of the point you are making

Quoting Effectively

As a general guide, quotations should be **accurate, brief and relevant**. Quotes should always support discussion points.

Words taken directly from the play should be placed within **quotation marks**, e.g. 'O Iago, the pity of it, Iago'.

A well-chosen quotation **enables you to comment effectively** on theme, character(s) and style. Apt quotes, derived from a thorough knowledge of the play, will help to develop your analysis effectively.

Try to **integrate quotes** seamlessly into your own sentences, e.g. *Desdemona appears to accept her 'wretched fortune'*.

You will be penalised for mechanical errors, so **take great care** with spelling, grammar and punctuation. Remember – examiners award marks for 'quality of language'.

I will not stay to offend you

Desdemona
Act 4 Scene 1, l.270

Writing Top-Grade Essays

SEC guidelines require examiners to mark the Single Text *Othello* question ex 60 by reference to the criteria for assessment, using the **PCLM** breakdown of marks.

P: Clarity of Purpose (18/60 marks) refers to addressing the task in the question. It is essential when developing a response to identify all the key elements of the question and adopt a viewpoint or stance: agree/disagree wholly or in part.

Note: Examiners will reward: focus/relevance of response/well-chosen, compelling points/originality of thought/understanding of genre/evidence of critical literacy, etc.

C: Coherence of Delivery (18/60 marks) refers to sustaining an effective response throughout the answer. It is vital to sustain a coherent response over the entire answer. Successful responses demonstrate clear management of ideas, suitable references and/or quotation, and close engagement with the play.

Note: Examiners will reward: sustained focus/appropriate management and sequencing of ideas/coherence.

L: Efficiency of Language Use (18/60 marks) refers to the management and control of language appropriate to the task.

Note: Examiners will reward: effectively substantiated/apt use of examples, key moments, engagement with the text, etc. Language managed and controlled to achieve clear communication throughout/fluency/quality of expression, etc.

M: Accuracy of Mechanics (6/60 marks) refers to **spelling and grammar**, appropriate to the register. Marks for M are essentially independent of P, C and L marks.

60 marks	H1	H2	H3	H4	H5	H6	H7	H8
Total 100%	54–60	48	42	36	30	24	18	0–17
P/C/L 30%	17–18	15	13	11	9	8	6	0–5
M 10%	6	5	4	4	3	2	2	0–1

Remember!

Examiners will penalise unfocused narrative. Avoid retelling the story of the play or merely summarising.

Chief Examiner's Report Observations

- It is the question set which must be answered.
- Students should be assisted to develop the skills needed to shape, manipulate and adapt their knowledge to produce measured, informed and reflective responses.
- Some examiners identified candidates who were able to demonstrate knowledge of a text ... but were less able to deliver this knowledge in a lucid and coherent fashion.
- It is essential that candidates fully engage with the terms of any question attempted, challenging the terms of the question, perhaps disagreeing with some part or the entire premise outlined.
- Examiners were impressed when candidates presented lucid responses to questions based on their knowledge and understanding of the texts, augmented by a well-reasoned argument, point of view or opinion.
- Examiners were pleased when they saw candidates trust in their own personal response and demonstrate a willingness to challenge the 'fixed meaning' of texts.
- Careless use of quotation served to undermine answers.

www.examinations.ie

Sample Essays and Plans

Sample Essay 1

Q. 'The love between Othello and Desdemona, whether obsessive or unconditional, adds to the fascination of their relationship for the audience.'

Discuss this statement, developing your answer with reference to the play *Othello*.

Marking Scheme Guidelines

Candidates are free to agree and/or disagree with the statement, but they should engage with the terms: 'obsessive or unconditional' love 'adds to the fascination of their relationship'. Pay particular attention to the quality of the discussion and the extent to which the answer is developed with reference to the text.

Mark ex 60 by reference to the criteria for assessment using the breakdown of marks below.

P: Focus/relevance of response/well chosen, compelling points/originality of thought/ understanding of genre/evidence of critical literacy, etc.

C: Sustained focus/appropriate management and sequencing of ideas/coherence/points effectively substantiated/apt use of examples, key moments, engagement with the text, etc.

L: Language managed and controlled to achieve clear communication throughout/fluency/ quality of expression, etc.

M: Accuracy of mechanics

Code L/FR for obsessive/unconditional love adds/lessens fascination of relationship.

Indicative Material

- Joys/dangers of romance and passion engages audience
- Fragility/strength of the couple's complex relationship is/is not intriguing
- Dramatic tension/suspense caused by their lack of communication
- Impact of Iago on the love between Othello and Desdemona
- Contrasting consequences of tragic love are/are not absorbing, etc.

1 Othello is a play about an army officer from Africa who marries a rich lady in venice but whose downfall is jealousy from 'loving not wisely but too well'. The love affair she has with cassio is just a total lie that is made up by the villian Iago to destroy Desdemona and Othello's love for each other. He succeeds totally in this act and he is the main character who the audience find fascinating in this unfortunate story about the two star crossed lovers who are totally not suited and end up in tradgic circumstances because of this.

2 The audience knows that love is not perfect because Desdemona and Othello are not all that prepared for their inter-racial marraige. For a start, her father has no time much for Othello and in fact it could also be said that he hates the moor. In fact all of venice is filled with racial revenge against the likes of the moor because of his racial background.

3 But this does not stop him from loving Desdemona with a passion and she returns his love on account of what she calls 'the danger he passed'. She would of done nearly anything to please him and that includes deserting her father and in fact disgracing the whole family by running away with Othello behind his back and eloping.

4 This shows she had no conditions when it came to loving Othello and was under his spell. But it all turned bad when they went to live in Cyprus and the villian Iago put his evil revenge plans for the downfall into action. The plan was to get the moor thinking that his wife was in a relationship with cassio who was the local man about town and interested in other women. Anyone knows that love affairs are fascinating and that's what happens when the villian starts planting gossip and doubt in the jealous mind of Othello. He keeps hinting that there is something romantic going on involving cassio and his wife behind the scenes. This changes the moor into a totally different lover. In fact it could be said that his love more or less turns to hate.

5 The love gets totally obsessive after a while when Iago takes posession of a fancy handkerchief giftset that Othello gave his wife. Iago would of done anything to bring down the moor and he knows that he is inseccure as a husband and has no experience much of rich white girls from venice. It is fascinating for the audience to watch how Othello goes from adoring his wife who he calls 'gentle Desdemona' to suddenly waning to murder her as an unfaithful 'strumpet'. In one scene on a street in Cyprus, he calls her out and also hits her across the face which shames his wife who is actually an inoccent person in the wrong place at the wrong time. This is a shocking act for everyone who sees it and the audience finds it totally fascinating that even worse is to come. So much for his obsessive love for his wife.

6 The love in which the moor and Desdemona share goes from bad to worse and becomes like a war between them. Othello gets so jealous that nothing will do him but actually kill his own wife who he says 'will betray more men'. This shows that he is no longer a loving husband but is now treating her like one of his enemies on the battlefield.

7 In total contrast, she is unconditional. The worse thing he does and that includes trying to murder her is something that she is fully prepared to put up with and even forgive. When the maid finds her dying from being smothered by the moor, Desdemona tells a white lie and says 'comend me to my kind lord and husband'.

8 At the end of the play the moor finds out the true facts that his wife loved him all along

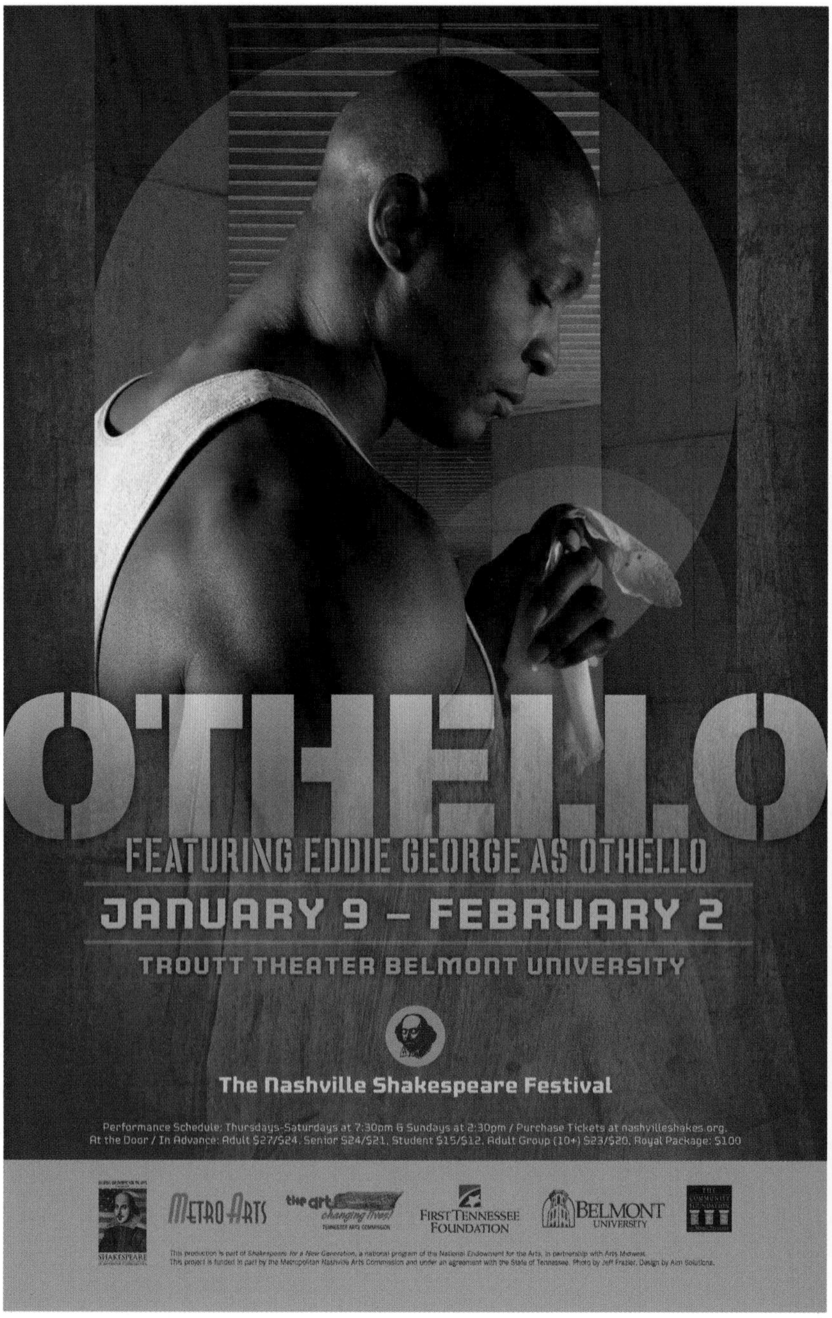

and she was certainly faithful. The maid calls him a 'gull' and that he was 'ignorant as dirt'. This is bound to be fascinating because the tradgic truth has finally come out in a dramatic way and involved the death of Desdemona and other innocent victims of Iago's evil revenge. There was always a bit of hope that the truth would of been discovered earlier and the audience was kept in suspense until the very end when the murder took place.

9 By the time the play is over the audience has seen a tragedy and this is totally fascinating. Othello seems to know that both he and Desdemona failed to really understand each other and they're both victims of the power of love, whether obsessive or unconditional.

(*c.* 785 words)

Marking Scheme		
P	10	18
C	9	18
L	9	18
M	4	6
	32	60

GRADE: H4

Examiner's Comment

- Reasonable focus overall on 'love' and 'fascination'.
- Reliance on summary; very little analysis.
- Some points could be developed and improved, e.g. in paragraphs 3 and 7.
- Basic use of references and quotes (including some misquotes).
- Basic vocabulary, expression needs to be improved.
- Capitals omitted; some flawed expression ('would of done', 'in which').
- Spelling errors ('villian', 'tradgic', 'marraige', 'posession', 'inoccent', 'inseccure', 'comend').

Improving the Essay

Paragraph 3 includes a worthwhile point about the nature of Desdemona's love for Othello. With more development and analysis, the standard could be improved significantly.

Desdemona's absolute love for the Moor is evident from the start of the play. In choosing Othello, she challenged the racial prejudice of Venice and risked being disowned by her father, Brabantio. For her, love was obviously a more powerful force than the traditional attitudes of society. Othello describes the couple's early attraction, 'She loved me for the dangers I had passed'. It's clear that Desdemona has an idealised view of the Moor and sees him as courageous and heroic. Audiences are likely to admire her strength of feeling, but they might also consider her naive. The fact that she deceives her father by eloping might well be romantic, but it is also dangerous. The elopement is not fully explained, but it might suggest that the couple's love would never be completely accepted in Venice. Brabantio also adds to the audience's early doubts about the marriage when he says, 'She has deceived her father, and may thee'. (155 words)

- Developed argument
- Focused on one element of the question
- Supported by relevant reference
- Accurate quotation
- Controlled expression and mechanics

Class/Homework Exercise

Rewrite paragraph 7, developing the key point about Desdemona's final act of selfless love for Othello. (Aim for about 150 words.)

Sample Essay 2

Q. 'Othello's complex character comprises contrasting elements which fascinate and repel in almost equal measure.'

To what extent do you agree or disagree with this statement/view? Develop your answer with reference to the play *Othello*.

Marking Scheme Guidelines

Candidates are free to agree and/or disagree with the statement, but they should engage with the terms: 'complex character' and 'elements which fascinate and repel'. Pay particular attention to the quality of the discussion and the extent to which the answer is developed with reference to the text.

Mark ex 60 by reference to the criteria for assessment using the breakdown of marks below.

P: Focus/relevance of response/well chosen, compelling points/originality of thought/ understanding of genre/evidence of critical literacy, etc.

C: Sustained focus/appropriate management and sequencing of ideas/coherence/points effectively substantiated/apt use of examples, key moments, engagement with the text, etc.

L: Language managed and controlled to achieve clear communication throughout/fluency/ quality of expression, etc.

M: Accuracy of mechanics

Code CE/F for Othello's complex character comprises elements which fascinate

Code CE/R for Othello's complex character comprises elements which repel

Indicative Material

- Initial impression of Othello raises interesting questions about his character
- Appealing effect of his love for Desdemona and dignified response to racial slurs
- Protagonist's personal insecurity and lack of judgement attract/repel sympathy
- Impact of conflicting roles as soldier and husband is compelling/repellant
- Audience's response is affected by attitudes of other characters towards Othello
- Inconclusive outcome fascinates – enigmatic tragic hero/delusional murderer

1 At the start of the play, Othello is protrayed in two ways. The Duke needs a brave general to defeat the Turkish navy, so he hires him on account of this. But Iago hates Othello and protrays him as inferior. Othello has run off in secret to marry Desdemona, a young white woman. Venice is a hypocritical place. On the one hand there's racism against outsiders like Othello. But they also use him when it suits. All this means we see different sides to Othello, so the first impression of the noble 'Moor' has elements which fascinate and repel in equal measure.

2 Othello is respected in public by the Duke but insulted by Iago and Roderigo. To some extent, this makes him a complex character. It shows different elements to his character. But the most fascinating thing about him is his jealousy. Iago plans to get revenge on Othello and this means he comes up with a false rumour that Desdemona is seeing Cassio behind Othello's back. In fact Othello genuinly loves her. The strange thing is that Othello soon believes Iago's lies. This makes the audience feel angry about why he is so easily fooled. The key scene is the play is the

turning point of scene 3 in act 3 when Iago manages to 'enmesh' the Moor under his spell. It is fascinating to watch how Othello changes from the honourable husband who trusts his wife to a jealous bully who plans to kill her.

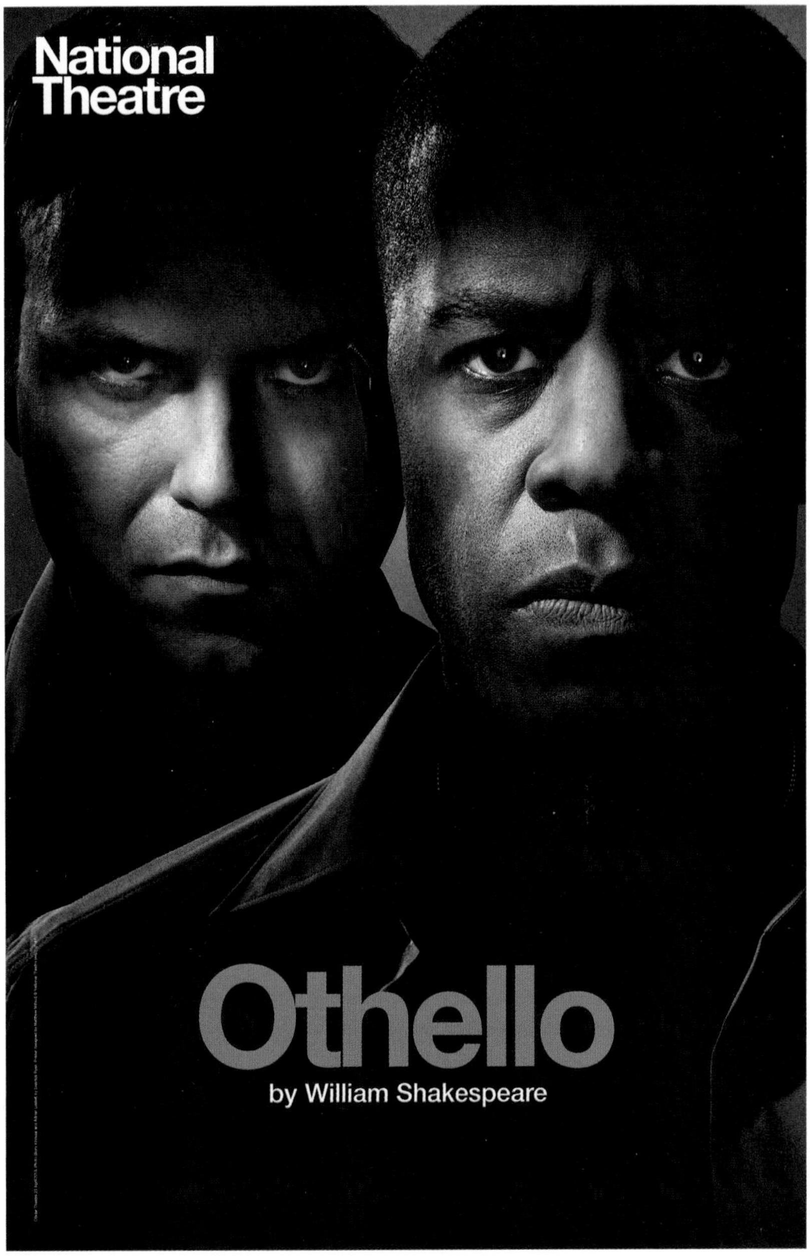

3 Iago warns him to 'observe' Cassio when he is with Desdemona and reminds Othello that she once deceived her father Brabantio in marrying in secret. The fascinating question is why Othello trusts Iago more than Desdemona. His 'honest' Iago has made him blind to the truth. The audience now sees a man who is only used to a male military world and is unable to deal with people outside of the battlefield envoirment. Iago is subtle and he deceives Othello. It could be said that Othello is not very complex by comparison. He does not think about things. Instead, he is a shallow character, judging on appearances. He is also completely unfair to Desdemona.

4 By the time the end of the play comes around, Othello is filled with anger and jealousy. Othello is honourable in ways, but turns out to be a violent revenger killing his innocent wife and trying to justify his terrible crime at the end. This means the noble soldier is a foolish husband. His downfall is shocking. The one thing that prevents him from being regarded as totally evil is that he eventually regrets his great mistake at the end. To some extent, it could be said his suicide also makes up for his evil and so he deserves some sympathy.

5 Othello has a weak side to his character. He is exploited for this weakness by Iago and is happy to receive complements from him. Jealously rules the Moor and he is also self-destructive. This means there is a lot of complexity about him. He is correct in saying that he 'loved not wisely'. He does not fully want to kill Desdemona, but feels it is for the best. This is yet another serious error of judgement, to think that he is stopping his wife from betraying 'more men'. Othello has many conflicting feelings. He describes Desdemona as being both 'sweet' and 'fatal'. These opposites show his personal confusion and uncertainty. This suggests he is never sure about what he really feels for her.

6 The transformation in Othello from the romantic hero to the unhindged killer makes him a tragic character who fascinates and repels in almost equal measure. He is of a royal background and has been a heroic soldier. Othello always loved Desdemona, but his love was too possessive. His insecurity as an outcast in Venice might explain his. The strange thing is that even though the audience condemns Othello's terrible behaviour, they still have some sympathy for

him as a foolish character who was tricked by a very clever villain.

7 Othello wasn't the only one taken in by Iago. So was everyone else. But Desdemona forgives Othello and loves him to the end. Emilia condemns him outright as a 'gull' and she calls him out for the macho bully that he was. Lodovico is typical of all politicians and just focuses on the tragic events that have happened, but mostly focuses on governing Cyprus. He promotes Cassio as the new governor to replace Othello. Cassio praises Othello, but then again, Cassio has never been a good judge of character either. This means that we are still unsure about Othello despite his actions. He has qualities and faults, but there's general agreement that he is a most 'unfortunate man'.

(*c.* 790 words)

Marking Scheme		
P	15	18
C	13	18
L	12	18
M	5	6
	45	60
GRADE: H3		

Examiner's Comment

- Good overall discussion of Othello's contrasting characteristics.
- Some informed analysis of the protagonist's qualities and flaws.
- Reasonable textual support shows engagement with the text.
- The interesting point challenging Othello's complexity deserves development.
- Functional, note-like expression, repetitive at times (e.g. 'This means').
- Spelling errors ('protrayed', 'genuinly', 'envoirment', 'complements', 'unhindged').

Improving the Essay

Paragraph 3 includes a worthwhile point about Othello's lack of complexity. With more development and analysis, the standard could be improved significantly.

It could be argued that Othello is not a complex character. His elopement with Desdemona shows poor judgement. He acted hastily and did not consider how Brabantio was likely to react. The Moor is hopelessly blind to 'honest' Iago. The audience soon sees a man who is only used to a male military world. Othello is clearly unable to deal with people outside of the battlefield environment. Iago is much more subtle and easily deceives Othello. The Moor is unimaginative and never considers the consequences of his rashness in promoting Cassio or trusting Iago so much. Unlike Desdemona, who is naive but honourable, Othello allows his foolish nature to become vicious. He is outwitted by Iago from the start. For the most part, Othello is simply a failure. He fails in love, in his military career as Governor and he even fails to know himself. (145 words)

- Focused on Othello's limitations
- Argument is developed effectively
- Well supported by relevant reference
- Clear, varied expression and accurate mechanics

Class/Homework Exercise

Write a paragraph suitable for inclusion in the above essay exploring the impact of Othello's conflicting roles as soldier and civilian. (Aim for about 150 words.)

Some of the following points might be used to develop your answer:

- Othello is an outsider whose military background limits his social skills.
- His love for his 'fair warrior' is based largely on passion or blind emotion.
- He seems to have little understanding of Desdemona's unconditional love.
- He mistakenly views his wife as a prize who loved him for his military 'dangers'.
- His disastrous decision to kill Desdemona stems from military values.

Sample Essay 3

Q. 'Shakespeare's play *Othello* has all the main elements of powerful and absorbing drama.'

Discuss this statement, developing your answer with reference to the text.

Marking Scheme Guidelines

Candidates are free to agree and/or disagree with the statement, but they should engage with the terms: 'elements of powerful and absorbing drama'. Pay particular attention to the quality of the discussion and the extent to which the answer is developed with reference to the text.

Mark ex 60 by reference to the criteria for assessment using the breakdown of marks below.

P: Focus/relevance of response/well chosen, compelling points/originality of thought/ understanding of genre/evidence of critical literacy, etc.

C: Sustained focus/appropriate management and sequencing of ideas/coherence/points effectively substantiated/apt use of examples, key moments, engagement with the text, etc.

L: Language managed and controlled to achieve clear communication throughout/fluency/ quality of expression, etc.

M: Accuracy of mechanics

Code E/PD for play has/does not have all the main elements of powerful and absorbing drama

Indicative Material

Main elements of powerful and absorbing drama:

- Othello's flawed character has a profound impact on himself, others and Venice
- Engrossing effect of Iago's forceful embodiment of evil
- Pathos of frailty of the human condition brutally exposed
- Compelling study of key themes – love, jealousy, patriarchy, deception, racism, etc.
- Impact of foreshadowing, imagery and irony creates tension and suspense
- Tragic ending eliminates a happy resolution for Othello and Desdemona
- Increases psychological pressure on audience

OR

Lacks elements of powerful and absorbing drama:

- Tragedy reduced to unconvincing melodrama
- Pathos turns to pantomime, fear to farce
- Unsympathetic caricatures and stereotypes fail to engage
- Lessens psychological pressure on audience, etc.

1 Shakespeare's poignant tragedy, 'Othello', contains all the compelling elements necessary to captivate an audience; a great general brought low through a character flaw, a villain who is the embodiment of diabolical evil and an ending which does not seem to offer redemption for the central characters, Othello and Desdemona.

2 Othello is first presented as dignified and noble, he is of 'royal siege'. He handles the bigoted Brabantio, Desdemona's father, well, refusing to be drawn into a public brawl. A brave, intelligent army commander, he is fully aware of his worth to the Venetian Senate, 'My services ... shall out-tongue his complaints'. But he suffers from the character flaw of insecurity because he is an outsider in this sophisticated world. The cunning Iago, who is furious that Othello passed him over for promotion, exploits this weakness with devastating consequences. His skin colour provokes racist comments, 'sooty bosom'. He is seen as a predator who is accused of engaging in witchcraft to win Desdemona, 'thou hast enchanted her'. Othello desperately desires to be accepted.

3 Iago has a huge role to play in Othello's downfall, 'Thou hast set me on the rack'. But Othello has to accept some blame for his tragic downfall. He is quick to rush to judgement. He accepts Iago's insinuations, 'Ha! I like not that'. He is deceived into believing his wife is unfaithful. Within a short space he is calling his wife a 'lewd minx' and plotting her killing. But his character flaw succeeds in destroying everything he holds dear. He knows he has lost his occupation of military life, 'Farewell the plumed troop, and the big wars'. He sinks so low that he even submits to becoming an eavesdropper. He is tormented to the delight of the villainous Iago by the jeers of Cassio who is gossiping about his lover, Bianca. The 'dolt' Othello mistakenly believes that he is speaking about his wife. His insecurity is destroying him. The audience is gripped by this.

4 In the 'jealousy scene' Iago delights in his spell-binding cat-and-mouse game with Othello. All the other characters believe Iago to be 'honest'. He triggers and warns against 'the green-eyed monster' of jealousy in the Moor. In a stage production of the play, I was fascinated by the changing body language between the two characters. As Iago began to control Othello, he circled him onstage, taunting him with word pictures of his 'unfaithful' wife, 'Lie ... With her, on her'. It seemed as if the hypocritical villain was growing in height while he trapped the noble general in his wicked scheme, 'Work on, My medicine, work!' Othello falls writhing on the ground in an epileptic fit. The audience was completely absorbed in this spectacular dramatic display of malevolence.

5 The play does reinstate law and order in Cyprus. Cassio is made governor of the island and Lodovico returns to Venice to report on the tragedy, this 'heavy act'. But Shakespeare has one more twist to frustrate the audience's expectations of a new civilised order. Iago is not fully defeated. He frustrates everyone by refusing to explain his actions.

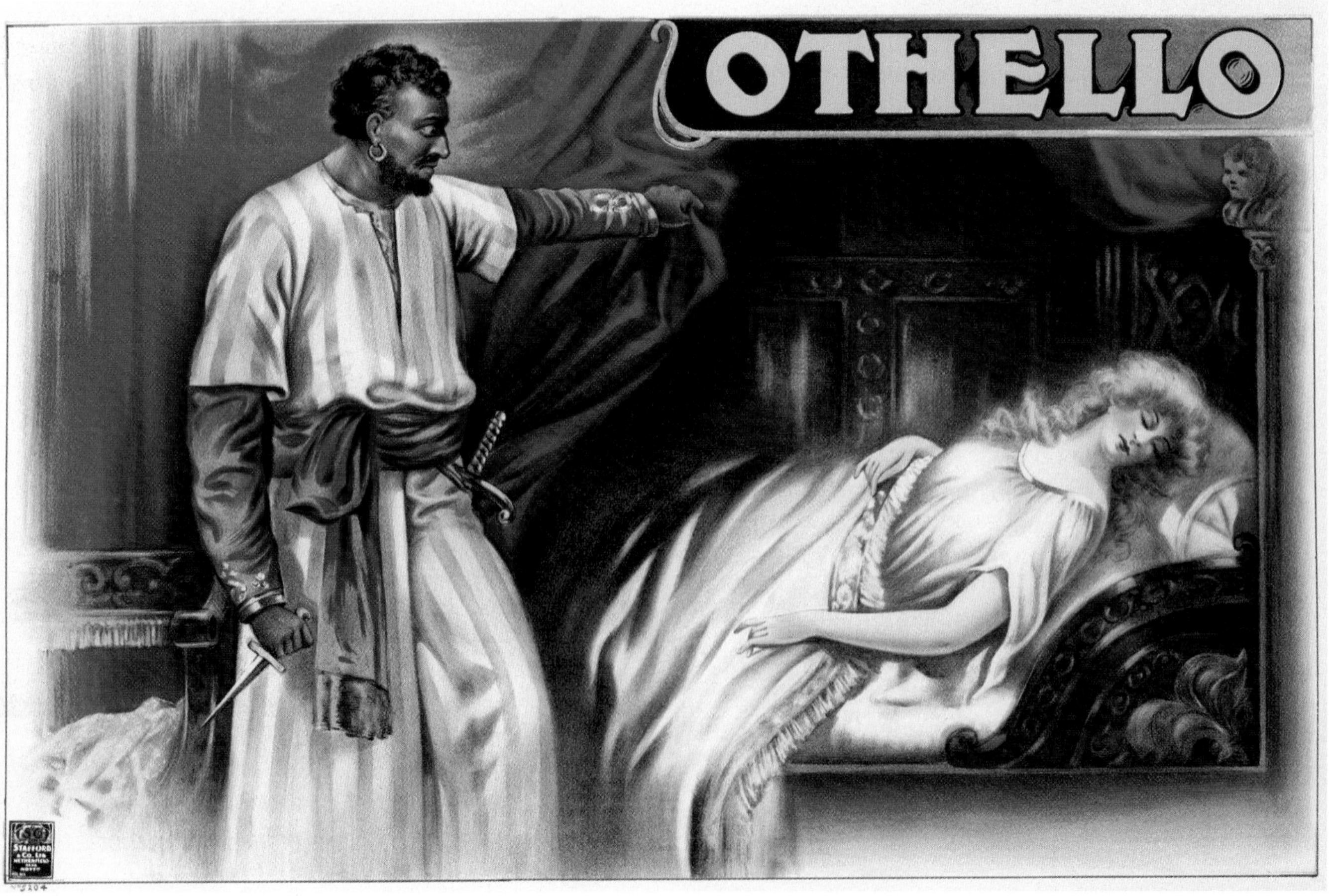

He sneers, 'what you know, you know'. Evil lingers over the new rule. Cassio will struggle to extract any information from the villain. Cassio was unreliable when given charge of the watch. He is easily led and has a weakness for alcohol, 'I have very poor and unhappy brains for drinking'. He also lacks patience, wanting to be reinstated immediately and pressures Desdemona mercilessly. He is absorbed in himself rather than understanding that he has to act in the best interests of the state. This concluding part of the play is not particularly convincing and is liable to leave the audience feeling uneasy.

6 The audience expects the protagonist to gain self-knowledge by the end of the play, yet Othello excuses himself as one who 'loved not wisely but too well'. He pays little attention to Desdemona who sacrificed everything for her 'filthy bargain'. Then the audience realises that she dies, still taking the blame for her own death and this is likely to confuse the audience to some extent. This tragic conclusion is not fully inspiring. The good characters, such as Desdemona and Emilia, do not seem to rise above the evil in this world.

7 I believe that the play is an engrossing exploration of the central characters' weaknesses, Iago's wickedness and Desdemona's naivety. Overall, the ending is tragic, a complex conclusion which shakes the audience while it looks at the 'tragic loading of this bed' which 'poisons sight'.

(*c.* 755 words)

Marking Scheme

P	16	18
C	15	18
L	15	18
M	6	6
	52	60

GRADE: H2

Examiner's Comment

- Generally sustained focus on 'elements of powerful drama'.
- Narrative is less explicitly focused in paragraphs 2 and 3.
- Well-supported and developed analysis in paragraphs 4 and 6.
- Paragraph 5 includes interesting ideas about the end of the drama.
- Overall, engaging insights demonstrate a close knowledge of the text.
- Impressive vocabulary; good expression – although repetitive at times (e.g. paragraph 3).

Class/Homework Exercise

Write a paragraph suitable for inclusion in the above essay about the impact of foreshadowing in creating absorbing dramatic tension throughout the play *Othello*. (Aim for about 150 words.)

Some of the following points might be used to develop your answer:

- Brabantio's early warning about Desdemona's deception is ominous.
- Disturbing effect of Iago's soliloquies on the audience's expectations.
- Foreboding signs of Othello's jealous nature heighten tension.
- Audience anxiety caused by the handkerchief plot.
- The willow song foreshadows the tragedy.

And yet, how nature erring from itself –

Othello
Act 3 Scene 3, l.255

Sample Essay 4

Q. 'The relentless deception that occurs within the play *Othello* creates gripping moments of dramatic tension and maintains suspense to the end.'

To what extent do you agree or disagree with this statement/view? Support your answer with reference to the play.

Marking Scheme Guidelines
Candidates are free to agree and/or disagree with the statement, but they should engage with the terms: 'relentless deception', 'gripping moments of dramatic tension' and 'maintains suspense to the end'. Pay particular attention to the quality of the discussion and the extent to which the answer is developed with reference to the text.

Mark ex 60 by reference to the criteria for assessment using the breakdown of marks below.

- **P:** Focus/relevance of response/well chosen, compelling points/originality of thought/ understanding of genre/evidence of critical literacy, etc.
- **C:** Sustained focus/appropriate management and sequencing of ideas/coherence/points effectively substantiated/apt use of examples, key moments, engagement with the text, etc.
- **L:** Language managed and controlled to achieve clear communication throughout/fluency/ quality of expression, etc.
- **M:** Accuracy of mechanics

Code D/TS for relentless deception creates/does not create moments of tension and suspense

Indicative Material
Relentless deception:

- Pretence, lies, duplicity – real and imagined

Creates dramatic tension/maintains suspense:

- Moments of revelation and soliloquies affect audience
- Effect of unexpected developments/plot twists
- Suspense caused by foreshadowing and irony
- Extreme violence is compelling/unconvincing
- Impact of intense/heightened emotional experiences
- Audience is involved/distanced by tragic/shocking events
- Ending fulfils/thwarts expectations, etc.

1 'Othello' is largely based on deception and self-deception. From the opening scene, the audience is caught up in the complex story of revenge. The play moves relentlessly towards its tragic outcome through a series of intense dramatic moments which create a heightened state of suspense right up to the terrible conclusion.

2 From the start, Iago operates in the shadows, directing proceedings and causing confusion. The foolish Roderigo openly declares himself to Desdemona's father while the hidden Iago offensively shouts 'an old black ram is tupping your white ewe'. We see Iago play out his double game of informant and loyal follower, 'I must show out a flag and sign of love'. The embittered soldier explains his reasons for hating Othello. He has been passed over for promotion, so he pretends to like the Moor, 'I follow him to serve my turn

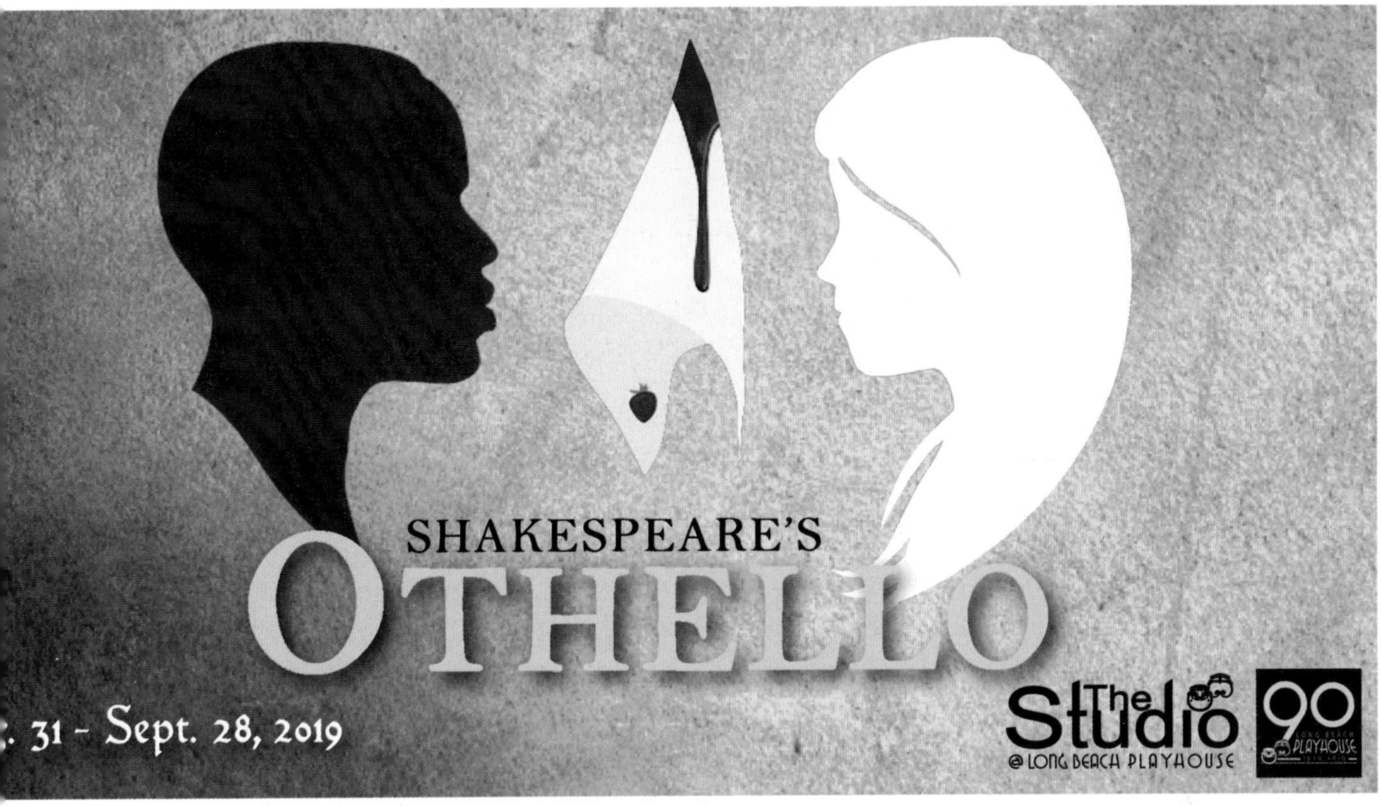

upon him'. We are aware of Iago's self-centred plan of vengeance, 'I am not what I am'. He deceives everyone else. As a result, we are more informed about his hypocrisy and the tension is all the greater. We want to warn his victims.

3 Iago promises to use Desdemona's decency to destroy his enemies and 'make the net that shall enmesh them all'. But Desdemona has also practised deception. She hides her relationship with Othello from her father by eloping. Her intentions were probably good, she wished to spare her father anguish. But in doing so, she deceives herself. When Brabantio finds out, he warns the Moor, 'She has deceived her father, and may thee'. Iago uses this later to discredit her with Othello and plant suspicion in his mind, 'She did deceive her father, marrying you'. This creates unease in the audience. We wonder if Desdemona can be fully trusted. Later on, she lies to Othello when he asks for her handkerchief, telling him 'I have it not about me'. She compounds the lie by declaring 'It is not lost' even though it is. Again, she is acting out of good intentions, wishing to spare her husband grief because he values the handkerchief so highly. Unlike the audience, she is not aware at this time of how suspicious Othello has become or the full impact of her deceit.

4 This leads to the final dramatic scene where Desdemona tells another lie. Just before her unfortunate death. She seeks to pursue blame for her own murder. It was 'Nobody; I myself'. This desperate effort to keep hurt from her guilty husband could result in sending her soul to 'burning hell'. Desdemona practises deception. Both on others and self-deception in an effort to spare those she loves grief. The irony of this has a distressing effect and we sense the tension. Desdemona's naivety prevents her from realising the terrible outcome. All will be revealed to rebound on her. No matter what she does to try to protect her husband. She will soon pay a terrible price.

5 It is only in the play's last lines that the truth about 'honest' Iago is revealed by Emilia. She dramatically accuses her husband of a 'wicked lie' if he told Othello that Desdemona was 'false' with Cassio. But Iago excuses himself by saying that he just offered his opinion. If Othello chose to believe it, that was the Moor's own fault. Othello acted out of his inherent insecurity, 'what he found himself was apt and true'. From this point, however, Iago refuses to explain the true motives for his evil actions. The playwright succeeds not only in creating suspense until the conclusion of the play but beyond it. The audience is left to wonder what Iago meant by his cryptic statement, 'what you know, you know'. What exactly do they know?

6 Shakespeare concludes this scene's shocking and compelling plot twists in Othello's final soliloquy. The Moor has gained some self-knowledge. He recognises himself as the 'dolt' and 'gull'. But, like Desdemona, right to the end, he deceives himself. He demands that he 'must' be spoken of as 'one who loved not wisely but too well'. We are left to evaluate what he has done. Othello was fully aware of the gravity of his action, that he cannot give 'vital growth' back after he has 'plucked the rose'. As the play reaches its climax, he murders Desdemona. We are shocked that he could not 'see' what was before him, his beautiful innocent wife. Instead, he 'sees' the distorted image Iago placed before him, a 'strumpet', a 'lewd minx'. So the playwright maintains suspense, asking the audience to consider whether it is really true that Othello loved 'too well', thereby increasing the dramatic tension to the play's heart-breaking end.

7 Through gripping moments of dramatic tension that force the audience to re-examine previous events in light of the tragic ending, Shakespeare succeeds in maintaining suspense to the conclusion and beyond. 'Othello' is a tense and disturbing play which explores the practice and horrific consequences of relentless deceit.

(*c*. 820 words)

Marking Scheme

P	17	18
C	16	18
L	16	18
M	6	6
	55	60

GRADE: H1

Examiner's Comment

- Sustained and assured focus on 'deception', 'tension' and 'suspense'.
- Well-supported and developed analysis throughout most of the essay.
- Paragraph 3 makes an interesting point about Desdemona's impact.
- Apt quotations are integrated effectively into the critical discussion.
- Overall, good clear expression – although awkward at times, e.g. in paragraph 4.
- Some impressive vocabulary (e.g. 'compounds', 'inherent insecurity', 'compelling plot twists').

Class/Homework Exercise

Write a paragraph suitable for inclusion in the above essay about the significance of racism in creating absorbing dramatic tension throughout the play *Othello*. (Aim for about 150 words.)

Some of the following points might be used to develop your answer:

- Dramatic impact of prejudice against the Moor by Iago and Brabantio.
- Ironic outcome of Desdemona's idealistic attitude.
- Othello's insecurities as an outsider create moments of tension.
- The language of racism and prejudice adds to tense atmosphere.

O, banish me, my lord, but kill me not!
Desdemona
Act 5 Scene 2, l.94

Sample Essay Plan 1

Q. 'Iago's complex personality comprises disturbing features which horrify and repel audiences, but he is still the most fascinating character in the play.'

To what extent do you agree or disagree with this statement/view? Develop your answer with reference to the play *Othello*.

Intro: Address the two main elements of the question ('features which horrify and repel' and 'most fascinating character'); adopt a viewpoint (agree or partially agree); outline approach by giving a very brief overview of Iago's malicious character and his dominant presence in the tragic story.

Paragraph 1: Initial impression of Iago's hate-filled character is negative. A larger-than-life figure, he controls Roderigo and is cruel to Brabantio. The fact that he has been passed over for promotion may gain him some sympathy. His desire for vengeance against the Moor foreshadows tragic events to come.

Paragraph 2: Dramatic impact of Iago's powerful soliloquies; audience is involved in his obsessive revenge. His ingenious plan ('It is engender'd') to ruin the happiness of Othello and Desdemona is shocking. The fixated tone and imagery reveal Iago's deeply disturbed personality.

Paragraph 3: The vengeful ensign's multi-layered character is illustrated in his compelling ability to read the characters of others and to take advantage of their weaknesses; he flatters Roderigo and Othello, is witty and playful with Desdemona, targets Cassio's weakness for alcohol and bullies Emilia. Only the audience knows the real Iago.

Paragraph 4: Act 3 Scene 3 marks a turning point in Iago's control of Othello. The subtle cat-and-mouse power game is absorbing. Iago's sadistic delight in the suffering of Othello is alarming. He is innovative and imaginative in manipulating the man he hates, leaving us asking how Othello can be so trusting and naive.

Paragraph 5: As the suspense increases, Iago's plans become more involved and he takes further risks; the audience wonders if the truth will emerge. His misogynistic attitude to women is increasingly disturbing – particularly his treatment of Emilia.

Paragraph 6: His final act of defiance ('From this time forth I never will speak word') highlights his inscrutable nature and enduring enigmatic presence. Associated with devilish demonic language at the end.

Conclusion: Iago is central to the play's horrifying outcome. His complex character is filled with contradictions. By turns hypocritical, conniving, sociopathic and thoroughly evil, on occasion he is intelligent, inventive, charismatic and insecure. From start to finish, he intrigues the audience.

Class/Homework Exercise

Using one of the Sample Plan paragraph outlines above as a starting point, write a developed paragraph in response to the essay question. Support the points you make with reference to the play. (Aim for 150 words.)

Sample Essay Plan 2

Q. 'Shakespeare's presentation of women characters in the play *Othello* inspires outrage, admiration and compassion in the audience.'

To what extent do you agree or disagree with this statement/view? Develop your answer with reference to the play *Othello*.

Intro: Address the main elements of the question ('presentation of women characters' and 'inspires outrage, admiration and compassion'); adopt a viewpoint (agree or partially agree); outline approach with a brief overview of the way women are presented in this tragic story.

Paragraph 1: Desdemona initially an ambiguous character – loving and obedient daughter who challenges tradition by eloping with the Moor. Can be seen as strong-willed and independent or impetuous and naive.

Paragraph 2: As Othello's wife, Desdemona's unconditional love and idealism prove tragic; her passivity contributes to her unfortunate downfall and image as a pitiful victim.

Paragraph 3: Key moments in the drama illustrate mistreatment of women; Iago ridicules women, Othello strikes Desdemona in public, Cassio demeans Bianca.

Paragraph 4: Emilia is a likeable/engaging character who balances duty to Iago with loyalty to Desdemona. Pragmatic and self-serving, but also courageous and ultimately heroic.

Paragraph 5: Abuse and violence by male characters is shocking/outrageous. In contrast, Desdemona and Emilia display courage, honesty and forgiveness. Bianca also endures Cassio's mistreatment with some dignity.

Paragraph 6: Audiences will react to the fact that all three women are subject to the patriarchal and misogynistic values of their time. They struggle to assert themselves beyond the traditional roles of daughter, wife, mistress.

Conclusion: It is possible to respond to the many qualities of Desdemona, Emilia and Bianca while sometimes questioning their actions. Our sympathy can vary throughout the play and can be tempered by modern views.

Class/Homework Exercise

Using one of the Sample Plan paragraph outlines above as a starting point, write a developed paragraph in response to the essay question. Support the points you make with reference to the play. (Aim for 150 words.)

Sample Essay Questions on *Othello*

Note: 60 marks/60 minutes. Aim for at least 800 words.

1. 'Throughout the course of the play, both Othello and Desdemona share a common tragic fate, but Desdemona emerges as the more admirable and heroic figure.' To what extent do you agree or disagree with this statement/view? Develop your answer with reference to the play *Othello.*
2. 'The cultural and social values evident in the play *Othello* have a profound effect on the tragic outcome of the story.' Discuss this statement, developing your answer with reference to the text.
3. 'Iago's complex personality comprises disturbing features which horrify and repel audiences, but he is still the most fascinating character in the play.' To what extent do you agree or disagree with this statement/view? Develop your answer with reference to the play *Othello.*
4. Identify three moments of emotional intensity in the play *Othello*, and discuss how Shakespeare uses language and dramatic techniques to heighten the emotional intensity.
5. 'Desdemona's self-assured defiance and fatal submissiveness make her the most intriguing and tragic figure in the play.' To what extent do you agree or disagree with this statement/view? Develop your answer with reference to the text.
6. The fine balance between power and powerlessness throughout Shakespeare's play *Othello* intensifies our experience of the play's tragic and dramatic qualities.' Discuss this statement, developing your answer with reference to the text.
7. 'Over the course of the play *Othello* Shakespeare presents a morally chaotic world where hatred and love can be seen as equally destructive forces. To what extent do you agree or disagree with this statement/view? Develop your answer with reference to the text.
8. There are several compelling reasons to explain Othello's tragic downfall, but it his personal impulse towards self-destruction that ultimately destroys him.' To what extent do you agree or disagree with this statement/view? Develop your answer with reference to the play.
9. 'Shakespeare's presentation of women characters in the play *Othello* inspires equal measures of outrage and compassion in the audience.' To what extent do you agree or disagree with this statement/view? Develop your answer with reference to the play.
10. 'Shakespeare's effective use of imagery and symbols heightens our experience of the tragic drama in the play *Othello*.' Discuss this statement, developing your answer with reference to the play.

'Twere now to be most happy
Othello
Act 2 Scene 1, l.204

Using *Othello* as a Comparative Text

Introduction

- The Leaving Cert Comparative Study section is worth **70 marks** out of the 400 total.
- In the Comparative section, plays, novels and films are all referred to as **texts**.
- A **mode** of comparison is simply a framework in which to explore a text.

There are **four** Higher Level modes:

1. The Cultural Context
2. Theme or Issue
3. Literary Genre
4. The General Vision and Viewpoint

You are required to study **at least two** of the three modes prescribed each year.

Only **two** of these three modes will appear on the exam paper.

Each mode that appears on the paper will have a choice of **two** questions.

These questions take two forms. Either:

- An **essay-type question** comparing three texts for 70 marks or
- A **question divided into two parts**
  - Part (a) requires discussion of **one text** (30 marks)
  - Part (b) requires comparison of **two other texts** (40 marks)

You are allocated 70 minutes for the Comparative section. Aim to write at least **1,000 words** in the single 70-mark answer.

For the two-part question, aim to write about 400 words for Part (a) and about 600 words for Part (b).

When answering Comparative questions, candidates may compare and/or contrast, i.e. address similarities and/or differences in both the subject matter and style of their chosen texts.

Note: At Higher Level, a play by Shakespeare **must** be one of the texts chosen. This play can be studied on its own (for the Single Text section) or as an element in the Comparative Study section.

1. The Cultural Context

The Cultural Context mode usually refers to the society or 'world' of the text. This includes social setting, values, attitudes and day-to-day rituals. Some societies are corrupt and violent while others are orderly and peaceful. Our understanding of a text is enriched by knowing something about the culture in which the story is set.

Key cultural context features include:

- power
- social class
- family
- violence
- freedom
- identity
- race
- wealth
- morality
- patriarchy
- religion
- traditions

Remember!

Various aspects of cultural context will overlap at times. For example, race, identity and power are closely interlinked in Othello.

The Cultural Context in *Othello*

Geographical locations

Shakespeare set the play in two contrasting locations, the bustling city of Venice and the isolated outpost of the island of Cyprus. Act 1 takes place in the autonomous city-state of Venice, which was a key trading destination for merchants. Enormous wealth came through trade and Venice was viewed as **a sophisticated place** of stylish civilisation.

It was important to the Duke and Venetian Senate that the **trading routes should be kept open** to facilitate the city's lucrative trade. They had a powerful army to protect these routes against the state's enemy, the Ottoman Turk. The Senate often employed a foreigner to lead this force because they were fearful of giving so much military power to one of their own citizens.

It was also easy to dismiss contracted foreign mercenaries, such as the Moor, 'there is especial commission come from Venice to depute Cassio in Othello's place'. This city's setting is one of power, romance and culture, an appropriate background for Othello and Desdemona's love story. Yet in Shakespeare's time **Italy is also associated with villainy, racism, decadence and corruption** with many brothels and casinos. Bianca, the courtesan, and Iago embody these Italian vices.

In Act 2, the action of the play moves to the island of Cyprus. This far-flung part of the Venetian Empire was important because it was situated on a major trade route from the East to the West. At the start of the play, Cyprus is under imminent attack from the Turks. On a symbolic level, **the island's vulnerability and isolation mirror similar traits in the protagonist**, Othello. Its distance from the civilised world of Venice makes it a credible location for the uncontrolled passions that rage there.

Military setting

The domestic love story of Othello and Desdemona is placed against a **turbulent military background**. Othello will struggle to combine the conflicting demands of work and love. A person's job is often a reflection of character and reputation. The prestigious position of general has been conferred on Othello largely because of his reputation, 'You have been hotly called for'. He is admired for his heroism and leadership. This prominent position suggests that Othello is loyal, trustworthy and courageous. Montano admires the Moor as one who 'commands/ Like a full soldier'. Othello himself gloried in 'Pride, pomp and circumstance of glorious war'.

The rank of lieutenant is second-in-command. He **deputises for the general** when he is not available. As second officer, the lieutenant is expected to have the same qualities as the general. However, Michael Cassio lets Othello down and loses his reputation by giving in to Iago's temptation, ''Tis a night of revels: the gallants desire it'.

In Venice they do let heaven see the pranks
They dare not show their husbands

Iago
Act 3 Scene 3, l.224–5

Cassio conducts a 'private and domestic quarrel' in a 'town of war'. The ensign, Iago, is the rough-speaking non-commissioned officer who carries the flag into the field, 'I must show out a flag'. This requires bravery and loyalty because he identifies the location of the army on the battlefield. The ensign must maintain that position in the face of possible death. Iago is bitter because **he has been passed over for advancement** by Othello even though the Moor has 'seen the proof' of his military ability.

The **army culture of the time was defined by honour and status**. Iago is a seasoned and ambitious soldier, so it is strange that Othello promoted the inexperienced Cassio who 'never set a squadron in the field'. As a result, Iago decides to be deliberately disloyal, 'I follow him to serve my turn upon him'.

A patriarchal society

In the play's 'macho' society, **men are dominant and controlling**. They make the decisions for the family. Fathers often choose their daughters' future husbands, usually men of equal or higher social and economic rank to maintain the family's status. Brabantio had already refused Roderigo, 'I have charged thee not to haunt about my doors'. Women are subordinate and expected to be subservient.

But Desdemona has **challenged societal norms** because she 'shunned/ The wealthy curled darlings of our nation'. Iago, the cynical misogynist, criticises her behaviour as 'one may smell in such a will most rank'. A man was expected to ask the father's permission before courting his daughter, yet Othello and Desdemona elope. Brabantio is appalled that his daughter has chosen to 'fall in love with what she feared to look on'.

Desdemona's assertive character is seen when she demands to accompany her husband on his tour of duty to Cyprus rather than be 'left behind,/ A moth of peace'. However, **Desdemona soon reverts to society's expectations** when she defers to her husband. After Othello abuses and strikes her in public, she leaves submissively, 'I will not stay to offend you'. Later, she instructs Emilia to lay her wedding sheets on her bed in an attempt to reconcile relations with her angry husband. She even exonerates him of her murder and dies murmuring, 'Commend me to my kind lord'.

Emilia is more assertive and provides a contrasting picture of womanhood. She is a worldly-wise servant who **criticises society's double standard of expected social behaviour**, 'have not we affections,/ Desires for sport, and frailty, as men have?' When she learns of Iago's guilt, she is not afraid to call him out publicly, ''Tis proper I obey him, but not now'. Emilia dares to 'speak' to defend her young mistress's reputation. She accuses her husband of telling 'an odious, damned lie' for saying Desdemona was unfaithful. In the end, Iago fatally stabs her. Assertive women were seen as a threat to the social order in Elizabethan times. Yet Shakespeare dares to challenge the traditional role of women.

Outsiders

For much of the play, Othello is referred to as 'The Moor'. In the early 17th century, this term was used for non-whites, usually of North African descent. The hostile Iago gives us the conventional attitude describing Othello as a **barbarous, foolish outsider** who did not understand the subtle ways

If I do die before thee prithee, shroud me
In one of those same sheets

Desdemona
Act 4 Scene 3, l.25–6

of the city, 'In Venice they do let heaven see the pranks/ They dare not show their husbands'. Roderigo, the disappointed would-be lover of Desdemona, resorts to racist abuse, calling Othello 'thick-lips'.

But Shakespeare **uses the character of Othello to subvert society's assumptions**. He presents him as a man of 'royal lineage', an exotic person who enthrals Brabantio and his daughter with fantastic tales of 'rocks and hills whose heads touch heaven' and 'Cannibals that each other eat'. However, he also has some of the expected characteristics of a stereotypical Moor; jealous, superstitious and easily moved to anger.

Othello is a 'credulous' man who demands 'ocular proof' of Desdemona's infidelity. He threatens to 'chop' his wife 'into messes' because he believes she has cuckolded him. But **Shakespeare, once again, subverts the norm**. The audience is asked to consider Othello as a complex person who is unsure of himself, 'Rude am I in my speech' who has become 'Perplexed in the extreme' because of Iago's insinuations. The playwright teaches the audience compassion for the outsider who did the state 'some service'. It is not the North African outsider, but the manipulative white Venetian, Iago, who is the play's great villain.

Religion and superstition

The play's action has an epic backdrop of a fierce **conflict between the Christian Republic of Venice and the Muslim Ottoman Empire**. Desdemona, the symbol of innocence, is associated with heavenly imagery, the 'grace of heaven', 'full of most blessed condition'. Iago is linked to evil through the imagery of hell and the devil, 'Hell and night/ Must bring this monstrous birth to the world's light'.

Othello comes to regard his malicious ensign as a 'demi-devil' and looks 'down towards his feet' to see if they are the cloven feet of the devil. Although Othello is a converted Christian, **he still harbours the superstition of his country of origin**. The handkerchief he gave to Desdemona is 'dyed in mummy' from 'maidens' hearts'.

The clash of cultures is obvious in Desdemona's frustrated comment about the love-token, 'would to God that I had never seen it!' Othello re-enacts his heroic action for the state when he killed 'a turbaned Turk' who had 'traduced the state'. Interestingly, it is Iago who is the cynical atheist and believes that men are in control of their own fate, ''Tis in ourselves that we are thus or thus'. Throughout this tragedy, **Shakespeare has sabotaged the accepted norms of society**.

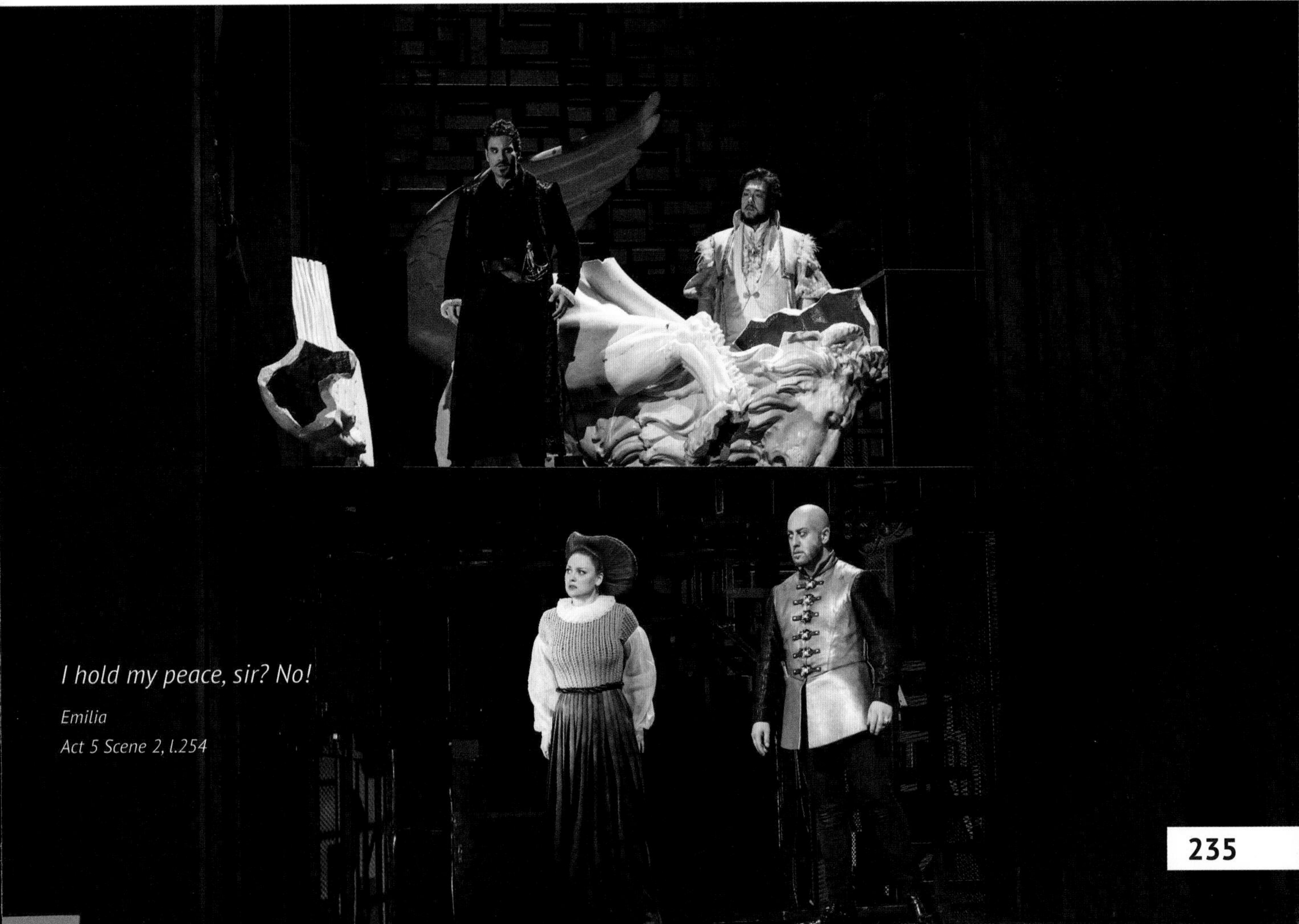

I hold my peace, sir? No!

Emilia

Act 5 Scene 2, l.254

Useful Quotes: Cultural Context

I know my price, I am worth no worse a place **(Iago to Roderigo)** *Act 1 Scene 1, l.11*	Rank is important in the play's military world. Iago has been passed over for a promotion that he believes he deserved. Othello has chosen Michael Cassio, who 'never set a squadron in the field'. Iago is criticising the Moor for being impressed by the education that he himself lacks, 'Rude am I in my speech'. From Iago's viewpoint, Othello has breached the hierarchy of military promotion by choosing the inexperienced Cassio.
Is there not charms *By which the property of youth and maidhood* *May be abused?* **(Brabantio to Roderigo)** *Act 1 Scene 1, l.181–3*	The outraged father cannot believe his daughter has eloped with the outsider, Othello. So he blames magic and drugs for subverting Desdemona's nature. This widespread belief in superstition is later mirrored by Othello's own reaction to the lost handkerchief, which he believes is imbued with magical properties to keep a couple together.
My parts, my title and my perfect soul *Shall manifest me rightly* **(Othello to Iago)** *Act 1 Scene 2, l.34–5*	A confident Othello refuses to heed Iago's advice to hide from the irate Brabantio's search party. He believes that his military rank and his clear conscience will save him from any accusation. Here is a man who seems to have experienced no racism in the civilised city of Venice. The Duke even declares that he is 'far more fair than black' at the trial.
I do perceive here a divided duty … *I am hitherto your daughter. But here's my husband* **(Desdemona to Brabantio)** *Act 1 Scene 3, l.194–8*	While acknowledging her duty to her father, who gave her life and education, Desdemona asserts that she has a higher duty now to her husband. In this patriarchal society, the subordinate woman defers to her husband before her father – just as Desdemona's mother did when marrying Brabantio. Desdemona does not believe she has violated society's norms by her actions.
you the blacker devil! **(Emilia to Othello)** *Act 5 Scene 2, l.157*	Despite Iago and Roderigo's initial racial slurs against Othello (and each believed they had cause to hate the Moor), it is only when he has committed the murder of Desdemona that his skin colour is held against him. Othello's irrational behaviour has now alienated others, resulting in a criticism of his character, 'as ignorant as dirt'. Lodovico laments that he was 'once so good'.
in Aleppo once, *Where a malignant and a turbaned Turk* *Beat a Venetian and traduced the state,* *I took by the throat the circumcised dog,* *And smote him, thus* **(Othello)** *Act 5 Scene 2, l.403–7*	In his final speech, the converted Christian Othello seeks to re-establish his position in mainstream Christian society by using religious prejudice against the Muslim Turks, the enemy of Venice. He re-enacts what he considered a great service to the state and kills himself because he has dishonoured himself in his and society's view by the murder of his innocent wife.

Using *Othello* in Comparative Questions

Sample Part (a) Question

Q. Identify at least one type of behaviour considered to be unacceptable within the world of <u>one text</u> on your comparative course. Explain why such behaviour is considered unacceptable in this cultural context and discuss the response or responses of society to such behaviour. Support your answer with reference to the text. *(30 marks)*

Remember!

Discussion points in the 30-mark Part (a) sample answer can also provide the basis for developed comparisons in the 40-mark Part (b) and 70-mark single questions. To write successful examination answers, it is essential to study the wording of questions closely. Marks can easily be lost if attention is not paid to each element of the question.

Indicative Material

Types of behaviour considered to be unacceptable:

- All forms of dishonesty, e.g. lying, cheating, stealing, etc. considered unacceptable in the cultural context
- Forming relationships deemed inappropriate within a society
- Violent or criminal activity considered unacceptable
- Behaviour at odds with the social/moral/religious/political norms of the society, etc.

The response of society to such behaviour:

- Punishment of various forms, including imprisonment or execution
- Social ostracisation/stigmatisation/loss of reputation/social standing
- Withdrawal of rights
- Various forms of repression
- The behaviour is tolerated, ignored, denied, etc.

Sample Answer

In the patriarchal society of 17th-century Venice, women were subordinate and subservient. They were expected to accept and defer to decisions made by the men in their family. Neither Desdemona nor Emilia behaves in accordance with this social dictate. At the beginning of the play 'Othello', Desdemona asserts her right to choose her husband, and at the conclusion Emilia upholds her right to denounce her husband's wicked behaviour.

Desdemona is presented by the playwright as the embodiment of goodness in the tragedy. She is the 'gentle Desdemona', 'tender, fair and happy' who 'paragons description'. Yet, she has 'shunned/ The wealthy curled darlings of our nation'. She has chosen to elope with the Moor. Her father is appalled at her choice, believing she will 'incur a general mock'. Iago, who has been presented as an acute observer of others' characters, also comments that she must have 'foul disproportion, thoughts unnatural'. Emilia forcefully expresses her disgust at Desdemona's choice, 'she was too fond of her most filthy bargain'.

Emilia also challenges society's norms when she realises her husband's 'villainy'. She acknowledges the reality of the patriarchal society when she says, 'Good gentlemen, let me leave to speak'. She realises that society requires her duty to her husband, ''Tis proper I obey'. Yet bravely she continues to defend her mistress's reputation, 'Moor, she was chaste, she loved thee, cruel Moor'.

Emilia succeeds in exposing the truth about 'honest' Iago's 'odious, damned lie' that Desdemona was 'false with Cassio'. She reveals that it was her husband who had 'begged of me to steal' the infamous handkerchief that he used as irrefutable proof in Othello's eyes that Cassio and Desdemona were having a secret love affair.

However, both women pay the price of challenging society's norms with their lives. Desdemona, 'the sweetest innocent', dies smothered by her husband, still deluded by her love for Othello, accepting the blame for her own murder. According to Christian belief, she will be punished for dying in a state of sin, not only in this life, but also in the next.

Emilia also dies, stabbed by her husband, but she is confident of salvation in the next life because she has spoken 'true'. In Elizabethan times, assertive women were regarded as a threat to order in society. These women have been severely punished. *(385 words)*

Examiner's Comment

- Focused top-grade response that addresses the question directly.
- Clear discussion of society's expectations of women.
- Informed understanding of Cultural Context mode throughout.
- Good use of supportive reference and integrated quotes.
- Expression is clear and controlled.

Class/Homework Exercise

Using some of the points from the Indicative Material above, write your own response to the Part (a) question. (Aim for 400 words.)

Exam Guide

To structure your comparative essay answer on the Cultural Context, a useful exercise is to practise making an outline of the **key points** you wish to include. The following Draft Plan uses *Othello* as one of the comparative texts.

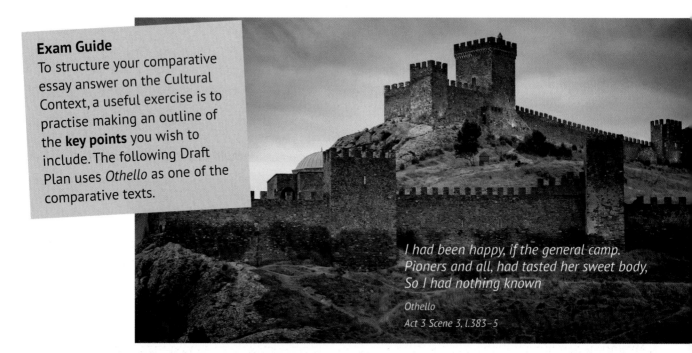

I had been happy, if the general camp.
Pioners and all, had tasted her sweet body,
So I had nothing known
Othello
Act 3 Scene 3, l.383–5

Sample 70-mark Question

Q. 'Aspects of cultural context affect the extent to which a character can be happy or successful within the world of a text.'

Identify a central character in each of three texts on your comparative course. Compare the aspect of the cultural context in each of these texts that, in your opinion, most affects the extent to which your chosen characters are happy or successful.

You may refer to the same or different aspects of cultural context in each of your chosen texts. Support your answer with reference to the texts. *(70 marks)*

Indicative Material

- Wealth and affluence/poverty, deprivation and economic insecurity affect happiness/success
- Norms and values, liberal, permissive society/ conservative, repressive society influence happiness
- Powerful friends/family/useful connections can contribute to success
- Extent of social cohesion, inclusivity/social division helps/hinders success/happiness
- Levels of social stability/instability, violence and oppression/peace and prosperity cause/ prevent happiness
- Impact of social class, religion, race, gender, matriarchy/patriarchy, etc.

Sample Draft Plan

INTRODUCTION

Characters achieve or fail to achieve success and happiness in their own world due to violence, social cohesion and religion/superstition in the three comparative texts I have studied. Othello fails to hold on to his high position obtained by his military achievements and destroys his chance for happiness with his loving wife. *Similar/different situations exist in my other* ***two texts*** ...

POINT 1

Othello's life is played out against the turbulent background of the Venetian/Turkish war. He is successful on the battlefield and is highly regarded by Venetian society. However, his violence against the innocent Desdemona damns him in society's eyes. He loses his social status, his military position and his chance for happiness. *In contrast/Similarly, the protagonist in my* ***second text...***

POINT 2

Iago fractures Othello's belief in social cohesion by reminding him of his hidden insecurities, of race, age and lack of sophistication. He succeeds in destroying Othello's chances for happiness and success in Venice. *My* ***third text*** *echoes/does not echo this situation ...*

POINT 3

Superstition – particularly about the handkerchief – plays an important role in hindering Othello's ability to gain acceptance and contentment in his world. *There are revealing similarities/contrasts regarding religious beliefs in my* ***other texts...***

POINT 4

Patriarchy diminishes Othello's chances of gaining joy. In a male-dominated world where women are seen as possessions, Iago is able to exploit Othello's jealousy and shame about Desdemona's apparent infidelity. *This is very like/unlike the situation in my* ***second/third texts...***

CONCLUDING PARAGRAPH

My knowledge of how aspects of society affect individuals' prospects for happiness/success has been broadened by my exploration of the impact of violence, social cohesion and religion/superstition on the central characters, particularly Othello ...

O, thou art wise, 'tis certain

Othello
Act 4 Scene 1, l.86

Sample Paragraph: **POINT 1**

Othello's journey towards self-fulfilment is both helped and hindered by violence in his society. At the play's start, he is 'hotly called for' by the Senate to lead the fight against their enemy, 'Valiant Othello, we must straight employ you/ Against the general enemy Ottoman'. Othello is happy and confident, secure in his position in society because of the 'services' he has carried out for 'the signiory'. But personal violence topples him from that position. Lodovico is horrified when Othello hits Desdemona in public, 'My lord, this would not be believed in Venice'. He is sorry he is 'deceived' in him. Othello fails to regain society's respect even when he reminds them of the time he 'smote' a 'malignant and a turbaned Turk' in his last soliloquy. His final act of violence against himself when he commits suicide is regarded as questionable or 'marred' by Gratiano. Violence has both created and destroyed Othello's chances for success and happiness in 17th century Venice. *Violence in my* ***second/third comparative text*** *helped/hindered the central protagonist's ability to achieve happiness/ success ...*

Examiner's Comment

- Well-developed discussion point on violence in the play.
- Effective use of apt reference and quotations.
- Good understanding of the Cultural Context mode.
- Comparative approach evident at the end.
- Successful top-grade response.

Useful Comparative Links

Successful comparative answers include clear links between texts.

The following phrases might be useful in pointing out similarities and differences between texts.

Similarities	Differences
• Both authors take a similar approach.	• These two texts could not be more different.
• The two stories have much in common.	• These two key moments illustrate contrasting aspects of ...
• This is also evident in the film's most disturbing scene.	• In an entirely different way ...
• Common to all three narratives is ...	• In contrast, the opening scene in the novel ...
• In an almost identical way ...	• The complete opposite is seen in ...
• This is mirrored in the way the heroine of the story acts when ...	• On the other hand ...
• The same effect occurs later in the text.	• This is certainly not the case in the film, where ...
• Likewise, in my other texts ...	• All three endings are completely different.
• This viewpoint is echoed at the end of my second text ...	• The novel takes a much more unexpected approach.
	• This aspect is contrasted in my second/third text, when ...

Class/Homework Exercises

1. Choose **one** of the other points in the Sample Draft Plan and write a paragraph of your own in response to the question above. (Aim for 150 words.)
2. 'Understanding who holds power and who is powerless helps to reveal the cultural context in texts.'
   Compare how the distribution of power within each of **three texts** on your comparative course helps to reveal the cultural contexts in these texts. Support your answer with reference to your chosen texts. (Aim for 1,000 words.) *(70 marks)*

2. Theme or Issue

A theme or issue in a text is **a central idea** or topic of interest within the story. There are many universal themes in literature, including relationships, morality, identity, conflict and power. The author's presentation of a theme often challenges the reader to think about human nature and to distinguish between right and wrong.

Comparing themes can broaden our understanding of what it means to be human and allow us to experience, at a safe distance, the struggles characters go through as they confront and seek resolutions to their difficulties.

We all **need to know ourselves**, to distinguish between appearance and reality, come to terms with growing up, face the finality of death, understand the destructive consequences of hatred and violence – and the redeeming power of love. Great writers provide ways of enabling us to do this.

The **impact of a key scene** or turning point in a Shakespearean play such as *Othello* will influence our understanding of the theme or issue. Are questions raised in the scene? What point is the playwright making? Are the main characters developing or not? What techniques is the playwright using to communicate his theme? Is the treatment comic or tragic?

> **Remember!**
>
> *Various themes are likely to overlap at times. For example, identity, gender and power are all closely interlinked in* Othello.

Exploring Theme or Issue in *Othello*

Drama conveys its message primarily through:

- character
- plot
- setting
- dialogue
- atmosphere
- mood
- movement
- sound
- imagery and symbols
- soliloquies, asides

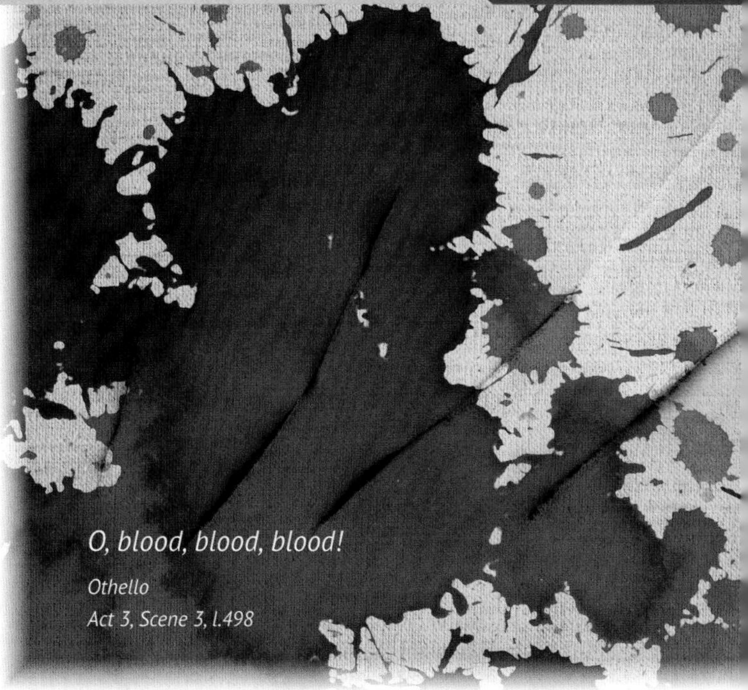

O, blood, blood, blood!
Othello
Act 3, Scene 3, l.498

Exploring the Theme of Relationships through Character Study

Othello's **dysfunctional relationships** with himself, his society and other characters leads inescapably to the play's tragic outcome. Othello, originally a heathen Moor and now senior military officer, wants to be part of Venice, a white Christian society radically different from anything he has previously known.

'Valiant Othello'

At the start of the story, the protagonist is introduced to the audience at the height of his power, 'hotly called for' to defend the state against the Turkish enemy. He is 'brave Othello', who is respected by all those who 'served him'. Initially, he is **comfortable facing up to challenges**. Under threat from Brabantio's search party, he uses his military experience to judge the right time to engage in violence, 'Were it my cue to fight, I should have known it'.

From the age of seven, Othello has spent his life in 'feats of broil and battle' at the centre of an all-male world where he has pursued 'Pride, pomp and circumstance of glorious war'. The heroic leader on the battlefield demands certainty and will act decisively, 'once in doubt/ Is once to be resolved'. The Moor is a highly competent professional soldier, but he lacks self-knowledge and is unaware that not all situations can be dealt with by military tactics. This leads him to make a series of ***disastrous decisions in his personal relationships***.

A rejected follower

The Moor **shows poor judgement** in his dealings with others, often failing to recognise the consequences that will arise from his decisive actions. He broke military tradition when he passed over Iago for promotion, abandoning 'by old gradation, where each second,/ Stood heir to the first'. Othello had not considered the effect on his bitterly offended ensign, who now follows him 'to serve my turn upon him'. Why did he choose the inexperienced Florentine Cassio who is a 'bookish theoric'? What does his choice tell us about the Moor?

Is Othello insecure about his lack of education and civilised manners? He **admits to being unsophisticated**, 'Rude am I in my speech,/ And little blessed with the soft phrase of peace'. Did he choose Michael Cassio because he was the go-between in his courtship of Desdemona? Was he not aware that Cassio had 'unhappy brains for drinking?' It seems that as an outsider living in a white urban society, Othello is never really at ease in Venice.

An abused father

Brabantio, Desdemona's father, once accepted the Moor as a welcome guest in his home. This was presumably because he admired Othello as a military officer who had experienced 'hair-breadth scapes i' the imminent deadly breach'. Yet Brabantio's attitude changes dramatically when Othello elopes with his daughter. The elderly Venetian senator feels betrayed and embarrassed, fearing that Desdemona will 'incur a general mock'. He reacts by **judging Othello as a cultural stereotype who must have resorted to witchcraft**, 'practices of cunning hell', to win his daughter. Was Brabantio naive in allowing this 'extravagant and wheeling stranger' into his home?

There are several other questions about the relationship between the two men. Why did Othello elope? Did he suspect that Brabantio would object to the marriage? Did Othello not consider that he might be abusing Brabantio's hospitality by deceiving him? Or did he think that he had acted honourably in marrying Desdemona? What is clear is that **Othello's status in Venetian society directly affects all his relationships**. Unfortunately, he is not fully aware that he may be accepted for his 'service' to the city-state, but not as a member of a prominent Venetian family.

A demoted friend

Othello's soldierly skills are not equal to the task of administering the island of Cyprus. When confronted by a drunken street brawl involving his lieutenant, he becomes flustered and reverts to his military background. The Moor demands certainty, 'Give me to know/ How this foul rout began'. Having initially misjudged Cassio's character weaknesses, he now **acts decisively, dismissing their friendship**, 'Cassio, I love thee/ But never more be officer of mine'. He has made an 'example' of the lieutenant and deprived him of rank and reputation. Othello prides himself on being an honourable man who upholds justice even at a terrible price to himself and others.

A dishonest friend

Ironically, Othello relies heavily on the man he passed over for promotion, 'honest' Iago. **The two men have a complex relationship** and the embittered ensign reprogrammes the Moor to view himself through the prism of racial

This fellow's of exceeding honesty

Othello
Act 3 Scene 3, l. 287

stereotypes. Although Othello is originally depicted as a black outcast, old and uncivilised, he tries to resist, 'For she had eyes, and chose me'. But Iago plays on Othello's insecurity as a naive outsider in this white society, 'In Venice they do let heaven see the pranks/ They dare not show their husbands'.

The ensign also reminds Othello of Desdemona's deception of 'her father, marrying you'. As the lies and doubts continue, Iago soon begins to take Desdemona's place in Othello's mind. Act 4 Scene 1 marks a turning point. Overcome by jealousy, the Moor collapses in an epileptic fit, which Iago contemptuously dismisses as a 'passion most unsuiting such a man'. **Othello is now 'bound' to Iago forever.** His desire to banish uncertainty outweighs his regard for Desdemona. He has destroyed not only his wife but also his peace of mind, 'Farewell the tranquil mind!'

Othello's downfall is a direct result of his dependency on Iago. He blindly accepts the ensign's flimsy story of Cassio's guilt based on a dubious account of a dream and the incriminating 'evidence' of the handkerchief. Othello now sees himself as an agent of justice and swears a 'sacred vow' with Iago to bring 'swift means of death' to his supposedly adulterous wife. He is pleased at the 'justice' of strangling her in 'the bed she hath contaminated'. The Moor has reverted to his heathen side.

A scorned wife

Desdemona's relationship with Othello raises many questions. She is portrayed as a character who lacks self-awareness. Idealistic and romantic, Desdemona 'saw Othello's visage in his mind'. She forsakes all for love, 'my soul and fortunes consecrate' and believes so completely in her image of Othello as an exotic, courageous hero that when his behaviour towards her changes, she attributes this to his administrative concerns as Cypris's governor. Desdemona tactlessly persists in pleading on Cassio's behalf despite her husband's obvious displeasure, 'leave me but a little to myself'.

Shortly after Desdemona is viciously struck on the face by her enraged husband, she timidly leaves so as not to 'offend' him. When he accuses her of being 'that cunning whore of Venice', she instructs Emilia to lay her wedding sheets on her bed. She also refuses to accept Emilia's cynical advice that husbands should 'use us well'. Desdemona dies exonerating her husband from blame for her own murder, totally deluded by the romantic picture in which she has so heavily invested. **The audience is left wondering if Desdemona and Othello ever really knew each other.**

Self-knowledge

Othello's reasons for loving Desdemona and his hasty elopement suggest a man who is infatuated rather than in love. He admits that he loved her because she admired his bravery in battle and 'did pity' the dangers he had endured. But **their relationship is never stable**. At times Othello is clearly obsessed by her, 'when I love thee not,/ Chaos is come again'. Towards the end of the play, he sees himself as an arbiter of justice, killing his wife 'else she'll betray more men'. He continues to fool himself that he is 'merciful' by killing her when she revives.

Othello reaches his **lowest point of self-delusion** when he tries to excuse himself of his wife's murder by claiming 'You heard her say herself, it was not I'. When Emilia reveals Desdemona's innocence, he begins to realise what he has done and how he has damned himself by this unjust murder, 'That look of thine will hurl my soul from heaven'. He feels dishonoured, 'why should honour outlive honesty?/ Let it all go'. The Moor's tendency towards self-dramatisation remains right up to his suicide. Has he redeemed himself in Venetian society's eyes?

The inter-racial relationship between Othello and Desdemona was troubled from the outset. The Moor struggled to be a husband to a wealthy white Venetian woman. Othello was confident and successful as a military leader and found it **difficult to relate to people away from the battlefield**. He is such a poor judge of character that Iago has little trouble exploiting Othello's insecurities about love and marriage.

Audiences continue to speculate about Othello's relationship with Desdemona. Has he damned himself to eternal hell by committing an act of despair? The play's characters also disagree about Othello. Gratiano regards his epitaph as 'marred' and questionable while Cassio pronounces him 'great of heart'. Through his creation of the 'noble Moor' Shakespeare has presented a complex study of the devastating consequences for a person and others when self-knowledge is lacking.

Useful Quotes: Theme or Issue

Her father loved me; oft invited me; Still questioned me the story of my life **(Othello to the Duke of Venice)** *Act 1 Scene 3, l.140–1*	The theme of self-delusion is evident in Othello's failure to realise his true worth to Venetian society. He is praised for his prowess on the battlefield and his usefulness as a mercenary soldier against the Turkish threat. He is easily dismissed later when the threat ends and he is soon replaced by the Florentine Cassio. Othello is not really welcome as a member of Venetian society.
a frail vow betwixt an erring barbarian and a super-subtle Venetian **(Iago to Roderigo)** *Act 1 Scene 3, l.377–8*	Iago has a way with words and is able to persuade Roderigo to help him take revenge on Othello and Cassio. The sleek alliterative phrase 'super-subtle' reflects the scheming ensign's malicious character, highlighting the theme of evil at the core of the play.
a subtle slippery knave, a finder of occasions, that has an eye can stamp and counterfeit advantages **(Iago to Roderigo)** *Act 2 Scene 1, l.260–2*	Appearance and reality is another of the play's central themes. In this ironic statement, Iago ridicules Cassio, but what the ensign says is actually an accurate description of his own evil character. Sibilant alliteration emphasises Iago's underhand schemes.
Demand me nothing: what you know, you know: From this time forth I never will speak word **(Iago to Othello)** *Act 5 Scene 2, l.349–50*	The theme of power is explored largely through the complex relationship between Iago and the Moor. For most of the play, Iago has used his skill with language to control Othello and others. Persuasive speech has been the medium of his evil vengeance. After his villainy is revealed and Othello asks why Iago has tried to 'ensnare' him, the unrepentant villain refuses to explain himself. He attempts to regain control by sullen silence, frustrating his victims.

Remember!

Discussion points in the 30-mark Part (a) sample answer can also provide the basis for developed comparisons in the 40-mark Part (b) and 70-mark single questions. To write successful examination answers, it is essential to study the wording of questions closely. Marks can easily be lost if attention is not paid to each element of the question.

Exam Guide

A theme should not be confused with plot or storyline. In responding to the Theme or Issue mode questions, focus on central ideas or messages presented by authors. Think about how different authors establish and develop themes in texts. Be careful to avoid unfocused narrative that simply retells the story rather than tackling the question.

Perdition catch my soul,
But I do love thee!

Othello
Act 3 Scene 3, l.99–100

Sample Part (a) Question

Q. 'The same theme or issue can appear more relevant to life today in some texts than in others.'

In relation to <u>one</u> text on your comparative course, discuss the aspects of the text that, in your opinion, make your chosen theme or issue appear more or less relevant to life today. Support your answer with reference to the text. *(30 marks)*

Indicative Material

- The author's approach to a theme can make that theme or issue seem more/less relevant to life today
- The social morals and mores may/may not make a theme or issue seem remote to modern life
- The story may be timeless or dated or contemporary, making the theme or issue seem more or less relevant to life
- A particular setting (historical or contemporary) may/may not make a theme or issue appear more/less relevant
- Characterisation can contribute to our sense of the relevance of a theme or issue appearing to be contemporary regardless of the time in which the character lives
- The presentation of a theme or issue through music/imagery/symbolism/visual effects, etc. can make a theme or issue appear more or less relevant to life today
- Views and values (outmoded or contemporary), expressed implicitly or explicitly, about matters such as the role of women, social equity, etc. can make a theme or issue appear more/less relevant to modern life, etc.

Sample Answer

In 'Othello', Shakespeare's approach to the difficulty of establishing loving relationships is explored in a way that makes that theme appear modern and relevant. The romance between Desdemona and the Moor who 'loved not wisely but too well' is as relevant today as it was in the 17th century. The recklessness of an obsessed man who is willing to sacrifice everything for love remains true when the disastrous consequences of excessive passion are revealed. Shakespeare's story about foolish love and lack of communication is timeless.

Today's world travellers meet and marry, often coming from different backgrounds. Desdemona and Othello are from very different cultures. She is from a refined, sophisticated city, Venice, and has led a sheltered life under her father's 'guardage'. She is revered by all her society. Cassio calls her 'divine Desdemona', Roderigo believes she is 'full of most blessed condition'. Her father describes her as 'so still and quiet'. Into this cultured world comes 'an extravagant and wheeling stranger', Othello. He is a mercenary soldier whose world is the violent battlefield, but who now wishes to marry Desdemona.

The clash of cultures occurs when Othello demands of Desdemona to 'Lend me thy handkerchief'. When she cannot produce it, the Moor reverts to his superstitious North African background when he insists 'there's magic in the web of it'. He believes that as long as his wife has the handkerchief, all will be well between the couple. Desdemona is completely out of her depth with this, 'would to God that I had never seen it!' Their intense feelings for each other are expressed in terms of excess, 'it is too much of joy' (Othello), 'My downright violence and storm of fortunes' (Desdemona). Passion and physical attraction do not necessarily guarantee a lasting relationship – a universal theme that is just as relevant today.

To the end Desdemona cannot let go of her love for Othello for whom she sacrificed everything. She dies without gaining self-knowledge, 'Commend me to my kind lord'. Othello only achieves partial self-awareness when he speaks of 'these unlucky deeds' – he is not accepting his responsibility for them. He gave in to jealousy and chose to murder his wife. Excessive feeling, 'a violent commencement' that blinds a person to the reality of a situation, is shown to have dire consequences for all. Shakespeare warns of the dangers of extreme passion whether between those of a similar or different background. It is important to love 'wisely'. *(405 words)*

Examiner's Comment

- Good top-grade response that addresses the relevance of a particular theme in the play.
- Impressive introduction and effective third paragraph on the universality of the theme.
- Generally focused – but drifts at times into general discussion on self-awareness.
- Clear understanding of Theme or Issue mode.
- Apt, supportive reference and clear expression.

Class/Homework Exercise

Using some of the points from the Indicative Material above, write your own response to the Part (a) question. (Aim for 400 words.)

Exam Guide

To structure your comparative essay answer, a useful exercise is to practise making an outline of the **key points** you wish to include. The following Draft Plan uses *Othello* as one of the comparative texts.

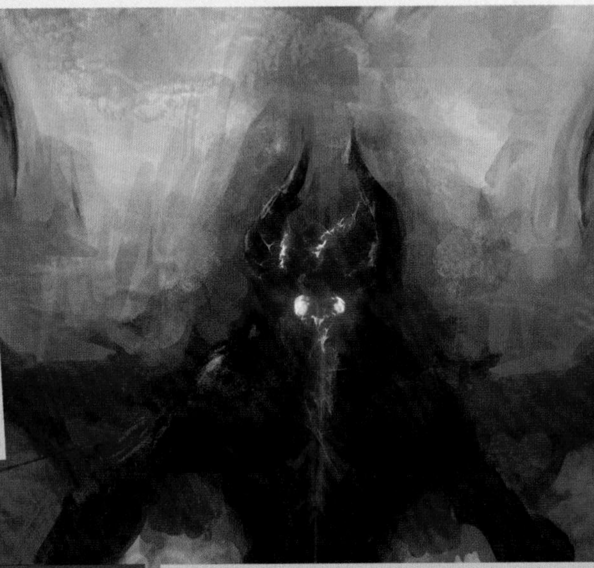

When devils will the blackest sins put on,
They do suggest at first with heavenly shows

Iago
Act 2 Scene 3, l.351–2

Sample 70-mark Question

Q. 'There are many reasons why the exploration of the same theme or issue can be more entertaining in some texts than in others.'

Compare the reasons why you found the exploration of the same theme or issue more entertaining in some texts than in others. Support your answer with reference to <u>three texts</u> you studied on your comparative course. *(70 marks)*

Indicative Material

- Engaging storylines, plot twists, key moments, unexpected endings, etc. can make a theme or issue more/less entertaining
- An author's approach to the theme or issue, e.g. comic, tragic/realistic, etc. can be more/less entertaining
- The presentation/behaviour of characters can make the exploration of a theme more/less enjoyable
- Insights gained through the exploration of a theme or issue can entertain, amuse, involve, disturb, bore, inspire, etc.
- Particular features of different genres, e.g. colourful costumes/music/sound effects/camerawork/special effects, etc. used in the exploration of a theme or issue can increase/reduce the appeal/entertainment value of the theme or issue, etc.

Sample Draft Plan

INTRODUCTION

Othello is a mesmerising study of evil presented through the character of Iago. The smooth-talking villain fascinates, repels and frustrates not only the characters onstage but also the audience through his chameleon-like behaviour and total lack of remorse for the havoc he has wrought.

POINT 1

In my comparative course, the three texts I studied allowed me to focus on the intriguing theme of evil and its consequences. In *Othello* a bitter ensign's knowledge of human frailty is so great that he can adapt to suit any character's circumstance. On the surface, he is adviser to Cassio and confidant of Desdemona, fellow conspirator to Roderigo and loyal follower of Othello. His indispensable advice earns him the title 'Honest Iago' while he becomes the characters' inner voice, tempting them to become his puppets for his own benefit. *My other* ***two texts*** *presented similar/contrasting views of their villains ...*

POINT 2

Iago, unlike all the other characters in the play, has an awareness of self, 'I am not what I am'. He accepts that he is envious of the educated, courteous Cassio who 'hath a daily beauty in his life/ That makes me ugly'. I was fascinated that the only main character left alive at the play's conclusion was Cassio, who will be in charge of the ensign's punishment. Perhaps Iago was not as successful as he thought he would be. *The self-awareness of the other characters in my* ***second text*** *was similar/different ...*

POINT 3

The audience's reaction to Iago is mixed, combining fascination and repulsion. At different times, he can be terrifying, charismatic, charming, witty – even sympathetic. This logical, modern man makes the audience omniscient and in a way collaborative in his evil plans through his subtle use of language, 'When devils will the blackest sins put on/ They do suggest at first with heavenly shows'. *This ambivalent reaction to the villain is/is not used in my* ***third text ...***

POINT 4

The complete villain revels in causing hurt and destruction. Love to him is 'merely lust of the blood and a permission of the will'. We wonder if his risks will succeed. He delights in the havoc he is about to wreak in the scene when Othello and Desdemona are reunited in Cyprus. *In my* ***second/third text****, the central character does/does not take pleasure in their evil actions ...*

CONCLUDING PARAGRAPH

The audience remains spellbound right to the unexpected end, which frustrates and disturbs everyone. Shakespeare does not allow Othello to defeat Iago, 'If that thou be'st a devil, I cannot kill thee'. Are humans powerless in the face of true wickedness? Iago also refuses to explain why he acted as he did, 'what you know, you know'. The audience is left to sift furiously through the evidence presented to try to work out as Othello demanded, 'Why?' *This is an absorbing study of evil. In comparison, the endings of my* ***other two texts ...***

Sample Paragraph: **POINT 4**

Iago delights in ruining the key moment of Desdemona and Othello's happy reunion in Cyprus. He confides in the uneasy audience, predicting that he will use Cassio's friendship with Desdemona to 'ensnare' all. He fools Roderigo into misinterpreting what has happened, 'Didst thou not see Her paddle with the palm of his hand?' Yet earlier he told the audience that it was Cassio who 'takes her by the palm'. At first, Roderigo excuses this behaviour as 'but courtesy' – actions acceptable in Venice. Iago's sneaky language foreshadows the trick he will also pull off on the 'credulous' Othello, causing him to mis-see what he is actually witnessing. The audience is amazed at Iago's ingenuity in getting the foolish Roderigo – who regarded Desdemona as 'full of most blessed condition' – to believe that she is about to embark on an affair with Cassio. *In my **second/third text**, the central character does/does not exult in his/her devious schemes ...*

Examiner's Comment

- Solid mid-grade response that includes general comment and detailed narrative reference.
- More direct focus needed on the 'entertaining' impact of the presentation of the theme.
- Expression is clear and there is close engagement with the text.
- Good comparative approach at the end of the paragraph.

Remember!

Modes overlap. For example, Theme or Issue is often influenced by both the Cultural Context and Vision and Viewpoint of a text.

Useful Comparative Links

Successful comparative answers include clear links between texts.

The following phrases might be useful in pointing out similarities and differences between texts.

Similarities	Differences
• Both authors take a similar approach. • The two stories have much in common. • This is also evident in the film's most disturbing scene. • Common to all three narratives is ... • In an almost identical way ... • This is mirrored in the way the heroine of the story acts when ... • The same effect occurs later in the text. • Likewise, in my other texts ... • This viewpoint is echoed at the end of my second text ...	• These two texts could not be more different. • These two key moments illustrate contrasting aspects of ... • In an entirely different way ... • In contrast, the opening scene in the novel ... • The complete opposite is seen in ... • On the other hand ... • This is certainly not the case in the film, where ... • All three endings are completely different. • The novel takes a much more unexpected approach. • This aspect is contrasted in my second/third text, when ...

Class/Homework Exercises

1. Choose **one** of the other points in the Sample Draft Plan and write a paragraph of your own in response to the question above. (Aim for 150 words.)
2. 'The presentation of a powerful theme or issue can add greatly to the impact of the story on a reader.'
   With reference to **three texts** on your comparative course, compare the ways in which the presentation of a theme or issue in each text was presented and its impact on you. (Aim for 1,000 words.) *(70 marks)*

3. Literary Genre

Literary genre refers to the **craft of story-telling**. Authors make use of various narrative techniques that are commonly found in novels, plays and films.

These include:

- plot or storyline
- characterisation
- setting
- dialogue
- conflict and tension
- resolution

Other Aspects of Literary Genre

Narrative voice Point-of-view
Foreshadowing Flashback Climax
Plot twist Action Atmosphere
Mood Language Imagery
Symbolism Contrast Soliloquy
Irony Humour Sound
Lighting Music

Othello: Literary Genre

Othello is a Shakespearean **tragedy** in five acts. The hero has the potential for greatness, but he has a fatal character flaw (*hamartia*) and that weakness leads to his downfall, with disastrous consequences for himself and others.

Othello's initial fault is his **jealous nature**. He is also gullible and this makes him irrationally quick in his wrong judgements and actions. At the beginning of the play, he makes the rash decision to believe Iago's insinuations that his wife Desdemona is having an affair with Cassio. He then demands 'ocular proof' so that he can be sure of her guilt. Othello's jealousy becomes obsessive and he resolves to kill his wife so that she cannot deceive more men. His error is pointed out by Emilia, Iago's wife. Othello recognises the truth and commits suicide. Iago is arrested and order is restored. Othello's flawed judgement leads to his own demise and several other deaths.

'Stagecraft' is a general term for the playwright's skill at writing for dramatic performance. There was minimal use of scenery or props on Elizabethan stages, such as London's Globe Theatre. Audiences relied on their own imagination based on the play's language to understand setting and mood. Unlike modern dramatists, Shakespeare did not use stage directions. In *Othello*, **a range of dramatic techniques**, including contrast, irony, soliloquies and imagery, create tension and pace within the drama.

be merry, Cassio
For thy solicitor shall rather die
Than give thy cause away
Desdemona
Act 3 Scene 3, l.28–30

Key Aspects of Literary Genre in *Othello*

Structure

The genre of tragedy is **rooted in ancient Greek drama**. Shakespeare's famous tragedies have a five-act structure, each act corresponding to a section of the story. Analysing the **plot structure** can help us to understand the play's action as purposeful and unified. We can see how the main plot and secondary storylines work together to develop the key themes of the play. In *Othello*, the tragic central relationship (between Othello and Desdemona) together with the minor stories concerning Roderigo and Cassio all focus the audience's attention throughout the drama.

The first act is used for **exposition** and introduces the main characters, setting and possible signs of conflict ahead. *Othello*, Act 1 establishes the noble character of the Moor. It also signals Iago's motivation for vengeance – his jealousy at being overlooked for promotion and his suspicion that his wife has had a relationship with Othello. Desdemona and Othello's hasty elopement takes place just before he is sent to Cyprus as governor. Iago encourages Roderigo's obsession with Desdemona to get revenge on Othello.

Act 2 is the **complication** (or 'rising action') when characters act in response to the opening conflict and key relationships are developed. This complicates the play's action, involving the audience. Iago encourages Cassio's weakness for drink and gets him demoted. The ensign also encourages him to use Desdemona's influence with Othello in the hope that he will be reinstated as lieutenant. This will later fuel Othello's jealousy. Iago continues to use Roderigo to destroy Cassio's reputation.

Act 3 marks the play's **climax**. The action reaches a turning point and the main crisis occurs. There is no going back for the protagonist (central character). Characters or circumstances change (for the worse and/or the better). In this act, Desdemona pleads Cassio's case for reinstatement despite her husband's obvious displeasure. Iago convinces Othello that his wife is being unfaithful. He uses the flimsy 'evidence' of a dropped handkerchief and a tale about a dream Cassio had. Othello and Iago enter into a pact to kill the alleged 'lovers', Cassio and Desdemona.

Act 4 is the **falling action** and features the unravelling of complications and the resolution of conflict. Iago continues to 'poison' Othello's mind about his wife. He has placed him to 'overhear' Cassio speaking. But the subject of the conversation is really Bianca (Cassio's mistress) and not Desdemona. However, Othello is duped into believing that Cassio is ridiculing his wife. He falls into an epileptic fit and, later he strikes Desdemona in public. Roderigo and Emilia are becoming suspicious. In one poignant scene, Desdemona is depressed and submissive, despite Emilia's best efforts to teach her about the world's cruel ways. As tragedy envelops the central characters, the suspense grows and we await the final outcome.

Act 5 concludes the tragedy and is sometimes called the **catastrophe** or final resolution. This brings the conflict to its conclusion, and death to the play's tragic hero. As the drama draws to a close, Roderigo is fatally wounded and Desdemona is suffocated by Othello. But Iago's evil plans are undone by Emilia's revelations. Cassio clears his name. Roderigo's letters provide more evidence against Iago, who is arrested and imprisoned. Othello finally realises the truth too late and asks the ensign why he 'ensnared' him. Iago refuses to explain his actions and is threatened with torture. In an attempt to regain some honour, Othello commits suicide. Emilia and Desdemona also die. The restoration of moral and social stability comes at great cost. Public order is restored with Cassio's appointment as the new governor of Cyprus. Tragedy evokes pity and fear in the audience, leading finally to **catharsis** (the release of these passions).

Revenge drama

Othello is often categorised as a classic revenge play. The story is dominated by Iago, who is a villain and malcontent. He can be seen as an evil and sadistic **Machiavellian figure**, someone who deceives and exploits others to achieve his aims. The term comes from the medieval Italian writer Niccolò Machiavelli, who gained a reputation for promoting the philosophy that 'The end justifies the means'.

Iago has grudges against authority and women. Passed over for promotion by Othello, losing out to Cassio who has less experience, Iago has to make do with the lower rank of ensign (flag-bearer). This motivates him to exact revenge. He is amoral and inventive, **using every situation and**

manipulating other characters to his advantage. Iago convinces Cassio to ask Desdemona for help in regaining his position as lieutenant and plants in Cassio's room the handkerchief Othello had given to Desdemona, which leads Othello to suspect her of infidelity. When his wife, Emilia, reveals the truth of his plotting, Iago kills her. In the end, he is arrested and sent to trial without ever explaining his actions.

Soliloquies and asides allow the audience to know a character's state of mind. We see the real Iago in a series of informative soliloquies. Early on, he reveals, 'I hate the Moor', his suspicions 'that 'twixt my sheets/ He has done my office'. Iago also accuses Cassio 'with my nightcap too'. After convincing Othello of Cassio's affair with Desdemona, Iago gloats over the fallen Othello, 'Work on,/ My medicine, work!' Shakespeare has placed the audience in the uncomfortable position of being aware of Iago's every move before he makes it. This has the effect of almost involving them as unwilling accomplices in the ensign's diabolical schemes.

In Othello's first soliloquy (Act 3 Scene 3), the Moor praises Iago's 'exceeding honesty'. The ensign's vengeful plans have worked. Othello denigrates his own colour and lack of 'those soft parts of conversation/ That chamberers have'. He questions Desdemona's love and comes to the conclusion, 'She's gone'. Othello's only other soliloquy takes place just after he tries to smother Desdemona and before the entrance of Emilia. The fragmented rhythm, questions and short asides reflect his obvious confusion. Confronted with the horror of his situation, **Othello begins to show some regret**, 'My wife! My wife! What wife? I have no wife'.

Killings and corpses are on prominent display in this play, particularly in the final scene, 'the tragic loading of this bed'. There are three murders, two attempted murders and one suicide, all of them onstage. Desdemona's body lies in view for the last part of the story, emphasising the cruelty of her tragic fate to the audience. Meanwhile, Othello seeks to justify himself as someone who acted not 'in hate, but all in honour'. The series of violent deaths emphasises the terrible price innocent victims pay when those in power act rashly.

Unexpected events

Shakespeare uses many of the staple elements of modern horror films today. These are designed to **maintain dramatic tension**. Roderigo is shocked when his co-conspirator Iago stabs him, 'inhuman dog'. Desdemona's revival after suffocation is alarming and increases the depth of Othello's guilt in the audience's eyes. The Moor does not repent but continues in his self-appointed role as judge and executioner, 'I that am cruel am yet merciful;/ I would not have thee linger in thy pain'. Incidents such as the unexpected murder of Emilia and Othello's suicide involve the audience right to the end of this intense tragedy.

Subplots

The subplot is a common literary technique found in plays, novels and films. Subplots are secondary stories or offshoots of the main storyline and are often connected to it through minor characters. In *Othello*, several strands of the main plot – particularly involving Roderigo, Cassio and Emilia

Thou art sure of me. Go, make money

Iago

Act 1 Scene 3, l.385

– add depth to the drama and increase tension. However, the sense of claustrophobia in the play is heightened by the fact that there is no single significant subplot. The action throughout focuses very closely on Iago's manipulative role and Othello's reactions to his vengeful scheming.

Roderigo's story

Roderigo's desperate, futile hopes of winning Desdemona's affections open the play. Both her father and Desdemona herself have rejected him. Iago convinces him that the way to Desdemona's heart is to flatter her with lavish gifts. Even when Desdemona is married to Othello, Iago convinces his 'fool' that he can still succeed, 'She must change for youth'. He convinces Roderigo that Desdemona has fallen for Michael Cassio and persuades him to murder the lieutenant. When he fails and only wounds Cassio, he is no longer of use to Iago, who kills him. Roderigo finally serves the interests of justice by revealing Iago's treachery.

Dramatic significance

This subplot mirrors the main plot because it highlights the tragic consequences of rash, uncontrollable desire. Both Othello and Roderigo pay dearly for their passion. Roderigo provides some comic relief because the audience's sympathy is never really with the ridiculous, gullible young man. However, his story reveals the cold-blooded behaviour of Iago, who regards Roderigo as a 'snipe' and a 'quat' while tricking him out of his fortune. This prevents the audience from admiring the cleverness of Iago's deceitful schemes.

Cassio's story

Cassio's life provides a contrast to the rough, uncultured world of the battlefield in which both Othello and Iago operate. He is the young, cultured lieutenant who enjoys a close friendship with Othello's wife. He worships the 'divine Desdemona' in a chivalrous manner. However, he uses his connection with her to ask her to intercede on his behalf in his hour of need, 'I being absent, and my place supplied,/ My general will forget my love and service'.

Dramatic significance

Shakespeare uses the lieutenant's casual relationship with Bianca as a contrast to the grand passion between Othello and Desdemona. This subplot also highlights the loveless marriage between Iago and Emilia. All three women are let down by their partners. Desdemona's genuine love for Othello is echoed in Bianca's genuine affection for Cassio. Bianca and Emilia are much more realistic than Desdemona. However, Bianca does not share Emilia's cynicism. Like Othello, she is distressed by jealousy, 'This is some minx's token'. Cassio and Bianca do show some genuine affection for each other ('sweet Bianca', 'dear Cassio') and, perhaps, represent a more worldly, attainable relationship with which the audience can identify.

Symbols and Imagery Patterns

In Shakespeare's time, religious belief was prevalent. God was regarded as the head of the universe. Almost everyone in England was Christian, believing in Hell as a very real place, and that the Devil was a specific person. Othello's tragic story shows how if people debase their soul by losing their reason, they are no better than animals, such as Cassio in his drunken brawl and Othello in his excessive passion. The playwright depicts human degradation through his use of animal imagery. Shakespeare illustrates how humans 'transform ourselves into beasts' by referencing dogs, horses, toads, asses, monkeys, snakes, beasts and monsters.

Iago

Iago indicates how corrupt he is by his constant use of animal imagery, 'you'll have your daughter covered by a Barbary horse'. He regards Othello as a stupid, worthless person by 'making him egregiously an ass'. He swears 'exchange me for a goat'. The ensign's tainted character is evident throughout the play. Roderigo calls him 'inhuman dog'. Lodovico calls him a 'viper'.

Othello

Othello's controlled poetic language disintegrates as he becomes consumed with jealousy at the thought of Desdemona's supposed infidelity. He calls his wife a 'minx', or a mischievous pet dog. He regards her tears as fake, 'crocodile'. Under Iago's influence, his love has become poisoned like a 'cistern for foul toads'.

Magic

Shakespeare uses references to magic to show unnatural practices. Brabantio cannot believe his

in chains of magic
Brabantio
Act 1 Scene 2, l.77

daughter chose Othello of her own free will. He accuses him of witchcraft, 'foul charms' and 'chains of magic'. Othello also references magic in his description of the lost handkerchief. It was woven from the silk of sacred worms and had special powers that would bring harm to anyone who mislaid it. Loss of the handkerchief meant loss of fidelity in marriage. Magic underlines Othello's status as an outsider. The audience is left with an uneasy sense of the influence of witchcraft on the play's tragic outcome.

Remember!

Discussion points in the 30-mark Part (a) sample answer can also provide the basis for developed comparisons in the 40-mark Part (b) and 70-mark essay questions. To write successful examination answers, it is essential to study the wording of questions closely. Marks can easily be lost if attention is not paid to each facet of the questions.

Sample Part (a) Question

Q. Discuss how effectively two techniques are used to provide revealing insights into the minds of one or more central characters in <u>one text</u> on your comparative course.

Develop your answer with reference to the text. *(30 marks)*

Indicative Material

- Effective use of setting, narrative voice, dialogue, foreshadowing, flashback, back story
- Camera used effectively, e.g. close-ups, action shots, unusual angles or point-of-view shots, voice-overs, music, sound or special effects, editing, use of colour, black and white, etc.
- Soliloquies, asides, silence, special effects, lighting, body language, facial expression, costume, stage directions, etc. can all provide revealing insights
- Impact of choice of language, imagery, symbols, motifs, detail, use of diaries/letters, etc.

Sample Answer

In 'Othello', Shakespeare uses language and soliloquies to provide insight into the thinking of the central characters, Othello and Iago. Dialogue and vivid imagery allow us to comprehend the truth about both these two men and we witness the disintegration of their humanity.

At the start, Othello's language is formal and dignified. But the noble Moor, 'free and open', is soon corrupted by Iago's evil insinuations, 'I'll pour this pestilence into his ear'. He echoes Iago's animal imagery as he descends into depravity, becoming the 'green-eyed monster'. Instead of affectionately thinking of her as his 'fair warrior', he now roars that he will 'tear her all to pieces'. He demeans her with 'whore' and 'strumpet' as his love becomes contaminated by jealous rage.

Yet even as he plans to murder his innocent wife, he is still torn by love for her. This can be seen by his use of the gentle images of a candle and a rose to describe Desdemona. He knows he cannot give the rose 'vital growth' if he plucks it and it will 'wither'. His soliloquy reveals his trauma, graphically showing the torment created by Iago. Through Othello's transformed expression, the playwright allows the audience to see into his mind, which has been 'poisoned' by Iago. He was 'wrought/ Perplexed in the extreme'.

Iago's soliloquies and spiteful asides also reveal his depraved nature. When he observes the chivalrous behaviour between Desdemona and Cassio, he vows to use it 'catch' him in his 'courtesies'. When he observes the grand passion of Othello and Desdemona, he swears to 'set down the pegs that make this music'. The audience is shocked to observe the contempt in which he holds Roderigo, a 'snipe' and a 'quat' despite the fact the Roderigo has sold all his lands to give money to Iago to win Desdemona.

Having fascinated the audience throughout the play by informing them of what he is about to do before he does it, Shakespeare places them in the position of unwilling accomplice. They wait to see if Iago will succeed or not, 'This is the night/ That either makes me or fordoes me quite'. His silence at the play's conclusion leaves everyone in a state of frustration when he declares 'From this time forth I never will speak word'. No one is to be satisfied with an explanation of why this man acted this way.

Shakespeare has created a play that has provided the audience with an awareness of what the characters thought through his use of language and imagery. *(425 words)*

Examiner's Comment

- High-grade response, focusing mainly on how imagery and soliloquies reveal character.
- Impressive overview followed by three well-illustrated discussion points.
- Paragraph 4 lapses into more general comment and is less effective.
- Informed use of quotes, and good understanding of Literary Genre mode.
- Apart from some repetition in paragraph 4, overall expression is clear and varied.

Class/Homework Exercise

Using some of the points from the Indicative Material above, write your own response to the Part (a) question. (Aim for 150 words.)

Exam Guide

To structure your comparative essay answer on Literary Genre, a useful exercise is to practise making an outline of the **key points** you wish to include. The following Draft Plan uses *Othello* as one of the comparative texts.

When I have plucked the rose,
I cannot give it vital growth again
Othello
Act 5 Scene 2, l.13–14

Sample 70-mark Question

Q. Compare how tense moods or atmospheres are created in each of <u>three texts</u> on your comparative course. Refer to at least one technique used to create tense moods or atmospheres in each of your chosen texts. Develop your answer with reference to your chosen texts.

You may refer to the same technique or different techniques in each of your chosen texts.
(70 marks)

Indicative Material

- Use of narrative voice/dialogue/flashback/back story/setting/dramatic irony to create tense mood/atmosphere
- Soliloquies/asides/silence/special effects/lighting/body language/facial expression/costume/stage directions, etc. can all heighten tension
- Impact of choice of language – imagery, symbols, motifs, detail, use of diaries/letters can create sad/disturbing Gothic/surreal and unnerving moods
- Camera used to evoke suspense, e.g. close-ups, action shots, special effects, unusual angles or point-of-view shots/voice-overs/music, sound or special effects/editing/use of colour, black and white, etc.

Sample Draft Plan

INTRODUCTION

Writers use various literary techniques to create tense moods in my three comparative texts. Shakespeare uses dramatic irony in 'Othello' to build a suspense-filled, gripping atmosphere to involve the audience in the action. Only they know what is going on. The recurring motif of the handkerchief creates an exotic, disturbing atmosphere as the playwright threads it through the narrative, first as a love-token, then as damning evidence and finally as incontrovertible proof of Desdemona's innocence. *The authors in my **other two comparative texts** use similar/different techniques to create moods ...*

POINT 1

Dramatic irony is the gap between what appears to be and what is. The appearance of Iago's personality, 'Honest Iago' is very different from the foreboding reality, 'nothing can or shall content my soul/ Till I am evened with him'. Iago manipulates naive characters, Desdemona, Cassio and Othello, like obedient puppets. The disturbed audience is unsure whether to sympathise or judge these characters, to admire or abhor Iago. *However, in my **second text...***

POINT 2

Othello believes what's false and disbelieves what is true. Tension increases as he misunderstands Desdemona's pleas for Cassio. He is blinded by 'ocular proof', allowing himself to be diminished to the position of eavesdropper on Cassio's conversation by Iago, 'Look, how he laughs already!' He does not listen to Iago's ironic advice, 'beware, my lord, of jealousy'. The audience is distraught while Othello falls into Iago's devious trap. *Similarly/In contrast, the author of my **third text** relies on ...*

POINT 3

The handkerchief is a part of the 'ocular proof' that Iago manipulates to convince Othello of his wife's guilt. He uses it to paint a picture of Cassio's contempt for Desdemona. The coincidence of Bianca arriving with the handkerchief compounds the uneasy situation. The audience cannot believe how circumstances seem to favour Iago. *A similar mood is/is not created through a different literary device in both of **my other texts...***

POINT 4

In his ominous self-appointed role of dispenser of justice, Othello interrogates Desdemona about the handkerchief before he kills her, 'That handkerchief which I so loved and gave thee,/ Thou gavest to Cassio'. He will not listen when she denies it, 'I never gave him token'. Only after her murder, Emilia reveals the truth, that she 'found by fortune and did give my husband'. She confesses he 'begged of me to steal it'. The audience is distraught that the truth has emerged too late. This creates a very dark and edgy atmosphere. *The best example of irony in my* ***second text*** *is ...*

CONCLUDING PARAGRAPH

Shakespeare effectively uses dramatic irony and the recurrent motif of the embroidered handkerchief to build tension in this poignant tragedy. The audience has been gripped by the foreknowledge given by Iago in his soliloquies and asides and watch horrified, yet helpless, as the naive characters, Desdemona, Cassio and Othello, are manipulated by him. *This is similar to/different from ...*

Sample Paragraph: POINT 3

Iago uses the handkerchief, Othello's first love-token to Desdemona, to 'ensnare' them all in his web of deceit. He manipulates Othello's thinking by linking it to Desdemona's fidelity. Iago lies, saying that he saw 'Cassio wipe his beard' with it and then accuses Desdemona directly, 'It speaks against her'. There is a growing sense of discomfort as Othello's gullibility horrifies the audience. He has just seen the very same handkerchief in Desdemona's hand when he complained that he had 'a pain upon my forehead'. Iago 'poisons' Othello's mind through a devious association. He links Desdemona giving the handkerchief to Cassio with her giving her affection to him, both untrue. The atmosphere grows increasingly uncomfortable as the formerly articulate Othello descends into incoherence, 'Handkerchief – confession! – handkerchief!' He collapses onto the ground in an epileptic fit while Iago's 'medicine' does its 'work'. The mood of malevolent evil shocks the audience. *A similar/different effect is achieved through the use of a recurring motif in both* ***my other texts ...***

Examiner's Comment

- Well-sustained top-grade response that maintains focus on the question.
- Effectively developed point about the importance of the handkerchief in creating tension.
- Expression is varied and clearly controlled – and there is close engagement with the text.
- Rounded off with a comparative approach.

Remember!

Modes overlap. Literary Genre often influences the reader's understanding of Vision and Viewpoint, Cultural Context, and Theme or Issue in texts.

Useful Comparative Links

Successful comparative answers include clear links between texts.

The following phrases might be useful in pointing out similarities and differences between texts.

Similarities	Differences
• Both authors take a similar approach. • The two stories have much in common.	• These two texts could not be more different. • These two key moments illustrate contrasting aspects of ...

• This is also evident in the film's most disturbing scene. • Common to all three narratives is ... • In an almost identical way ... • This is mirrored in the way the heroine of the story acts when ... • The same effect occurs later in the text. • Likewise, in my other texts ... • This viewpoint is echoed at the end of my second text ...	• In an entirely different way ... • In contrast, the opening scene in the novel ... • The complete opposite is seen in ... • On the other hand ... • This is certainly not the case in the film, where ... • All three endings are completely different. • The novel takes a much more unexpected approach. • This aspect is contrasted in my second/third text, when ...

By heaven, I saw my handkerchief in his hand.
O perjured woman!

Othello
Act 5 Scene 2, l.73–4

Class/Homework Exercises

1. Choose **one** of the other points in the Sample Draft Plan and write a paragraph of your own in response to the question above. (Aim for 150 words.)
2. 'Authors make use of a variety of techniques to create scenes of great emotional intensity in texts.'
   With reference to **three texts** on your comparative course, identify and compare the techniques used by authors to create scenes of great emotional intensity. (Aim for 1,000 words.) *(70 marks)*

4. The General Vision and Viewpoint

The General Vision and Viewpoint mode refers to the **broad outlook** of a particular text. Authors challenge readers to look afresh at our beliefs and prejudices, while entertaining us with the craft of story-telling. Stories show us different ways of looking at people and the world.

For example, if a writer is critical of a society, events or central characters, the vision of the text is likely to be **dark and negative**. If the outlook in the text is **positive and life-affirming**, the author might well be acknowledging the courage and resilience of characters as they overcome or come to terms with their problems and circumstances.

Texts can usually be described as pessimistic, optimistic or realistic – or any combination of these. In the end, the **readers and audiences will decide for themselves** about the vision and viewpoint.

The **ending of a story is very important** in determining the viewpoint. Whether happy or sad (or a mix of both), the central conflict should be resolved. The conclusion should also be credible within the context or 'world' of the story.

Students will be expected to **compare the broad outlooks on life** presented within texts.

- Is the story positive or negative? Is it convincing and true to life?
- What aspects of human experience does the text concentrate on?
- How effectively is the viewpoint expressed?

The focus in the General Vision and Viewpoint mode is on the **overall impact** the text makes on the reader/viewer and on how this is communicated.

When studying *Othello*, we can identify the general viewpoint as something that **is expressed through the story's tragic events and the playwright's narrative voice** (Shakespeare's own viewpoint). The viewpoint in the play can also be formed through **a central character**. The villain Iago, for example, epitomises evil and an unforgiving world.

In coming to an understanding of the play's vision, we can **consider a range of key questions**.

- Is Othello's story told sympathetically, compassionately or cynically?
- Does the drama reflect the age in which the story is set?
- Is the era secular or religious?
- Is the playwright making moral or political points?

And nothing can or shall content my soul
Till I am evened with him

Iago
Act 2 Scene 1, l.314–5

Aspects of style, such as dialogue, poetry and prose, convey the atmosphere of the play as we listen to the conversations of the characters reacting to their circumstances. Imagery and language also affect the mood. In stage productions, visual and aural effects (lighting, sound, music, colour and costume) can show a world of good or evil, beauty or oppression.

The impact of a **key scene** or turning point in the play will influence our understanding of the vision and viewpoint. The **concluding scene** usually has a crucial effect on the audience's outlook. Are questions raised by the text resolved happily or unhappily? Or do these questions remain unanswered?

And what's he then that says I play the villain?
When this advice is free I give and honest
Iago
Act 2 Scene 3, l.336–7

How is Vision/Viewpoint Established in the Play?

The vision of a text is set by the writer's use of character, plot, setting, language and narrative voice.

Plays 'hold, as 'twere, the mirror up to nature' (*Hamlet*). A mirror does more than reflect reality; it shows reality from a different perspective. In *Othello*, Shakespeare gives us a **dual vision** – hopeful and despairing – while exploring some of the worst experiences that human beings can endure. He shows how human happiness is vulnerable when faced with the forces of evil, 'Thus credulous fools are caught'.

Using Characters to Establish the Outlook of *Othello*

Shakespeare's tragic drama *Othello* is dominated by Iago, one of the most sinister and fascinating villains in literature. This agent of fiendish cunning is an individualist who decides what he wants and works hard to achieve it, 'I follow but myself'. He believes in self-discipline, 'Our bodies are our gardens, to the which our wills are gardeners'. He establishes a conspiratorial intimacy with the audience through confessional soliloquies and sly asides. In this way he can 'ensnare' the audience as well as the characters in the play in his **claustrophobic web of evil**.

The audience will be disquieted to find themselves at times identifying with the values and viewpoint of this villain, 'But we have reason to cool our raging motions, our carnal stings'. Shakespeare has created a warped and sadistic human being who undermines authority because of his love of power over others. Iago **delights in malice** and despises the gullible people around him, particularly Roderigo, Othello and Cassio. He sneers at how easily the 'credulous' are fooled.

Iago has no problem using Desdemona's 'goodness' for his own despicable ends, 'turn her virtue into pitch'. The playwright portrays him as a callous director who creates convincing, deceptive illusions so that the characters in the play see, overhear and interpret what he wishes them to see. He supplants reality with his version of truth. Iago brings 'this monstrous birth to the world's light' by sowing seeds of distrust on every occasion. Shakespeare has produced a **very dark vision of life** in his play.

Iago is the epitome of the modern self-made man, the cynical opportunist. He manipulates language to convince Roderigo to act, promising that he can easily break 'a frail vow betwixt an erring barbarian and a super-subtle Venetian', playing on

Roderigo's prejudice against Othello and Desdemona's inter-racial marriage. His total control of the 'snipe' Roderigo is shown in the list of imperative commands he issues to him, 'Go to', 'provide thy money'. The audience watches to see what happens. A convinced Roderigo vows to 'sell all my land'. The audience understands, almost approves, that Roderigo's 'unbitted lusts' for Desdemona have been used against him by Iago. This is **a bleak image of the human condition**.

The scheming ensign uses the same technique against Othello. Furious at the disturbance of the night-time brawl in Cyprus, 'a town of war', Othello admits, 'My blood begins my safer guides to rule'. Iago uses the Moor's anger to **dim his perception of the truth**. He pretends to excuse the drunken Cassio, 'the best sometimes forget', while laying the blame on him. Othello swiftly decides 'never more be officer of mine'. He has foolishly accepted Iago's version of events. The audience watches helplessly while the predator encircles his prey. Iago is succeeding in leading Othello 'by the nose/ As asses are'. Shakespeare presents **an unsettling picture of what happens in a cynical world** when characters blindly trust one another rather than relying on their own observations or knowledge.

Throughout this **pessimistic play**, we see the amoral villain work his 'medicine', protected by a pretence of honesty. Othello alarmingly asks Iago to 'speak to me as to thy thinkings'. The master director now puts on a show for Othello, who has demanded 'ocular proof' of his wife's infidelity. Iago gradually poisons Othello's love for Desdemona, instructing him, 'Look to your wife, observe her well with Cassio'. Deviously, he develops the metaphor of 'seeing' to intensify Othello's suspicions, 'In Venice they do let heaven see the pranks/ They dare not show their husbands'. He makes innovative use of the handkerchief to cast even more doubt on Desdemona's character.

The audience is plunged, horrified, into this evil atmosphere, waiting to see if Othello will fall completely into Iago's evil trap. Like Roderigo, the gullible Moor has given up his will to Iago, and acts as he is instructed, 'Iago beckons me'. He will docilely stand to be educated about what he has 'seen' when Cassio speaks about Bianca and Othello believes that the lieutenant is mocking Desdemona, 'Did you perceive how he laughed at his vice?' Forewarned of Iago's villainy, we observe how it works and are saddened by the **disturbing perspective presented**.

In *Othello*, Shakespeare has depicted a universe where order and disorder co-exist. Human choices play a vital and potentially destructive role – especially when characters are manipulated by such a skilful villain as Iago. Although Desdemona is presented as the symbol of goodness and purity, a 'pearl', her decision to elope with Othello and betray her father's trust has set in motion the tragic events of the play. She has so immersed herself in her choice of love that she dies without gaining any self-knowledge, 'Commend me to my kind lord', and with a possibility of suffering in the next world, according to Christian belief. This adds to the **overall sense of failure** at the end of the play.

But Shakespeare springs a final surprise on the audience and Iago. The diabolical schemer who believed he could control everyone and turn every event to his own advantage is eventually brought down by **Emilia's selfless act of human decency**. The playwright does not allow evil to triumph. The forces of anarchy that the crass individualism of Iago unleashed are defeated by truth, 'He lies to the heart'. In a powerful display of the courage of the ordinary person, Emilia accuses Othello of ignorance and stupidity even at the risk of her life, 'I care not for thy sword'. She speaks Desdemona's epitaph, 'she was chaste, she loved thee, cruel Moor'.

Iago is caught and will face punishment for his 'work'. Order is ultimately restored despite Iago's final attempt at manipulation, 'From this time forth I never will speak word'. Cassio is charged with 'the censure of this hellish villain'. But will Iago explain himself? **The play concludes with a dual vision and viewpoint.** The audience respects Emilia's bravery, yet is horrified by 'the tragic loading of this bed'. They are shamefaced at having been positioned as onlookers and reluctant colluders by Iago's diabolical brilliance. They now realise, 'Knavery's plain face is never seen, till used'.

The audience can appreciate the importance of courage because we admire the ability of humans to stand up for what is right. **The duality of Shakespeare's vision not only reflects but also illuminates.** The Elizabethans believed that society functions well when order is maintained. Shakespeare's play illustrates the value of decency and love in the face of evil.

Remember!

Discussion points in the 30-mark Part (a) sample answer can also provide the basis for developed comparisons in the 40-mark Part (b) and 70-mark single questions. To write successful examination answers, it is essential to study the wording of questions closely. Marks can easily be lost if attention is not paid to each facet of the questions.

Sample Part (a) Question

Q. 'Our personal attitudes and values can influence our sense of the general vision and viewpoint of a text.'

With reference to <u>one</u> <u>text</u> on your comparative course, explain how your sense of the general vision and viewpoint was influenced by at least one of your personal beliefs. Develop your response with reference to the text. *(30 marks)*

Indicative Material

- Our personal beliefs in relation to gender, racism, sectarianism, ageism, politics, social responsibility, social class, etc. influence perspective/viewpoint
- Our ethical/moral values regarding loyalty, honesty, family, etc. colour our sense of the general vision and viewpoint
- Prejudice/bias affects our responses to texts either consciously or subconsciously
- Encountering value systems that run counter to our own can alter/reinforce our conception of the general vision and viewpoint
- Our sense of the general vision and viewpoint can be influenced by the extent to which we personally believe the ending is just/unfair/ambiguous, etc.

Moor, she was chaste, she loved thee, cruel Moor.
So come my soul to bliss, as I speak true

Emilia
Act 5 Scene 2, l.292–93

Sample Answer

I believe that loyalty, honesty and courage are important values in life. The playwright presented these in such a way that it negatively impacted my sense of the general vision and viewpoint in 'Othello'. The dark vision at the play's conclusion had only one spark of brightness, the extraordinary courage of the maidservant, Emilia.

Iago's dishonesty casts a dark cloud over the marriage of Othello and Desdemona. This villain is determined to disrupt the harmony of the love between the Moor and his wife. He knows Othello will be 'A most dear husband'. But he will exploit their vulnerability, he will 'set down the pegs' to create disagreement between them. Persuasive manipulation gets Othello to doubt his wife, unleashing 'chaos'. Iago lies about Cassio's dream and seeing him 'wipe his beard' with Othello's first gift to Desdemona. I was disgusted by the lies Iago tells to take revenge on Othello because he missed out on promotion to lieutenant. This left me with a bleak vision of the text.

I found the ending of the play so frustrating. I didn't think Othello, the tragic hero, achieved self-knowledge, which is to be expected in a classic tragedy. In my opinion, Othello does not really take responsibility for his actions. So I thought it was Desdemona, not Othello, who 'loved not wisely but too well'. I believe he was 'easily jealous'. I was also upset that Shakespeare allowed Iago to control events even when he was caught because he vowed to remain silent and explain 'nothing'. So I felt that evil was not truly vanquished. So I found the viewpoint depressing.

The only bright note lasted for a short time and that was Emilia's courage when she outed her husband about the handkerchief, 'He begged of me to steal it'. She dares to face Othello with the unpalatable truth that he is not an agent of justice. So I was devastated by the murder, 'he hath killed his wife'. Good is defeated through the overwhelming power of evil. The only positive viewpoint is quickly extinguished.

My belief in the power of loyalty and honesty to withstand evil was shaken by the fates of the characters in this tragedy. When Othello attempts to kill Iago, he taunts him, 'I bleed sir; but not killed'. Iago delights in his 'work' and refuses to satisfy the authorities with an explanation for his destructive behaviour, 'Demand me nothing'. I found this disturbing. I was also shocked that Emilia's bright moment of courage was dashed so suddenly. 'Othello' is a play with a dark, depressing viewpoint. *(425 words)*

Examiner's Comment

- Strong personal response, focused well in keeping with the question.
- Effective use of apt reference shows close knowledge of the play.
- Good expression, overall, but some repetition in paragraph 3.
- Solid high-grade standard with sustained discussion of the mode in the text.

Class/Homework Exercise

Using some of the points from the Indicative Material above, write your own response to the Part (a) question. (Aim for 400 words.)

Exam Guide
To structure your comparative essay answer on the General Vision and Viewpoint, a useful exercise is to practise making an outline of the **key points** you wish to include. The following Draft Plan uses *Othello* as one of the comparative texts.

Sample 70-mark Question

Q. 'Our view of the personal morality of a central character can help to shape our impression of the general vision and viewpoint of a text.'

Compare the extent to which your view of the personal morality of one central character, in each of three texts on your comparative course, helped to shape your impression of the general vision and viewpoint of your chosen texts. Develop your answer with reference to the texts. *(70 marks)*

Indicative Material

- Our view of the personal morality of central characters – i.e. his/her honesty, loyalty, moral/ethical behaviour, etc. – affects our response (sympathetic, antagonistic/ambiguous, etc.) to those characters, and contributes to shaping our impression of the general vision and viewpoint
- The ability/inability of central characters to behave with honour and integrity in the face of adversity can influence our sense of the general vision and viewpoint
- Our initial view of the morality/lack of moral standards of central characters can be accurate/misleading, influencing our impression of the general vision and viewpoint
- The extent to which the conclusion reveals/conceals the level of honesty and decency of central characters shapes our impression of the general vision and viewpoint, etc.

Sample Draft Plan

INTRODUCTION

The three texts on my comparative course offer a diverse selection of viewpoints on the personal morality of the central characters. This affects my response to those characters. My attitude towards the protagonist in Shakespeare's tragedy 'Othello' changes from an initial sympathetic response to one of antagonism by the play's conclusion. *My **other two texts** evoked similar/contrasting views ...*

POINT 1

Introduction of 'Valiant Othello', sought after by state to repel the threat by the Turks, is impressive. He springs into action with 'a natural and prompt alacrity', promising not to 'scant' the business of the state if the Venetian authorities allow his new wife, Desdemona, to accompany him. The overall outlook is initially positive, and I felt Othello behaved with honour and integrity, putting his duty to the state above his personal happiness. *In contrast/similarly, my **second text** ...*

Come, Desdemona: I have but an hour ...
To spend with thee: we must obey the time

Othello
Act 1 Scene 3, l.320–22

POINT 2

Othello is equally impressive in his calm, dignified dealing with Desdemona's outraged father, who insults him and accuses him of using 'witchcraft' to win his daughter. He answers the charges competently in front of the Senate, impressing the Duke, 'I think this tale would win my daughter too'. The vision of the text is bright because of the extraordinary composure of the general. *The central character in my **third text** does/does not impress me ...*

POINT 3

Othello's inability to bear uncertainty is exploited by the villainous Iago, 'when I doubt ... Away at once with love'. Othello is diminished in my eyes when he agrees to eavesdrop to find out if his wife has been unfaithful to him. On flimsy evidence, a lost handkerchief, a misinterpreted conversation and a lie about a dream, he declares, 'She's gone ... my relief/ Must be to loathe her'. His peace of mind is destroyed, and he resorts to violent outbursts, 'I'll tear her all to pieces'. I was disappointed in this behaviour from a man who was once so dignified. This influenced me to regard the play's vision presented to be dark. *The other central characters in my **other two texts** did/did not change so dramatically ...*

POINT 4

Endings contribute to the viewpoint in a text and leave us with a lasting impression of the vision. Othello's actions in the last scene appalled me and left me feeling antagonistic towards him. He deludes himself that he is an honourable agent of justice, preventing other men from being duped by Desdemona. I found his suicide to be an attempt to regain some of his lost status, 'I have done the state some service, and they know it'. The verdict of the Venetian Gratiano was similar to my own and reinforced the negative viewpoint, 'All that's spoke is marred'. *The ending of my **second text** is like or unlike ...*

CONCLUDING PARAGRAPH

Overall, I found the vision in 'Othello' bleak because my initial impression of the general proved misleading. He did not act with honour but allowed himself to be fooled through his own insecurity as an outsider. His deeds were not 'unlucky', but 'murderous'. My impression of the viewpoint in the text changed from one of admiration and sympathy to one of hostility towards 'the Moor'. *My **other two texts ...***

Sample Paragraph: POINT 2

Othello acts with courage and composure when Iago informs him of Brabantio's search party, 'I must be found'. He is confident of his worth to Venice, 'My services which I have done the signiory/ Shall out-tongue his complaints'. He performs well when brought before the Senate to answer Brabantio's charges that he won his daughter by 'witchcraft'. He calmly explains how he was 'oft invited' into the family home because 'Her father loved me'. He is confident that his wife loves him and is willing to have her testify to the court, 'Send for the lady to the Saggitary'. He confesses that he has 'married her'. He relates the wondrous tales of his exploits that Desdemona 'with a greedy ear' would 'devour'. The Duke was impressed by this noble display of love, 'this tale would win my daughter too'. Othello counters Brabantio's warning, 'She has deceived her father, and may thee' with the dramatic declaration of his devotion to her, 'My life upon her faith!' My positive impression of this noble man influenced my optimistic view of the text. *The behaviour of the central character in my **third text** was similar/different ...*

Examiner's Comment

- Good personal approach, closely engaged with the play.
- Rounded off with apt references to the mode and comparative link.
- Clear expression – but repetitious at times (sentences beginning with 'He').
- Overall, a sustained high-grade relevant response that takes on the question.

Useful Comparative Links

Successful comparative answers include clear links between texts.

The following phrases might be useful in pointing out similarities and differences between texts.

Remember!

Modes overlap. For example, the General Vision and Viewpoint is often influenced by both the Cultural Context and aspects of Literary Genre of a text.

Similarities

- Both authors take a similar approach.
- The two stories have much in common.
- This is also evident in the film's most disturbing scene.
- Common to all three narratives is ...
- In an almost identical way ...
- This is mirrored in the way the heroine of the story acts when ...
- The same effect occurs later in the text.
- Likewise, in my other texts ...
- This viewpoint is echoed at the end of my second text ...

Differences

- These two texts could not be more different.
- These two key moments illustrate contrasting aspects of ...
- In an entirely different way ...
- In contrast, the opening scene in the novel ...
- The complete opposite is seen in ...
- On the other hand ...
- This is certainly not the case in the film, where ...
- All three endings are completely different.
- The novel takes a much more unexpected approach.
- This aspect is contrasted in my second/third text, when ...

Class/Homework Exercises

1. Choose **one** of the other points in the Sample Draft Plan and write a paragraph of your own in response to the question above. (Aim for 150 words.)
2. 'The general vision and viewpoint in texts often presents us with an outlook that is optimistic or pessimistic, or a combination of optimism and pessimism.'
   Identify and compare the general vision and viewpoint presented in **three texts** on your comparative course. (Aim for 1,000 words.) *(70 marks)*

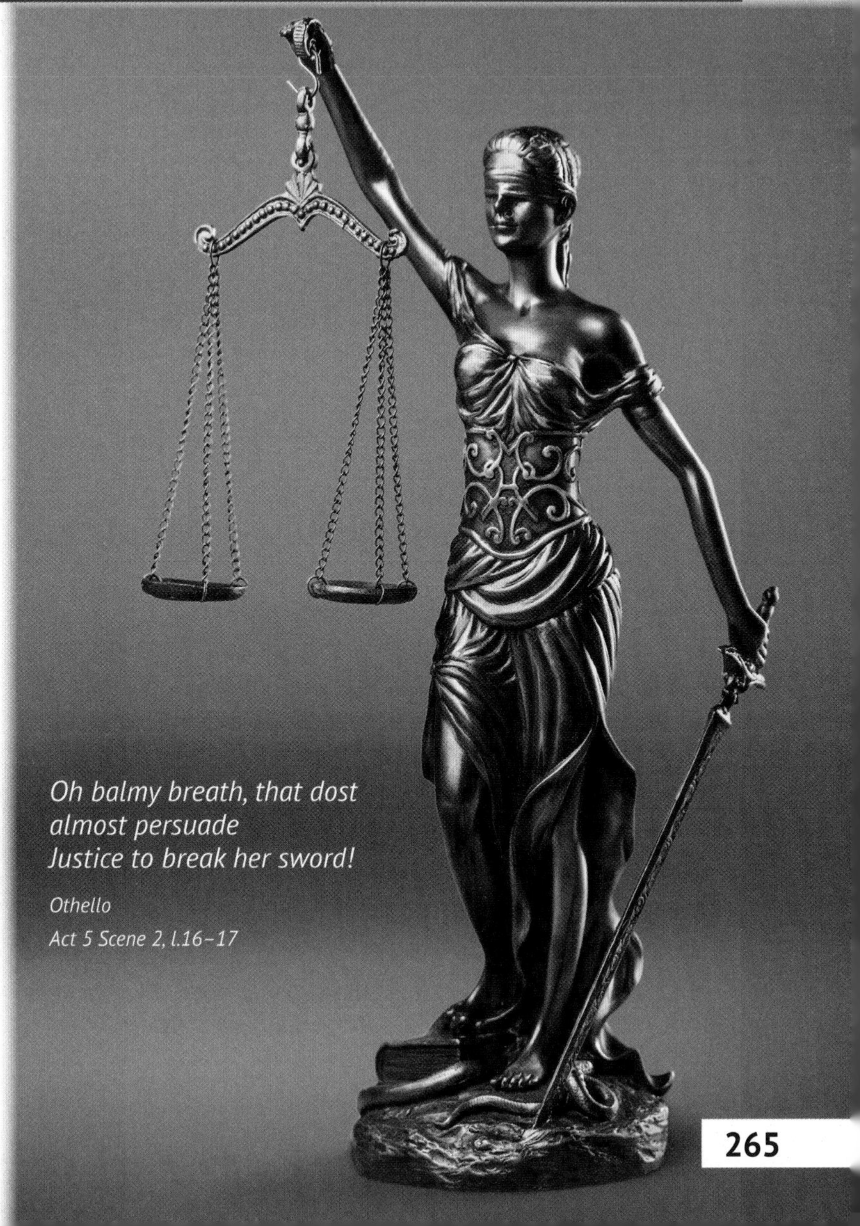

Oh balmy breath, that dost almost persuade Justice to break her sword!

Othello Act 5 Scene 2, l.16–17

Othello and the Critics

Most of the criticism of Shakespeare's *Othello* has focused on the central male characters, Othello and Iago. It is only in more recent times that Desdemona's role has been closely examined. Leading critics have taken very different – indeed, contradictory – views of the play.

Some of the earliest reviewers thought that *Othello* was unrealistic and could not be described as a classic tragedy. Others have concentrated on discussing the story's major themes, particularly jealousy, love, race, revenge and patriarchy.

Not surprisingly, critics have disagreed in their attitudes to the play's protagonist. Some show Othello in a positive light as noble and heroic, while others depict him as a highly unsympathetic figure. Shakespeare's great tragedy is open to many different readings. In the end, we are all free to consider the views of others, but we should interpret the play for ourselves.

The American writer and activist Susan Sontag famously said, 'Real art has the capacity to make us nervous.' *Othello* has a history of doing just that, and here are some examples of what critics and an actor who played Othello have said about the play.

'A very pretty lady sat by me and called out to see Desdemona smothered.'
Samuel Pepys (1660)

'... the most lamentable play that ever appeared on any stage. A noble Venetian lady is to be murdered by our poet, in sober sadness, purely for being a fool.'
Thomas Rymer (1693)

'[Othello] does not belong in our world, and he seems to enter it we know not whence – almost as if from wonderland. There is something marvellous in his descent from men of royal siege; in his wanderings in vast deserts and among marvellous peoples.'
A. C. Bradley (1904)

'Othello is both the best and the worst of men, he is both superior to passion and its slave.'
Mark Van Doren (1939)

'Othello, in his magnanimous way, is egotistical ... This self-centredness doesn't mean self-knowledge: that is a virtue which Othello, a soldier of fortune, hasn't had much need of.'
F. R. Leavis (1952)

'*Othello* is supreme in one quality: beauty. Much of its poetry, in imagery, perfection of phrase, and steadfastness of rhythm, soaring yet firm, enchants the sensuous imagination.'
Helen Gardner (1955)

'Iago is still serviceable to us, as an objective correlative of the mindless inventiveness of racist aggression'.
Germaine Greer (1986)

'In loving and marrying each other, Othello and Desdemona instinctively act according to principles of racial equality and sexual freedom which are still not normative, still far from generally accepted and practised even in our own day, let alone in Shakespeare's.'
Kieran Ryan (1989)

'I'm slightly allergic to Shakespeare ... At school we didn't know you were supposed to stand up and act it out ... It just felt like some ancient language that we didn't really understand.'
Lenny Henry (2009)

'There's a kind of a fast-paced, energy-driven thriller in there.'
Joe Dowling (2016)

Othello on Screen

Othello has been adapted for the screen many times, including four silent movies between 1907 and 1922.

Films

- 1952 *Othello* directed by and starring Orson Welles.
- 1965 *Othello* with Laurence Olivier, Maggie Smith, Frank Finlay and Joyce Redman.
- 1995 *Othello* with Kenneth Branagh, Laurence Fishburne and Irene Jacob. Directed by Oliver Parker.

Television

- 1981 *Othello* – part of the BBC's complete works of Shakespeare. Starring Anthony Hopkins and Bob Hoskins.
- 1990 *Othello* – a film version of the Royal Shakespeare Company production starring Michael Grandage, Ian McKellen, Clive Swift, Willard White, Sean Baker and Imogen Stubbs. Directed by Trevor Nunn.
- 2001 *Othello* – TV movie with Eamonn Walker, Christopher Eccleston and Keeley Hawes.

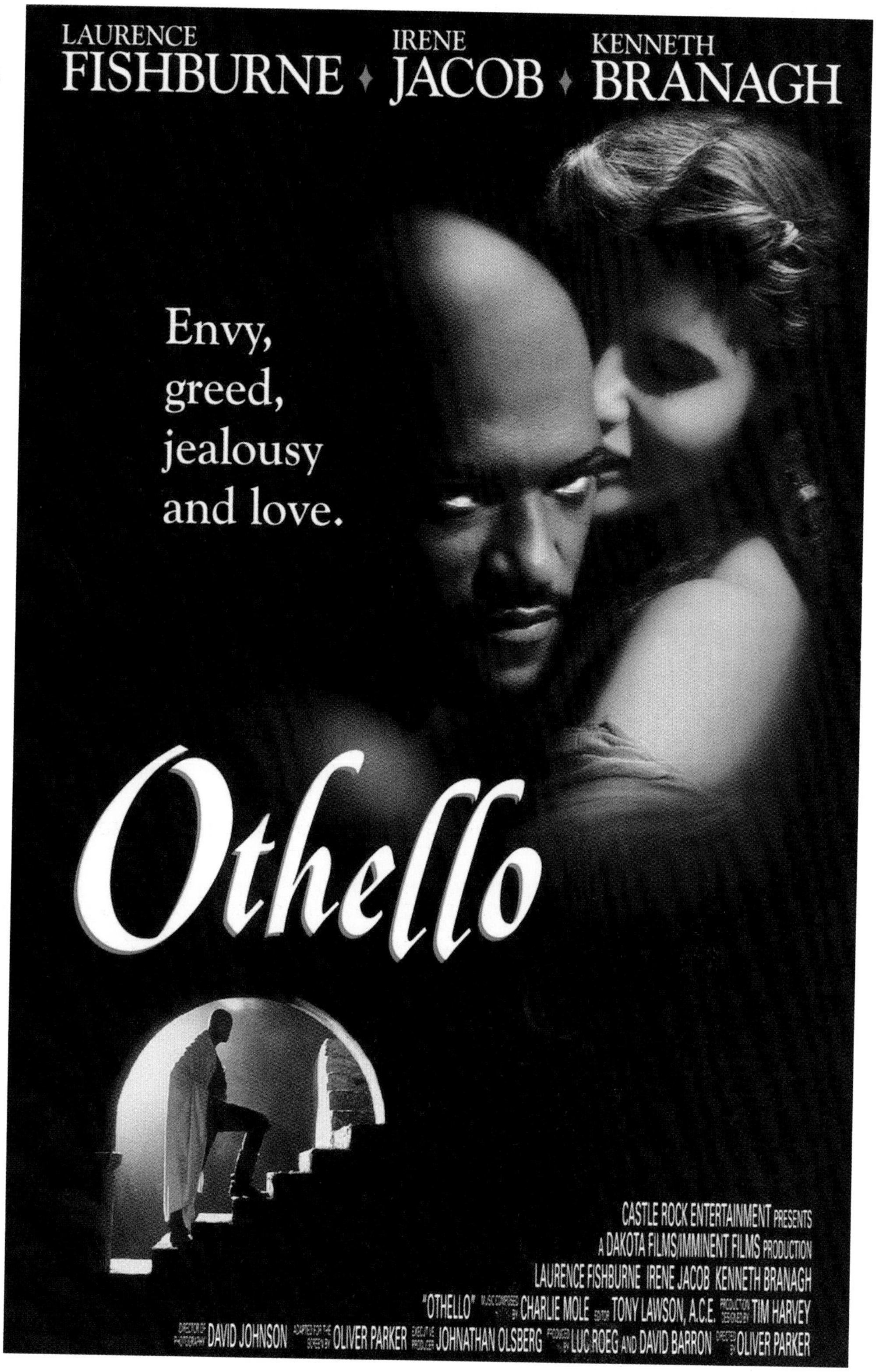

Leaving Certificate Comparative Study Practice Questions

The Cultural Context

1. 'The way in which family or social expectations liberate or restrict central characters can broaden our understanding of the cultural context of a text.'
   Compare the way in which central characters liberated or restricted by family or social expectations helped to broaden your understanding of the cultural context in three texts on your comparative course. *(70 marks)*

OR

2. 'Understanding attitudes to gender roles can offer the reader a valuable insight into the cultural context of the text.'
   (a) Discuss how understanding attitudes to gender roles offered you a valuable insight into the cultural context of **one text** that you have studied on your comparative course. *(30 marks)*
   (b) Compare the way in which attitudes to gender roles offered you a valuable insight into **two other** comparative texts that you have studied. *(40 marks)*

Theme or Issue

1. 'Exploring a significant theme or issue in different texts can often challenge or change the preconceived ideas of a reader.'
   With reference to **three texts** on your comparative course, compare the extent to which your study of a significant theme or issue challenged or changed some of your preconceived ideas. *(70 marks)*

OR

2. 'The experience of the central character can highlight the complexity of a theme or issue for a reader.'
   (a) Discuss the extent to which the experience of the central character highlighted the complexity of a theme or issue in **one** of the texts you have studied on your comparative course. *(30 marks)*
   (b) Compare the extent to which the experience of the central character highlighted the complexity of the same theme or issue in each of **two other** comparative texts you have studied. *(40 marks)*

Literary Genre

1. 'A variety of techniques can be used in a text to shape a compelling storyline.'
   Identify and compare the techniques used to shape compelling storylines in **three texts** you have studied on your comparative course. *(70 marks)*

OR

2. 'The author's use of imagery and symbolism can help to create the mood in a text.'
   (a) Discuss how the author's use of imagery and symbolism helped to create the mood in **one** of the texts on your comparative course. *(30 marks)*
   (b) With reference to **two other** comparative texts, compare how the author's use of imagery and symbolism helped to create the mood in these texts. *(40 marks)*

The General Vision and Viewpoint

1. 'Relationships between central characters which prove valuable or damaging often shape a reader's understanding of the general vision and viewpoint of a text.'
   In light of this statement, compare the extent to which the relationships in **three texts** you have studied on your comparative course helped to shape your understanding of the general vision and viewpoint. *(70 marks)*

OR

2. 'The general vision and viewpoint of a text can be interpreted by a reader's response to key scenes or significant moments in that text.'
   - **(a)** With reference to **one text** on your comparative course, discuss how key scenes or significant moments shaped your personal response and helped you to interpret the general vision and viewpoint. *(30 marks)*
   - **(b)** With reference to **two other** comparative texts, compare how key scenes or significant moments shaped your personal response and helped you to interpret the general vision and viewpoint in these texts. *(30 marks)*

poor lady, she'll run mad
When she shall lack it

Emilia
Act 3 Scene 3, l.352–3

Comparative Study Guidelines

(SEC Leaving Cert English Marking Scheme)

In all answers to questions in this section, candidates may compare **and/or** contrast, i.e. address similarities **and/or** differences in both the content and style of their chosen texts.

In shaping their responses to the questions set on the Comparative Study, it is expected that candidates will be involved in some/all of the following kinds of activities:

- Description/analysis of the text/s in the light of the modes for comparison
- Making general observations about texts in relation to each other
- Making connections between similar aspects of texts
- Recognising differences between texts
- Showing that similarities/differences need to be qualified
- Demonstrating awareness of themselves as readers, their reactions/responses/involvement.

Expect a wide variety of approaches both in the patterns of discussion and the manner of illustration.

Remember!
In your introductory paragraph, it's important to name the text/s, author/s and mode that you have chosen.

FAQs

Q. How many comparisons are expected?

A. There is no set number. Some candidates will focus in depth on a few key comparisons; others will range widely over texts, finding numerous similarities and/or differences.

Q. Do examiners expect a detailed summary of the plot of each text?

A. Unfocused summaries of the story are generally wasteful and time-consuming. A brief introductory overview will usually be sufficient, e.g. 'Shakespeare's *Othello* tells the story of a respected black army officer who murders his innocent wife.'

Q. What exactly is a 'key moment'?

A. This term usually refers to a revealing moment or scene, sometimes indicating a turning point in the story. It can be a brief exchange between characters, a soliloquy, an ironic remark, a violent incident, a grand occasion or even a seemingly unimportant event.

Q. How many key moments are expected?

A. Again, there is no set number. While some developed discussions include a range of references to revealing moments, others select a few and explore these in greater depth.

Q. Is it necessary to compare all three texts in every paragraph?

A. A paragraph will frequently refer to a key moment/scene from one text. A valid comparison with a second and/or third might be made – often at the start or end of the paragraph. Occasionally, there could be reference to all three texts.

Q. Should comparative texts be given equal attention in answers?

A. Although examiners are unlikely to have strict expectations, merely nominal or token discussion of any text will be penalised.

Remember!
*The **main aim is to take a comparative approach** and engage with the terms of the question. Examiners will reward relevant, well-written answers that demonstrate a good understanding of the chosen mode and the three texts.*

Chief Examiner's Report

Many examiners reported genuine engagement with the terms of the questions, combined with a fluid comparative approach. As in previous years, examiners also noted that a significant minority of candidates were hampered by a rigid and formulaic approach. In recent years there have been few instances of the use of invalid texts in answer to the questions on Comparative Studies. Nevertheless, it is worth noting that the use of some texts is not permitted in the Comparative Studies Section. Texts that are not valid are:

- a text already answered on as a Single Text
- a text not on the prescribed list for the current year
- the use of two films.

The Comparative Study is one of the areas where candidates have an opportunity to demonstrate skills in critical literacy. It is possible for candidates to challenge, wholly or in part, not only the premise put forward in questions but also the views and opinions they encountered in the course of studying texts. Many candidates showed **evidence of critical engagement** with the texts they had studied and a mature critical literacy was seen in the work of some candidates. Examiners were pleased when they saw candidates trust in their own personal response and demonstrate a willingness to challenge the 'fixed meaning' of texts. The best answers managed to remain grounded, both in the question asked and in the text.

www.examinations.ie

If she be false, O, then heaven mocks itself!
I'll not believe it

Othello
Act 3 Scene 3, l.307–8

Glossary of Dramatic Terms

Antagonist: an important character, such as Iago, who provides the main opposition to the protagonist.

Aside: when a character makes a remark that is only heard by the audience.

Blank verse: unrhymed verse in iambic pentameter, relatively close to spoken English.

Catharsis: the release of emotion (often sorrow or pity) that the audience experiences at the end of a tragedy.

Characterisation: how a playwright creates characters so as to attract or repel audience sympathy.

Conflict: involves tension or a struggle between two opposing forces. There is no drama without conflict. Conflict can be external (between characters) or internal (within a character's mind) and is generally resolved by the end of the play.

Dramatic irony: when the audience knows something that some of the characters don't.

Foil: a contrasting character, such as Emilia, whose realism highlights Desdemona's naivety.

Imagery: figurative or literary language (e.g. comparisons) that creates pictures in the mind.

Oxymoron: a figure of speech linking two contradictory ideas, e.g. 'fair devil'.

Pathos: a quality in a text that arouses feelings of pity or deep sorrow.

Plot: the sequence of events that make up a storyline.

Poetic justice: the idea that characters should get what they deserve, based on their behaviour.

Protagonist: the central or main character in a story.

Pun: word-play using ambiguity between words to create humour.

Rhythm: a pattern of sounds created by the arrangement of stressed and unstressed syllables.

Setting: when and where the story takes place.

Soliloquy: speech during which a character reveals his or her thoughts and feelings exclusively to the audience.

Suspense: the intense feeling an audience experiences while waiting for the outcome of certain dramatic events.

Symbol: an object that represents something else, e.g. Desdemona's handkerchief becomes a symbol of infidelity.

Tension: dramatic tension creates and maintains an audience's involvement in the story.

Theme: a central idea or issue explored in the play, e.g. deception in *Othello*.

Tragedy: a type of drama in which the characters experience a reversal of fortune, usually for the worse. In tragedy, suffering awaits many of the characters, especially the hero.

Tragic flaw: a weakness or limitation of character that results in the fall of the tragic hero, e.g. Othello's jealousy and too trusting nature.